Christopher Sandf[...] [...] careers in public re[...] [...] fiction writing. His [...] *[...]ing With Panthers* (1983), *Arcadian* (1985) and *We Don't Do Dogs* (1988), the last of which contains a fictional character called Mick Jagger.
Sandford still retains his interest in sports writing, and has published well-received biographies of Godfrey Evans (1990) and Tom Graveney (1992). He is a regular contributor to cricket journals in the UK and overseas. His music journalism includes profiles of Jagger and the Rolling Stones in a range of titles both here and in America. He lives in London and Seattle.

i

MICK JAGGER

Primitive Cool

Christopher Sandford

VICTOR GOLLANCZ

LONDON

For Victoria

First published in Great Britain 1993
by Victor Gollancz

First Gollancz Paperback edition published 1994
by Victor Gollancz
A Cassell imprint
Villiers House, 41/47 Strand, London WC2N 5JE

© Christopher Sandford 1993, 1994

The right of Christopher Sandford to be identified
as author of this work has been asserted by him in
accordance with the Copyright, Designs and Patents
Act, 1988

A catalogue record for this book is
available from the British Library

ISBN 0 575 05749 1

Photoset by Rowland Phototypesetting Ltd
Bury St Edmunds, Suffolk
Printed and bound in Great Britain by
Cox and Wyman Ltd, Reading, Berkshire

Contents

BRIAN JONES

Rumours about Brian Jones's death have regularly exercised tabloid writers and conspiracy theorists since the night he was pulled from his swimming pool twenty-five years ago. In particular, at least two books have been published suggesting that Jones was killed by 'revengeful drug-pushers', three workmen supervised by a fourth 'burly man wearing glasses . . . [who spoke in] a cockney accent' – by inference, Tom Keylock – or, most colourfully, agents of the Rolling Stones, to whom their recently fired and garrulous colleague had become an embarrassment.

As this edition of *Mick Jagger: Primitive Cool* was going to press, a new version of Jones's death came to light.

In late October 1993, Frank Thorogood, by common agreement the last man to see Jones alive, was admitted to North Middlesex Hospital, where he died on 8 November. On the 7th he was visited by Tom Keylock. Keylock found his old friend, who may have known it to be his final illness, in a confessional mood. After some discussion about domestic and family matters, the conversation turned to the events of 2 July 1969. In Keylock's account, Thorogood's exact words – spoken with chilling clarity – were 'I did Brian'.

There were few specific details. Thorogood, who was thought to have been on the verge of being fired, if not already dismissed by Jones, indicated a falling-out about money. After a heated discussion and fuelled by their running consumption of vodka and brandy, the two men, Keylock believes, resumed their debate alone in the swimming pool. No one can say whether Thorogood intended to kill or merely to frighten Jones by holding him under the water. Nor is it certain whether Thorogood, even hours before his own death, was being entirely candid. What is certain is that he struck Keylock (not known for his gullibility) as sincere, and that, referring to Jones's death, Thorogood used the words, 'My mind snapped'.

That leaves the problem of Thorogood's previous story – maintained for twenty-four years – which a number of critics, this one included, were happy to accept. As has been seen, neither the police nor Dr Sachs found evidence that Jones was ever manhandled. There are technical objections to any version of his death with implications of murder or suicide. The combination of mental exhaustion, alcohol, pills and warm water would have been enough to send a healthier man than Jones to a fatal sleep.

All the same, the account of Thorogood's confession bears conviction, and the phrase *My mind snapped* will be readily understood by anyone familiar with the tense, disgruntled and acutely paranoid court surrounding the Rolling Stones in 1969. Shocking as it is, there must be a possibility that Thorogood's final statement was a true one. On this reading, Brian Jones's death was the result of deliberate murder or, at best, a threat which went tragically wrong.

C.S.
April 1994

ACKNOWLEDGEMENTS

Although I spoke to Mick Jagger on a number of occasions between 1977 and 1989, this book was written without his consent or cooperation. It is not, in any sense, an 'authorized' biography. Jagger's parents, Joe and Eva, were kind enough to answer all but one of the questions I asked them; two of his cousins, Peter and Herbert Scutts, also provided background material. I was repeatedly told by those who know him 'not to expect anything from Mick' and, with the exceptions given above, I was not disappointed.

Of those who did make their time available, I should particularly thank Tom Keylock and Frank Thorogood, both of whom vividly conveyed their experiences of working for Jagger while at no time adopting the role of 'embittered ex-employees'. I was also lucky enough to interview the three members of Jagger's original group, Bob Beckwith, Alan Etherington and Dick Taylor, as well as the late Alexis Korner, all of whom witnessed – and, in Korner's case, abetted – Jagger's professional breakthrough.

For written material on Jagger and the Rolling Stones I am grateful to Tony Smith, headmaster of Dartford Grammar School; to Walter Stern, formerly Jagger's tutor at the London School of Economics; to David Wadman, HM Coroner for East Sussex, for depositions relating to the inquest into the death of Brian Jones; and to Kevin O'Brien of the US Department of Justice for portions of Jagger's FBI file.

Among those who provided recollections, photographs or other assistance were: Richard Allen, Luciano Amore, Walter Bennett, Ross Benson, Chuck Berry, Paul Bibire, John Birt, Gareth Bolton, Patti Boyd, Ben Brierley, Bob Clash, Albert Clinton, Denis Compton, Derek Diamond, Bo Diddley, David Drinkwater, Alan Dow, Andrew Etherington, Winnifred Etherington, Godfrey Evans, Chris Farlowe, Paul Getty, Eileen Giles, Tom Graveney, Ryan Grice, Jeff Griffin, Anthony Haden-Guest, Jane Hamill, Roger Hayes, Peter Holland, Colin Ingleby-Mackenzie, David Jacobs, John Keeble, Edith Keep, Arthur Key, Cecilia Lewis, John Mackereth, Gered Mankowitz, Nick Miles, John Murray, Mike Oldfield, Paul Ovenden, Arthur Page, Andy Peebles, Anthony Phillips, Cliff Richard, Mike Richards, Clive Robson, Jimmy Savile, David Scutts, Don Short, Chrissie Shrimpton, Jean Shrimpton, Winston Stagers, the late Ian Stewart, Graham Walder, Carol Ward, Adele Warlow, Walton Wilkinson, Tom Wolfe. Peter Tsappis was no help at all.

Finally, personally, I should again thank: Focus Photography, Malcolm Galfe, Johnny Johnson, Vincent Lorimer, Sue Pauliny, John Prins III, John Prins IV, Jan Ridley, my father Sefton Sandford, Peter Scaramanga, Fred and Cindy Smith, Hilary Stevens, Katrina Whone, Richard Wigmore, the staff of the New York, Seattle and British Libraries, my long-suffering friend and secretary Terry Lambert and, for the record, Kathy Ward, Caroline Forsyth and Lois Macnab, all of whom were there when called on.

C.S.
London, 1993

CONNECTION

BOAC Flight 505 landed in New York on 1 June 1964. Mick Jagger was first down the steps. Dressed in jeans and suede jacket, he walked with strides belonging to a man a foot taller, climbing the great tree of cameras and lights, carrying his own luggage. In the press conference reporters shouted at him like wild beasts. Bulbs crowded at the platform's edge. 'You play . . . the same kind of music . . . as the *Beatles*?' Jagger's hair puffed up and down, his lips pursed. 'No.' Another journalist swayed towards the stage. 'Who's the *leader*?' A long pause followed this. More than one individual seemed on the verge of speech. Finally Jagger came forward, his body so flat that fore looked identical to aft. 'We are,' he said. 'All of us.' The conference ended and the Rolling Stones were conveyed by Cadillac to the Astor Hotel. A girl jumped Jagger then backed off, hurriedly, like two cats tangling and thinking better of it. He stared at her open-mouthed, the dark ajar spot forming a hole in his narrow face, before the police escorted him upstairs.

The colour television spread light through the curtained room. Jagger looked outside: hundreds of girls (encouraged, it later transpired, by the group's management) were holding roses, love notes and furry animals, their faces turned upwards like radar dishes among the press. Media arrangements were elaborate. Jagger seemed to relish the prolonged focus on him, the drama of delay. An hour late, a second news conference began: 'You own a razor?' Jagger smiled. 'Ever use it?' Disarming grin. 'How about . . . a . . . *tie*?' Through the lobby, smoothly as if he were being paid, Jagger proceeded to engage, to enchant, obeying his manager's precept to 'under no circumstances, blow it' in New York. As if in confirmation he merely smiled when Murray Kaufman, the celebrated disc jockey, enquired, 'You want to lie down?' as, outside, yet more girls awaited the answer.

Midnight found Jagger in the Peppermint Lounge watching the Younger Brothers impersonate, among others, Mick Jagger. Girls repeatedly approached him with flowers, gifts and the information that their parents were out of town; boys, too, gave him a second glance. Drinks came to the table. Jagger discovered himself having dinner, like looking down into a food advertisement in a magazine, steaks the size of his head. At one the car appeared – more of a boat, it seemed to drift through oceans of dust, the pavements cracked from underneath, whole streets lifted up like crypts in a horror film. At the hotel the girls pounced, the police pushed, Jagger shuffled in. His feet made funnel-shaped tracks on the scarlet rug. In the suite the television was still on: Johnny Carson was interviewing Woody Allen. The phone was ringing. Girls shouted his name. Jagger went to the window as the voices beat up. 'Mick,' called one, 'is God.'

Jagger smiled, frightening himself.

Down a long concrete corridor, more of a tunnel, the Rolling Stones come up on stage. A canopy sends down blue light from a wedge of sky, blue scarves hang on balustrades, a film crew lights up, the group squeezes out by bearded carpenters, electricians, engineers, ritually late; chaos.

Stage left, draped in yellow breeches, blue kneepads, blue football shirt, Jagger lifts one foot, rotates, shuffles, legs rail thin, shoulders sloped, his check jacket darting like a shoal of carnivorous fish. Turning the corner, the clothes seem to precede him by a split-second. He may be the smallest adult ever to wear American football uniform. 'How long?' he asks a man identified as 'Roy Lamb – Access All Areas'. 'How *lonng*?' His voice is the squeak of a plastic toy accidentally stepped on.

Lamb ignores him. On the other side of the pink painted curtain the crowd wells up, 70,000 strong, the canopy actually quivering in the communal exhalation. Jagger goes back to his drill. Up close you can see the waxy shine of makeup. His body seems too slight for the heft and weight of his head. His mouth looks enormous, the puckered lips sharp in profile. Up comes a padded knee, little flips of his foot and a head toss. Jagger's mouth gives him the appearance of pouting even when he isn't. 'How long,' he asks, 'O Lord?'

This brings a laugh from the man who sits bulky in his coat at the piano. On cue Lamb looks back to where a bald, bearded man (Allan Rogan – Access All Areas) hands up a guitar, hangs it and lights a cigarette. Music pumps up, 'Take The "A" Train', the vaulted interior of the room starts to shake, a third noise cuts in: 'Would you welcome, please . . .', Lamb's arm rises, the curtain flares, the band starts 'Under My Thumb'. Jagger stands there for an instant, eyes closed, the smallest of the eight figures now on stage. The crowd catches him sullen and still, like a missionary hauled in front of a court – one whose jurisdiction he doesn't recognize; rigid. Remote, even. The curtain flaps. At the last second Jagger comes forward, eyes open, darts, feints, arms pumping and shouts *Hello* in a voice quite unlike that he uses offstage. *Under my thumb*, a bass line rolls, *There's a woman*, peaks, *Who once had me down*, and breaks, over and over, the seven musicians silent and scowling, Jagger pacing left and right, a curious way of using his free hand, pumping as if coiling a rope. In the guitar break he stamps the stage with his foot four, five, a dozen times, in the way of a talking horse. He starts to sweat. His eyes hooded. The lips. Jagger, you notice, is completely impassive as he sings. The motion is all in his arms and flailing legs – nothing to the face at all. 'Under My Thumb' wells again, the London of day-glo, ruffles and Chelsea boots translated to suburban Seattle, 1981. If Jagger has any nostalgia for this era he artfully conceals it from the crowd, who get only short shouted remarks like *Yeah . . . How you doin?* (a Jagger standard) and, 'Here's one for you women' ('Let It Bleed'). The last is greeted by prolonged silence. Jagger, for all his worldliness (this being his 239th American performance) can still, periodically, get it wrong. For ten minutes he engages in the sort of bad acting – hamming, snorting, streaming from the flues of his nose – only a gifted actor can produce. He recovers with a quick, hip-grinding 'Start Me Up', then crouches as the drummer plays 'Miss You', coiled like a half-open blade – or flick-knife. Two more numbers, Jagger, bare-chested now, howling and kneeing the stage, the bass rolling: the pianist removes his coat. On the last bar the four standing Stones come forward to give their rendition of a bow. Jagger stoops. His lips almost brush the stage. As he walks back his face is studiously calm. 'Not bad,' he says in a flat, ironic voice. The drummer shrugs. Alan ('Access All Areas') Dunn hands up a bottle of water. Jagger shuffles backwards on his toes. Two men in suits, one moustachioed, come forward, their faces wreathed in docile goodwill, beaming volts of excessive charm.

'Great,' says one. 'Mick.'

'Really,' the other.

'Sawright,' says Jagger. 'What's the house?'

'Seventy-two five . . . times sixteen' – he taps his briefcase, flat as a wafer – 'plus outside, we're looking at two, maybe three.'

In other words a quarter of a million dollars. As Jagger grunts, Dunn falls on him with a kind of luminous cape;

it turns out to comprise the American and British flags. 'Satisfaction,' he says cryptically. 'Now.'

Jagger stands there, a half-naked man wearing a cloak talking to his business advisers. 'Satisfaction,' he repeats, as in the darkness thousands of naked lights flare up like hearts. 'Now.'

Then Jagger is off and running again.

· II ·

THE DARTFORD DELTA

Mick Jagger was not born on 26 July 1944. The date was almost universally accepted until his twenty-fifth birthday. Throughout the 1960s Jagger's publicist Les Perrin, a man in the Hollywood tradition of George Evans (with whom he once briefly shared a client, Frank Sinatra), insisted over and over, with the precision of an engine: 'Name – Jagger, M.; born – Dartford, Kent; on – 26-7-44.' It became accepted, proverbial. As late as his marriage in May 1971 Jagger's age was widely misquoted. He did nothing to correct it. Perrin was a persuasive man. 'Twenty-six,' he told reporters in his plausible voice, flashing his *Me? Lie?* baby-blue eyes. Even Jagger was thought to believe him.

When, seven or eight centuries ago, a village youth was considered deficient in cunning or nerve, he was liable to earn the name Scutt. The word was originally used of the tail of the hare, particularly noticeable when the animal was fleeing. Later the Scutts became prominent in Micklesfield, Suffolk; a William Skutt (so spelt) appears in the Subsidy Rolls there in 1545. The family was granted a coat of arms: gold with three deer, and on a red stripe a tower between two silver shields. In the sixteenth and seventeenth centuries the Scutts were encouraged to migrate to Ireland, where they developed a skill for peat farming, mining and petty larceny. They were state-sponsored settlers who undertook to keep the faith (hence 'Undertakers') in return for lands previously occupied by native Catholics. Ireland being what it was, Scutts were later among those on board the White Sails to the New World. William and Mary Scutt settled in Virginia in 1741; William Scutts in 1754; Jacob Scutts and his wife Eva in Philadelphia in 1795. Eventually the family was drawn as far south as Washington.

After America, Australia. Not for nothing had Scuttses crossed the globe for seven centuries. Before World War I a branch of the family had emigrated from Greenhithe, Kent, to New South Wales, where they laboured and traded. Possessed in the female line of musical talent, Scuttses (as they became) were prominent in the local cathedral choir. They mined, farmed and they played cricket. The daughter of a neighbour of Alfred Charles Scutts remembers them as 'forever scheming, and planning to move'. Physically slight, their faces with closely set eyes, abundant lips, the Scuttses, she says, 'were always in a different dimension'. Her chief memory is that they seemed distant.

Alfred Scutts was a yacht-builder of excessive energy. Wrinkled under the chin, around the pale eyes that gazed longingly in the opposite direction, Alfred spoke frequently of going home. In the event, it was his wife Gertrude who returned without him; for her, migrating was only fulfilling the family tradition. Gertrude's neighbour remembers the statement 'we're leaving' as preceding departure by less than a month. Mother and five children set sail in January 1917. Alfred was in search of his fortune, but meanwhile his wife and offspring travelled steerage. Their ship, the SS *Rotorua*, arrived in Liverpool eight weeks later; it was snowing. ('Look,' said one of the children. 'White sand.') Immediately it set out on the return journey the vessel was torpedoed and sank.

The town where they settled was in a state of barely perceptible growth. The month the Scuttses arrived an incorporation inquiry concluded that 'this . . . is not a dormitory town for the Metropolis. The building of houses has been for a population which in the main makes its living locally . . . The *Daily Telegraph* Paper Mills have duplicated and construction is approaching completion of more works . . .' The inquiry put the town's population at 24,000 (including a number of Belgian and French evacuees having fled to Britain on the outbreak of war); the location as 'an important industrial area, comprising engineering, paper-making, chemicals, flour mills and other large works . . . employing many thousands'; communications as 'good', transport 'excellent', the weather (with some understatement) as 'moderate'. The name of this idyll was Dartford, Kent.

Gertrude and her children settled briefly at 20 Orchard Street in the town centre. Her only daughter, Eva Ensley, born 6 April 1913, did what any four-year-old would do. She attended the Church of England school. She learned to cook. She queued with her mother for food. (Local shops were frequently besieged in 1918, with meat rationing officially introduced in the southern half of England that February.) As soon as she was able Eva was sent to work in an office in Bexleyheath, where she remembers seeing a first flickering prototype television, and later still became a hairdresser. By then the family lived at 233 Lowfield Street, an avenue descending due south from Dartford Market. At weekends Eva attended dances at the nearby Glentworth Club or the no-less-adjacent parish hall. She rode the omnibus. She sang in Holy Trinity Church. A small, immaculately turned out teenager, personable and bright, Eva's looks were distinctive. Her hair, which she arranged herself, was cut diagonally over her high forehead. Smiling, each of Eva's features changed expression. Her heavy lips, the subject of much local comment, fell open; they looked pulled-on and swollen. To compensate she developed a severe look not unlike the actress Norma Shearer. Consequently friends found her odd. 'She always thought we teased her for being foreign,' says one. Wrongly: it was the lips.

Eva was not, herself, sensitive to being 'foreign'. She may have deflected questions about her upbringing, with its implied stigma of crudeness and colonialism; certainly she developed a marked English accent. Arthur Key, who lived in the same street, remembers her as 'shy and aiming to please'. Her own view is that 'I fitted in pretty quickly. I had to.' She seems never to have had a sense of being *deraciné* or even 'different', neither English nor Australian. She was, after all, bright, attractive, travelled and houseproud. The Scuttses' home was, like Eva herself, impeccable. It was a redbrick house of modest character and despite the relative roughness of the neighbourhood – a nearby house being burnt in mysterious circumstances – the Scuttses' was neat, tidy and replete with the chintz, the tea-sets and knick-knacks then demanded of Dartford society. 'Inside,' says Key, 'it was almost a museum.'

Credit for this lies exclusively with Eva. She dominated the house, she put up with her brothers, she organized family singsongs at which Gertrude ('Gran') joined lustily in. Eva's treatment of her family was, says Key, 'saintly', though she could be irascible (as, too, have been many saints). At a time when women married young, it was early 1940, approaching her twenty-seventh birthday, before Eva pushed open the black iron gate, entered the red door of Lowfield Street and announced to her mother, 'I'm engaged.'

Her fiancé was an almost morbidly shy man named Basil Jagger. The Jaggers were West Riding traders whose name (variations include Jaggard, Gager, Gigge and Gigger) denotes a carrier, pedlar or hawker. (In later years Mick Jagger preferred the etymology 'knifer', derived from the verb 'jag' – to pierce or cut in tatters.) The family were no less migrant than the Scuttses. As early as 1290 a branch settled in Glasgow, where Rudolf, Andreas and Finlay Jagger were traders in metal. They too were encouraged to take passage to Ireland; they too were among those en route to the New World. Jeremy Jagger settled in Pennsylvania in 1637; his cousin Jonathon in Connecticut a decade later. Eventually the family fanned west, where they were granted lands along the St Lawrence and in the Niagara Peninsula. A William Jagger was arrested for battery in Potsdam, New York, in 1861. Other members joined the Union armies in the American Civil War. The family crest was, aptly, a hand brandishing a sword.

In England the Jaggers remained settled in Yorkshire and, by the late nineteenth century, Kent. Only the offer of a teaching position brought David Ernest Jagger to Wickham Bishops, a village immediately east of Chelmsford in Essex. It was there that his second son Basil Fanshawe (his wife Harriet's maiden name) was born on 13 April 1913. For the remainder of the war, during which he served in the Royal Flying Corps, David's sons were raised by two uncles. Later he was appointed headmaster of a school at Lower Peever, Cheshire, then of St Mary's, Greenfield, Lancashire; Basil himself was enrolled there. Early on the boy showed unusual physical prowess. He excelled at all sports, particularly gymnastics, and was able to throw a cricket ball further than most adults. He was also, according to a schoolfriend, 'always the most unassuming in class'. Later Basil made it known that he preferred to be called henceforth by the more genial 'Joe'. Joe it was.

David and his family spent much of the next decade in Greenfield. As a headmaster he was both patient and progressive, with something gloomy about his outlook. Some of the austerity of Lancashire rubbed off on him. Joe, in turn, was a quiet, reticent youth whose chief distinction lay on the games field. His name is on a plaque in his Oldham grammar school as an outstanding footballer. The same schoolfriend describes him thus: 'Thin, wiry, almost rubberlike in the legs. In gym Joe was always being held up to us as an example.' He ends by adding, 'It rather embarrassed him.'

Later, faced with the bleak prospect of finding a job, Joe looked south, east – even west; a neighbour, Roger Hayes, remembers him 'talking vaguely about America'. He attended Manchester University, then King's College, London. After teaching briefly in Bedford he answered an advertisement for East Central School in Dartford where Joe arrived as a physical education instructor in 1938. His written brief was '. . . to offer the opportunity to study PE in detail . . . providing insight, understanding and knowledge of man's movement, performance and behaviour in sport and recreation'. According to Ian King, an East Central graduate, 'Joe was an able communicator, whose chief asset was an obvious love of sport.'

East Central was an all-boys school of three hundred students, later becoming the Downs School and admitting girls. The decor was spartan, the regime austere. The school log records 'Mr Jagger and Mr Buzzey' as having 'taken boys for a brisk walk . . . as a Sunday treat'. Conditions deteriorated in 1939 when, in a single week, 27,215 gas masks were issued in Dartford and eighty thousand sandbags were obtained to shore up local buildings. Hundreds, Jagger included, volunteered to serve as Air Raid Precautions personnel. Shelters were built at strategic points in the town. In the early months of the war it was widely feared that Germany would attempt poison attacks from the air. Children were issued with special 'Mickey Mouse' masks with red rubber face pieces and bright eye rims. Rooms in homes were gas-proofed with cellulose sheets or curtains. Even the tops of post office pillar boxes were given a coating of yellowish gas detector paint.

Rationing followed on 8 January 1940. Each adult received four ounces of bacon or ham and four ounces of butter per week. Sugar was limited to two pounds a month. Restrictions on meat came in March 1940. By June the bacon quota was down to three ounces, tea to two. At times water was rationed to a pump in the town centre. The apparatus was ornate and the water itself a faded cherry colour. Queues were long.

Joe Jagger lived in semi-detached lodgings at 147 Brent Lane in south-eastern Dartford. The house had its own garage, a vestibule, even a small front garden. The neighbourhood was a width upward of Lowfield Street. In late 1939 he met Eva Scutts through a mutual friend; by spring they were engaged. By then Eva had transformed into a confident, even glamorous young woman. Engagement agreed with her. She paid renewed attention to her hair. In the food queues she was seen reading improving books (*Tom Sawyer*, Key remembers). Her slight body was clothed in bargain Utility dresses bought at market, every purchase involving a battle with other bargain-hunters. Eva was dogged. She was determined. She it was who made arrangements to marry; she who confirmed plans. ('Now,' she was supposed to have told Joe, 'or never.') The couple took instruction at Holy Trinity. They were twenty-seven. The war outlook was grim: on 5 September 1940 a high explosive bomb demolished the women's wards at Dartford County Hospital, killing a nurse and twenty-four patients. That autumn bombs were dropped on sixty-nine of a possible ninety nights. On 5 December Joe and Eva attended a rehearsal at Holy Trinity. Inside the windows were dark and curtained; outside the day was mild, the river Darent at its second lowest winter level: mark twain.

On the seventh the Jaggers were married, and, after a reception at the Dartford Conybeare Club, honeymooned for a week in Cheshire.

The following two years were hard. Over eleven thousand homes in Dartford were damaged by bombs and at least 150 people killed. From June 1941 schoolchildren were evacuated in large numbers to the west country. East Central remained open with a skeleton staff and Joe was seen leading evacuees, crocodile-file, down Hythe Street to the station. He and Eva lived in Brent Lane, food scarce, the windows permanently shuttered. Only after their thirtieth birthdays was their first child born, a son, Michael.

He was delivered on Monday 26 July 1943. The previous day the RAF had dropped two thousand tons of bombs on Essen and US aircraft attacked the Solomon Islands; in Italy Mussolini resigned in favour of Marshal Badoglio, who undertook preliminary peace discussions with the Allies. The war situation had altered. Elements of normal life were returning. In Dartford a London cricket XI played opposite Brent Lane; Abbott and Costello showed at the State Cinema; the Dartford *Chronicle* carried advertisements for Mazawatte Tea ('The Cup That Cheers'). There was a feeling by mid-1943 that victory could, within the foreseeable future, be won. What was needed was patience. A friend remembers Joe stating that summer 'another year – two at most'. As a boy he had collected caterpillars and studied them for hours, awaiting metamorphosis. When the moment came they were instantly released.

Michael Philip Jagger was born in the Marina Wing attached to Livingstone Hospital, a small redbrick building of Dickensian gloom. His names, with the promising initials M.P., were 'dreamt up' over the next two weeks by Joe and Eva, both of whom had expected a girl. The birth was finally registered on 9 August, the delay having cost the family a fortnight's ration. The boy shared a birthday with Bernard Shaw, Aldous Huxley and Carl Jung – in whose theories he came to be interested. He was healthy, happy and widely admired. Surprisingly early he grew a head of ginger hair. 'Gorgeous' is the description of Mary Cannadine, who lived in nearby St Vincent's Road. 'And adored by Eva . . . She loved the fact that Mike once smeared an entire egg over himself. That was half the weekly ration.'

In June 1944 the V1s began. The *Chronicle* for that month and the next conveys the terror: 'Flying Bombs Night and Day . . . Parents, Daughter and Cook Killed . . . Old

Tavern Blasted ... Child Killed Running for Shelter ... Tragedy of Two Sisters.' On 26 August fourteen were killed and eleven injured in Carrington Road, less than a mile from the Jaggers'. That winter and spring were bleak. Snow fell in March, coal was rationed, chocolate and sweets for the child were minimal. Eva, as in 1918, stood in unending queues. Her lips grew pendulous as she waited, Mike rocking in his boxy pram. In air raids she took cover with him screaming under the stairs. Night fell with December speed, and even Joe looked pale and worn.

The war ended in May. On the eighth a victory party was held in the town centre. Ninety children were entertained to tea, after which there was music and dancing in the street, with floodlighting. Later, the *Chronicle* intoned, 'each child received a bag of sweets and a Savings Stamp'. Mike, still shy of his second birthday, was seen clutching his mother's hand. 'For some reason,' says Cannadine, 'a snarling dog kept running to the table, annoying the children. I remember Mike crying with fright.' The carnival atmosphere continued: in early June a funfair ('with Dodgems, Galloping Horses, Swings, and the usual side-shows too numerous to mention') arrived and fish and chips were distributed free to children. Black-out restrictions ended. (Mick Jagger's first memory is of Eva tearing down sheets from the windows.) Freed hostages, people were determined to act without knowing clearly what to do. Change was inevitable, and on 26 July, the boy's second birthday, a Labour government was elected.

Dartford itself returned a Socialist, Norman Dodds. War changed the town for ever. Power stations such as Richborough and Littlebrook were built, stimulating light industry in the Gray Valley and nearby Bexleyheath. The Wellcome company developed products – including Daraprim, still used in the treatment of malaria – providing hundreds of local jobs. Road and rail links were improved to London. There was renewed talk of a tunnel under the

Thames between Dartford and Purfleet. Cars – Austins, Morrises, Rileys – appeared in greater numbers. A garage was built in Brent Lane, where Joe liked to browse at weekends. At the Mobil station he was asked what size of car he might want. How large a family was he considering? He never answered.

The Jaggers' second son, Christopher, was born on 19 December 1947. By this time the family had moved to 39 Denver Road in west Dartford, a crescent of white pebbledash houses and identical gardens. To emphasize the change Joe was appointed to the staff of the Central Council of Physical Recreation where to his speciality, gymnastics, was added a lifelong love of basketball. Joe was among the founders of the sport in Britain. In 1948 he launched the Kent County Basketball League, working with Marine instructor Bob Clash. 'Joe,' the latter recalls, 'was a natural coach . . . superbly fit, keen, disciplined – but with genuine empathy for children. Young Mike was lucky to have him.'

In September 1947 young Mike was admitted to Maypole Primary School, where he was rapidly acknowledged as bright, energetic and extrovert. The last took form in two ways: while showing early promise as a sportsman he could be fractious, even aggressive. As Eva recalls: 'When he was four he had a phase of hitting people for no reason. Once, on holiday, we were walking along a beach when Mike knocked down every single sandcastle we came across. Even ones that little boys were still building.' And Chris Jagger? 'He was just a punch-bag . . . Mike used to beat him up regularly.'

At nearby 25 Heather Drive, John Spinks became Mike's companion in the wasteland separating their homes. Jagger, he recalled, 'possessed tremendous energy . . . He was always stamping his foot, tossing his head, screaming and shouting. Anything to let off steam.' On the other hand, he was a mother's boy. 'He did everything he was told by Eva,' said Spinks. 'I never saw someone about-turn so quickly.'

The boy's gifts included mimicry. Peter Holland, another

friend in adjacent Seaton Road, says he could imitate anything. Even as an infant, Eva confirms, Mike would pose in
front of the family wireless, accompanying tunes with lyrics
improvised on the spot. He became an active participant in
the family singsongs conducted by Eva and Gran Scutts.
The latter took him to hear the Salvation Army band in
Central Park. Mike's foot tapped appreciatively.

On 9 January 1951 he became pupil 112 at Wentworth
County Primary School. Both Spinks and Holland joined
him. Another student, Gareth Bolton, recalls Mike for two
things: his intense, almost manic energy and the pocket
chemistry set with which, he announced gravely, he
intended to blow up the world. Perhaps for this very reason
Jagger, concluded his teacher Alan Mills, 'could be insufferable . . . he mimicked his elders constantly'. Opinion was
divided between those who thought him intelligent and
liked him, and those who thought him intelligent and didn't.
Elsa Smith, a relief teacher at Wentworth, remembered:
'He was always the first out of his seat to collect books . . .
the first to say, "Please, Miss, can we play football?" . . .
Very popular with his friends, less so with staff.' Among the
former was a pale, unfed-looking youth with protuberant
ears and a love of Roy Rogers: Keith Richards.

Richards was born in Livingstone Hospital on 18
December 1943. His father Bert worked as a foreman at
the Osram electrical factory adjacent to the Hammersmith
Palais. He, his wife Doris and only child lived at 33
Chastilian Road, abutting the Jaggers'. Doris's father, Gus
Dupree, was a guitar and violin player in an amateur dance
band and was, his daughter states, 'a laugh'. Dupree spent
money like a Klondike miner. A loud, exotic figure, fractious
and extravagant, he was adored, even worshipped, by
his grandson. In the playground at Wentworth County
Richards repeatedly announced his intention to become a
cowboy and play the guitar. This was the first statement he
made to Mike Jagger.

Jagger was growing up in some comfort. The early fifties brought a release from post-war austerity. Dartford itself was expanding and much of the Victorian quality of the town vanished. At the same rate of speed council houses, parks and office blocks appeared. In an election address Dodds spoke of 'national optimism'. The 1951 Festival of Britain aptly followed the resignation of gloomy, ascetic Stafford Cripps as Chancellor. After the uniformity of war there was a renewed sense of the individual. That autumn Churchill offered an allegory of the distinction between the Conservative and Labour parties:

> The difference between our outlook and the Socialists' is the difference between the ladder and the queue. We are for the ladder. Let all try their best to climb. They are for the queue; let each wait in his place till his turn.

In October, aged seventy-six, he was returned as Prime Minister. Britain, subsidized by the US, committed to defence production, was palpably living beyond its means. No matter: to the grass-roots indicators of zero inflation and relaxed rationing was added a glimmer of American consumerism. The Dartford *Chronicle* in the early fifties bristles with references to Frigidaires, to Hoovers and radios. Immediately following the 1953 Coronation national television ownership rose by eight hundred thousand. It became possible to absorb foreign goods, arts and films. *High Noon* gave new credence to the cult of rugged Americanness. On a contemporary note advertisements appeared of exotic yachtlike cars. However slowly, imperfectly grasped, such things, as they will, left their impression. At Wentworth Mike Jagger now gave it as his ambition to own a red Cadillac.

His immediate horizons were restricted to suburban Wilmington. The Jaggers moved there in 1954. Newlands, a three-bedroomed stucco house, its rear garden fringed with apple trees, was a definite step up on Churchill's ladder. Joe, commuting to London as a lecturer and instructor, now described himself as a 'technical representative'. (Later Eva, with her interest in hair and make-up, became a cosmetics demonstrator – not, as has been said, an Avon Lady – working on a referral basis; always the practical one, she felt she must do something, and do it now. Somehow it always seemed to be up to her.) The house was one of a dozen homes in a private road. At night warm draughts of air lifted the lace curtains and blinds. There were other luxuries. The previous summer the family had holidayed in southern Spain; in 1954 it was St Tropez, where Mike acted as interpreter. In both resorts he was seen clutching a cheap flamenco guitar, but without any serious effort to play it. His brother noted: 'Mike had no interest in music . . . He didn't take piano lessons or anything like that. My memory of him is how much time he spent studying, always with his books. I really think he wanted to be a businessman. I think Mike's main ambition as a boy was to be rich. Money meant a lot to him.' Eva, forty years later, would insist 'he was always the least musical of the family'.

Mike's diligence paid off. In July 1954 he was confronted with the Eleven Plus. It is perhaps difficult today to convey the significance then attached to the exam: for those passing there was the promise of grammar school, with its prospect of university, the professions or the civil service. The alternative was the secondary modern. There only a minority of pupils progressed as far as O levels, still less further. The distinction, Joe knew, was stark. After a few mild pushes, his son set to work that summer with a vengeance. A fortnight short of his eleventh birthday he passed the exam and a subsequent test to Dartford Grammar School, seventy-second of 161 entrants. On 15 September 1954 he became Jagger M. P., admission number 4219, cycling up West Hill in his new uniform of gold-edged maroon blazer and cap.

The school, founded in 1576, was itself just entering the twentieth century. It had recently added a science building and new football fields. Ancient as it was it still pursued the normal British interests; outside the gate the Oddfellows Arms provided relief from the world of gowns, prefects and arcane rituals within. David Drinkwater, who entered the school that September, remembers it as 'a system of privileges, rewards and punishments ... very hierarchical ... like something out of *Upstairs, Downstairs*'. The headmaster's name was, aptly enough, Hudson.

For three years Mike Jagger was a model student. In 1955 his first-form exams placed him fifteenth out of thirty. His form master, Dick Allen, considers him to have been hardworking and possessed of 'intelligence without brilliance'. (His official report on Jagger reads, 'A good start'.) All parties were agreed he was willing to learn. In later years Jagger himself recalled: 'I never got to have a raving adolescence between the age of twelve to fifteen, because I was concentrating on my studies ... but then that's what I wanted to do and I enjoyed it.' In Drinkwater's estimate, Mike was neither popular nor the reverse. He was anonymous. His brother confirmed: 'As a teenager, I don't think Mike had many friends. He didn't go out very often and nobody much came around the house.' He drifted apart even from Keith Richards. The latter had not only entered technical school but moved to Spielman Road on the Temple Hill estate in far-off north Dartford. Dick Taylor, a classmate of Jagger's who later knew Richards well, says, 'That was a major thing between them. They were brought up on opposite sides of the tracks.' While Jagger cycled home to leafy Wilmington, Richards grew up in a zone of bleak redbrick flats and daubed graffiti. 'I was a complete lout,' he states.

In 1955 rock and roll happened. It reached England – specifically the Rialto, Dartford – in the form of *Blackboard Jungle*, a teen drama dealing with student anarchy, a theme reiterated in *Rebel Without A Cause*. It was followed by *Don't Knock The Rock*, wherein Bill Haley's ersatz rhythm and blues, played to a swing beat, was compèred by Alan Freed, and the pivotal *Jailhouse Rock*. Haley it was who invaded the British hit parade with 'Rock Around The Clock', 'See You Later, Alligator' and 'Rockin' Through The Rye'. Unlikely as he seemed, the portly middle-aged raver was the Francis Xavier of rock and roll. He spread the word. When in 1956 Haley and the Comets toured Britain they left behind a trail of smashed windows and damp theatre seats. Music, for the first time, became an issue. It became a conflict. Brooding in Spielman Road, for Keith Richards it changed everything. 'From then on,' he recalled, 'there was only one thing I was going to do.'

Jagger's reaction was different. He studied rock and roll like an anthropologist. Evenings found him in front of the Newlands television watching *Cool For Cats*, *6.5 Special* and *Oh Boy*. Even then he reserved judgement. ('I wasn't particularly fond of Elvis or Bill Haley,' he noted; 'for some reason they didn't appeal.') The truth is that for Mike – as for Mick – Jagger, music was part of something larger. What Jagger craved was style: a red car; money. Sex, even. As early as 1955 he developed a lasting fixation with America, where the cars were redder, the money greener, the sex – sexier. That autumn *The Seven Year Itch* reached Dartford, and was a sensation. Jagger's obsession had a definite origin. Aged twelve, he took a summer job on an American base outside Dartford. His brief was to coach gymnastics and running. In turn he played American football and baseball. (Thanks to Joe, he was already proficient at basketball; another friend, Robert Wallis, noted 'he was keen on that because it was American . . . Mike was the one with the real American boots to play in when the rest of us had only gym shoes'.) On the base, too, Jagger met José, a black cook who first played rhythm and blues for him. He watched the Stars and Stripes ceremonially lowered at dusk. He drank Coke.

He even developed a parody of an American accent. In short, the boy returning to school in September 1955 was changed for ever. His motive to be rich (and preferably famous) had met with opportunity.

Jagger, says Drinkwater, was now 'quite definite' in his ambitions. He wanted to be separate. He was filled with notions and plans as well as specific tactics. That autumn he announced his intention to be a millionaire. To another student, Clive Robson, he uttered the words 'The States are where it's at', memorable for one who had never been west of Marbella. There was the usual speculation about sex, with Jagger giving frequent hints of recent practical experience. A quarter of a century later he declared his 'first screw' to have been 'age twelve, with two girls in a garden shed'. Robson's verdict? 'Unlikely, to say the least.'

That autumn Elvis, Little Richard and Fats Domino could be dimly heard on American Forces radio. Peter Holland, who considered himself 'decidedly hip', realized that even then Jagger's tastes were more advanced: 'He always sneered at what he called "waffly pop", preferring – in quotes again – "real music" . . . by which he meant as black, and preferably obscure, as possible.' Among those Jagger considered 'real' were Big Bill Broonzy and Muddy Waters. His first love, though, was for Little Richard. His schoolfriend Dick Taylor remembers 'Jagger going into ecstasies at Richard's name . . . I distinctly recall him asking Joe for money to buy "Good Golly, Miss Molly", and being turned down'. (Jagger's own version: 'I tried to get money out of my old man . . . I said, "Richard's retiring. This is the last record. Gimme seven and six 'cause he's not gonna make any more . . ." And my father said, "I'm glad he's retired. I ain't giving you the money to buy that trash."') 'Waffly pop', meanwhile, continued its ascent that winter. In Britain it had its origin in the strange case of Ken Colyer's Lip.

Colyer played trumpet in a jazz sextet led by Chris Barber.

Perversely, he had a weak mouth. In order to give his star player a rest, Barber devised a four-piece group within the main unit to perform while Colyer recuperated. The quartet consisted of guitar, homemade bass, a suitcase banged by brooms and a washboard strummed with thimbles: skiffle. Barber acquired the name from that given to parties held to raise rent for the urban poor in, primarily, Chicago and New Orleans. The style caught on. The music was popular precisely because of its accessibility. Anyone could skiffle. Barber's *New Orleans Joys* committed the form to vinyl, an ex-serviceman named Tony Donegan (later changed to Lonnie in deference to Lonnie Johnson) spearheading the craze. Everywhere washboards, tea-chests, even cups, knives and forks were seized on by tremulous adolescents. Rage amounting to delirium swept Britain. And what, parents asked, for? The reasons for this new mania remained unclear.

Skiffle spread, in time, to Dartford. By 1956 the grammar school sported two competing groups, the Bucktowns and the Sidewinders. Jagger belonged to neither, remaining promised to the 'purer' blues. Another student, Graham Walder, remembers him as 'self-consciously devoted to the style he called "real" music ... Real being the word he used'. Jagger's commitment remained strictly theoretical. Short of reminding his immediate circle – Holland, Drinkwater, Robson, Taylor, Bob Beckwith, Alan Etherington – that America, and specifically American blues, were 'where it's at', Jagger had no definite musical plans. He neither sang nor played an instrument. His child's guitar remained in the Newlands closet. Jagger entered his teens almost without noticing. His school reports that summer are uniform: 'Very pleasing ... Doing well ... Has worked well'; a master, Arthur Page, describes him as 'immaculately well-behaved'. When Joe and Eva consulted Page on Parents' Day they were told they had nothing to worry about. Young Mike had a future – he was certain of that. Asked to speculate, Page shrugged, indicating the limitless range of Jagger's horizons. Journalism? Politics? Anything seemed possible.

Sport, even. Physically, Jagger was fast growing up in his father's image. The rear garden at Newlands was dotted with barbells, badminton nets and cricket stumps. (Eva's one great concern was that her elder son would be injured: 'He went through a Tarzan period when he would swing from tree to tree, giving out loud cries and screams. He used to terrify me.') At school Jagger was proficient at cricket, athletics and basketball; he dabbled in rock-climbing and was taken canoeing by Joe. His father believed 'he could have been a great athlete . . . he was excellent, but he didn't want to be tied down with all the practice'. The initial outcome was something of a disappointment to Joe.

On 26 July 1956 Jagger turned thirteen. That morning in Manchester England and Australia began the most dramatic cricket match in living memory. On a wider scale, 26 July was also the day Gamal Nasser nationalized the Suez Canal, precipitating a crisis of which the result changed Britain's world status for ever. There was a party at Newlands for Mike, attended by Robson and Drinkwater. At intervals the radio broadcast news from Old Trafford, engendering much good-natured ribbing of Eva as England's position strength-ened. This surprised Robson, to whom Jagger's mother had 'never seemed particularly Australian'; she had no accent. His overall impression was of 'a completely happy family'.

Things changed in 1957. For one, Jagger's voice broke. The ginger-haired cherub metamorphosed into leering adoles-cence. His face, says Robson, was what set him apart – not one sneer, but a greatest hits anthology of the hundred pouts already practised and the million that would follow. As if in confirmation he developed a haircut in the style of Tommy Steele, who topped the charts that January with

'Singing The Blues'. He was seen to arrive at school wearing moccasins rather than the prescribed black lace-ups. Worst of all, he appeared at Founder's Day sporting a dark jacket with luminous silver threads. 'The cheek,' says Walter Bennett.

Bennett taught Jagger for the following four years. He dates the boy's 'relative decline' from 1957. Between the bouts of brooding and teenage inertia he still had 'normal' periods, sometimes extending to a week – but from then on Jagger essentially lost interest. Adolescence, peer-pressure, even the distant influence of 'real' music may have contributed; they established the mood. But what really transformed Jagger was the awareness that, academically, he would always be average; once he realized that he succumbed. 'With Mike,' says a classmate, Paul Ovenden, 'you had the impression he had to be number one. When he found out he wasn't, he tended to give up.' Robson confirms that 'from about fourteen, he seemed to be freewheeling'. That summer Jagger's reports were merely average – 'Good on the whole ... Generally satisfactory' – they would deteriorate. Games, too, suffered. Joe remembers his son as having broken the unofficial record for the school half-mile, then immediately complaining that running was 'a drag'. Gone, too, was the 'lovely, looping bowler' compared by Robson to the England player Brian Statham. When Jagger played now he did so with a permanent scowl in clothing invariably soiled, where previously he had been laundered to almost ectoplasmic degree.

Girls, as they will, found this intriguing. Nineteen fifty-seven, rather than the more optimistic 1955, was the year Jagger discovered sex. A short walk down Shepherds Lane led to the girls' grammar school. There Jagger was the centre of heated analytical discussion. His very 'ugliness' was deemed by some attractive. Yet others took bets on the prospects of making him speak, let alone smile. (Few ever collected.) A girl of Jagger's age, Carol Ward, states there was 'intense competition' to escort him on to nearby Dartford Heath. It became a challenge. A number, she believes, succeeded – though never beyond the stage of 'heavy, mutual groping'. They were fourteen.

Girls were one way to solace the gap left by his academic demise. Music was another. That autumn Buddy Holly's 'That'll Be The Day' reached number one. During the year there were six million-selling hits by Elvis, three each by Little Richard and Fats Domino, two each by Holly, Chuck Berry, Sam Cooke and Jerry Lee Lewis. Jagger, his pale, aquiline cheek clamped to American Forces radio, now confessed that Presley and Holly, while not 'real' music, were listenable to. Lewis, he was heard to mutter, was 'a gas'. The vague feeling that Jagger was and would always be 'separate' began to find definite expression. Mike, his friends state, was en route to becoming Mick.

The actual transition is recorded on film. For more than a year Joe Jagger had acted as technical adviser to the ATV programme *Seeing Sport*. The idea was to promote physical fitness in children. In 1957 he periodically used his elder son as a model, so much that, according to the cricketer Alf Gover who was also employed on the series, 'it became usual to see this rather withdrawn teenager hanging around the set'. In the ATV vaults a segment can still be seen dealing with rock-climbing; with great crashes of music the set is revealed – John Disley, stage centre, in front of a cliff or precipice. Briefly he states the virtues of climbing and the concomitant need for proper equipment. On cue Disley is seen in close-up holding a dismembered foot. 'Here's Michael,' he states, 'wearing a pair of gym shoes.' The shoes are as nothing compared to the pout worn by Mike Jagger. The camera recedes to show a boy of fourteen in striped sweater and corduroys. His pursed lips and hooded eyes hint at complicated emotions (Boredom? Resentment? Yearning? – certainly none of the assertiveness of the later legend). At this stage Disley directs his victim to the rock face. Jagger shimmies down the twenty-foot ledge; the camera catches him skulking at the bottom. Immediately Joe (so introduced) appears. Father and son demonstrate the art of teamwork. Roped together they ascend, Joe glancing twice, three times, a shade anxiously at Mike. The boy bangs against the rock like an enraged ape in a monkey house. Disley appears again. He commends Joe, the leader, and Mike, the beginner. The latter is asked to abseil down the rock. The look with which he greets this is incandescent. Disley's skin must have been asbestos. With pouting lips and tremulous limbs Jagger sways earthwards. Disley utters the striking line, 'You want to wear thick trousers when you're doing this.' The camera pans back to reveal a stagey, artificial-looking hill, though the segment was filmed at the High Rocks near Tunbridge Wells (behind which Eva crouched off-camera, cooking sausages). Surreally, an announcer appears in full evening dress stage left. He thanks Disley and congratulates Mike and Joe. Next week's episode is trailed. Meanwhile, we are told, 'Look after yourselves – and, don't forget, look after dear old Mum' – whom the Jaggers can promptly be seen joining in the distance.

'Mike,' says Paul Ovenden, 'became something of a hero as a result. You can imagine how it set him apart.' Both Robson and Holland agree: whatever the rigours of being driven to a hillside in Tunbridge Wells early on Saturday morning, Jagger relished the chance to perform; he loved it. Looking bored was all part of the act. In later years he developed indifference to a virtual art-form. Where other entertainers preened, Jagger sneered or, in exceptional conditions, proffered a wolflike leer. His father and Disley were perhaps the first to receive the treatment in public. Dick Taylor, who was present on the first occasion Jagger sang professionally, states: 'He developed that put-down attitude at school, probably from *Seeing Sport* ... He was always moaning at his father for arranging it, though with underlying affection.'

Everyone liked Joe. Reserved, shy, buttoned-up, he was filled with inner discipline. He neither drank nor smoked. His voice was soft but carrying. Taylor recalls once going out with Jagger at the very moment his father called, 'Michael, your weight-training.' Mike duly returned and spent half an hour pumping barbells. Before meals Joe insisted on grace. This, says Taylor, brought a ripple of embarrassment from his teenage son, though no formal protest. Even then, he notes, 'he was chameleon-like . . . incredibly polite to his parents, for ever grousing behind their backs'. Joe also paid particular attention to the boy's education. Walter Bennett remembers him as 'quiet' – Eva fails to register at all – though asking perceptive questions at Parents' Day. Joe was instrumental in introducing basketball to the school. He coached there periodically, also organizing canoeing expeditions and walks. He was, says Bennett, a man of 'total northern integrity'. When Chris Jagger was given private maths tuition by a young grammar school teacher, Ian Harris, Joe returned the favour by washing Harris's car.

Dick Taylor was also fond of Jagger's parents – 'strict', he says, 'but understanding'. Taylor it was who alerted the Jaggers to the news that Charles Hardin Holly, a.k.a. Buddy, was to appear at the Woolwich Granada. An application was made to Joe who, Taylor recalls, 'agreed in a bemused sort of way'. Thus it was that on the night of Friday 14 March 1958 Mike Jagger attended his first concert. The curtain rose at six forty-five p.m. The compère, incredibly, was Des O'Connor, who introduced first Gary Miller and then the Tanner Sisters. Next week's attraction, the folk singer Peggy Seeger ('Big,' said Jagger, 'deal'), was trailed. Finally the Crickets appeared. They plugged in; they tuned up. Jagger at this stage gave one of his world-weary sighs. What, he seemed to ask, was all the fuss about? Just then Holly announced 'That'll Be The Day', followed by 'Peggy Sue' and 'Rave On'. By the last Jagger was clapping along. During 'Not Fade Away' he was out of his seat, hair puffing over his eyes, miming the – all too 'real' – lyrics, showing incredible levity for one whose precept was at all times to 'stay cool'. Leaving the cinema he went as far as to announce to Taylor, 'That was a gas.' They caught the return train tired but happy.

Everything changed from that moment. Jagger was transfixed, though even that might underestimate a process that bordered on reincarnation. From spring 1958 he dramatically increased both his appreciation and awareness of pop music, including that previously dismissed as 'waffly'. He spent hours at Taylor's home in Bexleyheath listening to Holly, Presley, Lewis – even the Shadows, whose guitarist Hank Marvin, Jagger admitted, had real panache. He was particularly taken by Howlin' Wolf and Muddy Waters, the latter of whom toured England that year for the first time. Waters had already scored a minor hit with the primeval 'Rollin' Stone', recorded whilst at the Ebony Lounge, Chicago, in 1950: Jagger admired the title. He also, says Taylor, still periodically embarked on a passionate defence of the blues, as if worried that his new, expanded interests might be considered deficient in 'cool'. Soon after the Woolwich concert he was back to his derisive self about 'waffly pop'. Where, Jagger asked, were the role models? That March Elvis joined the army. Within a year Holly himself would be dead.

Jagger's schoolwork now began to suffer in earnest. That July his report hinted darkly, 'Determined effort needed'. He and his friends Robson, Drinkwater and Taylor discovered the joys of the Oddfellows Arms. They drank beer; they smoked. During compulsory cross-country runs they found ingenious ways to go missing. Jagger's concentration, according to Robson, was now restricted to three topics: music, girls ('a gas') and everything else ('a drag'). His own memory seems a fair review of his last four years at Dartford Grammar:

School was a drag – all that peaked cap stuff. I suppose the masters had to try and keep discipline going, but if I could find a way to lose my school cap . . . I did. Apart from that, I suppose I was the sort of kid who really had to be pushed into getting any work done.

Walter Bennett remembers the teenage Jagger as 'moderately impossible'; another master, Arthur Page, 'as the sort you always thought was laughing behind your back'. Despite this, Page believes him to have been 'basically decent' and 'a different proposition alone than with his gang'. One evening a history master, Walton Wilkinson, was stocktaking the school library. Jagger entered, saw they were alone and promptly offered to help. 'For two hours,' says Wilkinson, 'he was the best behaved boy in the world.'

The autumn of 1958 was dismal. In September storms swept southern England. The Darent burst its banks. Jagger, alone of the grammar school gang, volunteered for mopping-up operations in the town centre. He was seen by a woman staggering along with sandbags nearly his own weight. For a week near-continuous rain overlay the Dartford gloom. In the course of shoring-up the bank at Overy Street, not far from Holy Trinity, Jagger asked Adele Warlow, forty-eight, how 'old folks' were coping. He meant it, she says, kindly.

It is certain that, of the hundreds who volunteered that week, Jagger's Wentworth schoolfriend was not among them. Early in life Keith Richards developed a powerful aversion to physical effort. In 1958 Richards was living in Spielman Road and periodically attending Dartford Tech. His journey to school took him within a few streets of Jagger in Wilmington. They never met. The latter thinks he may have seen Richards cycling down Oakfield Lane – 'and very erratically, too'. Part of the reason was that Richards invariably travelled in not one but two pairs of trousers. He arrived at school wearing the regulation issue; these were later removed to reveal a pair of stunning tightness. He also had a penchant for red sweaters with white stripes. 'Right before I left Dartford Tech I was considered a bit of a Teddy Boy,' he states. Doris's view was different: 'Actually he was a mummy's boy. He was too sensitive to be a Ted.'

In 1959 the soundtrack to the film *South Pacific* topped the British charts. It vied with selections from *The King and I*, *Gigi* and *West Side Story*. Elvis was in khaki, Little Richard retired, Buddy Holly dead. In the battle of the ages it looked as though the parents might stage a revival. 'The initial kick had gone,' says Dick Taylor. 'There was a definite sense of "What next?"'

Practical involvement, in Jagger's case. At this critical moment he chose to make his first effort at singing the blues. It was at the home of a boy called Michael Turner. Turner and his childhood friend David Soames were forming – in the sense of engaging in endless speculation about – a group. Both had known Jagger at primary school. By early spring they, Taylor, Beckwith and Etherington had formed an informal blues society. They listened to Muddy Waters, they watched *Jazz on a Summer's Day*, wherein Chuck Berry duck-walked across the Newport stage; they practised. It was thus in the unexceptional setting of 4 Marcus Road that Jagger discovered he could, after a fashion, sing – 'poorly' according to Taylor, and in a heavy, leaden-footed manner. The whole group was like that: on a bet Beckwith climbed a tree, holding his guitar. He couldn't get down again and grown-ups had to be sent for to free him. (Etherington's mother Winnifred thought they were 'young to the point of delinquency'.) After another session Jagger cycled home to Wilmington with Soames, discussing his O levels.

He passed seven. His GCE results that summer reveal Jagger to have been gifted at English language, French and history, adequate at maths, deficient in geography, Latin and literature. His successes owed more to intelligence than effort; he was by then blatantly coasting. Jagger's report for the year 1958–59 – 'Too easily distracted' – shows the corner had been turned. 'All that gang,' says Holland, 'were regarded as reprobates.'

The week of Jagger's results, also his birthday. Joe and son consulted the headmaster, and later Bennett: a decision was taken. The boy would enter the sixth form, with its promise of A levels and the prospect of university – no small decision. That summer Jagger set off for Italy with only a schoolfriend for company, an expedition which his father remembers as 'highly organized'. He subsequently announced his ambition to become a journalist, Joe having already issued the mandatory warning about there being 'no money' in music. That autumn Jagger made a final effort to knuckle down. Walton Wilkinson says that he was interested, even obsessed, in history; wrote fluently, wholly without style; and could, on occasion, remember names and dates. Both he and Bennett saw a change in Jagger in the sixth form. 'There was a sense,' says the latter, 'of a more serious attitude, which I, for one, hoped would last.'

It didn't. Waiting for Jagger in both history and English class was Clive Robson. From there things deteriorated. The English master, Eric Brandon, was, says Robson, 'terrible'. While reading *King Lear*, one of the A level texts, Brandon's eyes would change colour; tears came into them. He had a high quivering voice. Naturally Jagger impersonated him. Brandon's classroom had a window overlooking the headmaster's garden. Through this inkwells, books and clothing would be hurled, their owners periodically joining them. 'You'd look up,' says Robson, 'and there was Jagger grinning at you like an ape.'

Trips to the Oddfellows and the Carousel Coffee Bar increased. At the Rose and Crown on West Hill they remember Jagger well. (He put on a 'Terry-Thomas accent' when ordering.) Liberties were taken with the clothing regulations. It was now that Bennett observed Jagger in his silver threads. On another occasion Bennett spoke sharply to him about his general attitude. Which was? 'Sullen, to the point of insolence.' And Jagger's reaction? 'Much the same.'

Contrary to what has been written Jagger and Robson never mutinied against the school Cadet Force. By 1959 it was apparent that National Service would, within a year at most, be phased out. Membership of the Force became voluntary. Jagger, says Robson, merely made known his disinclination for 'that military crap'; the headmaster duly copied. In small but significant other ways they registered protest. That winter a new extension was built to the school; mysteriously Jagger's footprints would appear in the cement. On 29 November 1959 he was reported for the heinous crime of losing his cap. When a protest was lodged at the paucity of Mrs Bannister's school dinners, Jagger and Robson were to the fore. 'Mike,' says the latter, 'was always fond of his stomach.'

Not surprisingly, he never became a prefect. Dick Allen says Jagger was 'less difficult than commonly believed' – but still difficult. Alan Dow, another schoolfriend, describes him as obsessed, in no particular order, with music, girls and 'world events'. The last included the launch of America's Little Joe 4 Spacecraft; Kennedy's election as President; the introduction and rapid availability of the Pill; the *Lady Chatterley* trial; and Yves Klein's Anthropometries, whereby nude women imprinted canvases with their paint-spattered bodies. ('A gas,' said Jagger.) He was unusually aware for a seventeen-year-old. Even Robson, among the most sophisticated sixth-formers, considered Jagger to have distanced himself from other mortals. He liked to drop heavy hints of his experience. America remained 'where it's at', New York 'a gas'. And Dartford? 'A real drag.' About his only consolation was the company of his first formal girlfriend, a local teenager named Ann McAulay. She was regularly invited for tea at Newlands, where her chief memory is of sampling Eva's cosmetics. By all accounts Jagger was a gentleman; he might make lurid observations at school, but one-on-one he was shy to the point of withdrawn. 'I don't think he got beyond first base with Ann,' says Robson, whose grounds for such an observation are compelling: he later married her himself.

Jagger's other passion was basketball. Encouraged by Joe he became secretary of the school club. According to Dow, he was a player of average ability but abundant energy, rarely without a quip on court. The coaches Arthur Page and Warwick Willeard once spoke to him about 'intimidating' an opposition guard. 'He liked to make these cracks,' says Dow. Another team mate, Mike Richards, remembers him as the star of an otherwise indifferent team. For someone who slouched through the latter part of his schooldays, Jagger came startlingly alive in the gym. He leapt. He bounded. He ran back in defence. 'A lot of what came later,' says Richards, 'was learned on court.' By 1960 it was the one point where Jagger's interests and his father's met. Joe lent the team the family Dormobile to travel to away matches. Newly-qualified Mike took the wheel. The tyres pounded erratically. He was a terrible driver, rushing, slowing, weaving eccentrically, all the while his eye on the girls.

Jagger played no further part in the organized life of the school. He debated in the John Duncan Historical Society; he was dragooned as a stagehand in the annual play; otherwise nothing. The *Dartfordian* makes no mention of him until after he left, and even then it remains ambivalent. By July 1960 his report, 'Attitude rather unsatisfactory', was proverbial. Jagger would never actively contribute to the welfare of the school, and it in turn contributed little to his. At times the headmaster, Ronald Loftus Hudson ('Lofty' for his dwarflike stature) despaired. Jagger did an excellent impersonation of him.

He continued, whenever possible, to sing. Dick Taylor, by then a student at Sidcup Art College, had inherited a second-hand drum kit. This quickly became the focal point of a group comprising himself, Jagger, Beckwith and Etherington. They called themselves Little Boy Blue and the Blue Boys ('We loved,' says Taylor, 'the blues'). Their tastes ran to Muddy Waters, Little Walter, Howlin' Wolf, Chuck Berry, Bo Diddley and Jimmy Reed. The last made a particular impression on Jagger. Reed, an epileptic hellraiser from Dunleith, Mississippi, spent much of his career playing for bar money at clubs such as the Peacock, Shangri-la and Pussy Cat-A-Go-Go. He recorded at least two standards, 'Bright Lights, Big City' and 'Honest I Do', teamed memorably with John Lee Hooker, lived hard and died in middle age. It was Beckwith who first drew Jagger's attention to Reed. As with his initiation to Holly he responded with the zeal of a convert. For a while, says Beckwith, you couldn't have a normal conversation with Jagger; he answered you in song lyrics.

The lyrics were what first attracted Jagger to the blues. 'They seemed,' he later said, 'more mature.' Among the Blue Boys' repertoire was 'Around and Around', 'Susie Q' and a primal twenty-minute version of 'La Bamba' with Jagger improvising verse after verse of pidgin Spanish and tossing his head like a tied bull. He was some way from writing original material, but was, Beckwith notes, already interpreting freely. The group rehearsed at Taylor's or Beckwith's homes in Bexleyheath or, more rarely, at Jagger's. Eva's first concern was for the neighbours. 'It was lovely,' she says, 'but so loud.' She and Joe were forever banging on the bedroom door. 'Mike,' said Eva, 'you'll wake the dead.' 'Jungle music,' muttered Joe.

They were genuinely perplexed. Jagger's parents neither liked nor understood his fondness for the blues. They shuddered at the animal noises emanating from the back bedroom. At meals they noticed their son's lips seemed to move to some interior thought process. A nearby fence became covered with writing. The penmanship was legible. 'CHUCK,' it said. 'KANSAS CITY.' When Joe asked the boy what he intended to be, he replied, 'A failure.'

For a time he was inseparable from the other Boys, notably Taylor. It was he who Jagger approached with the news: one morning in the school gym Mike leapt from one rope to another only to find it frustratingly out of reach. In the ensuing fall he bit through his tongue. Taylor remembers Jagger being terrified at that night's rehearsal – he thought it would affect his singing. The first number the Boys rehearsed that evening was 'Around and Around'. Etherington taped it on his primitive Philips recorder. Jagger, he says, sounded 'fuzzier'; bluesier. That was all right with Jagger, who wanted nothing more than to sound like Jimmy Reed. Reed, Waters and Berry were the three names Jagger always mentioned whenever he and the others went record-hunting in London. At Dobell's in Tower Street he picked up a copy of *One Dozen Berries*. Elsewhere he was lucky to find anything bluesier than Cliff or Adam Faith. Eventually Jagger resorted to writing to Chess Records in Chicago to buy the albums direct; 'even then he was the organized one,' says Taylor.

Among Taylor's classmates at college was Keith Richards. Richards's attitude (surly) and clothes (jeans, denim jacket, purple shirt) never varied. At Sidcup his main activities were smoking, eating period pills and playing the guitar, in particular Elvis's 'I'm Left, You're Right, She's Gone'. Despite having a foot in both camps, Taylor never thought to introduce Richards to the Blue Boys. 'Keith,' he states, 'was a loner . . . the idea of him in a group was incredible.' (Even more incredible, when Richards bumped into Jagger – the latter slouched against the town War Memorial selling ice-cream – that summer, they exchanged only a dozen words. Typically Jagger made a sale.) Throughout the winter of

1960–61 the Boys continued as a quartet. In a mock press release they described themselves as:

Vocals – Mike Jagger
Drums – Dick Taylor
Guitar – Bob Beckwith
Miscellaneous background noises – Alan Etherington

– the last of whom describes Jagger as already more 'focused' than the others: 'We were on the side of the angels, whereas Mick ... if not on the side of the devil, was definitely on the side of Mick.' Richards, meanwhile, worshipped Berry and Scotty Moore. The bathroom at Sidcup became clogged with pill bottles and cigarette butts.

In fact neither Richards nor Jagger had even remote ideas of becoming musicians. The latter, says Etherington, who had himself been a promising chorister, was strictly basic as a singer – plenty of enthusiasm and little or no finesse. If he admitted to career plans, they still revolved around journalism or the Foreign Office. In his final year at school, Jagger seems to have made a decisive effort to secure a place at university. He even, says Robson, buckled down in English.

That winter Hudson wrote the following confidential report:

8 December 1960

Michael Philip Jagger has been a pupil at this School since September 1954. His general record has been satisfactory and he passed the General Certificate of Education in seven subjects in the Summer of 1959 with the following marks: English Language 66, English Literature 48, Geography 51, History 56, Latin 49, French 61, Pure Mathematics 53.

In the sixth form he has applied himself well on the whole and has shown a greater intellectual determination than we had expected. He should be successful in each of his three subjects though he is unlikely to do brilliantly in any of them.

Jagger is a lad of good general character though he has been rather slow to mature. The pleasing quality which is now emerging is that of persistence when he makes up his mind to tackle something. His interests are wide. He has been a member of several School Societies and is prominent in Games, being Secretary of our Basketball Club, a member of the First Cricket Eleven and he plays Rugby Football for his House. Out of School he is interested in Camping, Climbing, Canoeing, Music and he is also a member of the local Historical Association.

Jagger's development now fully justifies me in recommending him for a Degree Course and I hope that you will be able to accept him.

Head Master

Alan Dow, meanwhile, adds that 'with Jagger, you always had the impression he was coasting until the last possible minute ... when he pulled his finger out'. Both he and Mike Richards remember Jagger as determined to do well in A levels, and talking vaguely of writing as a career. Further evidence of his resourcefulness came in January when he complained to Robson about Eric Brandon's teaching. The man, he said, was a drag. A levels loomed. Jagger's solution was to subscribe to a correspondence course – which again, says Robson, 'was typical ... when something needed to be done, Mike usually did it'.

Jagger's last report – 'Harder work this term' – bears witness to his determination. In his final year he engendered more goodwill amongst the staff than in the previous five. (It should be noted that Jagger was never an authentic school rebel. Mike Richards, now a headmaster himself, says that on a scale of ten his friend's antics rarely exceeded five.

Joe Jagger's view is that 'while the grammar school teachers undoubtedly knew their subjects, not all knew how to teach them'.) Dick Allen was a particular fan. As Jagger's form master he was responsible for the boy's moral welfare. 'Strangely enough,' he says, 'I always thought of him as a conservative, rather cautious character. He could give a different impression, but basically he was well behaved.' In June Jagger sat and passed history and English A level – ironically failing French, once his special subject.

By then, based on Hudson's recommendation, he had been accepted at the London School of Economics. The choice at first appears unusual for an arts student and was also, says Walton Wilkinson, exceptional for Dartford pupils generally. The truth is that it was prearranged – as Jagger realized when he went for interview that spring; it owed much to the informal contact between one institution and another. That March Hudson had lobbied vigorously among his university contacts. The result was that Robson won a place at New College, Oxford; Robert Pynegar, a student in Jagger's history class, at Christ Church; another boy, Brian Morgan, at the LSE. Hudson was friendly with the admissions tutor at the last and, according to a colleague, 'strongly suggested' to Joe Jagger that an application by Mike might be successful. So it proved; at the interview Jagger's director of studies, George Grun, exhibited almost cosmic disinterest. Jagger was asked a perfunctory question and dismissed. Subject to his passing at least two A levels, he was told, a place would be held for him.

The plan now was for Jagger to go into either politics or industry. Strongly drawn to the arts, he realized that job opportunities as either a writer or a historian were limited. Journalism, he curiously thought, 'seemed too much like hard work'. Joe was forever instilling in him the virtues of an education. He entered the LSE determined, says Robson, 'to prove something to his parents'. As he left Dartford Grammar he seemed resigned to ending up in business or finance – possibly (a salve to his creative ambitions) in 'marketing' a bank. His eighteenth birthday party was gloomy, Jagger talking about preparing for college with the relish of a man facing the electric chair. That summer he worked as a porter at Bexley Mental Hospital.

In late September, draped in a purple, black and gold scarf, armed with a £350 grant, he entered university. Jagger's routine rarely varied. After a cooked breakfast provided by Eva, he cycled or took the 486 bus to Dartford Station. The fast train to London took twenty minutes, the slow forty. At Charing Cross he turned right, ploughing through rush-hour Strand, then left into curving Aldwych. The main faculty building was in Houghton Street, adjacent to Lincoln's Inn and the law courts. Here Jagger would drink tea, listen to records or, more infrequently, sit in the school library. His tutor, Walter Stern, first met him on 2 October 1961. His impression? 'Jagger was very shy, very polite and obviously nervous at being at university . . . He announced his intention of going into business but was worried about mathematics . . . Figures were his weak point.' They addressed each other respectively as 'Mr Jagger' and 'Sir'.

According to a contemporary, the LSE was where Jagger 'got' politics. Though not the Marxist cornucopia it became later, the school in 1961 was open to radical ideas. Richard Crossman and Harold Wilson were among the guest lecturers. Peter Holland, studying at nearby University College, remembers his schoolfriend using words like 'bourgeois' and 'Fabian' as if for effect. 'Mike was never a rough-and-tumble radical,' he states; 'more an interested observer.' In Wilmington Joe and Eva found their son quoting John as well as Jimmy Reed at the table. (He always, says Holland, 'went home to eat'.) When, on 4 October, a young MP named Thatcher claimed at Orpington that 'every pound paid to pensioners is a pound taken away from working people', Jagger was incandescent with rage.

He didn't mean it, of course. Walter Stern is adamant that Jagger was a 'middle-of-the-road, normal adolescent' throughout his time at the LSE. Both Holland and Robson, with whom he kept in touch, detected no significant change. Walton Wilkinson, his old history master, swears he saw Jagger in October 1961 standing at Dartford Station in a grey suit reading the *Telegraph*. (Eva to this day is bemused by stories of her son's wildness as a youth.) Throughout his subsequent career Jagger would repeatedly demonstrate that a conservative approach to life is one of the best ways to enjoy it. People rich in imagination, rich in talent and invention, many of the highly gifted, remain forever innately cautious. Jagger, in his first term at university, had no serious ambitions beyond obtaining a degree. Had things not conspired as they did, he might have ended up a civil servant, a salesman, a provincial journalist, or even in public relations – a profession whose qualities eerily echo his own. (A half-dozen of his grammar school contemporaries, are, respectively, a solicitor, pharmacist, engineer, schoolteacher, taxi driver and Pretty Thing.) He might have been a theatrical agent or manager. Even, with renewed effort, a professional sportsman. Anything, in fact, but a musician. As Jagger stood at Dartford Station clutching his copy of *One Dozen Berries* on the morning of 17 October 1961, that option seemed singularly improbable. A minute later it became inevitable. Coming down the bleak curve of platform two was Keith Richards, lugging his guitar.

· III ·

METAMORPHOSIS

Later that morning Walter Stern found Jagger unusually excited. After repeating his doubts (in time fully shared by his tutor) regarding his mathematical ability, he went on to extol the 'jazz scene', adding gnomically, 'I hope to be doing some blowing.' He left it at that.

Jagger's cryptic utterance followed a ten-minute reunion with Richards, en route to Sidcup Art College. They usually left Dartford on different trains but Richards, for possibly the last time in his life, was early that morning. The intoxicating sight of a Chuck Berry album and Richards' Hofner guitar made the introduction; the train journey did the rest. They discovered they shared, first, a love of the blues; and second, at least one mutual friend in the person of Dick Taylor. Taylor remembers Richards cornering him at art college later that morning. 'He asked me if I knew someone called Mike Jagger. I admitted it . . . Keith seemed amazed I hadn't mentioned him before.' Taylor's observation – that 'other than music, the two didn't have anything in common' – was to prove particularly acute a quarter of a century later.

Within a week, Richards had been assimilated into the Blue Boys. His membership initiated a harder, more pneumatic sound. He and Beckwith played guitar, Etherington maracas, Taylor himself bass or drums. Jagger sang, refusing at this stage to countenance learning an instrument. Early on Taylor attributes Jagger with having pictured himself as The Vocalist, a figure in Cab Calloway tradition, quite separate from mere 'players', free to strut, slink and generally illustrate the group's songs. And strut he did. Taylor also reports his mother, interrupting a rehearsal, as being 'knocked out' by Jagger's antics. 'That boy,' she predicted, 'will go far.'

(Taylor's mother was more sanguine in this respect than Jagger's, who, with rare exceptions, banned the Boys from rehearsing at Newlands. The early schooling of the Rolling Stones thus took place at 34 Alexander Road, Bexleyheath.)

Jagger now began to strafe his parents in earnest. At the LSE he discovered Marx; he read Engels enthusiastically and Keynes without complaint. At meals he spoke with equal facility of the growing crisis in Berlin as of his own prospects with the Blue Boys ('We can make it'). He would also, he announced, no longer answer to the name 'Mike'. From henceforth it was to be Mick.

By late October he was complaining to Stern that the LSE's working day started too early. 'How,' he continually asked, 'am I expected to make it?' (Jagger's first lecture was at ten o'clock.) He confessed to finding maths both 'baffling' and 'a drag' and was advised to substitute political history. He also selected a course in British Government (presumably as an outlet for his new-found theories), but contrived to miss the first lecture by getting lost. In the course of four weeks from early October, says Stern, Jagger went from a 'scrupulously polite boy from the provinces' to 'a Ted'. On 3 November he appeared for a tutorial dressed in drainpipe trousers and winklepickers. As Stern attempted to mediate in the latest dispute between Jagger and his political history lecturer, Professor Stroud, the eighteen-year-old calmly crossed the room, picked up an ashtray and placed it by his ankles. An hour and several Players later it remained for Stern to replace.

In all this Jagger was heavily influenced by Richards. As he admitted, 'I always imagined I'd meet someone who would make the decision for me ... someone who shared [my] point of view.' Already several milestones further down the road to genuine delinquency, Richards drank, he took pills, he could – after a fashion – imitate Chuck Berry. Unlike Jagger he had no academic, still less professional, ambitions. As Beckwith says, 'With Keith, it was rock and roll or bust ... Mick was a complete innocent by comparison.' In Spielman Road Richards occupied a small room with a mirror, before which he stood practising poses. Downstairs Doris would prepare elaborate fish and chip dinners. Afterwards Richards would drop the leftovers in the sink. At a visit to Heal's, the London department store, he flicked burning ash on a sofa. 'Keith,' confirms Taylor, 'was a hoodlum.' When Jagger brought his friend to tea at Newlands he dropped a heavy plate to the floor, causing Eva to flinch. Richards, with his pet mouse, cigarette ash and acne, must have been among the last house guests she would have chosen.

It was now that Stern detected a serious transformation in Jagger. He missed tutorials; he was surly; as to baths – he appeared not to over-do them. Another student remembers him 'wandering around, a slightly querulous expression on his face, as if looking for trouble'. Neither could have been aware of the altered focus of Jagger's life, of his efforts to reconcile it with aspects of normal existence. That Christmas he went home to Dartford, working in the local post office.

While there he met Clive Robson, who recalls Mick (as he was instructed to call him) arriving at a pub with 'arguably the ugliest girl in England' in tow. Robson deduced the woman was either an example of the 'arty birds' whom Jagger to this day finds engaging or that, more prosaically, 'she screwed' – or, conceivably, both. When, a week later, Jagger arrived at a party at Paul Ovenden's house, he was escorted by a raving beauty. 'With Mick,' says Robson, 'a woman had to have brains, looks – or, later, breeding ...

Two out of three was a bonus.' Jagger's demeanour? 'A bit surly, but basically unchanged. On his own he was still a normal, mixed-up teenager.'

His parents checked in with him occasionally, Joe asking about sports facilities at the university; Eva was concerned with his diet. That winter Jagger hovered between the two worlds, school and music, openly admitting to Taylor, 'I can't decide.' The unpalatable truth was that, for the time being, there was no decision. The pop world was entering one of its periodic troughs. The charts that year were dominated by *West Side Story*, the George Mitchell Minstrels, by Dorothy Provine and Acker Bilk. There was no precedent for a blues group making money – none. As Taylor states, 'No one in 1962 was getting rich playing Muddy Waters, even Muddy Waters.' It was inevitable that a new form of music would eventually emerge – the stirrings from America were too many and various to be ignored – but even the Blue Boys despaired of it being the type practised nightly at Bexleyheath.

It is not the least of Jagger's achievements that he persevered with the group when morale at times touched bottom. All that winter and early spring they rehearsed, Richards in lead, Taylor compliant, Beckwith (also at the LSE) falling by the wayside. A photograph was taken of Jagger in corduroys and white sweater crooning into a microphone, framed by the drainpipe of the Taylors' back wall. It was that primitive. They were, Etherington now believes, on the verge of break-up. 'We'd done our repertoire, over and over, to an audience largely of our own mums ... It was depressing ... We felt we were the only people in England playing the blues.'

That spring they learned otherwise.

Alexis Korner was born in Paris on 19 April 1928. His father was an Austrian cavalry officer, his mother a Greco-Turkish refugee. As if already not exotic enough, their son was educated in Switzerland, North Africa and London. By 1940 he was attending St Paul's School, Hammersmith, and pilfering records from nearby Shepherd's Bush market, among them a 78 by the barrel-house pianist Jim Yancey. From that moment Korner's destiny was settled. He became another willing slave to the blues.

After serving with the army in reconstruction Germany, Korner returned to London in 1948. He became friendly with the jazz bandleaders of the time, among them Ken Colyer and Chris Barber. When Lonnie Donegan left the latter to perform National Service, Korner deputized as banjoist. In 1953 he met a shambling dishevelled panel-beater, Cyril Davies, who played striking blues harmonica. Slowly a group began to form comprising Korner, Davies, Geoff Bradford (guitar), Dick Heckstall-Smith (saxophone) and in later years Jack Bruce (bass) and a drummer named Charlie Watts. They consciously merged jazz with blues, importing seminal American artists like Big Bill Broonzy, John Lee Hooker and Memphis Slim as guests. As Korner said: 'Our whole act was pinched from those guys ... We constantly cursed the fact we weren't born black.' They christened themselves Blues Incorporated.

In the winter of 1961–2 the group played at the Round-house in Soho, the Marquee and sundry coffee bars, cellars and clubs. They made a provincial tour. On the latter, Korner (no shrinking violet himself) was constantly heckled by crowds expecting, as he put it, 'the old bowler hat and clarinet crap'. This confirmed his intention of finding a permanent residency for the group. That spring he was offered the lease on an unheated basement room in west London known, somewhat ambitiously, as the Ealing Jazz Club. The first performance, scheduled for 17 March, was duly advertised in *New Musical Express*:

Alexis Korner Blues Incorporated
The Most Exciting Event of the Year

Ealing Broadway station.
Turn left, cross the zebra and go down steps
between ABC Teashop and jewellers.
Saturday at 7.30 p.m.

In Dartford the Blue Boys noted the date.

In fact it was three weeks before Alan Etherington persuaded his father to loan the quartet his Riley Pathfinder car. While the others were meditating on Ealing, Jagger's mind was firmly on his struggles at the LSE. In early March he complained to Stern of being 'overwhelmed', 'fagged out' and, more tellingly, 'totally broke'. He was even, he said, going without his midday meal. Stern sympathized. Could not Mr Jagger bring sandwiches with him in the morning? Several seconds passed before Jagger answered. 'I don't,' he announced, 'eat sandwiches.' He nonetheless undertook to work in the School library for two successive Saturdays (the second coinciding with the opening of the Ealing club). He struck his tutor as 'desperately seeking something to get interested in'; in Dartford Etherington remembers Jagger lecturing the bemused Boys on the political unrest in Algeria. 'There must,' he insisted, 'be something more than music.' ('Like what?' asked Richards.)

Jagger was in exceptionally febrile mood. The Boys' lack of apparent prospects had left him drawn and depressed. The group was running out of ideas. Questions were raised about the point of holding continual rehearsals – 'like a football team with no fixtures'. Nor, after Richards' initial impetus, were they noticeably improving. 'We were getting bored,' says Taylor; 'Keith had done his Chuck Berry bit and Mick was in a rut as a singer. We were screaming out for something to happen.' When it did they were torn between curiosity at Korner's opening and cynicism that the journey would be wasted; there was also the question of Jagger's commitment to work in the School library. Not until Saturday 7 April did the four finally make the twenty-mile journey to London. They parked in Madeley Road and walked, as instructed, past the Broadway station. Down sixteen steps a urine-filled alley gave on to a single subterranean room. Inside two hundred people listened with varying degrees of patience as Dick Heckstall-Smith blew a long tenor sax solo. 'The place was a dump,' says Taylor. 'Sweat everywhere and the trains running right underneath. We weren't exactly bowled over.' In fact, despite Korner's efforts, much of the music, albeit earthier, bore a disturbing resemblance to the 'bowler hat and clarinet crap' previously disparaged. Jagger had just turned to Etherington with the opinion 'This is a wank,' when his attention was drawn to something happening on stage. Korner came forward. 'This' – he indicated a blond bouffant in the shadows – 'is Elmo Lewis. He's come from Cheltenham to play for you.' The group promptly launched into Elmore James's 'Dust My Broom'. It ended to polite applause.

Back at the bar the beer slopped from Jagger's mug. Even Richards seemed impressed. Elmo Lewis – in reality a twenty-year-old named Lewis Brian Jones – could play the blues. When the time came for him to perform a solo his bar slide guitar almost echoed the original. The Boys were transfixed. At the interval they almost fell over themselves inviting Lewis/Jones to the bar. He peered at them under the swept fringe of his hair and spoke in a strangely lilting, effete voice. He was, he announced, 'tight' with Korner, whom he had met when the latter played in Cheltenham. Where was he currently living? 'With the old lady and kid.' The Boys exchanged glances. 'You got a kid?' asked Jagger.
'Three.'

Sometime around midnight the Boys introduced themselves to Korner, to whom they had earlier supplied one of countless rehearsal tapes. (It was, he said, 'Godawful'.) He smiled indulgently at their new friendship with Jones. 'At the beginning,' he noted, 'Mick and Keith hero-worshipped

Brian. He seemed about twenty years older than them.'

Jones was in fact born on 28 February 1942 at the Park Nursing Home, Cheltenham. His father Lewis was an aeronautical engineer with Dowty & Company, his mother Louisa a piano teacher. At school Jones excelled at piano and clarinet, also cricket, badminton and swimming. Later he passed nine O levels and two As. As a teenager Jones developed a passion for jazz in general and Charlie Parker in particular. Like Jagger his mood altered when he discussed America, only more so. Between bouts of drinking and learning the saxophone he impregnated a fourteen-year-old girl. Expelled from Cheltenham Grammar School Jones drifted through a succession of jobs, studying briefly as an optician and fathering a second child. In January 1960 he met and bedded a local teenager called Pat Andrews; later she, too, bore his child, the boy, Julian Mark, being named in homage to Jones's jazz hero Julian 'Cannonball' Adderley. In late 1961 Jones and his friend Dick Hattrell saw Blues Incorporated perform at Cheltenham Town Hall. This, as he put it, changed everything; at the nearby Patio Wine Bar Jones was introduced to Korner and invited to visit him in London. He accepted with alacrity.

The mood in repressed, Edwardian Cheltenham was by then deeply anathematical to the serial seducer. For six months Alexis and Bobbie Korner virtually housed and fed him; Jones's bed was a rolled-up mattress under the kitchen table. At the Korners' he also met an Oxford singer named P. P. Pond, widely known as Permanently Pissed Pond and in later years as Paul Jones, singer with Manfred Mann. It was Pond/Jones who joined him that April when, at Korner's invitation, they performed their fateful version of 'Dust My Broom'.

Dick Taylor remembers to this day the impact the song had on Jagger and Richards. 'They were stunned,' he says. 'Just when it seemed there was no one else who understood, here was a kid, our own age, playing bar slide blues. Mick was knocked out.' A good case can be made for believing Jagger's opinion of Jones was never higher than at that first meeting. From then on they related in the way a train relates to rails.

Korner in turn was impressed, or at this stage perhaps merely intrigued, by Jagger. Despite the awfulness of the Blue Boys' tape, he felt the lead singer 'had something'. The result was that Jagger, like Jones, was invited to perform a guest spot with Blues Incorporated. When the moment came the singer was half drunk and tremulous with stage fright. He coughed. Behind him the group struck up their signature blues. Jagger jumped with startlingly real alarm. His performance that night was, says Taylor, 'nothing great . . . Though he did have that way of moving'. Korner was more specific: 'It was the way he threw his head around. He came on like a hair fetishist.'

The upshot was that Jagger, in rotation with a six foot seven inch youth named John Baldry, became Korner's featured singer. After that first night he seemed to relish climbing on stage. Nor was the money (17/6 a session) a problem. The problem was Richards. Blues Incorporated had, at best, ambivalent feelings towards rock and roll. Cyril Davies, for one, became apoplectic when Richards joined Jagger one Saturday for the obligatory 'Around and Around'. Korner had to physically separate them. Jagger, to his credit, again stuck by the original Boys. By early May a sub-group of Blues Incorporated had been formed comprising Korner, a brooding Davies, Jagger, Richards, Taylor and, on occasion, Jones. Alan Etherington returned to college. A guitarist called Clapton stood in.

The drums were played by Ginger Baker or Charlie Watts. The latter, displaying all the enthusiasm of the jazz purist he was, was born on 2 June 1941. He attended secondary modern school in north London, shone at football and cricket and showed an early aptitude for art. In 1955 Watts acquired his first drum kit. After two years at college he took a two hundred pound a year job at an advertising agency, Charles Hobson Gray. Like Jones he was captivated by Charlie Parker and in 1961 wrote and illustrated *Ode to a High-Flying Bird* in homage to the great saxophonist. Later that year he met Korner and was persuaded to play with Blues Incorporated – persuaded because Watts remained deeply suspicious of anything requiring a vertebrate back-beat. 'That first time,' said Korner, 'he sat down like a man in the dentist's chair . . . It took a year for Charlie to settle in.' Later, Watts admitted, 'it was amazing; a cross between rhythm and blues and Charlie Mingus, which was what Alexis wanted'. He was convinced.

Was Jagger? Within a month he became Korner's de facto vocalist. As well as Saturdays at Ealing, the group was offered a Thursday residency at Harold Pendleton's Marquee Club. Jane Hamill, then working as a London sales clerk, remembers Jagger dressed in tie, cardigan and grey flannels, shaking his hair and, brutishly, twisting his trunk – 'a complete animal'. Later Jagger appeared at the bar and in a 'quiet, rather fey' voice ordered drinks. Hamill's impression began to alter. Underneath, Jagger wasn't an animal at all. He was shy, polite, even self-effacing. She remembers him admitting, apparently without irony, to doubts about his singing. Over a second drink Jagger discussed economics. Evidently he was finding the LSE hard going. This was confirmed when he met Stern for an interview on 7 May; now, for the first time, his tutor felt Jagger might not last the course. He spoke darkly of the 'drag' of his daily journey from Dartford. He was, he announced, considering moving to London. Jagger also referred to his new-found employment with Korner, at one stage asking – with startling candour – 'What should I do?' Stern's advice was to do nothing. He had the impression of a young man 'with a lot of overlapping worries. He was actually pacing the floor.' In ninety minutes Jagger chain-smoked a dozen cigarettes.

Stern's assessment was correct. Jagger was worried. Obviously one of those people able to function in two seemingly contrary worlds, he was constantly under pressure to abandon one or the other. Early on both Richards and Jones urged him to quit the LSE; Korner and Davies concurred. Taylor remained silent. Jagger's parents and Stern, whom he respected, lobbied vigorously from the opposite direction. One night Eva went as far as to ring Korner and ask if, in his opinion, her son had 'any future in show business'.

'Future? He's the best singer I know.'

Joe's emotions can only be guessed. However, as a teetotal schoolteacher with a distaste for 'jungle music', it seems safe to assume that he, too, had doubts. Later that spring Jagger's father published *Basketball: Coaching and Playing*, which drew the following conclusions:

> The coach should quickly recognize the stronger and sounder personalities in his unit and make the proper use of them ... The flamboyant players accept a lead with delight and often rapidly increase it and thus appear to be gaining the greater glory.

And then:

> The acquisition of skill takes time and there are very few who will achieve a high degree of all-round ability unless there is someone to help and encourage them ... To be a good performer, practice goes hand in hand with play.

Finally:

> [The coach's] pleasure comes from the lively companionship of young people, his pride in the formation of an efficient team, and his satisfaction with the part

he has played in the development of youngsters into fine citizens.

At the same time Joe was appointed an instructor at St Mary's, Twickenham, where he was known, according to a colleague, for 'an exceptional ability to combine old-fashioned values with a genuine love of youth, as well as for his own youthful qualities'. In later years he lectured periodically at Dartford College of Physical Education, involved in theoretical aspects of the London B.Ed. The college existed to instruct 170 students in 'deportment and fitness' (both being Joe's specialities); among the maxims of its founder, Martina Bergman-Osterberg, was: 'You have the perfect liberty to do as you like, provided you do the right thing,' and, 'The figure must, at all times, be uniformly covered.' Joe, the same friend notes, had little difficulty in complying with either. The college was damp and faintly sour with floor polish. In an outhouse Joe lectured in multiple sweaters and muffler. In winter he looked like the Michelin Man in profile. When colleagues asked about Mick he invariably smiled, but gave no details.

Mick's horizons were expanding. Within a month of joining Korner his repertoire had grown to include 'Got My Mojo Working', 'Ride 'em on Down' and Billy Boy Arnold's 'Bad Boy'. The attendance at Ealing had doubled. On 19 May the pop weekly *Disc* reported, 'Nineteen-year-old* Dartford rhythm and blues singer, Mick Jagger, has joined the Alexis Korner group, Blues Incorporated, and will sing with them regularly on their Saturday dates at Ealing and their Thursday sessions at the Marquee Jazz Club, London.' Richards and Taylor sporadically joined in; Watts drummed. Jones schemed madly in the background. His attitude to Korner veered between devotion and

---

* The only known occasion on which Jagger's age was exaggerated in print.

contempt. All his life Jones had the faculty of exuding public charm. In private he was rarely able to restrain his more churlish side. Korner, he now declared, was out. The Ealing scene was a drag. What was needed was a new scene altogether. When he said this Jones's and Jagger's eyes met. What about Richards? Richards, said Jones, was out. A fight ensued and for a week the Dartford and Cheltenham camps divided. Jones's response was to advertise in *Melody Maker* for musicians to join a new group under his leadership.

The first to reply was a twenty-three-year-old shipping clerk named Ian Stewart. His appearance in the rehearsal room at the White Bear, Soho, was sensational. Stewart arrived in leather cycling shorts carrying a meat pie which he proceeded to eat while playing Albert Ammons-like piano. Jones, observing Stewart's ample frame and protruding Cro-Magnon jaw (suggestive of the metamorphosis scene in a horror film), insisted on a prolonged formal audition. After effortlessly performing Howlin' Wolf's 'You Can't Be Beat' he was informed that his application had been accepted. By the end of June Geoff Bradford, a sometime Korner guitar-ist, and, with varying degrees of enthusiasm, Jagger, Richards and Taylor were also rehearsing every Wednesday and Friday under Jones's direction. In early July sessions transferred to the adjacent Bricklayer's Arms after Stuart Lovell, landlord of the Bear, had caught one or more of the putative group stealing from the bar. On 4 July Watts was formally approached but found unwilling. A second adver-tisement recruited a drummer named Tony Chapman, who recalls: 'We all met at Mick's house in Dartford, sat in his front room, and he played the album *Jimmy Reed Live At Carnegie Hall*. They asked me what I thought of it. I liked it and they said, "Fine, because that's the sort of music we want to play."'

By now Jagger's attention was divided between Dartford, Blues Incorporated, Jones's embryonic group and the LSE.

In mid-June he sat his BSc Part One with the following results.

Compulsories:	Economics	C	
	British Government	C	
	Economic History	C	
Alternatives:	Political History		C
	English Legal Institutions		C

On the twentieth Jagger appeared for a tutorial with Stern. He had, he said, suffered a bilious attack on the day prior to exams, a statement which Korner later found inconsistent with his memory of 'Mick having sung as usual' that night. The questions themselves, Jagger added, had been unfair. In fact, he stated – wearing the pained smile of an academic modesty earned several times over – they defied description.

'Try,' said Stern.

'Too narrow.'

'Really?'

'Too exact, too explicit.'

'Oh?'

'Too specific.'

This left a bad impression. All Stern's life he had listened to students complaining. He began to form a clearer picture of Jagger. Gradually it became very clear indeed. Like Paul Ovenden, Stern believed that with Jagger 'it was a question of all or nothing ... If he saw a chance to be top dog, he worked; if not, he gave up.' Had Jagger been miserable with love, ill, or abjectly poor his excuses would have been more dignified. As it was, Stern's impression was of a teenager who craved the prestige of success but without the intellectual weight to achieve it.

By early July, meanwhile, the Bricklayer's sessions had formed the basis of a group: Jones, Jagger, Richards, Taylor and Stewart. Geoff Bradford left. The drum stool was occupied by Chapman or Mick Avory – the latter commuting from far-off and soon to be sainted Liverpool. At Jones's insistence on 10 July they joined the Jazz Federation to increase prospects of work. That same week he proposed the name Rollin' (*sic*) Stones after the Muddy Waters song previously admired by Jagger. Stewart, for one, objected: 'People would expect to see a group of Irish acrobats, I told him . . . Of course, a name's not important until you start to get booked – and we were a *long* way from that.' Taylor, too, had misgivings about the name, recalling it as 'very much Brian's idea, which the rest of us just went along with'.

On the same day Korner was contacted by a phone call from the BBC. Blues Incorporated were offered a chance to broadcast on the Light Programme's *Jazz Club*; that was the good news. The bad news was that neither Jagger (superfluous to the five-man format required by the Corporation) nor Watts (not a professional musician) was included. Further, the booking was for a Thursday, clashing with Korner's weekly engagement at the Marquee. Jagger's response was immediate: Blues Incorporated would handle the *Jazz Club* and the Rollin' Stones provide cover in Soho. Harold Pendleton was contacted and agreed with the following proviso: John Baldry's new band would head the bill. The Stones were strictly in support. The following appeared in the 'stop press' column of *Jazz News*:

Mick Jagger, R & B vocalist, is taking a rhythm and blues group into the Marquee tomorrow night while Blues Incorporated does its *Jazz Club* radio broadcast gig.
    Called 'The Rollin' Stones' ('I hope they don't think we're a rock and roll outfit,' says Mick), the line-up is: Jagger (vocals), Keith Richards, Elmo Lewis (guitars), Dick Taylor (bass), 'Stew' (piano) and Mick Avory (drums).

When Jones saw the above he almost wept.

The Rollin' Stones were not taken anywhere by Jagger. They were led, indisputably and at his own constant insistence, by Jones. He it was who arranged rehearsals, lobbied endlessly for work, conceived the group in the first place. Taylor is adamant that 'it was basically Brian's baby'; while the bassist who replaced him six months later writes, 'The Rolling Stones that I joined was led by Brian Jones . . . [He] called the shots partly because he had pulled the musicians together, but mainly because what mattered most at that stage was music, and Brian was by far the most knowledgeable about what we were playing.' Others, like Korner, agreed that technically Jones was in a different bracket to his colleagues. Stewart, on the other hand, always insisted that 'if Brian and the rest hadn't existed, Mick and Keith would have still formed a group that sounded exactly like the Stones'. Not that their ability particularly impressed him – Richards was 'stiff'; Jagger 'off-key and rather self-conscious' – but Stewart realized what others would discover later. Jagger had genuine flair. He was highly organized. At the Bricklayer's rehearsals would be called for seven p.m. Jagger and Richards were invariably the first to arrive. Even at this stage Jones would go missing for days on end. When he reappeared he was sometimes sober, sometimes not. Always the practical one, Jagger would lead the group in his absence. 'Mick,' states Taylor, 'was always very together.'

The Rollin' Stones – so apostrophed – took the stage at the Marquee Club on Thursday 12 July 1962 (the very night on which Harold Macmillan sacked a third of his Cabinet, an act of carnage unprecedented in domestic politics). At the time Frank Ifield topped the British charts. The Beatles were still two months short of their first single. Across London an obscure group named the Detours considered changing identity to The Who. In New York the twenty-one-year-old Bob Dylan had recently released his first album. The phrase 'rock and roll' had only imperfectly entered the public lexicon. Long hair in males was still considered evidence of sexual ambiguity – or worse. When the group took to the Marquee's cramped, splintered stage they were viewed with polite curiosity; no more. Dick Taylor remembers at least one catcall from the house. They played, in full: 'Kansas City', 'Honey What's Wrong', 'Confessin' the Blues', 'Bright Lights, Big City', 'Dust My Broom', 'Down the Road Apiece', 'I Want to Love You', 'Bad Boy', 'I Ain't Got You', 'Hush Hush', 'Ride 'em on Down', 'Back in the USA', 'Up All Night', 'Tell Me that You Love Me' and 'Happy Home' – an extraordinary number for a fifty-minute set. Jagger barely moved throughout. He wore a striped sweater and corduroys, Jones a fringed jacket, Richards a suit of funereal darkness. 'You could hear people muttering between songs,' says Taylor. Afterwards the group proceeded to the bar where they were joined by Harold Pendleton. 'Not bad,' he allowed. 'And?' Pendleton shrugged, adding nothing. In the next three months the Rolling Stones had a total of six more bookings.

Pendleton, like Korner and Jones before him, valued Jagger more highly than Richards. At this point the latter was little more than a Chuck Berry acolyte (whose own motif derived, anyway, from jazz piano). Jagger, with his bull Negro voice and flapping hair was recognizably different; original, even. By midsummer he was playing proficient blues harmonica – on occasion, said Stewart, brilliantly. To his credit, at a time when his star was rising dramatically more rapidly than Richards', Jagger remained loyal. When Pendleton suggested paring the group to a quintet he was quickly disabused; at their next booking Richards was on stage as usual. 'For a while,' says Taylor, 'you never saw Mick without Keith.' That August the two went on holiday together in Devon, even playing as a duo in a local pub. Afterwards Richards confided to his mother, 'I wish we had a manager.'

The summer passed slowly. Rehearsals – on which the

group appeared almost to have a fixation – continued. Taylor remembers Jones as having been alternately 'great' and 'lousy', Jagger improving, Stewart continuing to play 'breathtaking' piano while leaning backwards to look out of the window for girls. Richards, meanwhile, developed his repertoire. In time he gave the group, as he had the Blue Boys, a harder, more aggressive mien. While Jones spoke endlessly of being a star and Richards wanted merely to play, Jagger's ambitions included traces of both. As Korner later said: 'A musician comes into this business for one of two reasons. There are compulsive players who have *got* to play. If they make money, great, but they've *got* to play. Then there are people who think, "Ah, this is how I'm going to make it." Mick is of the latter, Keith of the former.'

Jagger may have admired Richards; he may have liked him. Undoubtedly he was influenced by him. By late summer Jagger was unrecognizable from the grammar school student of a year before. In August he approached his parents with the information that he was leaving home. From henceforth, he stated, he would 'hang out' in London. What, asked Joe – here his voice grew distant and quiet – about money? 'Don't worry,' said Jagger. 'I'll get it together.'

He got it together at 102 Edith Grove, a tenement block of epic squalor located in, aptly enough, World's End, Chelsea. The rent was fifteen pounds a week. The plan was that Jagger would occupy one bedroom, Jones, his girlfriend Pat Andrews and their baby the other. Andrews and the baby lasted a week. They were replaced by Richards. From being merely filthy the flat became putrid. 'The first time I walked in,' recalled Stewart, 'the stink almost knocked me over. There was rotting food and old cigarette butts all over the place, dirty clothes flung around and that disgusting smell, like rotting cabbages.' Doris Richards described living conditions as 'awful'.

It was at Edith Grove that Richards made a decisive jump

into the group. He and Jones (fired from a job at the department store, Whiteley's, for shoplifting) stayed at home all day with their guitars. They practised duets, exchanged notes and may even have written embryonic songs. In Stewart's view: 'They really got off on that two guitar-player thing . . . They were young enough to be influenced in the heart rather than the head.' What Stewart was witnessing, among the piled dishes and festering laundry, was the genesis of the Rolling Stones. 'The whole secret,' says Richards, 'is the way we work two guitars.'

Jagger had a different perspective. Every morning he emerged from the back bedroom (Richards and Jones sharing the front), washed, shaved and took the bus to college. No one at the LSE detected anything amiss. Jagger continued to attend lectures (still citing, as the cause of his lateness, the 'drag' of his daily journey). He worked in the library. He even played football for the school second XI. In the afternoon he returned to Chelsea to find Jones and Richards still supine in bed. His reaction, so the latter told his biographer, was to 'go through his first camp period, wandering around in a blue linen housecoat. He was into that kick for about six months . . . Brian and I used to take the piss out of him.' There were nightly discussions about 'making it' and about their respective families, Jagger referring warily to his mother. Jones and Richards merely shrugged. At weekends they practised while Jagger went home to Dartford.

In the next flat lived a chemistry student named Judy Credland. In addition to supplying constant potatoes, chocolate and instant coffee she also offered to read her neighbours' palms. Taking Jagger's hand one night she announced, 'You've got the star of fame! It's *all there*.' It took some time for the laughter to die down.

In late October the group played at the Flamingo Club, Soho, travelling in by bus. They all, notably Richards, continued to suffer at the hands of the jazz devotees effectively regulating London's clubland. 'Rhythm and blues can hardly be considered a form of jazz,' Jones stated loftily in a letter on the twenty-fifth. 'It is not based on improvisation as is the latter . . . The impact is, and can only be, emotional. It would be ludicrous if the same type of psuedo-(*sic*) intellectual snobbery that one unfortunately finds contaminating the jazz scene were to be applied to anything as basic and vital as R & B.'

On the twenty-seventh the group entered a studio for the first time. Jones, Jagger and Richards paid the equivalent of a week's rent to record an acetate of Bo Diddley's 'You Can't Judge a Book by the Cover', Muddy Waters' 'Soon Forgotten' and Jimmy Reed's 'Close Together'. The pressing was subsequently sent to Neville Skrimshire at EMI who took all of a minute to reject it. After that Chapman passed it to a contact at Decca who announced: 'It's a great band, but you'll never get anywhere with that singer.' A quarter of a century later the record was sold at auction for £6,000.

At this point things, already apparently at their darkest, turned black. In November Dick Taylor left. Frustrated in his desire to play six-string guitar and overawed by Jones, he announced his intention to return to art school. Refused by the Royal College, he later re-emerged to found the Stones-influenced group the Pretty Things in whose career, at least at first, Jagger and Richards took a personal interest. Ironically, at the very moment Taylor walked out of the Edith Grove door another ex-Blue Boy, Bob Beckwith, arrived. He was greeted ambivalently, though with underlying warmth; 'one of my straight friends,' said Jagger, not entirely disapprovingly. Beckwith describes conditions at Edith Grove as 'resembling a war zone'.

Jones applied and applied and applied again for bookings, though to little effect. Such dates as they had were desultory affairs in Ealing or Sutton when the group, permanently broke, jammed with their equipment on to a tube or bus.

The drum stool was filled by Chapman, Avory or an exhibitionist named Carlo Little. Ricky Fensen replaced Taylor on bass. Hire-purchase payments were sometimes kept up, sometimes not. The band's going rate was five pounds a night.

Compounding the problem was the weather. On 1 December fog descended in London and the south-east. It was followed by snow. In Edith Grove the pipes had to be thawed with blow-torches while Jagger brooded over Keynes or practised the harmonica. After a barely animate performance at Ealing on the fourth Chapman mentioned a friend whom, he believed, 'might be persuaded to audition' on bass. The silence that greeted this was deafening. 'With,' the drummer added, 'his own equipment.'

'Send him up,' said Jagger.

The figure who arrived at the Wetherby Arms, a pub adjacent to Edith Grove, introduced himself as Lee Wyman, quickly amended to Bill. His actual name was William Perks. Born in Penge on 24 October 1936 he attended Beckenham Grammar School and later performed two years' National Service in the RAF. In 1959 he married a local girl, Diane Cory, and fathered a son. Using the name of an Air Force colleague, Lee Wyman, he joined a semi-professional dance band called the Cliftons – 'The second funniest band in the world after ourselves,' says a member of the Barron Knights. In June 1962 the group had lost their drummer when Tony Chapman answered an advertisement in *Melody Maker* placed by Jones.

The scene that greeted Wyman in the Wetherby Arms astounded him.

> We entered the pub through a side door, directly into the back room where the Stones were rehearsing. I spoke to Ian Stewart ... who introduced me to Mike (*sic*) Jagger, who was quite friendly; I then met Brian Jones and Keith Richards, who were at the bar. For

musicians, their appearance surprised me: they had hair down over the ears and looked very scruffy – Bohemian and arty. This was quite a shock: in the pop world where I came from, smartness was automatic . . .

I bought a round of drinks and offered cigarettes. These were jumped on as if I were delivering famine relief. Still Brian and Keith hardly spoke. Mike asked me if I knew the music of any black blues players . . . I drove back that night to south London, wondering about the bizarre world I was entering. How on earth had this group of layabouts got together to play minority music with such conviction?

Later in the month Wyman was introduced to the 'disaster zone' of Edith Grove. It was, he wrote, an 'absolute pit'; Jagger, Jones and Richards 'took a strange delight in pointing out the various cultures that grew in about forty smelly milk bottles lying around'; anyone using the communal lavatory was likely to be tape-recorded, or worse. Wyman, with his mohair suit and Tony Curtis hairdo, already middle-aged, was appalled. The Stones, he noted with disdain, were delinquents; beatniks. Only Jagger – in whom Wyman detected elements of self-conscious 'slumming' – had an eye on the future. 'He talked about becoming a lawyer, journalist or politician . . . Keith, on the other hand, had no plan to work. Brian just felt that music was his vocation.'

This sense of ambiguity, of lingering between worlds, was Jagger's trademark. Throughout that winter he commuted from squalid, rundown World's End to suburban Wilmington, from all-night blues sessions to lectures at the LSE. Capable of insufferable rudeness, he wrote to a seventeen-year-old schoolgirl, Cleo Sylvestre, whom he met at the Marquee Club, 'I want somebody to share everything with, someone to respect, not just someone to sleep with . . .

Please make me happy, it's the one thing missing from my life now.' Wyman was stunned that this 'intelligent, well-spoken' youth should choose to live with known reprobates like Richards and Jones. His reason? 'Bohemian *angst*, most likely.'

The thankless job of caretaking Edith Grove – more damage control than cleaning – was shared by Doris Richards and a teenager named Eileen Giles. The latter particularly recalls the kitchen, a room in which Jones appeared to be conducting a biological experiment, through whose window he would periodically eject cups and plates. Not surprisingly, she nominates he and Richards as 'the louts' of the establishment. Jagger, on the other hand, was charming, polite, even witty, 'laughing as if the whole thing was something of a joke'. You had the impression, she adds, he was living there because it amused him. 'Both the other two could be nasty, while the most Mick ever did was tease.' When Giles inadvertently burnt Jagger's prize shirt, his solution was straightforward: 'Give us yours.' She did.

Another neighbour, the journalist Ian Gilchrist, informed that 'really crazy' musicians were living on the floor above, once knocked at Jagger's door.

> I waited, and Mick appeared, naked and looking very angry. I asked if the landlord had been round lately. Mick didn't answer at first. He stood there looking at my feet and slowly moved his gaze upwards until it was level with my face. Then he spoke: 'Fuck off!' and slammed the door in my face.

Later Jagger, Richards and Jones woke Gilchrist at five a.m. demanding to be let in. Next night Richards smashed his guitar case through the front door; on another occasion Jagger swung a frying pan on a rope through Gilchrist's window. 'Strangely enough,' he says, 'I decided to move.'

Christmas was bleak that year. On the twenty-first the

group played to an audience of ten at the Piccadilly Jazz Club. The next night at Ealing was no better. The holiday itself was the coldest in London since 1897. Jagger, Richards and Jones spent the afternoon in a working man's café debating the group's line-up. Wyman, it was agreed, was in; Chapman, Avory and Little out. By then Watts had graduated to drumming in a Korner off-shoot called Blues By Six, though he retained his job at Charles Hobson Gray. In early January Jagger and Jones suggested – insisted – that Watts join. After consulting Korner ('I told him I thought they were likely to get more work than the others, in the long run') he accepted. The amended line-up – Jagger, Jones, Richards, Wyman, Watts, Stewart – gave its first performance at the Flamingo Club on 14 January 1963.

The six weeks that followed were the coldest in living memory. By day fog descended, leaving spectacular rime deposits on streets and houses. At night the sea froze solid. The group's mood, according to Stewart, was one of 'grim determination . . . as always when things looked bad'. Jones penned yet another letter ('Dear Sir . . . I am writing on behalf of the "Rollin' Stones" Rhythm and Blues band . . . We already have a large following in the London area') to the BBC *Jazz Club*; Richards and Watts practised; Jagger, according to Wyman, began to miss lectures at the LSE: 'On the whole the front-line trio was still clinging to a beatnik lifestyle and the notion that somehow the grind of club work might evolve into a career.' At this stage Jagger, by his own admission, 'had no idea of image at all'. Nor did he 'give a shit who was the leader of the band', unlike Jones who cared about little else. Jones wanted above anything to be a star; Jagger and Richards preached group success. Watts, Wyman and Stewart remained talented also-rans. The internal stress of the band was what gave it its drive. And diversity: within the Stones were two jazz diehards, a blues purist, the *ne plus ultre* of rock and rollers, an Eddie

Cochran fan and an overweight boogie pianist. 'We covered,' says Jagger, 'the whole gamut.'

At the end of January the group entered the IBC studios in Regent Street. Over five days they recorded six numbers – three by Bo Diddley, two by Jimmy Reed and a Willie Dixon blues, 'I Want to be Loved'. The tapes reveal Jagger to have been an enthusiastic shouter, wholly without restraint or finesse. His harmonies with Richards were, to put it mildly, crude. Not surprisingly the songs remained unreleased. Over the next month IBC's director, George Clewson, played the tape to every record company in London. The reaction was uniform: 'I'm sorry. It's not commercial enough.' Out of this the Stones drew satisfaction.

It was at this point that Jones met a twenty-nine-year-old Russian émigré, part jazz fanatic, part film-maker, Giorgio Gomelski. Gomelski had shot a documentary of the Chris Barber band in 1961 and subsequently co-founded the Piccadilly Blues Club. He was also friendly with the landlord, Chris Buckle, of the Station Hotel, Richmond, whose back room became the venue for regular jazz sessions. The result was that, after hearing the Rolling Stones at the Red Lion, Sutton, Gomelski promised 'when possible' to book them at Richmond. The day came on 24 February after the snowbound Dave Hunt Band failed to appear. The Stones played two forty-five-minute sets to an audience of thirty. They were paid seven pounds. Afterwards Gomelski and the group plastered fly-posters – 'R & B with the Inimitable, Incomparable, Exhilarating Rolling Stones' – over west London, mixing up the paste in the bath at Edith Grove (its only known function).

Gomelski was the group's first manager. He campaigned tirelessly on their behalf. He wrote to *Melody Maker*. He lobbied Buckle for a regular Sunday engagement in the hotel's back room, quaintly renamed the Crawdaddy Club. Even Jagger admits, 'The first cat we had who looked after the band was Giorgio . . . He was a kind person.' Gomelski himself remembers Jagger 'all prim and proper. He wrote these school notes in elegant writing and was very "into" Marxism.' His view of the power structure within the group? 'All Brian did was make a lot of noise. Mick and Keith are both doers, where Charlie and Bill are content to go along. If Bill and Charlie had big egos the band would have broken up ages ago.'

Within a month Jagger was a universal favourite at Richmond. At evening's end he climaxed by singing the eponymous 'Crawdaddy' for twenty minutes, tossing his hair, with flared eyes, his Negro strut and little girl's dance steps. The audience doubled and doubled again. On 7 April, the anniversary of their meeting at Ealing, the group played to three hundred. Afterwards a reporter from the *Richmond and Twickenham Times* filed their first review:

> Save from the swaying forms of the group on the spotlit stage, the room is in darkness. A patch of light from the entrance doors catches the sweating dancers and those who are slumped on the floor, the long hair, suede jackets, gaucho trousers and Chelsea boots. How sad and unfortunate that the Station Hotel is to be demolished. The Stones will go on Rolling.

The same week, in Wilmington, Joe and Eva Jagger turned fifty.

On 14 April 1963 the group were halfway through their scheduled Sunday performance when four figures appeared in silhouette wearing identical black leather overcoats: the Beatles. Jagger, Stewart recalled, went rigid. At the time the Mop Tops' single 'From Me To You' was an international hit. They had money; they had a manager. (Inducting the Beatles into the Rock 'n' Roll Hall of Fame in January 1988, Jagger recalled: 'When the Stones were first together we heard there was a group from Liverpool with long hair, scruffy clothes and a record in the charts with a bluesy harmonica riff ... The combination of all this made me sick.') Reciprocally the Beatles admired the Stones. In Edith Grove the two groups talked and stayed up through the night, Jones asking for, and receiving, a signed photograph.

On the eighteenth he, Jagger and Richards went backstage at the Beatles' concert at the Albert Hall. Jones was mistaken for one of the group and mobbed. 'That's it!' Gomelski remembers him yelling. *That's* what I want.' Jagger stood in the shadows in his sweater and jeans. At the screams his whole face crinkled like a teenybopper's. Feverishly excited, he was filled with incommunicable thoughts. 'Meeting the Beatles,' says Wyman, 'was a spur to all of us.'

The reason Jagger succeeded was that he was in touch with his ambition. If Jones wanted to be a star and Richards a musician, Jagger insisted on both. After meeting the Beatles he began to press Gomelski for more bookings, more money, more coverage. Before the next performance at the Station Hotel Gomelski rang Peter Jones, a journalist with *Record Mirror*. He arrived to find fans queuing outside and, within, Brian Jones – 'who supervised every move they made' – waiting to talk. Next day, at the *Mirror* office, he enthused to two people – a reporter, Norman Jopling, and an itinerant teenager named Andrew Loog Oldham.

Oldham was last in the trio of exotic quasi-Europeans who fathered the Stones. Ironically he was younger than any of them – born on 29 January 1944 to an English mother and Dutch-American father who was killed in the war. In 1955 Oldham discovered rock and roll and invested both time and ingenuity in playing truant in Soho. His idol was the film star Laurence Harvey. At sixteen Oldham was expelled from Wellingborough College, worked briefly for the designer Mary Quant and made a forlorn effort to become a pop singer under the names Sandy Beach and Chancery Laine. In the end he settled for a PR job with the publisher Leslie Frewin, and in February 1963 offered his services to Brian Epstein to promote Gerry and the Pacemakers – not, alas, the Beatles. Epstein fired him in April. Dropping by the *Record Mirror* office in the hope of finding work, Oldham found Peter Jones deep in conversation with Jopling.

'Wild,' was the first word he heard.

It was then that Oldham made his move. The next Sunday the Stones played to an audience of four hundred at Richmond. Oldham's memories of that night are crisp: 'They made an immediate impact on me and my first reaction was: "*This is it*." I felt they were magic . . . I knew what I was looking at. It was sex.' Immediately Oldham approached Brian Jones and proposed himself as the group's manager. (Gomelski, conveniently, was in Switzerland, attending his father's funeral.) Oldham quickly impressed the Stones as being equally anarchic as – possibly more than – themselves. Most managers, he readily concurred, were 'erdies'; agents ditto. 'The business', Oldham stated loftily, would be handled by his partner Eric Easton, a balding organist-cum-impresario impossibly old at thirty-five, leaving him, Oldham, with 'image'. On 1 May Jones went to Easton's office in Radnor House, Regent Street, to talk money. At one point he left with the contract to meet Jagger and Richards, waiting in a nearby café. (Watts and Wyman were never consulted.) The eventual deal, effective from 6 May, was signed that night. When Gomelski returned from Switzerland he was politely told he was out.

Jagger, meanwhile, had met a tremulous-lipped, teenage brunette named Chrissie Shrimpton. Shrimpton bet a girl-friend at the Ricky Tick Club, Windsor, that the Stones' 'groovy' singer could be induced to kiss her; she won. Jagger then invited her to see the group at Richmond on 28 April. When Oldham approached the hotel that night he saw 'two attractive people . . . arguing in the alley like lovers'. (Which they already were: Shrimpton's sister Jean recalls their mother entering Chrissie's room one morning to find Jagger asleep in bed. It was the start of an affair that lasted into a fourth year.)

Shrimpton, seventeen, commuted daily into London to attend secretarial college. She and Jagger would meet in Hyde Park after class; less frequently he induced her to Edith Grove. By midsummer, he announced, he was in love. He even proposed to her. According to her later memory Jagger's personality was by turns ambitious, tender, weak, strong – a typical domineering Leo – and 'lost'. She suggested they wait. It is doubtful that Shrimpton and Jagger were ever closer. By the time he broke off the relationship she was drawn, depressed and suicidal. 'He drained me,' she once told her sister. Jean believed her.

Incredibly, Jagger continued to attend classes at the LSE. He enrolled for a Special Subject in industry and trade. No one, Stern included, was given to believe he was on the point of departure. In World's End Jones and Richards teased him constantly. Jones further hinted that if Jagger 'wouldn't commit' to the group then he and Oldham would make other arrangements. Making arrangements was just what Oldham did best: at Eel Pie Island, Twickenham, Stewart was fired – 'too normal'. Next Richards was informed that the final 's' had been deleted from his name. Finally Oldham approached Dick Rowe, head of A & R at Decca Records, and insisted that he see the group at Richmond. Rowe did so. In the meantime Norman Jopling's review appeared in *Record Mirror*.

At the Station Hotel, Kew Road, the hip kids throw themselves about to the new 'jungle music' like they never did in the more restrained days of Trad.

And the combo they writhe and twist to is called the Rolling Stones. Maybe you haven't heard of them

– if you live far from London, the odds are you haven't.

But by gad you will . . .

Rowe's interest in the group was not entirely selfless. The previous year he had been approached by Brian Epstein to sign a quartet of mumbling Liverpudlians crooning 'My Feet's Too Big' and 'Besame Mucho'; he refused. By the end of the year the group had become the biggest phenomenon in showbusiness. Rowe, after a period of penance, was instructed by Decca's chairman Edward Lewis to sign someone 'bigger than the Beatles'. That was exactly how Oldham pitched them: bigger than the Beatles. Rowe saw the Stones at Richmond on 5 May and immediately opened negotiations. On the sixteenth a contract was drawn up. The group were offered the standard royalty rate of five per cent on each record sold. A tape-lease agreement gave Decca a first option on all Stones recordings for two years. In a separate move, for £106, the group bought back their recordings from IBC. Rowe's next suggestion was for the Stones to repair forthwith to Decca's facility in West Hampstead. This was met by audible yawns and Oldham's disclosure that time had already been booked at Olympic Studios off Regent Street. Lewis and Rowe quickly discovered what the rest of the world would know later: the Stones in general, and Oldham in particular, wanted it all – power, money, control. As an executive at Decca recalls, 'Andrew and Mick could be complete animals . . . I can picture them sitting with their feet on Dick's desk saying, "sod this" and "eff that" . . . They were the first really *arrogant* group to make it.'

Now and only now did Jagger quit the LSE. Even at this stage, with a contract and the prospect of recording a single, he hedged his bets. When Jagger approached the School Registrar he was told that, by all means, he was free to 'take off' for a year. That was how he put it to his parents: a year off. (Even now Joe Jagger insists that 'he took a sabbatical from his studies to sing.') At Edith Grove Jagger's announcement was greeted with war-whoops and slapped hands. Oldham came to the flat to discuss the choice of their first single. After prolonged debate they agreed on a Chuck Berry number, 'Come On', an obscure ditty with untypically dour lyrics. It was only the first of countless seemingly perverse career moves. The session that followed was, in Jagger's words, 'a bunch of bloody amateurs, ignorant as hell, making a hit single'. Musically the song was shorn of its original rumba beat and dramatically accelerated; lyrically Jagger inserted the word 'guy' for 'jerk'. The resulting shambles was, he later admitted, 'shit'.

Jones now launched his last major offensive to control the group. According to Wyman, outside Easton's office Stewart (retained as road manager) 'heard Brian say that Jagger had always had a weak voice and he had to be careful if he wanted to sing night after night. They'd just get rid of him if necessary.' Easton was known to share certain reservations about Jagger's ability. Jones had other motives: all too well he realized that the public demanded of each group a 'leader', and that all too frequently that meant the singer. Another consideration, in Easton's view, was that 'the BBC' – here his voice fell to a reverential murmur – 'wouldn't like him'. When Oldham heard of this he called Easton into his office. 'Do you want to tear up your contract,' he was asked, 'or apologize to Mick?'

Apologize to Mick.

'Come On' was released on 7 June. Eileen Giles remembers Jagger 'running into Edith Grove waving a copy. He put it on the turntable and kept shouting, "It's here!" ... He was like a kid.' Jagger also met his old schoolfriend Peter Holland, studying at University College, and announced theatrically, 'I've chucked it.'

'Chucked what?'

'The LSE.'

'Are you mad?'

Jagger's response was to explain for Holland's benefit the inevitable course the Stones' career would take: records, concerts, tours, finally America. That was the feverish pitch of his imagination – combined now, says Holland, with other changes. Already, by mid-1963, Jagger was affecting a wardrobe of crew-cut sweaters, Cuban heels and breath-takingly taut trousers. He sported a silver identity bracelet. His hair grew. 'It was now,' writes Wyman, 'that our appearance began to overtake our sound in people's perception . . . In the previous few weeks we had been refused service in various cafés and pubs, because of our hair.' (This at a time when the War Minister, John Profumo, resigned for, in Harold Wilson's words, 'debauching and corrupting public life' and the government itself came close to collapse.) During an interview with *Rave*, arranged by Oldham, the Stones were asked to leave a hotel lounge because of their 'demeanour'. Outside their demeanour promptly stopped traffic. This delighted Oldham.

Immense effort was put into the way the Stones looked and behaved. If every group has its characteristic selling point, one theme developed a million ways, then theirs was sex. From Oldham Jagger learned the virtues of appealing equally to both men and women, thus doubling the market. He began to develop an androgynous stage act wherein he danced, sang, preened, mimicked, joked: total entertainment. Over five hundred saw the Stones' final performance at the Station Hotel on 16 June. At the Richmond Athletic Ground a fortnight later Alan Etherington was intrigued to see Jagger perform for the first time in a year: 'The change was stupendous . . . He'd learned these tricks about teasing the audience, turning his back and shaking his rear. That was new.' Critics are divided as to whether Oldham 'made' Jagger or vice versa, but both knew precisely what they wanted. Early on Oldham had given it as his wish to be 'a teenage tycoon shit'. In a fan newsletter that summer Jagger's ambitions were to own his own business and record a million-seller.

'Come On' sold less than a hundred thousand. It peaked at number twenty-one. Meanwhile Easton had arranged for the group to appear on the Saturday night show *Thank Your Lucky Stars*. Oldham – in whom the 'showbiz' tradition was perhaps more deeply ingrained than he admitted – insisted they perform in matching black trousers and black and white houndstooth jackets with velvet collars. Even then they were treated by the compère, Pete Murray, like a disease. On a two-sided set, vaguely reminiscent of a western saloon, the Stones mimed 'Come On' to frenzied pre-recorded screams. Later the programme's switchboard was jammed with complaints. An ATV executive pulled Oldham aside and advised him repeatedly to 'lose the vile-looking singer with the tyre-tread lips', the singer himself muttering darkly, 'No more suits.'

Undeterred, Easton contrived for the Stones to perform a series of ballroom dates in far-off Wisbech, Dunstable, Margate. Conveyed in Stewart's decrepit Austin the group would appear backstage, hauling their own equipment, to be informed by the ruffle-shirted compère that they had ten minutes to change their 'gear'. Much slack-jawed amazement greeted Jagger's inevitable reply: 'This *is* our gear.' *Northern Beat* commented, 'They mount the stage wearing exactly what they please, be it jeans, bell-bottom trousers or leather jerkins. Individuality is their password.' On a typical night the Stones would play 'Poison Ivy', 'Fortune Teller', 'You Better Move On', adding, on rare occasions, 'Come On'. They were paid between twenty and sixty pounds a performance. The star of these shows, as much for his appearance as his still rudimentary stage act, was Jagger. At the Grand Hotel, Lowestoft, teenage girls flowed over the footlights like lava, removing Jagger's suede shoes and even clutching his socks. On other occasions underwear, some exotic items among them, would appear on stage.

Banners in the crowd proclaimed Liz & Julie's Love for 'Mik', or Jagger's status as 'God'. In the space of three months the public's lust for leadership had found expression in the pale, leering youth stage-centre with the rutting hips and animal howl. Credit for this – the exploitation of eternal adolescent dreams and cravings – lay with Oldham, though Jagger added refinements of his own: 'On stage,' he announced, 'we just go mad ... If people don't like us, that's too bad.' Truly it must have seemed that with the explosion of 'youth culture' – the young, for the first time since the war, consciously seeking to distance themselves from their elders – such a response was unlikely.

The next move was a purely arbitrary one (as so many would be) when the lease expired at Edith Grove. Jagger and Richard moved into a flat at 33 Mapesbury Road, Kilburn, later being joined by Oldham. Jones migrated to a girlfriend's house in Windsor. The axis thus formed effectively managed the group, Jagger's and Oldham's minds flickering daily from one ruse to another. Richard tagged along. A fan club, organized by Shirley Arnold, was established to exchange outgoing newsletters for incoming snapshots, love notes and other proposals. Jagger was offered for interview with *Fabulous*, *Valentine* and *Jackie*, an enterprising reporter from *Everybody* even tracking down Joe and Eva in Wilmington. ('Quite honestly,' said Mrs Jagger, 'I expected Mick to become a politician.') By early autumn the other voices had all but been silenced by Jagger's, and the public upheld their sacrifice.

Moving rapidly in his smoky blue glasses and cap, Oldham next designated Jagger and Richard the group's songwriters. Later he described this as a 'gut feeling', based on their known ability to interpret work in the studio. Oldham also had a healthy fear of running out of suitable material. 'We knew,' says Jagger, 'we couldn't go on forever recording old songs.' Whatever the cause, the effect was that late that year Oldham physically locked Jagger and Richard into a room 'about the size of a kitchen' in Mapesbury Road and demanded they compose a song. The result was 'It Should Be You', a mawkish ditty sold immediately to the late George Bean. 'The first ones,' Oldham admitted, 'were pretty shitty, but I had to keep pushing them'. Jagger promptly began to read all the books he could lay his hands on. He trawled the second-hand stores in Charing Cross Road, scene of his earlier expeditions with Taylor and Alan Etherington. He intended, he announced, to be eclectic. Richard paused, like an animal approaching a trap. 'Electric?' Yes, electric.

The trio now formed a sub-group. Jagger and to a lesser extent Richard were recognizably Oldham's favoured Stones. As Stewart said, 'Mick and Keith were quite prepared to go along with anything Andrew said. They fed off each other . . . We had very little contact with them in those days.' Some inferred a still closer liaison. Even in Edith Grove, Wyman remembers, there were mumblings that 'Mick and Brian had had some sort of gay relationship'. Now spurious allegations surfaced linking Jagger (who with make-up looked disturbingly epicene) and Oldham. Shrimpton, according to an interview she gave the author Anthony Scaduto, approached Oldham and was assured 'he and Mick were strictly friends and business associates'. She was also asked if Jagger and Oldham 'slept in the same bed' at Mapesbury Road.

'Not when I'm there. Because I sleep with Mick.'

In the same interview Shrimpton recounts that, approaching the flat one evening with Jagger, Richard, Jones and two girlfriends, she was shoved aside with the words, 'Get away for a moment.' Jagger had spotted a gaggle of fans at the gate. Oldham, Shrimpton believes, had forbidden any of the group to be seen with their partners and pressure was exerted on Watts not to marry his fiancée Shirley Shepherd. That night Shrimpton went quietly berserk, slapping Jagger, kicking at his shins and groin, perceiving herself 'just a piece of baggage carried by a star'. It set the tone for a relationship that on her own admission became harrowing. It is possible even then that she contemplated the idea of escape, but for three years she stayed loyal to Jagger. That autumn she was taken to Wilmington to meet Joe and Eva. The latter she found to be garrulous, extrovert, gossipy, 'not sophisticated enough' to understand her son's needs. Shrimpton also noted that Jagger had 'no patience' with his mother, to whom he spoke quite differently than the Cockney tone he affected on stage. Later Shrimpton returned the compliment by introducing Jagger to her father Edward. They discussed economics together.

By now Jagger was earning a living. On 11 September a music publishing company, Nanker-Phelge Ltd, was incorporated for songs to which 'members of the group' (i.e. Jagger, Richard) would contribute. It remained dormant for six months. That autumn the Stones began a British tour, third on the bill to the Everly Brothers and Bo Diddley. The fee was forty-two pounds a night. On 16 October the group received their first weekly accounts from Easton and were each handed a cheque for £193. (Roughly a tenth of its current value.) Later Jagger opined, 'You mustn't get too hung up about money . . . not so much having money, but what money can buy.' Visitors to Mapesbury Road confirm that, while lacking the Gothic squalor of Edith Grove, the accommodations were anything but luxurious. Jagger's quarters were a small bedroom overlooking the street. There were few amenities: a piano, Richard's guitar, a primitive Grundig tape recorder. Jagger's tongue was firmly in his prominent cheek when he insisted to the Dartford *Chronicle* on 29 November, 'I spend money freely.' The same article gave his age as nineteen and his 'day job' as the London School of Economics.

Oldham, having considered and rejected 'Poison Ivy' as a new single, was brooding in Great Newport Street when a taxi drew to a halt. Inside were John Lennon and Paul

McCartney. The dialogue, Oldham recalled, went: "'Ello, Andy. You're looking unhappy. What's the matter?' 'Oh, I'm fed up. The Stones can't find a song to record.' 'Oh – *we've* got a song we've almost written. The Stones can have that if you like.' The two Beatles repaired with Oldham to Studio 51 and completed the work, 'I Wanna Be Your Man'. Such things actually happened in the sixties. A fortnight later, on 7 October, the Stones went to Kingsway Studio, Holborn, with Easton; Oldham, not for the last time, had decamped for France. The resulting single was a miniature classic. Jones, in the very throes of losing control to Jagger and Oldham, reverted to his Elmo Lewis persona on bottleneck; Richard chimed in; Jagger screamed the primal vocal. Released on 1 November, the song reached number twelve in the UK charts. It was also briefly, and unsuccessfully, launched in the US. 'The backing is wild but too prominent,' said *Melody Maker*. *Beat Monthly* demurred: 'The Stones are rolling again.'

Oldham now further consolidated Jagger and Richard as the group's song-writers and de facto leaders. 'Success came,' writes Wyman, 'and confusion set in with Brian. Mick and Keith, egged on by Andrew, saw the golden chance to break through. Brian instinctively pulled back . . . he could easily have developed his song-writing, but he lacked confidence.' Jones himself made the same point to the reporter Don Short, complaining of the 'creative thing' having been 'stitched up' to his own prejudice. Wyman reiterates: 'Andrew . . . pushed Keith against Brian for second place in the band . . . Nobody except Mick and Keith got the opportunity to write.' When Bo Diddley saw the group backstage that autumn he felt Jones was 'burning out'; the singer Chris Farlowe that 'the song-writing thing finished him'. The producer Glyn Johns adds: 'A lot of [early] Stones records were built of riffs, and Brian invariably played those riffs. Then Mick and Keith were encouraged to write and the whole balance of power shifted.' Jagger went home to Wilmington that Christmas looking, says Alan Etherington, 'very dignified'. Not to have laughed out loud was dignified. At one stage he signed autographs for a queue outside his parents' door.

Support for the group now picked up in earnest. The Stones began their second British tour on 3 January 1964. On opening night girls tore down the dressing room door. Inside they fanned out, dividing equally between Jagger and Jones. Later a reporter asked a representative sample (plastic macs, mascara) what it was they liked about the Stones:

'Mick!' (The voices ascending almost into animal pitch.) *'Mi—ck!'*

'What about him?'

'His feet' – more squeals. 'His legs.'

'What else?'

Here a dark-haired child of thirteen came forward and breathed, *'Everything!'* before swooning in a parody of Jagger on stage.

Even he must have been impressed. In the space of three months that winter the Stones went from provincial novelty act to national fixation, largely on the basis of Jagger's unerring ability to convey sex to a mass audience. He did so by dancing, preening, darting, shuffling, strutting – and by standing stock still, his eyes drooping under his fringe, with none of the apparent *joie de vivre* associated with, for one, the Beatles. 'This Mersey Sound is no different from our River Thames sound,' he stated; 'as for these Liverpool blokes proclaiming themselves better than anyone else, that's rubbish.' The North v South, Beatles v Stones debate now raged in fact. 'Who,' the *Sketch* asked, 'would have thought that half Britain's teenagers would end the year with heads like hairy pudding-basins?' (Not the *Sketch*, obviously. They seemed genuinely perplexed.) Even Jagger, later in the year, would attribute the rage only to 'some kind . . . of . . . chemical reaction' wherein the two groups had, in different ways, tapped the modern vein of one generation's desire to be separate from another. Without the need to analyse this Jagger played on it intuitively.

On 13 January the jet-setter of his age boarded a plane for the first time. Jagger, Wyman states, looked nervous throughout the ninety-minute flight to Glasgow. It took less than a tenth of that for the ensuing concert to dissolve in chaos. So went the tour: Mansfield, Bedford, Swindon, the Stones' fee three hundred pounds, their clothes permanently wrinkled, Stewart's van lumbering down suburban vistas, wheels pounding eccentrically, Jagger navigating, Jones alone, Richard asleep, the others along for the ride. Between shows Jagger was introduced – largely by Shrimpton – to names whose acquaintance would have seemed outlandish a year before: David Bailey, Mary Quant, Richard Lester. By spring he was already established as the most personable of the Stones. He learned instinctively what Jones never did – how to manage people; to adapt. To his mania for books was added a lifelong interest in the theatre. In a not unrelated move Jagger became the first group member to use make-up. The previous Christmas a musician named Joe Flannery had showed him how to apply rouge and mascara; Little Richard (attached to the Everly Brothers tour at the last moment) added touches of his own. He further developed his stage act to encompass burlesque. One of his moves was to spin an article of clothing on his finger like a stripper: another Richard motif.

The group returned to IBC Studios to record the Buddy Holly standard 'Not Fade Away', though Oldham later considered this the first song Jagger and Richard ever wrote, so enhanced was the beat. They even played the Woolwich Granada, scene of Jagger's encounter with Holly in 1958. As 'Not Fade Away' rose to number three in the chart, the Rolling Stones in the space of two weeks cut the raw material for their first LP. At various stages Phil Spector, Graham Nash and Alan Clark of the Hollies, and later Gene

Pitney appeared in the studio. The resulting mêlée produced two songs, 'Andrew's Blues' and 'Spector and Pitney Came Too', in which Jagger mimicked, amongst numerous others, Edward Lewis, chairman of Decca. Unamazingly, they were never released.

By now everything Jagger did, on and off stage, was characterized by a sense of exuberant, extrovert egoism. Something of this communicated itself to the press. Reporters' eyes turned to him wherever he went. 'While Brian,' notes Wyman, 'was losing his confidence, Mick's was increasing by the day. He took to stardom like a fish to water, while affecting an air of nonchalance with the press, whom he could disarm with his natural charm,' a point confirmed by Don Short, who remembers Jagger 'giving me a long speech on the way to a party – it was all about my writing and how much he admired it'. 'Mick's trick,' Wyman adds, 'was to portray himself as indifferent, whereas in fact he cared very much.' Oldham pulled a masterstroke by singling him out as the group's spokesman; he was the perfect mixture of boorishness and charm. When *Melody Maker* penned its headline on 14 March: 'WOULD YOU LET YOUR SISTER GO WITH A ROLLING STONE? (They don't wear uniforms, don't need mirrors as they hardly bother with examining themselves before they wander on stage)' Jagger was almost apoplectic with joy. By that March he was being written of as some impossible exotic who instilled ribaldry if not actual riot wherever he appeared. All this in a year.

The Beatles, meanwhile, had made their inaugural tour of the US. An estimated seventy-four million people saw them perform on the *Ed Sullivan Show*; they oozed their Goon Show humour ('What do you do when you're cooped up in your rooms?' 'We ice skate'); records, wigs, rings, buttons, posters, shoes and bubble-gum bore their imprimateur. In London *Melody Maker*, Oldham's noticeboard of choice, proclaimed the inevitable consequence:

'STONES FOR STATES (They call them the ugliest pop group in Britain . . . the five dishevelled young men America wants)'. The truth is that, on the issue of song-writing alone, the Stones were a full year behind their counterparts. While the Beatles occupied the top five places in the *Billboard* American singles chart, Jagger and Richard were penning a ditty entitled 'Shang A Doo Lang' promptly foisted on to the singer Adrienne Posta.

It was at Posta's sixteenth birthday party on 27 March that Jagger first met Marianne Faithfull. Born on 29 December 1946, she was the scion of an unlikely marriage between Glynn Faithfull, an English philologist, and one Eva Sacher-Masoch, Baroness Erisso, a descendant of the novelist who gave his name to the enjoyment of pain for sexual pleasure. Faithfull's parents separated in 1953, whereafter Marianne lived with her mother in Millman Road, Reading. Educated at a convent, where she was compelled to wear a smock in the bath in order to conceal her own nakedness, as a child she contracted TB, read voraciously, evolved at sixteen into dramatic beauty and lived, as she put it, 'in a Renoir painting'. In 1963 Faithfull became engaged to John Dunbar, a Cambridge undergraduate. Dunbar it was who escorted her to Posta's party, where she met Oldham ('Here was this pale, blonde, retiring, *chaste* teenager looking like the Mona Lisa, except with a great body'), who in turn summoned his celebrated protégé.

What happened next is open to conjecture. In one version Jagger deliberately poured champagne over Faithfull's dress; in another he lewdly introduced himself in his Cockney accent. What is certain is that the impression left on Faithfull could not have been worse. Also certain was that Oldham on the spot promised to make her a star. Moreover, he announced, 'Mick' and – indicating a swaying figure in the shadows – 'Keith' would compose Faithfull's first single. Jagger nodded assent. That summer he wrote 'As Time Goes By', later revamped as 'As Tears Go By', with which Faithfull had a number nine hit. Immediately she became a quintessential 'figure', identified with glamour and style and ultimately with Jagger himself, lapsing simultaneously into drug addiction and depression. In the end Faithfull spent much of the decade as a celebrity without portfolio. Between fluctuations and the deep qualms of delirium and despair she took her place among the catsuits, pantsuits, the Nehru jackets and miniskirts, the festivals, love-ins, be-ins, the bells, beads and mods and rockers in the pantheon of the sixties. She had her day in the sun.

The Rolling Stones' first LP was released in April 1964. It was a sensation. First the cover – five skulking profiles, their expressions not wholly endearing, no words or title. On the reverse Oldham's immortal quip, 'The Rolling Stones aren't just a group; they're a way of life.' The dozen songs within are a perfect documentary of the group as they played on stage. (Most of the tracks were, in fact, recorded live; there was no money for retakes.) Only one, 'Tell Me', was a Jagger–Richard original, derived strongly from the Mersey Beat with its warbling harmonies and descant. For the remainder there were covers of Berry, of Diddley, of Jimmy Reed. According to the critic Roy Carr the album exuded 'frenetic primal magnificence' possible only in a band of 'enthusiastic young activists'. *New Musical Express* limited itself to the epithet 'fantastic'. On 'King Bee' Jagger, to his credit, sounded as lascivious as the Slim Harpo original – he drooled rather than sang the vocal. There was also a definitive version of 'Route 66'. The record may have been the first British LP, not excluding the Beatles', devoid of fillers. Every track was a potential single. On 24 April, eight days after release, *The Rolling Stones* reached number one. It sold 110,000 in a week.

Easton left immediately for New York. Plans were made for the Stones to tour America that summer. The group's co-manager with his beaming forehead and pipe was an unlikely harbinger of the British Invasion; that was his great strength. In ten days Easton ruthlessly sold the Stones in the image of the Beatles, on which basis – and little else – an eight-city package was agreed with General Artists Corporation. In London this was reported as if the very future of the Western Alliance were at stake. 'What sort of picture of British youth will [the Stones] create across the Atlantic?' screamed the *Sketch*. A very, very bad one, was the answer. In the course of further debate Wallace Snowcroft, president of the National Federation of Hairdressers, announced – to their delight – 'the Rolling Stones are the worst'; his colleague in the Tie Manufacturers Association that 'the criterion for good manners seems to have been forgotten'. In Bristol on 10 May Jagger was barred from the Grand Hotel for wearing his usual corduroys and sweater. 'We dress like this,' he announced, 'and that's that . . . I have no intention of wearing borrowed clothes.' Even then his talent for social legerdemain was at work. Almost simultaneously he drank cocktails with Reginald Maudling and his daughter Caroline at 11 Downing Street. His last act before taking the plane to New York was to be photographed by his friend David Bailey for *Vogue*.

If a single key exists to the Rolling Stones collectively, and Jagger particularly, it lies in post-war British austerity. Everything the group did from 1964 onwards was in conscious – sometimes self-conscious – effort to reverse the privations of their parents. Even this approach had its drawbacks: Jagger found that to be young and affluent in Britain was to know only partial relief from the eternal queues, insipid fashions and all-too-cyclical fits of public morality; Swinging London was not yet. When, therefore, his feet first touched American soil at three-thirty p.m. on Monday 1 June, Jagger went quietly berserk. In his first twelve hours he absorbed as much of New York as a native. He entered and exited Cadillacs, he ran down corridors in the Astor

Hotel, he ordered steaks, waffles and blueberry muffins, and watched *Dragnet* and Johnny Carson. Little did he know that, of the three-week tour, this would be the highlight. In his rapacity to sell the group to General Artists, Easton had prearranged publicity almost exclusively limited to one town.

The *New York Times* reported on 2 June:

> Another British singing group, this one a rock 'n' roll quintet called the Rolling Stones, arrived in New York by plane yesterday . . .
>
> The young men with shoulder-length haircuts were greeted at Kennedy International Airport by about 500 teen-age girls. About 50 Port Authority and NY policemen were on hand to maintain order.
>
> Most of the teen-agers had been informed by (*sic*) the arrival of the singers by announcements made over the radio by disk jockeys.

Jagger's first brush with reality came two days later. In Los Angeles the group taped three songs for the *Hollywood Palace Show*, compèred by Dean Martin (everyone else having turned them down). Lurching towards the old-fashioned stand mike Martin delivered his monologue about 'smaller foreheads and higher eyebrows' before introducing a trampolinist as 'the father of the Rolling Stones – he's been trying to kill himself ever since'. Even before Martin's slur a producer had handed Jagger a crisp hundred-dollar bill backstage to buy the group uniforms. It was crisply returned.

Worse was to follow. After the first official concert at the Swing Auditorium, San Bernardino, where four thousand girls threw jelly-beans and became ecstatic, the Stones appeared to a backdrop of straw bales and horse manure at the San Antonio State Fair. Incredulous cowboys became apoplectic as Jagger strutted, swayed and shook his bony posterior. He was lucky to leave alive. Jack Hutton reported back to the *Daily Mirror*: 'The Stones are being treated as freaks in America . . . People gasp in amazement when they appear.' Barbara Collett, staying at the group's next venue, the Water Tower Inn, Chicago, remembers Jagger 'sashaying down the hall in white pants, silk shirt and a black girl in tow . . . You didn't *see* that in Illinois in those days'. That same night the group drove to 2120 South Michigan Avenue, headquarters of Chess Records, an address familiar to Jagger from his mail-ordering days. They recorded, among others, 'It's All Over Now', promptly designated their new single. Later Willie Dixon arrived and commended Jagger's singing; Chuck Berry also appeared. Next day as the Stones returned they noticed a small, squirrel-cheeked man with an Oriental moustache painting the ceiling: Muddy Waters.

In Minneapolis the group played to an audience of four hundred; at the Olympia, Detroit, to only twice that in a stadium seating thirteen thousand. Some days they drove three hundred miles; others they flew for fifteen minutes. It was that sort of tour. After two weeks away the best news was from home: on 15 June *New Musical Express* voted the Stones number one group in England, while in *Record Mirror* Jagger was 'top individual group member' and 'Not Fade Away' second best single. *The Rolling Stones* topped the LP charts.

At times in America the group almost floundered. There were mutterings about Oldham, and more especially Easton. Jagger hinted darkly: 'We feel we've been given the business here . . . We would never get involved in this kind of tour again.' Some nights he seemed to sag as he ran on stage surveying tier after tier of vacant seats. In Detroit there was exactly one paying customer in the first half-dozen rows. For all its size, its affluence, its diversity, there was nothing conspicuously tolerant in a society whose choice of presidency lay between Lyndon Johnson and Barry Goldwater.

New York and Los Angeles were one thing, the 'bits in the middle', as Jagger put it, another. The critic Lillian Roxon attributed resistance to the group as fear of their 'slummy English lout barrow-boy gutter-rat routine', and added, 'No one had ever seen a white man move on stage the way Jagger moved.' Ominous blurring of the traditional 'white man's' role was exactly what Jagger did best.

In New York he repeatedly asked Ronnie Spector to introduce him to James Brown. When she did, backstage at the Apollo Theatre, Jagger – 'like a scared teenager' – proceeded to watch Brown's act twice in an evening, immediately incorporating the Godfather's patent lurches, shuffles and twists into his own routine. At Carnegie Hall the Stones induced genuine New York mania. Between performances Jagger was kept prisoner in the dressing room as girls swarmed in the corridors, behind curtains and down airshafts. A strange amalgam of hostility and hysteria characterized their last days abroad. At the Park Sheraton Hotel the Stones were treated like dangerous, if exotic, wild animals. Bob Bonis, the tour manager, collected a hundred fan letters daily for Jagger. Hate mail also came in.

The Stones returned to London on 22 June. At the airport Jagger was met by Shrimpton, with whom he spent the afternoon before driving to Oxford. Six months earlier Easton had accepted four hundred pounds for the group to perform at the Magdalen College Ball; to their credit, despite subsequently commanding twice that amount, the Stones duly appeared. Less than a day after leaving New York Jagger found himself singing in a tent to an audience of inebriated, champagne-swilling undergraduates dressed in tails and calling for 'Moon River'. The group, contracted for three sets, settled on two.

The Stones made no money – none – from their tour. They were, however, reaping the benefits of both an LP and single in the charts. After a meeting with Oldham and Easton on 24 June Jagger and Richard moved from

Mapesbury Road into a flat in more modish Hampstead. Shrimpton, now working for Radio Caroline (whose flouting of the broadcasting monopoly laws Jagger deemed 'groovy'), semi-permanently moved in. Home, as Jagger put it, became 'where you finish up between tours'. He, Shrimpton and Richard were driven by armoured car to the BBC Theatre, Shepherd's Bush, on 27 June. Outside were five hundred delirious fans. Inside an equal number witnessed the Stones' notorious performance on *Juke Box Jury*, notorious in that, having voted all but one of the proffered selections a 'miss', they were portrayed in the press as 'rude', 'anthropoid', 'boorish' and even 'charmless'. 'If the producer had wanted sophistication,' said Jagger, 'he would have got a bunch of actresses.' It was another example of playing to the myth: *Jury*'s urbane host, David Jacobs, says today that 'they were perfectly behaved, even debonair' backstage. Fresh from his performance as a confirmed halfwit, Jagger attended a meeting on 1 July to incorporate the Rolling Stones as a limited company.

After holidaying in Ibiza with Shrimpton, he returned to the circuit on 11 July. At Bridlington, Leeds and Brighton Jagger was merely mobbed. At Blackpool he was nearly killed. The violence at the Empress Ballroom started with a roomful of swaying Glaswegians ('Many of them,' Wyman intones, 'drunk'); it was compounded by Jones, as usual, competing with Jagger on stage. 'Someone at the very front suddenly took exception to Brian's effete posturing,' wrote Roy Carr. 'So did his cronies. As Brian nervously bounced closer to the edge of the stage, this gang of sodden louts began a contest to see which of them could spit on the Stone. Not one of them missed.' When Richard was also targeted he extended a steel-toed boot in reprisal. Mayhem. Stewart promptly pushed Richard backstage, where Jagger, Jones, Watts and Wyman were already making for the door. In the ensuing riot amplifiers, drums and a Steinway piano were demolished. The theatre's red and gold velvet curtains were torn. A teenager climbed the shreds and, apelike, swung from a chandelier. The Stones themselves were smuggled out of the building over a roof and into a police van which deposited them at the station. The Deputy Chief Constable later opined that 'such scenes cannot be tolerated'.

The next morning Jagger was interviewed on BBC radio and confirmed airily that 'it was really violent'. A renewed debate raged over the disease called rock and roll; headline writers had no sooner excelled themselves than they were called on to make one more effort. At the next concert on 26 July Jagger was pelted with eggs, hundreds of stones, underwear beyond number, books, bottles, decaying food, newspaper, notepaper and toilet paper; demonstrators singled him out. In the street a middle-aged woman swung at him with her handbag, repeating over and over, like a machine, 'Ashamed ... you should be ... ashamed' as Jagger ducked for the car, his convict's striped jersey slipping from his shoulders.

He was twenty-one.

· IV ·

COULD *YOU* WALK ON
THE WATER?

'Mick,' trilled Oldham, 'has such *personality*'. He may have been alone in identifying it: Jagger's personality in 1964 was by turns churlish and coy, his voice childishly weak with phony Cockney aspirations. Once he lay supine on stage, smiling gently as chaos broke all around him. Another night he discussed art with the Marquess of Bath. Parents, he informed Paul McCartney, were a drag. At weekends Jagger returned to Wilmington, not omitting to bring chocolates. One more side to him, it seemed, and he would have been circular.

The public Jagger, performing Jagger, was perfected that summer. In August a tenth of the five thousand present in Ulster Hall, Belfast, fainted in the space of two numbers; police begged Jagger to stop after a third. At Longleat braying debutantes became delirious as he descended a flight of steps into their presence. 'If they keep on at this rate,' noted a policeman, 'there'll be a disaster.' Leaving the *Ready Steady Go!* studios the roof was torn from Jagger's Daimler and he drove convertible-style before being transferred to an armoured van. Later the Stones played alfresco in Richmond to seven thousand fans, among them a seventeen-year-old named Ronnie Wood, who smashed his leg against a protruding tent peg.

Next night anarchy broke out during a performance in Holland. As Jagger announced 'I Wanna Be Your Man' the – predominantly male – audience responded. In the ensuing bedlam electric leads were twisted, chandeliers broken and spotlights shattered; in the wings Stewart was felled by a bottle. The police formed a firefighter-like chain and passed troublemakers methodically hand-to-hand, pausing to administer a quick, impersonal beating to each. The Stones left under escort. In Brighton bouffant Mods busily set about Rockers, studiously ignoring Jagger who twisted in the mid-distance. Next there was a police dog on stage at the Isle of Man which became distraught at Jagger's singing and tried to bite him. Overwrought teenagers were laid out in blankets in the lobby. In Jersey tomatoes and eggs were thrown on stage. Returning on Channel Airways, the stewardess enquired when Jagger had last had a haircut. She also referred to hygiene. Jagger retaliated and was banned for ever from the airline.

In August the critic Fred Newman wrote that 'whether he cares to acknowledge it or not . . . [Jagger] provides the visually suggestive symbolism that sparks the mass orgy'; he also considered the 'psychology of concert-hall hysteria' and discerned a 'group protest against society'. Jagger himself was less ingenuous, stating only, 'I don't think I [try] necessarily to be outrageous . . . I move on stage the way I do because I enjoy it.'

Somewhere between lies the key to the frenzy that, despite certain incidents afforded maximum treatment in the press, was less apocalyptic than the headlines suggest. The temperature at these concerts fell the moment the Stones ceased playing. There was no deeper sense of *angst* or youthful unrest. The crowds who rioted at Wimbledon, Luton and Liverpool were fully capable of engaging in dramatic scenes without themselves living dramatically. Jagger understood this perfectly. As early as 1958, returning on the train from Woolwich, Dick Taylor remembers him talking 'quite coolly' about aspects of his O level curriculum. There was no mention of Buddy Holly.

Jagger's reputation extended. He was greeted warmly by McCartney, without insult by Lennon; on 12 August he attended a party with both at Brian Epstein's. Of all the Stones he was singled out for special attention by Oldham ('Andrew's association with Mick,' states Wyman, being 'clearly much warmer than with the rest of us'). From his manager Jagger learned brilliantly how to manipulate the press. The playfully menacing quote – 'If people don't like us, that's too bad' – was another Oldham refinement. By late 1964 he was almost morbidly protective of his charge. Oldham also fell into dispute with Easton, with whom he argued constantly about money; there were conflicts about the 'image' and 'deportment' of the group, one manager wanting them changed for the better, the other greatly for the worse. That autumn Oldham sold his consultancy agency to a PR colleague, Tony Calder, and began spending weekends in voluntary seclusion in a convent or monastery in France. After marrying in September Oldham withdrew still further from day-to-day management of the group. 'I don't enjoy it any more,' he informed *Melody Maker*; 'someone else' would have to do it.

Almost inevitably Jagger stepped forward with Richard. For almost three years the two had been inseparable; they co-habited; they roomed together in hotels. They wrote songs. With Oldham detached, Jones diminished, Wyman and Watts (as from October) both married, Jagger and Richard effectively took over. When Easton suggested something 'pop' for the next single the two principals closed ranks: '"Little Red Rooster",' said Richard. 'You remember,' added Jagger; 'the *blues*.'

In August Jagger was in court to plead guilty to three motoring offences: having no insurance, failing to produce a licence and operating his Ford Escort at fifty in a thirty m.p.h. zone. He was fined thirty-two pounds. Driving problems of one sort or another became something of a theme. In November Jagger appeared in Tetenhall, Staffordshire, to be defended theatrically by his solicitor Dale Parkinson: 'The Duke of Marlborough had much longer hair than my client, and he won some famous battles. He powdered his, too, because of the fleas. My client has no fleas.' (Fined ten pounds.) Two years later he crashed his Aston Martin DB6 into the Countess of Carlisle's car. 'Mr Jagger,' intoned a statement, 'wishes to deny that he is dead.' The Aston Martin was traded in for a Mini.

Jagger also took – or extended – responsibility for the group's public profile. He granted, or more frequently denied, interviews. He insisted on control of photographs. According to Shrimpton's interview with Anthony Scaduto, she and Shirley Watts were permitted to join the Stones in Paris that October only on sufferance. 'You won't like being there,' said Jagger, 'and you'll get in our way.' Shrimpton came to attention in front of him, raised an arm and extended a Nazi salute. She went to Paris.

Also present that night was an Old Etonian army officer-turned-art dealer, Robert Fraser. Fraser in turn introduced Jagger to the film-maker Donald Cammell and the designer Christopher Gibbs; through Gibbs Jagger met Cecil Beaton. It became a kind of chain-letter to the more raffish elements of the aristocracy. For the first time the word 'decadent' was applied not entirely disparagingly. It would recur throughout the decade as first the Chelsea Set, then Swinging London itself embraced the Stones. Even in America they became fashionable.

America was Jagger's next stop. The Stones arrived there on 23 October. At the airport there was an authentic New York riot as five hundred screaming fans outflanked the police and rushed the tarmac. 'On our first trip,' allows Wyman, 'people were curious. This time there was excitement.' A middle-aged reporter, the bald summit of his head beaming in the sun, gleaned the following:

'Who do you prefer, the Beatles or the Rolling Stones?'

'I think that the Rolling Stones have a lot more sex appeal than the Beatles . . . When the Rolling Stones are performing on stage, there's a lot more excitement coming through.'

'Er . . . How about you?'

'I think they're the greatest, they dress different and they're the best thing that's ever happened in the United States.'

'Why do *you* like the Rolling Stones?'

'Because . . . they're so ugly, they're attractive.'

The next day the group's second LP was released in America. It kicked off with the mandatory 'Around and Around' before subsiding into the Drifters–Wilson Pickett material recorded in Chicago the previous June. Two songs were credited to the group's collective alias, two to Jagger–Richard. The old Irma Thomas hit 'Time Is On My Side' was released as a single. The LP went to number three, 'Time' to number six. Both served as a transition from the Stones as white English slaves of the blues to full-blown rockers; no small transition. (A number of the out-takes from the album were later issued on an LP called *Metamorphosis*.) That same night, 24 October, the group played two shows at the Academy of Music at which the writer Tom Wolfe (then guesting on the *Herald Tribune*) excelled himself:

The girls have Their Experience. They stand up on their seats. They ululate, even between songs. The looks on their faces! Rapturous agony! There, right up there, under the sulphur lights, that is *them*. God, they're right there! Mick Jagger takes the microphone with his tabescent hands and puts his huge head against it, opens his giblet lips and begins to sing . . .

And so on. (Today Wolfe notes merely, 'they were seismic'.)

On the twenty-fifth the group was conveyed by Cadillac to the *Ed Sullivan Show*. Sullivan ignored them. Backstage Oldham was ceremonially handed a pink telephone into which he purred, 'Edward . . . I have to remind you' – here his voice seemed to drop an octave in the gloom – 'Ties, right . . . yeah, suits.' After that he listened for a while and said 'I know' several times. 'Rehearsal? . . . Of *course*. Eddie, before you ring off, I wanted to ask you about . . . Rung off,' said Oldham. 'You'll have to change.' Jagger changed into a grey sweatshirt and walked on. The Stones played 'Around and Around' to continual screams and returned for 'Time Is On My Side', Jagger slapping his palm on to his raised knee once, twice, a dozen times; chaos. Later Sullivan confided to the Toronto *Globe*, 'I hadn't met the Stones until the day before . . . They were recommended to me by my agents in England. I was shocked when I saw them . . . I promise you I'll never invite them back on the show.' It took Sullivan six months to do so.

The full extent of the group's celebrity became apparent in California. The Teen-Age Music International (TAMI) Show had assembled a bill including Chuck Berry, Smokey Robinson, Marvin Gaye, the Supremes and James Brown. The Stones headlined. Afterwards Marvin Gaye informed *Rave*: 'See that guy Jagger stand suddenly still, then whirl around . . . He doesn't plan it but it's sure exciting.' Jagger, in turn, paid more than casual attention to Gaye's own act and Berry's. He began to incorporate elements of both. He experimented with the splits and the slide. He learned in America what a thousand singers would learn later: how easy it is to animate the average rock audience. It needs to hear only the vaguest facsimile of a hit record, suitably dramatized, Jagger realized. To the barely audible drone provided by Richard, Jones, Watts and Wyman he added a further series of lunges, lurches, shuffles, struts and scowling immobility. Very few of the twelve- and thirteen-year-olds who comprised the Stones' audiences were, after all, there to listen. 'That's when the Mick Jagger we know began,' says Gomelski. 'After that second trip to America. When Mick got off the plane in London, he was doing the James Brown slide.' Later Jagger and Richard wrote their first hit using Brown's famous put-on, pleading routine as the basis for 'The Last Time'.

On 27 October the group assembled at RCA Studios, Hollywood, to record six numbers. Jack Nitzsche and Dave Hassinger, respectively the studio's arranger and engineer, had seen nothing remotely like the Stones. 'Mick,' Hassinger told Barbara Charone, 'came in bobbing and weaving and snapping his fingers'; adding, 'After a playback you had to get an OK from the Stones. And an OK from the Stones meant Mick and Keith ... not even Andrew.' According to Nitzsche: 'They were the first rock and roll band I met that were intelligent.'

The inevitable riots: Cleveland, Milwaukee, Fort Wayne ... After a while the names tended to swarm and mingle. The Stones returned to New York on 5 November. Black porters at Grand Central Station shouted, 'Are you girls?' 'Are you the Harlem Globetrotters?' snapped Jagger. After registering at the Astor Hotel he and Richard drove immediately to Harlem to see – yet again – James Brown. Backstage Jagger sat on a stool as Brown drank champagne, holding a telephone, while an assistant lacquered his hair. He certainly, says Wyman, 'made an impression'.

The tour ended on 15 November. Jagger sat backstage signing autographs while fans filed past, in the manner of feudal tenants paying rent, presenting: Thanksgiving cards, postcards, playing cards, bubble gum, chewing gum, toy animals – and one live puppy. Eventually four tables were filled. 'Thanks ... mmm ... thanks,' mumbled Jagger in a twangy whine. Later a reporter edged forward in his suit and bow tie and conducted an interview of sorts:

'Er, you've now been on your second tour of the United States for two weeks. How was it?'

'Er . . .'

'Three weeks, excuse me.'

'Three weeks, yes. Very enjoyable . . . er, most enjoyable . . . very successful tour.'

'Now, er, that was not true of the first one, was it?'

'Ooh, *no*.' Jagger at this stage gave a dazzling boyish grin. 'We only came over here on the first one so we could get ourselves known, so to speak.'

'Uh-huhh.'

'And then we went back and things started happening for us.'

'Well, er . . . why did they start happening?'

'I really don't know.' Jagger shuffled and shrugged. 'Some . . . sort of chemical reaction . . . seems to have happened, somehow.'

In the space of three weeks Jagger had performed fifteen concerts, recorded a dozen songs, appeared on coast-to-coast TV, been described as 'scum' by Sullivan and 'immoral' by the Mayor of Milwaukee. Wolfe and Andy Warhol had noticed him. On stage Jagger had developed an act halfway between menacing and mincing, one aimed purposefully at the average teenager's midriff. It connected brilliantly. In Long Beach police with clubs beat twelve-year-olds who crawled insect-like over the group's car.

'It wasn't always pleasant,' said Stewart, 'to see what we did to people.'

———

From late 1964 Jagger subsumed (at times) name, honour, virtue, order and law in his rapacity to be a star. He refined his stage act. He shaved a year from his age. He accepted invitations. He constantly stressed the need for 'image' to Richard and Jones. And where was Jones? Hospitalized in Chicago and denying he was leaving the Stones.

Desire now met decision. Once Jagger was perceived as a threat he began consciously to act like one. In December viewers of *Thank Your Lucky Stars* were treated to an unnerving close-up of Jagger's larynx as he drawled 'Little Red Rooster'. On *Juke Box Jury* Lonnie Donegan spat at the Stones. The BBC again banned them. *Tailor and Cutter* wrote an editorial suggesting that 'with position comes responsibility'. 'The trouble with ties,' replied Jagger, 'is they dangle in the soup.' 'The Rolling Stones and such,' opined the Archbishop of Canterbury, 'are something one has to live with.'

Jagger's lifestyle might have surprised his numerous critics. He still lived with Richard and Shrimpton. He read; he went to plays. He visited Wilmington. Such life as existed outside the group was spent largely in the clubs – the Ad Lib, Bag o' Nails, the Scotch of St James – catering to the cultural elect, the Frasers, Cammells, Gibbses, the Lennons and McCartneys. It was through the last that Jagger was introduced to the merits of marijuana and the Musician's Best Friend, benzedrine. In a later interview Shrimpton recalled having said, 'I won't [take drugs] because Mick doesn't' – to which an Oldham employee responded, 'My God, Mick was in the office this afternoon, smoking and stoned out of his head.'

Jagger and Shrimpton fought on other fronts – when she lunged at him after a 'nasty comment', gouging his cheek with her rings, a fingertip in either nostril; or when, at their next flat, Jagger suggested to the maid that she use the back stairs. There were further rows, major and minor. All of which – the books, the plays, the clubs, the drugs, the brawls – may have been no more than a twenty-one-year-old's adjustment to sudden wealth. Because he was wealthy. A statement from London Records in New York shows that in 1964 each of the group received royalties of sixteen thousand dollars. None was slow to expand his social horizons. To the consternation of the pop-star-as-cretin school,

Jagger consorted freely with the established orders. 'There's no harm these days in knowing a Rolling Stone,' sighed the *Express*. 'Some of their best friends are fledglings from the upper class.'

The Stones' second British LP was released in January 1965. Only three of its eleven tracks coincided with its US equivalent; to confuse matters further a third record was then issued in America almost identical to the second British release. Both were considered merely competent, no more. Such was the group's status that the British LP reached number one for thirteen weeks. Again there was a front cover devoid of title, again a photograph of epic nastiness in which heads were almost surreally displayed with no apparent effort to conceal the many blotches, blemishes and crevices of Richard's complexion. 'Cast deep into your pockets,' wrote Oldham, 'to buy this disc ... If you don't have bread, see that blind man – knock him on the head.' Not for the last time, questions were asked in the House.

The Stones flew to Australia. In Sydney Jagger visited his remaining cousins, to whom Eva had helpfully written advising them to 'take earplugs'. At the Agricultural Hall the group were hailed and hated ('Ugly Looks, Ugly Speech, Ugly Manners') in equal measure. This was also the tour in which the word 'groupie' became a recognized entity. In Melbourne, according to Wyman, Jagger slept with both the hotel owner and her daughter. (Wyman himself had fans delivered to his room in shifts.) On stage in Invercargill Jagger announced, 'There are no bathrooms ... You can't blame us if we smell.' And at tour's end he dared support act Roy Orbison to sing 'the worst record you've ever made'. 'Agreed,' said Orbison, 'if you will,' whereupon he performed his 1955 ditty 'Ooby Dooby' only for the Stones to give ... exactly their usual performance. 'Just kidding,' said Jagger.

*

En route to Australia the group had spent a day in Hollywood recording 'The Last Time'. Released in late February 1965 it reached number one in Britain and number nine in America: the first authentic Jagger–Richard hit.

'The Last Time' revolves around a repetitive, four-note guitar rhythm. It also illustrates Oldham's affection – even fixation – for Spector's 'wall of sound' technique, the more-or-less arbitrary combining of random noises. The vocal influence was Brown's. 'Best thing they've ever released,' noted *Disc*; Jagger was mobbed the first time he sang it, on *Ready Steady Go!* Millions saw him dragged from the rostrum by his twisted ankle. The following week a British tour began at the Regal, Edmonton. The primitive force of these shows was captured on an EP entitled *Got Live If You Want It*. Announced by the chant 'We Want The Stones' (credited, bizarrely, as a group composition), it proceeded with 'Everybody Needs Somebody to Love' and 'Pain in My Heart', peaked with 'Route 66', faded on 'Moving On' and 'I'm Alright'. The full stage performance also included 'Down The Road Apiece', 'Time Is On My Side', 'Little Red Rooster' and 'The Last Time' – thirty minutes of raw frenetic energy. At times Jagger was singing with girls clinging to his neck.

The tour ended on 18 March. Around midnight the group's Daimler was travelling up Romford Road, a bleak zone of derelict flats and stucco shop fronts, when Wyman felt the call of nature. The car stopped at the Francis Service Station where the attendant, Charles Keeley, was confronted by a 'shaggy-haired monster' (Wyman) asking in 'disgusting language' to use the bathroom. Keeley refused. Thereupon 'eight or nine youths and girls' exited the car, including Jagger uttering the memorable line, 'We piss anywhere, man.' He, Wyman and Jones then availed themselves of a nearby wall witnessed by a Mr Eric Lavender, who dutifully noted the Daimler's number.

The three Stones were charged with insulting behaviour.

At East Ham Magistrates Court Jagger testified that the group 'had every reason to be happy' that night before adding mysteriously, 'I've never been in a bad enough mood to want to hit anyone . . . We have played in many places from Texas to Miami (*sic*) to Helsinki (*sic*) and this is the first time we have been in any trouble with the police'; fined five pounds. The Magistrates' chairman then issued a warning, laughed off at the time, which appeared all too prescient later:

> Because you have reached the exalted heights in your profession, it does not mean you have the right to act like this. On the contrary, you should set a standard of behaviour which should be a moral pattern for your large number of supporters. You have been found guilty of behaviour not becoming young gentlemen.

That April a teenage photographer named Gered Mankowitz, previously involved in the promotion of Marianne Faithfull, was contacted by Oldham. Mankowitz, still an innocent in the world of commercial portraiture, was surprised to be asked – 'prompt at two' – to receive the Rolling Stones. Prompt at three-thirty they arrived at his studio in Masons Yard off Piccadilly. Mankowitz was quickly made aware of the group's disinterest in being photographed. A full hour passed; then another. Comments were made. Suddenly, as if by prearrangement, the Stones stopped complaining. They looked at Mankowitz. They posed. Under the surface, he realized, they weren't disinterested at all. Just the reverse. 'Once they'd committed to something, they threw themselves into it.' To whose direction? 'Andrew was incredibly important in PR terms. He understood the angles. Mick dominated the Stones under Oldham's general guidance.'

The same conclusion was reached by a thirty-nine-year-old ex-paratrooper, veteran of Arnhem, who met the Stones that spring. Tom Keylock ran a two-man car-hire firm from his base in Outram Road, north London. After driving Jagger and Richard to the airport – delivering them through swarms of screaming fans, reporters and strangely silent police – Keylock was offered the job full-time. He looked incredulously at Jagger in his floral shirt and necklace. 'Me. Mind *you*?'

'You're a minder, aren't you?'

The truth of this was irrefutable. All his life Keylock had employed his considerable talents, not least of them pugilistic, in 'minding' his own interests. Gradually, over the course of a month, he was persuaded to apply them on behalf of Jagger's. Like Mankowitz, Keylock had a negative impression of the Stones at their first meeting. Like Mankowitz he rapidly revised his opinion upwards. Under the shades, the flowered shirt, the jewellery borrowed from Shrimpton, Jagger, he concluded, was 'straight'; he respected people who stood up to him (Keylock in this respect giving uniform satisfaction). 'Mick,' he further determined, 'specialized in combinations' – combinations no one else would have dreamed of – exotic clothes, affected accents, a strange amalgam of courtesy and cheek. When Keylock enquired about wages he was told, 'Thirty a week.' As to 'duties' Jagger merely shrugged. (Over the course of six years, these included: driving, cooking, guarding, procuring, putting Jagger 'up', bringing Jagger down, career advice and touches of marriage guidance.) He agreed to think about it.

When Joan Keylock heard the above she almost fainted. The *Rolling Stones*. The East Ham trial had taken place that same week, 'MONSTERS' being among the mildest epithets attached to the group. She was genuinely disturbed. What would the neighbours say? And what was this . . . Mick Jagger . . . *like*?

'Straight,' said Keylock.

'You surprise me.'

Later at the Keylocks' flat Jagger, with his lifelong interest in the subject, asked Tom about the war.

'You know I was injured at Arnhem? Burnt.'

'I didn't know.'

'They grafted most of my arse on to my face.'

'So that's why you talk so much crap.'

'Take the job, Tom,' said Joan.

The Stones spent late April and May in America. 'Mick the Magic Jagger' he was called in the official programme. No stranger to adulation, even he was surprised by his reception: girls crouched in his shower at the Astor; Brown asked to see him; even Sullivan invited the group back, pleading amnesia.

Throughout all this songs were being written. On Thursday 6 May Richard woke at the Gulf Motel, Clearwater, with a recurring noise in his head. 'Some kind of folk song,' he called it. On 10 May the group tried, without enthusiasm, to record it. The next day in Hollywood Richard adjusted the sound by use of a fuzz-box; Watts accelerated the tempo; Jagger improvised. At two in the morning he added a title: 'Satisfaction'.

There was no lightning, no peal of thunder. Richard himself was unimpressed by the song, deeming it 'simple', 'unfinished' – even 'derivative'. As Jagger recalled:

I think Keith thought it a bit basic. I don't think he really listened to it properly. He was too close to it and just felt it was a silly kind of riff. I had to fight like crazy against Keith to put it out, and he'll tell you the same thing. He didn't think it was anything.

Wyman, on the other hand, attests to a group meeting on 12 May at which he, Jones, Watts, Oldham, Stewart and Hassinger voted for 'Satisfaction' as a single, Jagger and Richard against. It was released at the end of the month.

'Satisfaction' spent twelve weeks at number one in America and Britain. It generated 250,000 orders in the latter before release. Eventually it became a standard, a matrix for all the Stones were and would become later. As a song it had everything: blues words, a soul sound in a rock idiom; and attitude. Before that pop, at worst, had treated of broken love. 'Satisfaction' was different. It dealt with the perfidy of promotion, the tedium of touring, frustration, apathy, *angst* – and sex. When the Stones performed the song on *Shindig* the line 'Trying to make some girl' was promptly bleeped. This thrilled Jagger.

'Satisfaction' changed him. On stage Jagger became yet more sexual; in 'Off The Hook' he practically feigned the act. Elsewhere he was described as 'arrogant' and, in Keylock's phrase, 'aware, to put it mildly, of his fame'. On the tour's last night in New York the disc jockey Scott Ross, a fan since 1963, remembered 'Mick and Keith in some room, smoking. We didn't have anything outside . . . I started kicking on the door. Mick opened it and said, "What do you want?" I said, "What have you got in there? Can we have some?" And he said, "Oh, we can't do that." I said, "Oh! You're a big star now?" and started pushing on the door. We were yelling at each other, and I remember grabbing him and pushing him up against the wall.'

Jagger's credit had always been good. By early 1965 he had only to sign for something in one of the countless bistros or boutiques whose cachet was enhanced by his patronage to possess it. Cash was another matter. Even as 'Satisfaction' rose to number one, Jagger, like all the Stones, continued to draw fifty pounds a week. Mutterings were heard about 'management' in general and Easton in particular. By midsummer Oldham was explicitly instructed to 'get it together'.

He did so by introducing a thirty-three-year-old New Jersey accountant, manager of a new wave of British acts (though not yet the *primus inter pares* themselves): Allen Klein. Oldham had met Klein at a record convention that July. By the twelfth he was writing to him, 'You are hereby authorized to negotiate in (*sic*) my behalf as the producer of the Rolling Stones and the co-manager of said group for a new phonographic recording agreement.' A fortnight later Klein was introduced to the group as a fait accompli. His first act was genius: the Stones were instructed to accompany Klein – 'Don't say nuthin' – to a meeting in the Decca boardroom. They left an hour later $1.3 million richer. The money was to be paid into the group's collective company, Nanker-Phelge Music. Meanwhile Jagger, Richard, Jones, Watts and Wyman were each handed a cheque for £2,500.

In late August, in residence at the London Hilton in his red T-shirt and sneakers, Klein announced, 'Easton's out.' He also fired General Artists in America. Personal Accounts were opened for the Stones at the Chemical Bank, New York (bearing, as it turned out, very little resemblance to personal accounts). There was talk of a merchandising agreement, of a major film project. The *Mirror*'s Don Short, invited on board Klein's private yacht that summer, confirms 'he was fantastically ambitious for them – if equally so for himself'. In September Klein wrote formally to the Stones: '. . . Because of your phenomenal success in the recording business, which we gratefully appreciate, we have decided to increase your royalty on all record sales so that all royalties received on gramophone record sales from inception will be divided equally – 50% for the Rolling Stones and 50% on behalf of the producer.'

'Impressive,' said Richard.

He and Jagger now moved apart. The latter rented a flat at 13A Bryanston Mews East, Marble Arch. He continued to look for something 'not just thrown together, but to suit my personal taste', while giving limited evidence of what that was. He also continued to visit Wilmington, despite

Eva's wish that 'I could see more of him... I miss the times when, after being out late, he came to my bedroom and chatted to me.' Alan Etherington's brother Andrew remembers Jagger and Shrimpton appearing that summer; Edith Keep saw them in Dartford hailing a taxi. Keylock was given specific instructions to 'mind' Joe and Eva whenever they appeared at the dressing room door. Rumours of Jagger's alienation from his parents were, he says, highly exaggerated.

Madly excited, Jagger expanded in other areas. He encouraged Klein to seek film scripts for the group, the first of which, *Only Lovers Left Alive*, was actually drafted but never produced. He renewed his connections with the connected; he and Shrimpton attended a coming-out ball for the Ormsby-Gores. He discussed theatre with Princess Margaret. ('Mick loved it,' said Richard; '... the social thing, the whole Hollywood bit.') According to Mike Gruber from the Klein-appointed William Morris Agency, Jagger intended to 'start dating girls like Julie Christie... He was growing up and didn't want to have the girls he had when he was starting.' And, as stated by the minutes of a meeting of the Rolling Stones Limited on 20 September – 'To appoint Mr Michael Philip Jagger as chairman of the company in place of Mr E. C. Easton' – he exercised increased personal control over the group.

He also, to his credit, found time for music. The Rolling Stones gave 240 concerts in 1965. They released three LPs and four singles in the US, two LPs, three singles and an EP in Britain, selling more than fifteen million copies. They made fifty television appearances and gave countless interviews. In Dublin in September braying rockers rushed the stage, lifting Jagger bodily through a door, his clothes in shreds, still singing. He goosestepped to 'Satisfaction' in Germany. He was even punkish before his time, manhandling the mike, sporting southside Chicago shades. And, in a memorable duet, Jagger and Oldham crooned 'I Got

You Babe' on *Ready Steady Go!* while stroking each other's hair.

On 30 July the fourth American LP, *Out of Our Heads*, was released and reached number one. The critic Lillian Roxon considered this the group's acme, ranging as it did from 'Satisfaction' to Marvin Gaye's 'Hitch Hike' to the Don Covay standard 'Mercy Mercy'. It also included a ballad entitled 'That's How Strong My Love Is' in which Jagger contrived to sound both soulful and sincere, not always synonymous. The same album was released in Britain in September in different format; it reached number two. Christmas saw yet another American release, *December's Children*, wherein Jagger's vocal on 'Blue Turns To Grey' (compared by critics to 'Yesterday') was widely praised. To his surprise he was being taken seriously as a singer.

Hours off the plane in Los Angeles, he and Richard wrote two Beatles-like songs, 'I'm Free' and 'Looking Tired' and a third, 'Get Off Of My Cloud', quintessentially their own. 'Cloud' became the group's first simultaneous number one in the US and UK and their fifth consecutive British number one. Musically in the 'Twist and Shout', rock and roll tradition, lyrically it exceeded even 'Satisfaction':

I live on the corner, on the ninety-ninth floor of my
    block . . .
I sit at home looking out the window, imagining the
    world has stopped.

When critics heard the above they used terms like 'garbled' and 'word salad'. They were genuinely puzzled. What did it *mean*? In 1965 'beat' lyrics, 'Satisfaction' notwithstanding, were meant to convey love or non-love – either you got the girl or you didn't. The trend embodied by Dylan, whose lyrics for *Highway 61*, released that summer, veered from cryptic to merely odd, was beyond *Rave*'s comprehension. Even *Rolling Stones Monthly* seemed bemused.

With 'Satisfaction' and 'Cloud', Jagger–Richard entered a world only marginally less exalted than that of Lennon–McCartney. Thrown together twelve, fifteen, twenty hours a day, off stage and on, they constantly improvised, constantly wrote. The very idea of being a 'writer' was significant to Jagger. It included, among other things, being a card, an artist, a genius, and a clown. He had an innate flair for the last: after 'Cloud', the Stones released the risible 'As Tears Go By', which reached number six. The duo became a separate corporate entity. Like Oldham, Klein actively developed Jagger and Richard as a sub-group. They, and they alone, were encouraged to write. This estranged them from Jones, Watts and Wyman, the last of whom notes:

> ... song-writing and publishing effectively made Mick and Keith more the leaders than Brian, Charlie and me – their names carried the weight. They'd bring a song in, suggest a style and what the bass line and drums might do, and then we'd play around with it, and throw in our own ideas. And they'd say: 'Yeah, that's better, let's do that' – but that input by me or Brian or Charlie was never recognized.

Song-writing was one way Jagger established himself, performing another. The group's fourth American tour opened in late October 1965. Mankowitz accompanied it. In New York the Stones arrived at the City Squire Hotel where, the photographer notes, 'all hell broke loose ... There was an enormous crowd of girls ... Our driver was terrified ... The weight of the girls on top of the car caused the roof to buckle, so that Mick, Keith and I were literally holding it up with our hands.' Next morning Jagger's Cadillac was conveyed to the top floor of the Hilton by private freight elevator. 'Fame,' he noted; '... at last.'

In Times Square Jagger's very face loomed from a hundred-foot-high billboard. Dylan asked to see him. Ken

Kesey appeared bearing marijuana. This was the first year in which a definable American 'counter-culture', actually a series of collective social, sexual and other fantasies (with a concomitant interest in drugs) was established, with a matching requirement for role models promoting means of success other than hard work and perseverance. Jagger realized this and exploited it tirelessly. On tour he came across as a composite agitator and sexual athlete, inspiring, said Stewart, 'a whole new phenomenon . . . the chick wanting to get laid as quickly and often as possible'. Mankowitz remembers 'an endless stream of notes, often pinned to bras and underpants, with telephone numbers, quite lurid love poems and very explicit offers, quite complicated messages like "Mom and Dad are away – ring me before eleven" '. (Not that such offers were always accepted: Wyman calculates that from 1963 to 1965 he slept with 278 women, Jones 130, Jagger 'about thirty', Richard six and Watts none.) Mankowitz also recalls having a three-hour conversation with Jagger one night, 'both of us missing our girlfriends like hell'.

Shrimpton herself appeared in Los Angeles. She and Jagger stayed at the Bel-Air Hotel, after which they flew to Jamaica. Throughout the American tour he sent her flowers and letters, as well as twenty pounds p.w. allowance. (Jagger earned $50,418.62 during the month.) According to a later interview Shrimpton now became agitated at 'not being able to understand' Jagger, shouting at him, demanding to know what was 'going on'; she was also heard by a habituée of the Ad Lib Club, Cecilia Lewis, deriding her lover for his 'meanness' and apparent indifference to sex. Jagger in turn called her neurotic. Later Shrimpton came to believe the song '19th Nervous Breakdown' was written about her.

The no-women-on-tour rule (expressed by Jagger thus: 'There's really no reason to have them, unless they've got a job to do . . . The only other reason is to screw') was relaxed in America. In Miami Jones was joined by a twenty-two-year-old German-Swiss model, Anita Pallenberg. The couple had met the preceding September in Munich, where Jones spent the night crying in Pallenberg's arms after arguing with Jagger. Arguing became a Jones *leitmotiv*. According to Keylock, 'he was constantly complaining about Mick "undermining" him, though most of it was imaginary . . . Brian was paranoid as hell.' Don Short confirms 'there was friction'. Jones is described by Mankowitz as 'manipulative', by Pallenberg herself as 'moody'. As she told the journalist A. E. Hotchner:

> I was aware that the other Stones didn't approve of me when Brian brought me around. Especially Mick. They looked at me like I was some kind of threat. Mick really tried to put me down, thereby putting Brian down in the process, but there was no way that this sort of crude, lippy guy was going to do a number on me. I was always able to squelch him – I found out, you stand up to Mick, he crumbles. He tried to get Brian to stop seeing me, called me poison. He ordered his girlfriend, Chrissie, not to go near me. I figured he was jealous because I was the one close to Brian.

Despite this deeply unpromising beginning, Pallenberg's relationship with the Stones extended into a third decade. Even then, she insisted, 'Mick resented me . . . I brought this new positive force into Brian's life. It seems to me that Brian could have regained control of the Stones [in 1965] except for one thing – much as he tried, he couldn't compose songs.'

At year's end *Disc* had the original idea of asking each Stone to describe another. Wyman drew Jagger:

He's changed considerably (since 1962) – he was a lot quieter and less confident. He was very friendly when I first met the group. In fact he was the only one who spoke to me for the first couple of hours.

Now he's more difficult to get on with. He's automatically on guard with people he's not sure about – if they're trying to hang on . . .

He gets depressed sometimes and we have to bear with it.

He's a bit careful with money – not extravagant like Keith . . .

Jagger on Richard:

From time to time, we've had arguments. In fact we disagree quite a lot, but we usually come to a compromise. There's never any hard feeling . . . He's forgetful and so he doesn't remember to bear a grudge.

He's very good at his song-writing now and we've got a relatively efficient way of going about it . . .

He's very good about the group. Very optimistic. This cheers me up when I'm feeling low.

I think people find it difficult to know Keith. Sometimes he's shy, other times he can't be bothered to take an interest in people.

———

'His main worry was that they were laughing at him,' says a friend of Jones's, Dave Thompson. Richard defined his co-worker's attitude at the time: 'Brian's only solution was clinging to either Mick or me . . . He always tried to be friendly with somebody just to get at other people.' 'As soon as he got any real taste of money,' said Stewart, 'he just went mad.'

The group's ninth UK single (tenth in America) confirmed Jones's decline. '19th Nervous Breakdown' featured

Jagger, Richard, even Wyman, with his diving Framus bass-runs, to advantage. It also established the group's respective creative roles for all time: Richard supplying the sound, Jagger the words, the others (uncredited) embellishments. Jones, Thompson adds, was 'acutely paranoid' of making esoteric suggestions. He seemed odd enough already. Like Shrimpton, he took 'Breakdown' personally. In fact the title was Jagger's aphorism about touring.

In February, after a recording stop in Los Angeles where, said Brian Wilson, the studio 'overflowed with booze, drugs and food', the Stones returned to Australia, now to grudging respect. 'Whatever they have, and it's indefinable, the audience loved it,' said a report. 'Cultivated arrogance,' suggested another. In his two weeks away Jagger earned $7,063; he also collected record and song-writing royalties. That spring he moved from Bryanston Court into 52 Harley House, an apartment block moored, rather than built, at the southern end of Regent's Park. The flat itself suggested a liner with its flaking white paint and leaden doors, to which Jagger added studded black furniture, Oriental rugs – and at least one full-length mirror. 'This,' says Mankowitz, 'was to be his home.' Workmen were delegated to unload the books, the wine racks, the clothes (including a newly purchased kangaroo jacket); appliances were delivered from Harrods. It was at this stage, 1966, says Keylock, that Jagger's domestic life began to resemble something out of P. G. Wodehouse.

In public he continued to affect the ruffles and flares, the composite accent, the smirks and sneers, epitome of Swinging London (itself a relative of the Baby Boomer revolution occurring in America) whose primary objective was negative: the avoidance of dull, boring, conventional reality. Those who knew Jagger best knew that his act – the demotic 'Mick' with his south London slang – retained strong conventional undertones. Keylock to this day groans in memory of unloading Jagger's 'thousand or so' novels. Apostates of the London 'scene', and the yet more outlandish Hippies emerging in California, might have been surprised by the demure, even docile figure dining (and frequently omitting to pay) at the Casserole before retiring to his Victorian mansion block.

Books, as they will, began to influence Jagger's writing. The hook-line of 'Paint It, Black' – 'I turn my head until my darkness goes' – was lifted from *Ulysses*; 'Lady Jane' from *Lady Chatterley's Lover*. The latter issued from an LP, initially entitled *Could You Walk On The Water?*, released in Britain that April. *Aftermath*, as it became, was the first album consisting entirely of Jagger–Richard compositions. It established them on level creative terms with Lennon–McCartney and lent credence to the notion of working-class cultural supremacy on which television, stage and film came increasingly to depend. 'Not a single track,' says Don Short, 'missed its mark.' They varied from 'Mother's Little Helper', a single in 'Black's saturnine tradition, the Beatlesque 'Out of Time' and an eccentric twelve-minute blues odyssey called 'Goin' Home'. Musically *Aftermath* confirmed Richard as the group's overseer, with Jones relegated to the role of in-house exotic (marimbas, dulcimer, sitar); lyrically, the album contained at least three songs offensive to feminist sensibilities, while a fourth, 'Under My Thumb', seemed to further unhinge Shrimpton with its reference to 'squirming dogs' and its assurance that 'a change has come'. *Aftermath*, all agreed, was a masterpiece.

'Out of Time' (with its leering refrain, 'You're obsolete, my baby') was subsequently hawked to the young rhythm and blues singer Chris Farlowe. Farlowe was signed to the Immediate label formed by Oldham and Tony Calder that summer. He was promptly summoned to Harley House where a 'very businesslike' Jagger suggested 'Time' and another *Aftermath* track, 'Think', as suitable singles. The former went briefly to number one. Farlowe's chief memory is of Jagger working diligently in the studio while Oldham (still 'the evil genius' in the shadows) blinked distractedly behind his octagonal lenses. 'Mick,' states Farlowe, 'was a professional.'

In this and other ways he began to separate from the rest. While Jagger remained in the heart of London Richard retreated to a fourteenth-century cottage near West Wittering. Redlands, for twenty thousand pounds, included three bedrooms, a minstrel's gallery, a study/studio, even a Saxon moat. There were no fewer than four fireplaces and a thatched roof, later to prove an incendiary combination. Richard himself spent increasing time with Keylock – an authentic 'character' of the sort the Stones admired – who rotationally guarded him, Jagger and Jones, the last of whom had moved to a mews flat in Chelsea with Pallenberg. Her influence was dramatic. Under Pallenberg's direction Jones withdrew further into a social demi-monde. On one occasion he was seen dressed like the French singer Françoise Hardy, on another as a Nazi stormtrooper. 'He began,' said Richard, 'to think less and less about music.' Jones became 'seriously unstuck' in public, glazed-eyed, morbid, argumentative, forever dependent on Pallenberg – one of the many people with artistic weaknesses without artistic strengths. 'The worst possible choice,' says Keylock.

Pallenberg was duly waiting when the Stones arrived in Paris on 28 March. Outside the George V there was the familiar riot, with Jones demanding 'Accelerate! I want to see him bounce!' as a fan attached himself to his car. Next night the Stones played an eleven-song set at the Olympia – mayhem – after which Brigitte Bardot appeared backstage. Bardot's request that the group appear in her next film was refused by Klein on the basis of 'conflict of interest' with the Stones' own – still unscripted – project.

(There was a footnote: to his dying day Stewart maintained that the only moment he was ever jealous of Jagger was when the latter 'had Bardot'. This, Stewart alleged, was the night.)

In Marseilles Jagger was badly hurt when a wooden chair hurled from the crowd gashed him over the right eye; he needed six stitches. 'It took thirty minutes to find the emergency ward,' he noted later. 'Then I saw an incredible thing, running down the corridor of the hospital . . . A huge rat!' Next night he gave two performances through shut tight peepers, as Oldham would have put it.

On 3 June Jagger drove a hundred yards down Harley Street to consult a specialist, Samuel Weinstock. He was pronounced to be suffering from 'nervous exhaustion' and 'completely unfit for work'. Keylock remembers him that summer as 'carrying baggage' (under the eyes), the result of 'going everywhere, seeing everyone'. As well as recording, performing, producing and writing, Jagger was invariably the one called on to 'explain' his latest lyric – 'It means paint it black . . . "I can't get no satisfaction" means I can't get no satisfaction' – to a waiting public. Tabloids now joined the music press in doorstepping Jagger at Harley House. Even Shrimpton had taken to writing a column called 'From London With Luv' ('Recently I had my twenty-first birthday. It wasn't too painful, as these things go. Mick gave me a huge rocking horse on big rockers which I named Petunia . . .') which may have further aggravated a relationship already at best turbulent.

Jagger's unfitness for work lasted three weeks. On 23 June the Stones flew to New York. For the first time they encountered teenagers, working men, even young professionals, with hair longer than their own; a combination of race riots, civil rights demonstrations, unfulfilled Democratic promises and the Vietnam War had created an unusually volatile atmosphere wherein hard drugs, previously restricted to the fringe districts of Soho and Little Italy, circulated freely. 'The kids,' confided Klein, who met them in his patched cardigan and sneakers, 'may be different this time.'

They proved not to be. On opening night in Lynn, Massachusetts, twelve- and thirteen-year-olds broke through police cordons and stormed the stage. Torn planks were brandished like spears. It was an authentic mob orgy from which the Stones escaped as palms flailed on the roof of their car (a write-off) and tear gas canisters exploded in the crowd. In Hartford there was bedlam, in Toronto and Montreal merely chaos; bouncers karate-chopped girls as they made for the stage. Jagger's perceptible sneer merely hinted at how predictable such scenes had become.

An extraordinary press conference on board the SS *Sea Panther*, reported in *Village Voice*, further emphasized the head Stone's attitude:

The motors churn and the yacht begins to move. Mick says: 'It's ninety-five out and you'd never know it here.' Charlie says: 'Don't let those photographers make you nervous; ask your questions.' Keith says efforts to censor rock songs because of their subject is 'typical American prudery'. Brian says: 'The next thing in pop won't happen for another three years . . .'

Meanwhile, Mick is responding to a question. 'What's the difference between the Stones and the Beatles?'

'There are four of them and five of us.'

A pop writer compares the old and new Stones: 'I think now there's a feeling of – don't touch me, I'm a Rolling Stone. Even their manager is so hung up on himself, it's unbelievable. And Mick is a hippy in the true sense of the word. When someone says something honest, he goes blank. He can't relate to honesty . . .'

But Mick defies approach. The others are shorter, pudgier, softer than they sound on record. But Mick . . . a while ago, he was hospitalized suffering from 'nervous exhaustion'. Now you observe him smiling, chatting, responding. You watch him 'circulate'.

You notice his tired grin, his oval eyes and sagging
lips; his yachtsman's jacket is an irony . . . You want
to touch Mick Jagger? You can't even come close.

Among the photographers on board the *Panther* was Linda
Eastman, later McCartney, with whom, Wyman notes
simply, 'Mick spent a night'.

A fortnight later Jagger tripped down the steps of his
charter plane in Houston. 'We don't create images,' he
announced. 'We perform hoping everyone will enjoy
themselves. You make your own opinion.'

Then: 'I'm not trying to put you down, but you ask old-
fashioned questions. People were asking us [about image]
two years ago.'

'Is "Paint It, Black" about blindness?'

'It's about somebody dying, a funeral.'

'What about "Satisfaction"?'

'Frustration.'

In America the Stones reverted to type. For two, three,
sometimes seven nights Richard omitted to sleep. He brandished knives and guns. He wandered alone around Harlem
and Greenwich Village, a moneyed delinquent. Wyman and
Watts went to ground. Jagger, acutely aware of his enhanced
status, spoke only in epigrams. He captivated the press; to
Village Voice he expounded on Vietnam, to *Town and Country*
on fashion. He was highly organized. (The Houston *Chronicle* has him informing the other Stones of their very where-
abouts.) On stage he looked distracted, even bored, his lips
twisted into a permanent leer. Performing, he implied, was
all part of the act – as was touring; 'mass funny entertainment', he called it.

And Jones? Jones's chief contribution was to steal an
American flag lying backstage at Syracuse, whereupon
ushers seized all five Stones and threatened to arrest them.
The incident was defused by Jagger's intervention with the

chief of police. (The Stones were all long accustomed to being waylaid by local officials, instructed to 'sign here' for their daughters and then leave town – something similar to which happened in Syracuse.) Jones also, admits Wyman, 'dabbled in drugs' – though dabbled may underestimate a habit that included, at minimum, marijuana, LSD and amyl nitrate. According to Mike Gruber, 'We'd get to a hotel and I'd call the drugstore . . . I'd ask for some toothpaste, shaving cream, deodorant and a hundred boxes of amyl nitrate. I'd ask how many amyl nitrates were in stock as they were legal then and only five pounds a box. We'd get them all.'

The tour went west. At Sacramento the Stones played for the first time in almost total silence: 'the kids' foretold by Klein sat cross-legged smoking pipes – this being the year in which the first wave of Baby Boomers, largely the off-spring of middle-class, affluent Republicans, hit college, experimenting with drugs, opposing Vietnam, investing rock music with a significance greater than the 'good time' claimed for it by its practitioners. In San Francisco thousands of leaflets were dropped on stage as Jagger sang 'Satisfaction' on 26 July, his twenty-third birthday:

> We welcome the Rolling Stones . . . They themselves are our fellows in the desperate struggle against the mad people who got the power. We fight in guerilla groups against the imperialist invader in Asia and South America. We make noise at every rock and roll concert. In Los Angeles we set on fire and kill everywhere and the bulls (*sic*) know that our guerillas will be going back there . . . Fellows, you'll come back to this land when it is free from state tyranny and play your wonderful music in the factories which will be led by workers among one million red flags fluttering above an anarchic community of two million people. Rolling Stones, the young people of California listen to your message – Long live the revolution!

In Harley House, meanwhile, Keylock was taking possession of a Regency bath and four-poster bed for his master.

———

They reached Hawaii. Shrimpton appeared in Honolulu, as did Pallenberg and Shirley Watts. At the Sports Center Jagger introduced 'Satisfaction' in his mock southern drawl: 'I can't tell you how wonderful it is to be here, everybody. It's really wonderful, the best audience ... ever ... and this is our last concert ... ever.' The Stones walked off. It was their 112th American concert extended over five tours. There were no plans for a sixth. That same week radio stations in Alabama broadcast John Lennon's assertion of being 'more popular than Jesus', inciting record-burnings and marches by the Ku Klux Klan. A month later the Beatles too gave their final performance.

Both groups elected simultaneously to return to the studio. Both had become increasingly drawn to the concept of 'the album', a largely untried format in 1963 with its emphasis on interminable package-tours and singles. After three years of endless airports, of braying fans and reporters, of hotel rooms surrounded by the above, of rodeos and ballrooms, and finally arenas where they could barely hear themselves play, the Rolling Stones called a halt. Except, being the Stones, they didn't. After a week off, Jagger summoned the group to Hollywood where, on 7 August, they completed a song he described as the 'ultimate freakout'. 'Have You Seen Your Mother Baby, Standing in the Shadow?' was badly recorded, badly mixed and sold (comparatively) badly, reaching only number nine in Britain. The song featured brass, guitar feedback, a bitter, even brutal vocal – also an arresting sleeve later blamed for the single's relative failure. 'Those photographs,' said *Disc*, 'didn't help.'

The Stones first met Jerry Schatzberg in October 1964; he threw a party after their ('Rapturous agony!') concerts at the Academy of Music. Schatzberg was a photographer in the Cecil Beaton mould – given to sweeping into rooms in his black cape and fedora – only more so. In New York he buttonholed Oldham with the assertion, 'These guys would look great in drag.' Two years later he found out. By means of razor, rouge, resin and not a little uplift, Keith, Brian, Charlie and Bill were converted into Molly, Flossie, Millicent and Penelope; 'Sarah' Jagger meanwhile reposed in her wrinkled hat and frilly gloves. 'Stunning,' intoned *Disc*; 'shocking,' thundered *The Times*. 'The English,' says Jagger, 'don't need much convincing to dress up as women.'

In September they were back in America, topping the *Ed Sullivan* bill with Louis Armstrong, Robert Goulet, Red Skelton and 'Holiday on Ice sensation' Robbie Robertson. Jagger in his vaguely military khaki jacket, grey trousers and boots, the sail-like expanse of his white tie, ground through 'Mother', 'Lady Jane' and 'Paint It, Black', lips puckered, his eyes clamped permanently upward. To his right Jones sat cross-legged strumming a sitar. Observant viewers noticed his bandaged left hand. The official version – 'the real story', as Jones put it – was a household accident. In fact he broke his wrist punching Pallenberg. After *Sullivan* the Stones went to a party at Schatzberg's, where they declined to reprise their drag act. They dressed as Nazis instead.

Incredibly, Jagger had reached this stage in his career without recourse to a press agent. In late 1966 he hired Les Perrin, a forty-five-year-old Fleet Street veteran who, with Oldham, Klein, Tito Burns (their European booking agent), Stewart and Keylock formed the Stones' inner circle; they also employed a small personal office. Perrin's first assignment was almost his last. At the Albert Hall on 23 September Jagger was pulled to the floor during 'Paint It, Black'. Girls swarmed over the orchestra pit to reach Richard and Jones. While Keylock frog-marched the group offstage, Perrin – a slight, balding figure in a grey suit – was seen blinking distractedly, clenching the white silk handkerchief knotted in his fist like worry-beads. At a reception that night the Stones each received four gold records for their American sales. When Keylock opined that the discs would play music other than their own he was bet five pounds by Jagger that they wouldn't. The presentational copy of *Aftermath* was duly heard to play: Beethoven, Sibelius, snatches of Mantovani, Buddy Holly and the soundtrack from the film *Bambi*. The singer paid up.

It was Jagger's decision to perform again behind 'Have You Seen Your Mother', 'Mick,' says Keylock, 'being addicted to playing. After a month he'd get bored: "What am I going to do – sit home and get fat?"' The others, with varying degrees of enthusiasm, concurred. Shell-shocked they may have been but retiring – finally – was unthinkable. In October Jagger was back on stage, neither caring nor complaining. He staggered a bit, true, and more than once Keylock delivered him to Harley House the worse for wear. But most days Jagger was remarkably calm, remarkably cheerful and remarkably cordial. He continued to insist that the Stones were 'semi-detached' from the business of touring while stating in private, 'The Beatles are finished – it's up to us.' He still drove to Wilmington to see Joe and Eva. They still drove to London to see him. A privileged few were still invited to meet in restaurants and clubs, where Jagger regaled them in the new lowlife tones – 'What's your game?', 'Streuth', 'Strike a light' – appropriated from Keylock. He still brought flowers and chocolates to Shrimpton. And in Dartford Alan Etherington was surprised to be handed a telegram on his wedding day signed by Little Boy Blue.

The circus reached Liverpool, Newcastle, Glasgow, Leeds. In Manchester Keylock prevented an overwrought fan from entering Jagger's hotel room; she embedded her stiletto in his leg. The supporting act that tour was Tina Turner, over whom, Keylock observed, 'Mick's eye frequently roved'. Turner later remembered Jagger 'wanting to learn a dance

I did with my back-up group, the pony. I knew he'd been watching us every night from the wings. He tried, and I said, "Look at the rhythm on this guy! God, Mick, come on!" We laughed because Mick was serious – he wanted to get it. He didn't care about us laughing at him. And finally he got it . . . in his own kind of way.' Keylock also states it as 'certain' that Jagger and Turner had a sexual encounter in Bristol. 'I tripped over them backstage.'

If so Jagger must have been more than usually active. It was also in Bristol that he first spent the night with Marianne Faithfull. After performing at Colston Hall on 7 October, Jagger, Richard and Jones drove with Faithfull – whose career, after 'As Tears Go By' and an eponymous LP, had stalled – to a nearby hotel. Reefers were smoked. Faithfull was vaguely aware that people were sporadically leaving the room. Eventually she was alone with Jagger. The suite was densely clogged and dripping, and Faithfull suggested a walk. In the morning dew she told Jagger he resembled King Arthur; a long silence followed this as the moon sent chopped-up light through the trees and the couple returned to the hotel. That same day Faithfull flew to Italy. On her return she was informed by Richard that 'Mick was in love with me, and all that'. Her initial reaction? 'Disappointment. I preferred Keith.'

There were other complications. Jagger was still technically involved with Shrimpton, Faithfull with John Dunbar and their infant son. For two months the lovers met furtively in clubs, in hotels, in Harley House, where Shrimpton once encountered Faithfull on the way out (Jagger growing 'more and more agitated, spilling a drink', she told Scaduto). They attended a party together in Paris. Even then, according to an interview she later gave A. E. Hotchner, Faithfull had doubts:

The last person in the world I would discuss anything with was Mick. We never talked about anything really personal, anything that really mattered ... After the beginning Mick was never very interested in having sex. I always felt that whatever sexual drive Mick had, he used it up on stage and there was little left over for his personal life ... Even when we climbed into our draped, four-poster bed Mick was only interested in reading a book.

On the other hand, Faithfull was sufficiently disenchanted with marriage (as was Dunbar) to be receptive to change. Jagger, while 'straight', even conventional, was undoubtedly caring. In Italy he bombarded Faithfull with letters; in London the inevitable chocolates and flowers. 'This,' said Faithfull, 'made me feel safe. I liked the thought that somebody who was somebody in this world was being romantic about me.' Jagger, she further learned, was a different proposition off-stage than on. He was shy, sensitive, submissive, even. For eight weeks Faithfull enjoyed the high voltage of being wanted. 'If Mick hadn't been hanging around and courting me,' she told Hotchner, 'I would have stayed with John. But Mick's life was a bit too tempting, this very powerful man with lots of money promising me the moon with my name on it. I fell for it.'

There remained the question of Shrimpton. For weeks she and Jagger had planned to spend Christmas in Jamaica. As the day approached tickets were bought and reservations made. Still Jagger prevaricated. Keylock was instructed to make different arrangements; then yet more. On Thursday 15 December, the day of their intended departure, Shrimpton rang the office 'pleading for Jagger', even as Jagger – promising a clear-the-air meeting that afternoon – went shopping with Faithfull instead.

The showdown came on the eighteenth. 'We had loads of rows and it reached the point where a split was the only thing left,' said Jagger. As to the exact cause of the break, his practice of 'never leaving one woman before you see another coming' – comparing them thus to musical styles – might be indicative. In the week before Christmas Shrimpton's account with the Stones' office was closed. Her belongings were removed from Harley House. On Christmas Eve she was reported to be in the Greenway Nursing Home after attempting suicide; the hospital bill was sent to Jagger, who returned it. Shrimpton revived and, not without reverse and misfortune, recovered. A decade later she made a half-hearted effort to sell a number of love letters. 'It's not,' she says today, 'something I'm proud of.'

Down a long grey corridor, almost a gangway, Jagger's raised voice could be heard answering his hairdresser:

'All right, all right . . . You wouldn't believe it, some people think just 'cause I'm a big pop star that I'm helpless and I have to have everything done for me. I was up at the office the other day, and I mentioned to one of the girls that I was going to use the phone, so she asked me if I could manage, if not she'd dial for me – honestly, just 'cause I'm a big name doesn't mean I've got big fingers as well. They still fit in the phone dial.'

At this point Jagger eyed the row of skull-like driers.

'All right, all right' – a device was clamped on his netted head – 'you'll have to yell. I can't hear a thing.'

'Have you changed much?'

'Na . . . I still want to act, produce records and write books. At the moment I have no time for acting, but when it's all over I think I'd like to go to drama school. I rather go for the contemporaries.'

Jagger sighed, returning to his magazine.

At the very moment he fell for Faithfull Jagger recorded a new single. 'Let's Spend The Night Together' was ingeniously twinned with 'Ruby Tuesday', the idea being that nobody could object to both. Because there were objections: 'Night' was banned by some, shunned by others. When the group returned to New York in January Ed Sullivan became apoplectic. 'Either the song goes,' he boomed, 'or you go.' It was close; in the end Jagger compromised, altering 'the night' to 'some time', turning his eyes theatrically upwards to register protest.

The accompanying album was the Stones' first critical flop. *Between The Buttons*, featuring a cover by Mankowitz, reached only number three in Britain, number two in America; 'a turkey' Roy Carr called it. *Buttons*, with its emphasis on nursery-rhyme lyrics and vague psychedelia, was a virtual throwback to vaudeville. Only 'Connection', co-sung by Richard, was authentic pop: 'Back Street Girl', with Jones on accordion, was pure waltz. Others ranged from the mundane ('Please Go Home', 'Cool, Calm and Collected') to the mawkish ('She Smiled Sweetly'). Shrimpton's sensibilities may have been further offended by the obvious sneer of 'Yesterday's Papers'. Richard later disowned much of the album. Jagger described it as 'more or less rubbish', viewing it as a transition from the 'pop thing' to destinations unstated. *Buttons* was the last in the sequence of manic, on-the-road LPs, poorly recorded, ineptly produced, completed in the days or even hours between concerts. The very speed of some tracks suggested lateness for an appointment.

The new affair became official that January. Jagger and Faithfull were seen carousing at the San Remo Pop Festival, holding hands and smiling gamely for the photographer Dezo Hoffman. Jagger rented a yacht and sailed with Faithfull to Cannes, where her son Nicholas was collected from a nanny. In London they attended a record company dinner at the Savoy. Jagger, in his sweater and velvet jacket, sat among the accountants and A & R men, breaking off from a diatribe on royalty rates to squeeze Faithfull's knee, his head cocked to one side nuzzling her shoulder. Jimmy Savile made faces across the table. They also attended the opening of a club where an obscure Seattle guitarist made his second

British appearance. Immediately Jimi Hendrix played his last crotch-thrusting note he made for Jagger's table. He sat down. In Faithfull's subsequent account Hendrix propositioned her, dismissing the adjacent Jagger as 'a cunt'. (If so, his opinion soon altered. Hendrix's father insists today 'he admired that man tremendously'.) Jagger was also introduced to Glynn Faithfull, who later described him as 'very pleasant'. He charmed the academic, as he had Edward Shrimpton, by discussing economics.

Jagger and Faithfull became what he and Shrimpton never were: a public item, exemplars of Swinging London, compensating for the shortness of time in frequent, intense gratification. Don Short of the *Mirror* was the first to pronounce Jagger 'King of the Scene', a title flippantly endorsed by the Beatles. In his Regency bed, attended by Keylock, Jagger, calling for morning tea before dressing fastidiously in public, held court in Harley House, in clubs, in studios, in public, accompanied throughout by Faithfull. She was received ambivalently by the other Stones – notably Wyman, who wrote, 'Mick involved his current girlfriend to the exclusion of other members of the band'. Even Richard seemed put out. Having broken with his own girlfriend he briefly found himself alone of the group in lacking a partner. 'That was a period', he told his biographer, 'when Brian and Anita were together and Mick was getting into Marianne. And we were all enjoying getting stoned.'

Discontent with what seemed a full-time job, Jagger continued to press Oldham for new projects. As always impressed by the Beatles he mooted recording, as they had, a 'concept' LP. He discoursed on books, on films, on plays, even politics, tutored in the last by the Labour MP Tom Driberg. He exuded, not for the last time, boorishness and charm in the same package. On *Sunday Night at the Palladium* Jagger refused to appear for a curtain call, to even Oldham's manifest distress. He denied possession of any 'moral responsibility' to his fans and he announced in general: 'It's very unlikely that the Stones will still be going in ten years' time. I've worked out that I'd be fifty (*sic*) in 1984. Horrible, isn't it? Halfway to a hundred.'

'SECRETS OF THE POP STARS' HIDEAWAY.' The headline cut a slice from the morning sun that greeted Jagger on Sunday 5 February. After the mere mundanity of the *Observer*, *The Times* and the *Telegraph*, the lurid photos and breathless tone of the *News of the World* came like a small explosion. After informing its eighteen million readers of the 'growing epidemic' of drug use, the paper startlingly named Roger Burrows, 'a man in his early twenties, who runs a car-hire service below his flat in Brook Mews North, Paddington', as a supplier. That was dramatic. Worse was to follow:

> Another pop idol who admits he has sampled LSD and other drugs is Mick Jagger of the Rolling Stones ... Investigators who saw Jagger at Blases Club in Kensington reported: 'He told us: "I don't go much on it [LSD] now the cats [fans] have taken it up. It'll just get a dirty name.
> "I remember the first time I took it. It was on our first tour with Bo Diddley and Little Richard."
> During the time we were at Blases, Jagger took about six benzedrine tablets. "I just couldn't keep awake at places like this if I didn't have them ..."
> Later at Blases, Jagger showed a companion and two girls a small piece of hash [marijuana] and invited them to his flat for 'a smoke'.

Other than apparently confusing LSD and marijuana, the *News* made at least one critical error. The 'pop idol' in question wasn't Jagger. 'I'm shocked,' he announced, 'that a respectable newspaper can publish such a defamatory article about me.' That night on *The Eamonn Andrews Show* he announced a writ against the *News* and its editor Stafford Somerfield for libel.

It was a mistake of Wildean proportions. In the following week (while he was mysteriously reported to be dead), Jagger attended a Beatles recording session, took Faithfull to Wilmington and even wrote a song tentatively entitled 'Blues One'. On the evening of 11 February he and Faithfull in their white Mini S and Richard in his Bentley drove to Redlands. Also present were Christopher Gibbs, the photographer Michael Cooper, Robert Fraser, Fraser's Moroccan servant Ali Mohammed, George and Patti Harrison and two hangers-on of dubious aspect, David Schneidermann and Nicky Kramer. At midnight Ali Mohammed served dinner – at which very moment a voice was informing Chichester police that an orgy of drugs, sex and pop, possibly all three simultaneously, was about to overwhelm West Wittering.

The three bedrooms at Redlands were occupied by Jagger and Faithfull, the Harrisons and Richard. Downstairs the remainder lolled on the thrown Moroccan rugs, the fire smouldering in its iron gate. At noon Schneidermann circulated cups of tea and lurid red Sunshine capsules – LSD. At about the time eighteen million readers were absorbing the details of '"happenings" where drug experiences are simulated by sight and sound without the participants actually taking drugs' (illustrated, to make the point, by a gyrating topless girl), Jagger was lying peacefully dazed in an antique Chinese bed.

The party revived to walk, trek and stumble through the fields south of Redlands, Jagger angling his Mini like a rally-driver on to the shingle beach. At day's ebb they knew the unbearable joy of being rich and young. Richard was photographed cavorting in his Afghan coat, Jagger rock-scrambling in a parody of *Seeing Sport*. Seven o'clock found them together, vectoring over the moonlit grass, uncontrollably excited like two schoolchildren grown old. It may have been among the happiest days of Jagger's life.

An hour later a convoy of police cars turned up Redlands Drive. They parked in the gravel surround. After a preliminary reconnoitre (the front door, helpfully, being located at the back) they knocked. Richard, suspecting nothing more than curious fans, opened up. 'I have a warrant,' intoned Chief Inspector Gordon Dineley, 'pursuant to the Dangerous Drugs Act.'

Richard stood aside.

The events that followed can be quickly recalled: the police fanning through the galleried living room, hung with ornate tapestries and drapes, wheezing in the incense and smoke; Faithfull, later described under oath as 'in a merry mood and one of vague unconcern' being led upstairs to be searched, or – since she was wearing only a fur rug which she promptly dropped to the floor – seen; the remaining eight (the Harrisons having departed) being frisked; the instant acceptance of Schneidermann's Sunshine collection as 'unexposed film'; the discovery of twenty-four heroin tablets ('for diabetes', he explained) on Fraser, and of four Stenamina pep pills in a velvet jacket belonging to Jagger; the removal of these and sundry tins, pipes, bowls and even soap and ketchup sachets; the cautioning of Richard that, if dangerous drugs were identified without specific proof of ownership he, as householder, would be held responsible; the withdrawal of the convoy; the silence, punctuated by Kramer's placing 'Rainy Day Women' on the turntable with its insistence that 'everybody must get stoned'. The phone calls to Klein, Perrin and Keylock.

Jagger's reaction was muted. He entirely missed the significance of the raid. The LSD, after all, had gone undetected. Jagger himself had an oral prescription for the Stenamina, which in fact belonged to Faithfull. Nor had the police unearthed evidence of diabolism, voodoo, or more exotic rites. (The story of Jagger having been found in an orgy of cunnilingus involving Faithfull and a Mars Bar was invented later. Its origins are obscure, but may have derived from Richard's avowed sweet tooth; when the barrister Michael Havers was briefed at Redlands he found 'several Mars Bars on top of a bookcase . . . That's all there was to it, some Mars Bars plus the vivid imagination of tabloid writers'.) There was even, according to Gibbs, 'a rather philosophical feeling – "It had to happen and it's happened."' Years later Cooper remembered Jagger assuring the room, 'We'll handle it.'

He handled it by summoning Keylock. His brief was to find whoever had informed the police – the prime candidate being either Schneidermann or Kramer. The 'insider' theory was lent further credence when, on 19 February, the *News*'s readership was treated to an account of a 'nationally known star' having had pep pills seized from him; of proceedings against two 'nationally famous names' being active, and of a third leaving the premises minutes before. By an elaborate process of elimination Keylock deduced the following: Schneidermann, a Canadian known popularly as Acid King David, of otherwise nebulous background, had first rung the *News* on 11 February. The paper in turn called Scotland Yard, who helpfully advised contacting drug squad officers connected with West Sussex Police. That was the theory: the fact was that Schneidermann, while charged with possession, immediately left the country and no serious effort was ever made to find him. The subsequent trial confirmed it:

Havers: 'Was your source a well-known national newspaper?'
Detective-Sergeant Cudmore: 'Yes, sir.'
Havers: 'A well-known national newspaper gave information which led to the raid at Redlands. Who tipped off the paper? . . . Schneidermann was at the party loaded to the gunwales with cannabis resin, the

only man at the party found to have cannabis on him, but when the charges were made, he had gone.'

Keylock was further instructed to improve security against future incursions. He promptly hired a north London neighbour and schoolfriend, Frank Thorogood, who over the next year braced, buttressed and built Redlands to resemble a fort, his first suggestion being to erect a six-foot surrounding wall. 'Make it ten,' said Richard.

Finally Jagger sub-contracted 'Spanish Tony' Sanchez, a known Soho habitué, to negotiate with the police. According to Sanchez:

> In those days police corruption in the West End was commonplace. I knew cops who took regular bribes ... Someone in the forensic laboratories at Scotland Yard might be prepared to say [Fraser's] heroin was glucose if the price was right. Robert was ecstatic when I broke the news, and he phoned Keith immediately to tell him that if he paid the money, the whole case would be dropped. The same day Mick Jagger sent across a messenger with the cash in a suitcase.

Possibly. Undoubtedly Jagger telexed Klein on 17 February: 'Please cable by Saturday morning £5,000 and credit Rolling Stones Number 3 account at Westminster Bank'; undoubtedly this was added to the two thousand raised by Fraser; undoubtedly Sanchez at some stage met a policeman in a bar in Kilburn. Equally undoubtedly a month later the *Mirror* announced that Jagger, Richard, Fraser and the vanished Schneidermann were to be tried on drugs charges, bribe notwithstanding. 'It went to the wrong man,' says Keylock. 'Either that or Tony never delivered. Mick was furious.'

Klein, in a rare show of support, not only supplied the necessary five thousand pounds; he cabled further that 'in respect of the other matter' Jagger was to 'do nothing at all until I see you. Repeat: do nothing until I arrive.' On the twentieth Jagger and Richard were summoned to the Hilton. Also present were Perrin, Keylock and two lawyers, Timothy Hardacre and Victor Durand. Keylock gave his opinion that the *News* and Schneidermann had, indeed, been conspirators ('Bastards,' said Jagger) and made his interim report on Sanchez's pay-off. Jagger and Richard expressed the view that elements of the press were out to 'get' the Stones and Perrin hastened to join such consensus. There was a suspicion that phones had been tapped; Jagger also reported being followed. Such was the level of paranoia, albeit justified, that Klein was forced to advise his two charges – now sullen, like errant schoolboys under threat of punishment – to 'cool it', preferably together, preferably abroad.

They settled on Morocco. While Jagger and Faithfull flew via Paris to Marrakesh, Richard, Jones, Keylock and Pallenberg began the most complicated continental journey of modern times. The plan was for the quartet to drive through France and Spain in Richard's Bentley – the Blue Lena – eating well, drinking well and placing as much distance between themselves and Fleet Street as possible. That was the plan. So far as Paris, where a fifth passenger, Donald Cammell's girlfriend, was collected, so good. In Toulon Jones, plagued by asthma, was hospitalized. The party continued as a foursome, being detained in Barcelona where hoteliers refused to accept Richard's credit card proffered, to their further mystification, by Keylock. A telegram was received instructing Pallenberg to return for Jones. It was ignored. At Marbella, with a confirmatory wink to Keylock, Richard spent the night with Jones's lover. Finally crossing on the *Mons Calpe*, they reached Tangier on 8 March; Richard and Keylock made for the tenth floor of the Hotel Minzah where, according to the latter, 'Mick was already installed like a young lord, lying on a huge bed and complaining'. Also present were Fraser and Cooper. Pallenberg belatedly returned to Toulon to collect Jones.

The remainder proceeded to Marrakesh where they met the painter Brion Gyson, James Coburn, Paul Getty and Cecil Beaton, who reported 'Mick has much appreciation and his small, albino-fringed eyes notice everything. He has an analytical slant and compares everything he is seeing here with earlier impressions in other countries.' According to Beaton Jagger also advised him to sample LSD, adding that 'one's brain works not on four cylinders but on four thousand'.

In the week that followed many drinks were drunk and habits indulged. Getty and his wife Talitha rented a villa where, says Keylock, 'Paul wasn't averse to exotic practices'. (Asked to comment on this today Getty rolls his eyes.) Christopher Gibbs appeared, as did Pallenberg and Jones. The latter immediately summoned Keylock and insisted he procure a brace of local women for his 'health'. Keylock's response was to offer some medical advice of his own. Accomplishing the job himself, Jones then demanded that Pallenberg join them in bed. When she refused Jones did what eventually he always did: he beat her.

That was enough for Richard. Keylock was instructed to have Gyson remove Jones to the Djemaa el Fna, the local sook. While he was gone Richard, Keylock and Pallenberg left in the Bentley. Jagger and Faithfull, the former still complaining about his hotel bill, flew out. When Jones returned he was splenetic, though not incoherent, with rage. 'Judas!' he shouted. And 'Thomas Hobbes!' Gyson had him sedated while Jones cried and threw streamers of clothes into the street.

———

'A study in contradictions,' Korner called him; no sooner had Jagger insisted the Stones were 'semi-detached' from the work of performing than he instructed Tito Burns to arrange European dates that spring.

The tour that followed fulfilled the promise made in Hawaii. It was to be the final, the ultimate – the 'absolute last' – a three-week commitment prior to the group withdrawing into Beatle-like seclusion. It was also, notes Wyman, 'the worst possible time to hit the road': Jagger and Richard distracted, Jones demoralized, the whole group enrolled for ever on the customs international red list. In Copenhagen Jagger was ordered to unscrew the hinges of his suitcase when unable to find the key. He was searched and re-searched. According to Keylock, the singer's reception throughout Europe was 'scandalous' – constantly hounded, harassed, his planes subject to bewildering interminable delays; hotels, mysteriously and en bloc, lost track of the group's reservations. At airports they were greeted by snarling dogs and the snapping of rubber gloves. Even on stage guards lounged with studied contempt, slapping the sides of their military boots with drawn clubs. In Malmö Jagger was physically assaulted when requesting the police to 'cool it' in subduing unruly fans. Two nights later in Örebro five teenagers and a steward were taken to hospital.

After that things calmed down. In Vienna there were merely thrown eggs and smoke bombs; in Bologna hysteria. Twenty-eight shows in twenty-three days, attended by anarchy on stage and antipathy off. Jagger, separated from Faithfull, in the shadow of his trial, performed at the peak of his considerable powers. Keylock to this day puzzles how 'Mick kept it together, night in, night out, under that kind of pressure ... There were literally cops spitting at him on stage.' Between Austria and Italy Jagger detoured to London to meet his lawyers. He returned with Faithfull, who in Milan (she told A. E. Hotchner) witnessed her lover's public persona for the first time:

He came straight off stage to the hotel where I was waiting, and he was absolutely terrifying. I was really,

really scared. He was like some other person . . . I don't think he even knew who I was. He still had his make-up on, and there was a froth of spittle around his lips. His eyes were violent. He was making sounds, guttural sounds, and he was completely unintelligible. He was a berserk stranger. He picked me up and slammed me against the wall, several times.

Keylock also noted that 'after performing, Mick was an animal', while on tour generally he was 'hard to get through to'. His supposition was that the gap between Jagger off stage and on was wider than people knew: 'You could *see* him becoming Mick Jagger, doing exercises, psyching himself up, staring into space, while the others more or less just turned up.'

The official opprobrium surrounding the Stones was ingrained on that tour. Keylock gives a vivid description of his employer's *modus operandi* on these trips. On the plane Jagger would have Keylock or Burns sit outside him in the aisle seat, affording him at least partial protection from hostile businessmen, stewardesses and gaping fans. Once installed (under an assumed name) in the group's hotel, Jagger would rarely leave his room prior to the scheduled concert. The most intelligent, certainly the most inquisitive of the Stones, was thus restricted to a series of indistinguishable hotel suites, arenas, and the chauffeured limousine in between. 'That's when the aloof, movie star bit took over,' said Korner, ' – even though it was foisted on Mick from outside.' On Jagger's few unavoidable appearances evidence was invariably forthcoming that a secluded approach to life was the best one: in Paris immigration officials swore at him and jostled Richard; Keylock intercepted a punch; there was a row about passports. In Warsaw, their first visit behind the Iron Curtain, the Stones played to two thousand Party members while outside the army rioted – a stunning performance, says Don Short, who recalls Jagger's prophetic remark that 'sooner or later, rock and roll will catch on here'. At the finale Keylock was delegated to throw copies of 'Satisfaction' into the crowd on Jagger's command. Later still he was approached by a Polish photographer with evidence of the army menacing the numerous fans denied access to the stadium. Jagger was consulted and agreed to buy the film – the idea being to publish it in the English press – with the proviso that Keylock physically transport it through customs. Keylock compromised by dropping the spool in the *Mirror* man's pocket without telling him.

In Zurich a fan rushed a cordon of guards, mounted the stage, seized Jagger by the lapels and hit him; the police stood by. Keylock broke the man's jaw. He did the same to Jones's new factotum, Brian Palastanga, when Keylock discovered him charging drinks to the group's account. These were ad-libbed; Keylock's official duties that spring were expanded to include: rousing the five Stones (plus Stewart and Perrin) from bed, discouraging fans, encouraging fans (for Wyman), negotiating airports, handling hotels – and sending flowers to Faithfull. That April she made her debut as Irina in *Three Sisters* at the Royal Court Theatre. Her portrayal ('Marianne is unable to conserve her emotions, must offer them up wholesale, at once') was noted for its lavish, almost manic intensity. After a dozen performances she collapsed on stage suffering from exhaustion.

The tour ended in Athens. Having recently undergone a fascist coup Greece was in no particularly good mood to host a concert by the Rolling Stones. Jagger immediately showed his awareness of the situation by engaging an – obviously startled – military officer at the Athens Hilton in a long, erudite discussion on the need for 'appropriate' governmental control; the non-conformist espousing conformity. As Jagger sang that night in the vast bowl of Panathinaikos Stadium he handed Keylock a bouquet of carnations with the instruction to 'hurl them' at 'the cats'.

As Keylock did so he became uneasily unaware that he was alone on stage; the rest of the Stones had dropped their instruments and run. Even then, says Keylock, 'Mick was pretty cool, charming the military types backstage. He had them eating out of his hand. I always said there were two great performers in the world – the Pope and Mick Jagger.'

On 9 May 1967 Jagger, Richard and Robert Fraser lunched at a London gentleman's club, then drove to Chichester to face charges of threatening society.

At the hearing the next morning Jagger wore a white shirt and floral tie; accused of 'possessing four tablets of amphetamine sulphate and methyl amphetamine hydro-chloride', he nodded affably to his name and legal address (Perrin's office in Oxford Street). He pleaded not guilty. The three magistrates were informed by Anthony McCowan, prosecuting, that a chemist would testify as to the unavailability of the tablets found on Jagger at Redlands; the only question was whether they were obtained on pre-scription from a qualified doctor. With that all three defend-ants elected trial by jury in a higher court. They were bailed to appear at West Sussex Sessions on 27 June.

At the very moment of Jagger's committal, Jones was answering the doorbell at his flat in Courtfield Road, Earl's Court. It was the police. After picking through the debris, the empty gin bottles and overflowing ashtrays, they arrested Jones and his house guest, an exotic named Stanis-laus Klossowski de Rola, for possession – specifically, fifty grams of cannabis, methedrine and cocaine. He, too, elected trial by jury; he too, was bailed. Jones entered court already alone. He left it virtually alienated – advised by his lawyers to 'discuss nothing', not his case, their own, not even record-ing dates or sessions with Richard and Jagger. The last immediately instructed Keylock personally to 'look after Brian', keeping him cheerful or, failing that, to arrange a regular delivery of flowers from Chivers the Florist. Over the next two years Keylock ran an account with Chivers.

In the following six weeks Jagger recorded one song, 'We Love You' (Jones on off-key and far-off mellotron), helped the Beatles produce another, attended the launch of *Sergeant Pepper*, served on the committee of the Monterey Pop Festival (which he failed to attend) and returned with Faithfull to Tangier – possibly for the holiday denied them in March. Keylock remembers Jagger as 'calm' about the impending trial: 'My main memory is of Mick with Marianne's boy. He was incredibly patient with him – always on the floor playing.' When Nicholas accidentally put his foot through a guitar or soiled the rug Jagger shook his head as if to say, Kids!; as if to say, God bless them! He was genuinely affectionate. In June Keylock was instructed to find a house where the three of them – Jagger, Faithfull and Nicholas – could live.

'Rather too keen on the infernal WIRELESS' was the verdict on a wartime Lieutenant by his commanding officer, Leslie Kenneth Block. Later, as Fleet Navigating Officer, Block entered in the Royal Naval Club's suggestion book a plea for 'pray, SILENCE in the library'. He was a man inordinately given to capitals. Block also had a lifelong aversion to music in all forms – even as anodyne as Glenn Miller or, later, Des O'Connor. After the war Block returned to the Bar, serving as a judge on the Mayor's and City of London Courts, a commissioner of the Central Criminal Court and later as chairman of West Sussex Quarter Sessions. It was as the last that he appeared on 27 June 1967, a sixty-one-year-old Tory landowner of Naval mien, the very last person whom the frilled-shirted figure in the dock would have chosen to confront. 'Mick,' said Richard, 'came up against the brick wall of reality.'

The first sign of having done so came as Jagger emerged through the police, press, the fans, the T-shirt salesmen and hawkers outside the Chichester court. As he arrived in the vestibule he saw Havers sharing a joke with the prosecuting counsel, Malcolm Morris, laughing while – as Jagger now realized for the first time – his own future was at stake. Later the sheer intimacy of the occasion was Jagger's abiding memory. As he put it: 'They're all the same, the lawyers. You know, "Hello, Harry, how are you?" "Hi, Charlie. Groovy! Yeah, great! Have a brandy."' This was confirmed as, in an aside, Havers advised his celebrated client to 'restrict [himself] to his proper accent' – this to 'better impress the opposition'. His barrister then instructed Jagger to 'disregard everyone but me, never to guess at an answer but to say that [he] didn't know or forgot' and that, in his considered opinion, 'the prosecution had a very weak case'. Havers' overall assessment? 'I told him that I didn't think there was a chance in hell he'd be convicted.'

The sole witness for the defence was Dr Raymond Firth of Wilton Crescent, Knightsbridge, Jagger's GP since early 1965. He 'distinctly recalled' a conversation in which Jagger had asked him if 'Italian pep pills' were permissible in an emergency. He agreed that they were.

Block then ruled that 'the evidence given by Dr Firth does not in law amount to the issue of a prescription by a qualified practitioner'. Six minutes later the jury returned its verdict: guilty of illegal possession. Turning to Jagger, whose knuckle tightened visibly on the brass rail of the dock, Block announced his intention 'to defer sentencing until after the trial of your two friends', adding with customary emphasis, 'You will now be *remanded in custody*.'

Jagger was then handcuffed to Fraser (also found guilty) and driven to Lewes Jail. He was brought books and cigarettes. A request for a razor was refused. At ten o'clock – a sensation that for Jagger must have been as disorientating as jet lag – Lights Out was called. The next morning at seven he was served breakfast before being returned to Chichester, where he spent the day in a basement cell while Richard's trial proceeded overhead. Much of the testimony concerned the antics of 'Miss X', a woman whose 'unperturbed behaviour' and eccentric garb were plainly taken as evidence of having 'lost her inhibitions ... because of smoking hemp'. To the stench of drugs and rock and roll was added an intoxicating whiff of sex; as Morris delivered the line *All she was wearing was a light-coloured fur rug*, there was something akin to a brawl in the rush for the court's three available public phones. Miss X herself sat demurely in the public gallery.

'I hope,' intoned Havers, 'she will remain anonymous. She is described as a drug-taking nymphomaniac with no chance of saying anything in her defence. Do you expect me to force that girl to go into the witness box with no chance to refute the allegations? I am not going to tear the blanket aside and subject her to laughter and scorn. If I can't call the girl, and Mr Richards is in agreement with this, I will not call anyone else.'

On that note the court recessed. Faithfull – whose reputation became proverbial from that day on – was allowed ten minutes alone with Jagger. She brought him a jigsaw puzzle, more cigarettes and fresh fruit. Michael Cooper surreptitiously filmed the scene but had his camera impounded. More successful was the agency photographer who caught Jagger, handcuffed once more, his raised arm joined to that of his guard as the latter beamed in the high current of publicity. He may even have smirked.

This proved justified. Next morning Richard took the stand in his own defence. After informing Morris that 'we are not old men ... and we are not worried about petty morals' he firmly endorsed the suggestion that 'because the *News of the World* did not want to pay libel damages to Mick Jagger, it was arranged to have Indian hemp planted [at Redlands]'. An hour later the jury returned its verdict: Guilty. (This after Block had belatedly instructed them to 'disregard ... the evidence as to the lady who was alleged by the police to have been in some condition of undress' – in other words, the bulk of the trial.) At four o'clock on Thursday 29 June Jagger was again brought to the dock. He stood between Richard and Fraser. In reverse order of trial, Block then passed sentence: twelve months, six months and – turning to Jagger – 'three months'. Immediately Faithfull was ushered downstairs by Keylock, where she sat surrounded by leering warders and the rasp of jangling keys.

Jagger wept.

That night he became Jagger M. P., Prisoner 7856 at Brixton Jail. It was among the very bleakest outposts of a system known for its bleakness. While fans demonstrated in Piccadilly Circus and, more pertinently, at the *News of the World*, Jagger was photographed, fingerprinted, and exchanged his velvet jacket for blue overalls and regulation black shoes. He was locked in a cell he later described as 'not much worse than a motel room in Minnesota'; he completed his jigsaw. He wrote the lyrics of a song whose very title, '2000 Light Years From Home', would become the basis of a cult, proving yet again the consolatory nature of art.

Havers, meanwhile, worked overnight to obtain leave for Jagger and Richard to appeal. Mysteriously he was drawn aside by Morris, his opposing counsel, and told that the latter had 'direct instructions' not to oppose him. At the Court of Appeal Havers stressed his opinion that Dr Firth's endorsement amounted to 'moral authorization' for the tablets and that 'there is no question of peddling . . . no question of vast quantities'. In a bewildering reversal Lord Justice Diplock then freed Jagger on bail, as well as Richard. Fraser's application was refused.

At four-thirty that afternoon Keylock edged the Blue Lena to the gates of Brixton Jail. Jagger emerged wearing a composite of prison and Carnaby Street chic: sports coat, ruffled shirt, black lace-up boots. His first words to Keylock were, 'I need a drink.' An hour later, after collecting Richard from Wormwood Scrubs, they were in a pub in Fleet Street. Jagger ordered vodka. 'I just went dead when I was sentenced,' he admitted. Later he informed a reporter, in tones that could only have been supplied by Perrin, 'We had very good treatment, though no different from the other prisoners. They all wanted our autographs. The other chaps showed a great interest in the case and wanted to know all the details ... We don't bear a grudge against anyone for what happened. We just think the sentences were rather harsh.'

Jagger's complaint was rendered compelling by *The Times* editorial, inspired by Pope's *Epistle to Dr Arbuthnot*, on 1 July:

> ... In the courts at large it is most uncommon for imprisonment to be imposed on first offenders where the drugs are not major drugs of addiction and there is no question of drug traffic. The normal penalty is probation, and the purpose of probation is to encourage the defender to develop his career and to avoid the drug risks in future. It is surprising, therefore, that Judge Block should have decided to sentence Mr Jagger to imprisonment, and particularly surprising as Mr Jagger's is about as mild a drug case as can ever have been brought before the Courts.
>
> ... If we are going to make any case a symbol of the conflict between the sound traditional values of Britain and the new hedonism, then we must be sure that the sound traditional values include those of tolerance and equity. It should be the particular quality of British justice to ensure that Mr Jagger is treated exactly the same as anyone else, no better and no worse. There must remain a suspicion in this case that Mr Jagger received a more severe sentence than would have been thought proper for any purely anonymous young man.

When Jagger read the above he immediately phoned his mother in Wilmington.

If, as some supposed, the trial's primary end had been to close the Establishment ranks, in which presumably could be included the Establishment newspaper, then it failed abjectly. The *Evening Standard* had already bridled at the use of handcuffs ('To the public it must seem an act of unnecessary harshness'); to *The Times*'s leader was added the following by the *Sun*:

There are teenagers who do not accept the law and the conventional approach because they think that both are unreasonable and falsely based.

Teenagers ask why there is no stigma in being a drinking driver who may kill people, while smoking marijuana, which they consider less harmful, is banned.

The *Observer*:

For the many hundreds of thousands of youngsters, those for whom the Rolling Stones are part of the pop Pantheon of heroes, it was like a drum-head court martial on the battlefield where the war of the generations is conducted.

The *Sunday Express*:

Was Jagger convicted of taking one of the evil drugs like heroin or cocaine? Or LSD, with which some of the Beatles confess they have been experimenting? Not at all. Did he smoke marijuana which some experts say is evil but others, equally expert, say is not so evil? That wasn't alleged against him. He merely had four benzedrine tablets, legally purchased abroad, which, with the knowledge and approval of his doctor, he took to keep him awake while he worked.

In the revised view of Jagger's fate in which the word 'flash' was tempered by 'hard done by', only the *News of the World*, for reasons of its own, maintained the offensive.

> [The charge of planting Schneidermann] was made without a shred of evidence ... It was made within the privilege of a court of law ... which denied us the opportunity of answering back ... These outrageous allegations are of course totally unfounded. We have had no connection whatsoever with Mr Schneidermann directly or indirectly, before, during or after this case.

Whatever the altered prevailing climate of opinion, the same forces previously bent on chastening Jagger now rapidly reversed themselves. On 4 July Havers received word that the Lord Chief Justice had personally intervened to bring forward the date of his client's appeal to the thirty-first. (Havers later noted that this was without precedent in his experience.) In the interim Jagger reassembled the Rolling Stones, who recorded a half-dozen desultory songs at Olympic Studios in Barnes. Keylock recalls the atmosphere on these occasions as 'dead', Jagger himself as 'zombie-like' and morbid – a description also endorsed by Havers. When a young Granada TV researcher, John Birt, rang to invite him to appear on *World In Action*, 'Mick ... seemed hardly able to grasp the question'. An interview was nonetheless agreed for 31 July – neither party referring to the fact that Jagger's availability on that date was by no means secure.

On the twenty-second Robert Fraser lost his appeal and had his sentence upheld.

At the end of the month Jagger and Richard (the latter having developed chicken pox) appeared at the High Court.

'The spectators' gallery,' Havers told Hotchner, 'was chock-full of young squealing girls, all there to catch sight of Mick ... Before the judges appeared, the bailiff announced that the court would not convene unless there was order in the gallery ... "Leave it to me, Uncle Mike," said Jagger, whereupon he stood up, faced the gallery and raised his arms in a quieting gesture like Moses parting the water. The girls immediately fell silent.' Two hours later Lord Parker ordered the conviction against Richard quashed since 'Judge Block erred in not warning the jury there was no proper evidence ... that the girl clad only in a rug had smoked cannabis and that [Richard] must have known about it'. He turned to Jagger. The court, he was told, upheld his conviction. Jagger's sentence, however, would be reduced to probation: 'That means,' said Parker, 'if you keep out of trouble for the next twelve months, what has happened will not go on your record.' In a level voice he added, 'When one is dealing with somebody that has great responsibilities as you have, because, whether you like it or not, you are an idol of a large number of the young in this country, you have grave responsibilities ... Accordingly, if you do come for punishment, it is only natural that those responsibilities should carry a higher penalty.'

Jagger was hurriedly driven to a Granada press conference, having changed en route into silk trousers and an embroidered smock. Heavily sedated, he appeared – to use an earlier phrase – in a state of mild unconcern; in the car park he took a toss on a concrete abutment and sprinted face first into a pillar, but recovered to take his place at the table between Perrin and Ian Stewart. Behind them stood Faithfull, sporting a thigh-length white skirt that success-fully diverted attention as Jagger, mumbling, shaking his head, ground to a halt. According to Faithfull, she was 'really happy everything [had] turned out all right' and that 'all the things we have been worrying about have dis-appeared'.

The couple were then driven at frenzied speed across London to a waiting helicopter. Once aloft Jagger immediately attacked Faithfull, kissing and fondling her while Birt, squeezed on to the same narrow seat, studied the view. On arrival at Spain's Hall, a Georgian mansion house outside Ongar, the lovers promptly made for the bedroom. 'We assumed they'd have an hour to themselves before we started filming,' says Birt. 'Suddenly I was told we were ready. I had to go up and knock on the bedroom door. I waited about five minutes before Jagger appeared. It was pretty obvious what I'd interrupted.'

Outside, the events of an already dreamlike day continued dreamily. Jagger, the new hedonist, was confronted with three apostates of the Traditional Values: Lord Stow Hill, former Home Secretary; a Jesuit priest, Father Thomas Curbishley, and John Robinson, Bishop of Woolwich. William Rees-Mogg, editor of *The Times*, presided. Asked if he felt 'responsibility' to the young, Jagger's inordinate head lurched sideways. 'The influence we have has been pushed on us – especially during this drug thing.'

'What are the qualities,' asked Rees-Mogg, 'you think your generation is going to bring forward?'

'I don't really want to format a new code of living, a new code of morals.'

Again and again he denied it: no power, no sway, no dominion, just the desire, 'like everyone else', to have as good a time as possible. 'I never set myself up as a leader in society. It's society that has pushed one into that position.'

'But wouldn't you say that some drugs – heroin, for example – represent a crime against society?'

'Against a *law*,' snapped Jagger. 'I can't see it's any more a crime against society than jumping out a window.'

The Establishment sat in their starchy suits as the hedonist lounged and, lizard-like, flicked his tongue. At one stage he confessed to enjoying influence 'in the public sector', then immediately retracted by saying, 'My personal habits are of no consequence to anyone.' For an hour the debate had the attention of society, and it taught it nothing.

In Wormwood Scrubs, meanwhile, Fraser served four of his six months' sentence. Jagger wrote him a letter.

· V ·

THE BUTTERFLY...

Oldham left that autumn. By means of mysterious agreement between Jagger and Richard the Stones conspired to fire him. Even then the end was oblique. 'At some stage they realized that Andrew's ideas on production were only ideas he'd got from them in the first place,' said Stewart. 'There must have been some sort of bust-up, because all of a sudden they wanted to get rid of him . . . We went in and played a lot of blues as badly as we could. Andrew just walked out. At the time I didn't understand what was going on.'

Mankowitz also witnessed the end. 'The band would turn up later and later each night and achieve less and less,' he says. 'They'd arrive either really morose, or totally stoned . . . Andrew was pissed off, because he couldn't get anything done; he turned round several times and said, "This is ridiculous. What am I doing here?" It was all quite unpleasant . . . time-consuming, exhausting, tense, unproductive. I was there because Andrew wanted me to photograph the sessions, and you could feel these undercurrents going on. The end when it came was traumatic . . . At one of the sessions Michael Cooper approached Andrew and said, "Mick's asked me to talk to you about the new album cover." I knew instantly that I was out, and I think it was the final straw for Andrew as well.' Don Short, who interviewed Jagger at Olympic, felt that it was a 'more-or-less natural progression . . . Mick had moved on, and he didn't want the same manager he'd had when he was starting. He was ruthless like that.' Oldham himself recalled: 'It was very simple . . . It was like, "We know what's what, let's let Allen Klein work it out." It was at the time of *Satanic Majesties* and I don't think they needed a manager like I'd been managing them before. *That's* hindsight. At the time it was just confusing.'

The announcement was made on 14 September. The ever-amenable Perrin was instructed to say that the group had 'parted from our recording manager . . . because the Stones have taken over more and more of the production of their own music'. Jagger added pointedly: 'I felt we were doing practically everything ourselves anyway. And we just didn't think along the same lines. But I don't want to have a go at Andrew. Allen Klein is just a financial scene. We'll really be managing ourselves.'

In fact responsibility for day-to-day management of the Stones reverted to Jagger himself. From late 1967 the group were administered from an attic office at 46 Maddox Street, Mayfair. It was nominally managed by a young Californian, Jo Bergman, former assistant to Faithfull, who, in Wyman's words, 'took all her instructions from Mick', a view fully endorsed by Stewart. There were additional mumblings that the group had effectively become a Jagger–Faithfull consortium; Keylock, retained as tour manager, notes that 'with Andrew gone, Mick basically took over. Suddenly it was him calling the meetings . . . I'd never thought of him like that before.' Jagger it was who summoned Richard, Wyman, Watts and, more sparingly, Jones to the studio; Jagger who scripted a film wherein he, Faithfull and Richard cavorted as Oscar Wilde, Bosie and the Marquess of Queensberry to accompany 'We Love You' (promptly shelved); Jagger who mooted the idea of a joint production company with the Beatles. The man emerging from his trial in 1967 was no longer a team member. He was player-manager of the Rolling Stones, his reputation extended and enhanced as one who had fought the law – and drawn.

As if in illustration Jagger renewed his upward domestic momentum. That autumn he paid forty thousand pounds for 48 Cheyne Walk, a Queen Anne mansion on the Chelsea side of Albert Bridge. He, Faithfull and Faithfull's son moved in before Christmas. Christopher Gibbs was commissioned as designer; among other items he supplied ornate Venetian blinds and Moroccan drapes – one or both of which remained permanently drawn – and a crystal chandelier for which Jagger paid six thousand pounds. David Mlinaric provided additional touches. The Regency bath and four-poster bed followed from Harley House, as did the extensive library, wardrobe and wine collection. The house itself was bare-floored – Jagger preferring hand-sewn Persian rugs to carpets – with something gloomy about the interior. In the three years he visited Cheyne Walk Keylock never once saw the windows open. Upstairs were three guest rooms, a study and Jagger's own bedroom, whose red velvet curtains and chaise-longue reminded more than one visitor of Versailles.

Jagger also invested twenty-five thousand pounds in a country house near Newbury, implausibly named Stargroves. The estate agent Savills piqued their client's interest by alleging the building had 'served as field headquarters of Oliver Cromwell, Supreme Lord Protector of England' (no historical evidence of which exists); they omitted to stress the equally supreme disrepair of much of the interior. After the inevitable delay papers were exchanged and Jagger and Faithfull took possession that winter – though 'possessed' exaggerates an arrangement largely restricted to weekends. Faithfull took personal responsibility for the thirty-seven acres of garden and parkland, assuring the resident couple, Mr and Mrs White, 'You'll be looked after.' (A decade later the Whites were evicted.) With the construction of a mobile studio, the manor's sixteenth-century rafters were regularly raised by The Who, Hendrix or the Stones themselves – while, incredibly, up the gravel drive crunched a convoy of fifteen horse-drawn caravans led by Sir Mark Palmer, formerly a page-boy at the Queen's coronation. Palmer's revised *modus vivendi* was to live out, eat *au naturel* and sleep rough, late and with whomever he could. Surprisingly Jagger tolerated and even encouraged Stargroves as a venue. Villagers became inured to the sight of Palmer's numerous acolytes appearing in the local shop to buy cigarette papers or a magazine of astrological data. At night campfires could be seen flickering in the distance. Later Palmer gave an interview in which he stated: 'In reality it was a grim place, and Mick never really intended to fix it up and move in' (a view seconded by Frank Thorogood, briefed to make improvements to Stargroves specifically designed to 'tart it up for resale'); 'it did have big stables and all that sort of thing, so when winter came and we couldn't graze the horses any more, we all moved inside. We did that for a couple of winters. Mick and Marianne stayed for a bit but before long they took off ... We had this great benign feeling, everybody loving everybody. Great masses of people were coming down from London to join us ... We had communal eating, and at night we listened to music together and smoked dope ... people looking up at the stars, touching ... arms around ... sex ... Life as it should be lived. I'm not sure Jagger was as comfortable with all this as he pretended to be; Marianne was.'

Palmer's suspicions were correct. While Jagger applied himself as chairman of the Rolling Stones, Faithfull searched for a role away from the singalongs and shared bonhomie of Stargroves. Ever the actress, she earned respectful reviews in *Three Sisters*; appeared dolefully in a film entitled *I'll Never Forget What's 'is Name* with Oliver Reed (having declined *Women in Love*), before starring in *Girl on a Motorcycle*, aptly described in *Halliwell's Film Guide* as 'an incredibly plotless and ill-conceived piece of sub-porn claptrap, existing only as a long series of colour supplement photographs'. As for singing: after the LP *Love In A Mist*, promoted by Decca as 'a beautiful singer singing fourteen beautiful romantic songs in wistful mood', was released in February 1967, Faithfull was silent for nearly a decade. Drugs: by her own admission Faithfull had a 'romantic idea' of narcotics from reading De Quincey, Baudelaire and Wilde; her second husband believed she spent 'at least ten years unhinged' by the experience. And sex: Faithfull enjoyed sex. In addition to the conquest of 'three Rolling Stones' (by implication Jagger, Richard and Jones) Faithfull was far from averse to experimentation: Keylock cites Jagger having found her in bed at least once with another woman. 'He knew about my girlfriends,' she says. 'He didn't mind.' The prevalent impression? A restless soul, doomed to wander for ever down vistas of triteness, her only salvation the unconsciousness foretold by altered visions of reality. 'A right raver,' says Keylock.

Jagger himself carried an almost equal number of masks. Concurrent with organizing the Stones, he was a kindly and ironic employer, much given to the sarcastic remark followed by immediate retraction, an indulgent guardian of Nicholas and devoted supporter of his mother. He actively encouraged Faithfull to make *Girl on a Motorcycle* and was more than once found asleep, receiver in hand, after an early-hours call to his absent (and presumably equally comatose) lover. At night he was full of good intentions to rise early. Keylock or occasionally Thorogood would be instructed – by means of a note pierced with a dagger – to 'wake me WITHOUT FAIL at nine'. Jagger would arise unfailingly at noon. Both his houses were permanently full. He had a chronic fear of appearing unsociable, preferring subterfuge as when Keylock was instructed to appear at Cheyne Walk and remove Jagger from his house guests on the pretext of 'a meeting'. He still drove to Wilmington to see Joe and Eva, who were in turn invited for weekends at Stargroves.

Faithfull, in a subsequent interview, said of the period, 'The prevalent belief was that to take LSD or smoke hash was a pure sort of organic thing ... and that alcohol was going into the straight world of parents' – meanwhile blaming drugs for the fact that she and Jagger 'didn't talk'. Stewart also noted that, pharmaceutically, 'Mick tried almost everything'. Keylock's view is blunter: 'There was a lot of smoking done by Mick and Keith. With Brian it was pills and brandy. The difference is that they could handle it and he couldn't.' The essence of Jagger's strength was that 'he could get out of it and still operate'. Operative or not, the shadow of his drugs conviction pursued Jagger unceasingly. Landing in New York on 13 September he was detained for forty minutes by immigration officials and his luggage systematically dissected. After Klein's intervention he was given permission to enter America for a fortnight, with the proviso that 'we will not decide whether [Jagger] will be able to enter the USA again until we have studied reports of the drugs cases in Britain'.

Jones's state was more perilous. Pending his own trial he began to see a Harley Street psychiatrist. The doctor in turn referred him to a clinic in Roehampton. Evidently confused as to the purpose of his visit, Jones arrived demanding 'a suite' for his new girlfriend Suki Poitier and himself and 'a room for my man Tom'. He was promptly shown to a cubicle. Jones, the clinic noted, was 'anxious, depressed and even suicidal ... without a great deal of confidence in himself'; still, the report concluded, 'trying to grow up in many ways'. In August he arrived with Poitier and a friend, Tara Browne, in Marbella, where his swaggering gait and patent leer immediately persuaded a visiting English schoolboy, Anthony Phillips, that the pop business was for him. (Phillips went on to co-found Genesis.) In September, surreally, Jones was reported to have applied for a pilot's licence. Finally, on 30 October at Inner London Sessions, he was sentenced to nine months for, like Richard, allowing his premises to be used for the taking of drugs. Like Richard he was imprisoned in Wormwood Scrubs. In a demonstration that night eight teenagers, including Jagger's younger brother, were arrested for abusive behaviour. The next day Jones was freed on bail. On 12 December Lord Justice Parker – having heard evidence of Jones's 'extremely precarious state of adjustment' and 'fragile grasp of reality' – quashed his prison sentence in favour of probation. Jones immediately collapsed and returned to Roehampton, where he was said to be 'tired and suffering from over-strain'. Suicide, his doctor added, remained a possibility.

At the studio Jagger drew Keylock aside and discussed Jones in an undertone. Brian, he noted dryly, was 'a druggy'. He was a mess. On a material note Jones's conviction further jeopardized the group's precarious immigration status in America. The self-pity, always close to the surface with Jagger, boiled over: 'That's all we need,' he said. He continued to complain to Keylock, though with underlying concern. Contrary to the theory that Jagger diminished – in certain versions, destroyed – Jones, some form of higher emotion remained. He was genuinely saddened. When Jones passed out one night at the studio Keylock was delegated to drive him home. Jagger also arranged for Jones to be chaperoned and asked Poitier to watch him. He even telephoned Jones's parents. At the Appeal Court Jagger sat in the public gallery for moral support. He was visibly pleased when Jones was freed. Outside, after posing for pictures, they announced their intention of 'getting back to the music'.

They urgently needed to. The album released that month was the group's weakest to date. *Their Satanic Majesties Request* was an uneasy composite of studio doodlings and vague ephemera whose highlight, '2000 Light Years from Home', was originally written in Brixton Jail; it formed the

B-side of the new single, 'She's A Rainbow'. Other offerings included 'Sing This All Together', wherein free form was confused with formlessness; 'Citadel', a rocker diminished rather than the reverse by warbling brass; 'Gomper', best described as whimsical; and 'On With the Show' (perversely, the closing number), a cacophony of under-rehearsed mayhem. *Satanic Majesties* limped to number three in Britain and number two in America without threatening to set either market alight. 'Rainbow' sank without trace. Poorly recorded, pretentiously wrapped, the album was the first to go unpromoted on tour – or even by personal endorsement ('Complete crap,' said Jagger). In the confusion a Wyman composition was even released as a single: chaos.

The strong suspicion was that *Majesties* had tried, and failed, to emulate the Beatles' breakthrough LP *Sergeant Pepper*. Both records featured opening numbers later reprised; both included background noise, dialogue* and tape effects in the normally sacrosanct silence between tracks. Both featured a similar cover by the same photographer. Both, in the idiom of the moment, were hailed as 'way out'.

The Beatles' influence was mutual. As early as 1964 both groups had extended their success into America, appealing to the same privileged, mainly white, mainly middle-class audience, though – by deliberate contrivance between Oldham and Brian Epstein – never overlapping, never intersecting and above all never confusing their quite separate propositions (the Beatles wanting to hold your hand, the Stones any other part of the anatomy). Twenty years later Jagger admitted to 'a sense of sharing a joke [with the Beatles] that people were taking it all so seriously.' The musical affinity also preceded *Sergeant Pepper*: in April 1966 Lennon and Harrison had been pictured in *16* magazine flourishing copies of '19th Nervous Breakdown' under the

* Including Jagger asking, 'Where's that joint?'

caption, 'Wait a minute, Paulie – George and I are coming up with a couple of really original ideas.' Don Short was one of a number of journalists asked to relay information between the Beatles and the Stones – the release date of each other's singles, for instance – 'as much out of genuine interest as anything devious'. For a while, that year and the next, the two groups became almost indistinct. In June Lennon and McCartney supplied back-up vocals on 'We Love You'; Jagger reciprocated by appearing on the Beatles' 'All You Need Is Love' telecast, *Our World*. In August Jagger and Faithfull joined the Beatles at the Maharishi's ill-fated seminar in Bangor, during which it was learned that Brian Epstein had died. Jagger's agent Tito Burns then declared it an 'excellent idea' for the two groups to pool their resources. Jagger instructed his solicitors to register the name Mother Earth as a title for the joint venture. The moment passed, but not without one voice registering concern at the Stones' apparent identity crisis. In Wyman's words, 'Mick and Keith . . . couldn't accept that people had different views or tastes from theirs. If you weren't one of their gang, they thought you were *against* the gang. Childish. Anything they didn't want to do was wrong, and if they were in a bad mood, everyone was expected to join it. I came close to leaving on many occasions because of the various frustrations and what I considered to be selfishness. I also couldn't identify much with the music on *Majesties*. Altogether, it often felt that there really wasn't much of a future in the band.'

The Beatles were an obvious influence on *Satanic Majesties*. Books were another. In early 1967 Jagger appeared at the Indica shop and bought, among others, *The Secret of the Golden Flower*, an anthology of cryptic allusions and Middle Earth esoterica (green suns, flying disks and argosies of celestial travellers). He read *The Golden Bough* approvingly and *Morning of the Musician* without complaint. Suddenly, says Keylock, 'Mick would appear with four paperbacks under his arm and start babbling about "fiery oceans" ' (which very phrase occurs in '2000 Light Years'). 'Either that, or it was his workers-unite bit. Mick got very political that year. God knows who started it.'

Tom Driberg was who started it. The old radical, homosexual, security-risk Labour MP, godfather of Jagger's former girlfriend Cleo Sylvestre, had originally been introduced that spring. After more companionable advances were declined Driberg settled on a role as political tutor. Twice that summer he lent his name in Jagger's support: in early July Driberg tabled a Commons motion '. . . deploring the action of a Glasgow magistrate, James Langmuir, in using his privileged position to make irrelevant, snobbish and insulting personal comment ("Clowns . . . Filthy clothes . . . Complete morons") on the appearance and performance of the Rolling Stones, who are making a substantial contribution to public entertainment and the export drive'; he also signed a letter in *The Times* calling for the legalization of soft drugs in the wake of Jagger's trial. The Gay Hussar, a narrow, panelled restaurant – somehow giving the impression of the dining car in a Royal train – became the unlikely milieu for a series of political seminars. Jagger, in floral shirt and flares, would sit on the scarlet banquette opposite Driberg. The latter's thesis followed the orthodox Leninist line: thought was a function of reality; thought led to action; action changed reality. Driberg went on to assure his companion that any 'thinking person' owed it to himself to consider whether an anarchistic approach to life might not be the best one. A long silence greeted this as Jagger studied his Vagdalt Limbamell Solatell, his breast of goose and red cabbage. His politics still being largely a mélange of Utopian-socialist mumblings, his eventual response was to ask where, in the real world, such a person would fit in.

'The Labour party,' said Driberg.

Opinions vary as to whether Jagger ever seriously considered standing for Parliament. Driberg always thought so, although he had other motives for prolonging the relationship. Resigned to Jagger's sexual orientation – and indeed the presence of Faithfull – Driberg adopted a different approach: from 1967 the couple became his personal conduit to the 'young people' in whose subversive instincts he placed lifelong faith. That winter he repeatedly urged Jagger to 'toughen' his song lyrics, adding in Thorogood's hearing that 'you could really, *really* amount to something'. The following spring he wrote to the wartime activist Richard Acland '. . . I have been discussing the electoral possibilities, and the problems of revolution with two people, friends of mine, who could have some influence among the young: Mick Jagger and his lady, Marianne Faithfull – both more intelligent than you might suppose from their public *personae*. They would like to meet you. Would you?'

Despite further correspondence and at least one encounter at Cheyne Walk between Jagger, Driberg, Acland and the journalist Paul Foot (a new parliamentary party, to be called Logos, was discussed) nothing ever transpired. Gradually it became clear that Jagger's feelings about 'toughening' his lyrics, let alone more direct action, were ambiguous. Stewart, who once collected Jagger from the Gay Hussar, believed that 'Mick went along [with Driberg]', a view shared by Keylock, who considered it 'all a bit of a send-up of old Tom'. Certainly his young pupil remained silent as Driberg repeatedly pumped him for his 'plans'. To the direct question, 'Why not stand for the local council?' Jagger gave him a look of withering scorn. When next Driberg appeared for dinner at Cheyne Walk it was to be told by Faithfull that Mick was 'unexpectedly detained'. On another occasion at the restaurant Jagger interrupted a long monologue on the post-feudal acceleration of the means of production to ask for a glass of port. Albert Clinton, who waited at the Gay Hussar for twenty years, remembers 'the elder gentleman doing the talking, the younger one the eating'.

The following February and March anti-war demonstrations took place outside the American Embassy. Jagger's first reaction was to give an interview to the *Sunday Mirror* in which he eschewed Driberg's proposal of conventional politics – with its threat of effort and self-denial – in favour of the intoxicating idea of anarchy: 'Millions of marvellous young men are killed and in five minutes everybody seems to have forgotten all about it. War stems from power-mad politicians and patriots . . . Politicians? What a dead loss they are. There shouldn't be any Prime Minister at all.'

Next Jagger joined a demonstration organized by the Vietnam Solidarity Campaign on 17 March; he had Keylock drop him at the corner. For forty minutes he marched arm-in-arm with two – visibly starstruck – students down Park Lane and into Grosvenor Square. 'What do we want?' a man with a megaphone demanded. 'Peace,' mumbled Jagger.

'I can't hear you.'

'PEACE!'

His involvement ended there. By the time the crowd turned violent, with three hundred arrested and fifty injured, certainly by the time they assembled in Trafalgar Square to hear Vanessa Redgrave state, 'A Vietcong victory is the only way to peace', Jagger was safely back in his Chelsea mansion house, writing lyrics.

'Everybody Pays Their Dues' was a basic three-minute rocker conceived by Richard that winter. When the Stones gathered to rehearse at Redlands in March it was viewed as an album filler, no more. On the twenty-first Jagger appeared; he sat outside on the living room terrace and, in the course of an afternoon, improvised a story line concerning his experiences. After several false starts a chorus was added:

> Well, what can a poor boy do
> Except to sing for a rock 'n' roll band . . .

To Keylock Jagger called it 'direct action'.

In May he gave an interview to *International Times* in which the 'What to do?' motif recurred:

Q: I'm interested in the idea of an alternative society growing out of what's been happening in the last few years, a general re-evaluation of things that a lot of people are getting into, which is beginning to threaten a lot of the barriers which the old-style society has put up.

A: I think that about most cyclic changes. There's no doubt that there's a cyclic change, a VAST cyclic change, on top of a lot of smaller ones. I can imagine America becoming just ablaze, just being ruined ... but this country, it's very weird, you know, it always does things slightly differently. Always more moderately, and always more boringly ... most of it ... the changes are so suppressed. There definitely is this fantastic split, and it even cuts across class which shows how strong it is, because there's very few things in England that do transcend class. All extremes meet at the other end but that's not the point in this one. It isn't one of those.

In releasing *Satanic Majesties*, no less than by his flirtation with Driberg, Jagger had asked for trouble. Now that the Stones had stopped touring the group's standards were threatened by a plethora of acts – The Doors, Small Faces, Hendrix, Cream, even the Monkees – created to meet the new demand for LPs, eleven million more of which were sold in the UK in 1968 than 1967. What the Stones needed were new standards altogether.

They found them in the improbable setting of a rehearsal studio in Morden. On 26 March Wyman was doing what he did all too depressingly often – waiting for Jagger and Richard – when

> Sitting around, I began playing the electronic keyboard, messing around with a great riff I'd found. Charlie and Brian began jamming with me and it sounded really good and tough. When Mick and Keith walked in they said: 'Keep playing that, and don't forget it – it sounds great.'

Six weeks later Jagger appeared at Olympic and announced that the group would forthwith record their new single. It was Wyman's song adapted to guitar. Jagger himself had added lyrics ('I was born in a crossfire hurricane . . .') and a title, 'Jumpin' Jack Flash', little more than an in-joke between himself and Richard, whose size-fourteen-footed gardener, Jack Dyer, could be seen padding lugubriously around the Redlands moat.

'Flash' was previewed to a delirious audience at the New Musical Express Poll-Winners concert on 12 May. The Stones made a ten-minute cameo (as had the Beatles two years before) amidst almost nostalgic chaos: commissionaires fought with fans as Jagger threw his shoes into the crowd. They also released a promotional film to accompany the song. The crude lighting and tinsel sets then redolent of pop videos were literally shaken to their foundations; to a surreal backdrop the Stones, barefoot, faces smeared with warpaint, strutted, scowled and snarled for three minutes, Jagger's lips at one stage appearing to fellate the camera lens. ('Wicked,' says Richard.) The record was released on 24 May and promptly made number one.

Things now began to happen in earnest. There was renewed talk of a tour. Jagger was said to be 'actively considering' the film scripts delivered daily to Maddox Street. A new accountant, Fred Trowbridge, was hired to prise cash out of Klein and in late May handed Jagger cheques for

$11,250 (his guarantee from London Records) and $21,500 for song-writing royalties. It was, said Stewart, 'incredibly exciting, like nothing could go wrong.' Almost inevitably, Jones was arrested again.

At seven-thirty in the morning of 21 May four policemen variously shouting, knocking and, in one case, climbing in the rubbish-chute to his King's Road flat found cannabis inside a ball of blue wool in Jones's desk. According to police records the following ensued:

Dt. Constable Prentice:	I have just found this ball of wool in this drawer.
Jones:	Oh, no. This can't happen again, just when we're getting on our feet.
Dt. Sergeant Constable:	Is this your wool?
Jones:	It could be.
Constable:	When Prentice showed me the wool, you seemed to recognize it immediately.
Jones:	Why do you always have to pick on me? I've been working all day and night promoting our new record, and now this has to happen.
Constable:	I am arresting you and you will be taken to Chelsea police station where you will be charged with possessing cannabis.
Jones:	I never take the stuff. It makes me so paranoid.

Two hours later Jones appeared at Marlborough Street Magistrates Court; he pleaded innocent and was bailed to appear on 11 June. 'Our hearts,' says Wyman, 'sank.'

Ironically, Jones's arrest took place at the very moment he had forsworn drugs. Keylock states that after leaving Roehampton 'Brian started to clean up – to the extent of being a boozer, not a doper'. Suspicions were further raised when Keylock was invited to the Regent Palace Hotel by a policeman who promised to 'lose' the alleged evidence for a consideration. The general feeling was that, as with Sanchez's effort, it would be wasted.

Jones was one of two predominant problems for Jagger that early summer. The other was Klein. After the initial 'You want it – you got it' euphoria wore off, relations with New York had cooled to open enmity. By 1968 there were difficulties in extracting even basic expenses. In February Stewart telexed melodramatically: 'You are already aware of the fact that we are destitute, the boys are destitute, and only you can save us.' Later that spring Jagger himself signed a message ending: 'The phones and electricity will be cut off tomorrow. Also the rent is due. I am having to run the office despite your wishes. If you would like to remedy this please do so.' Bergman, in a private memo to Jagger, added: 'The Klein problem is more than a drag. We're puppets. How can you work, or the office, if we have to spend so much time pleading for bread or whatever? It's never going to be efficient till that is straightened out.'

Meanwhile Oldham served writs against Gideon Music, Mirage, Essex, Decca, London Records, Nanker-Phelge – and Klein. He claimed the last had 'diverted assets . . . for his own personal use and benefit'. In October the suit moved to the High Court in London, where Oldham was eventually persuaded to settle for a million dollars (payable on the instalment plan). That left only the Securities & Exchange Commission and IRS interested in Klein's activities. By this time, says Keylock, Jagger had 'had it' with the man he openly referred to as Fatso; not only was Klein dilatory in providing – as Jagger saw it – the Stones' own money, he made the cardinal error of alienating his two principal employers. Jagger was said to be 'incandescent' when his younger brother, much given to Himalayan trekking, was stranded in Kathmandu by Klein's failure to wire funds. Later Keylock had to fly to New York with instructions not to return without sufficient cash to buy Richard's new house.

Jagger's interest was piqued. According to Faithfull, 'Mick's obsession with business matters resulted from the problems he was having with Klein ... Mick really hated him ... It all began when [Jagger] suspected that Allen wasn't giving him a fair shake on the accounting ... All of the records were tied up by Klein so that the royalties went to Klein first and then to the Stones ... And, of course, Mick mightily resented getting what was left over rather than getting the chief cut of the pie. One thing about Mick is that he has a great head on his shoulders and he learns very fast ... He realized he could just as easily use Klein's tactics to make a record deal without using Klein.'

In public Jagger openly hinted that Klein's services would be required more seldom in future. In private he appointed the solicitors Berger Oliver to open a parallel accounting system. They wrote to New York demanding records of the Stones' tour receipts for 1966–7, as well as details of record guarantees and song-writing royalties for 'our client, Mr Michael Jagger'.

Jagger it was who negotiated a fifty thousand dollar fee with Jean-Luc Godard for the latter to shoot the Stones as part of a feature originally entitled *One Plus One*. Godard arrived in the studio and witnessed the genesis of a song whose title, he realized, was the perfect come-on for his film. 'Sympathy for the Devil' originally started life as an acoustic blues. Watts and the session pianist Nicky Hopkins accelerated it to a samba. Richard added guitar and a chorus including Jagger, Pallenberg and Keylock the 'oo-oos' that became its trademark. The title was another product of the Indica Bookshop. *The Master and Margarita*, Bulgakov's existentialist Soviet novel translated in 1967, leads with Satan crooning 'Permit me to introduce myself' – the hook for 'Sympathy'. Jagger, the A-level historian, added touches of the Russian Revolution, Hitler and Kennedy. 'It was just Mick writing an essay,' says Keylock; 'I remember him laughing about it in the studio.'

The question of satanism remained. At Kenneth Anger's request Jagger composed the soundtrack for a film called *Invocation of My Demon Brother*; later he was abortively cast in the title role of Anger's *Lucifer Rising*. Certainly Pallenberg periodically dabbled in black magic. (She actually once pierced a wax effigy of Jones, causing him, apparently, to suffer stomach pains.) While a number of the group's more credulous fans saw 'Sympathy' as a call to the dark arts it was, like most of Jagger's output, ironic. 'The whole thing,' says Keylock, 'was a wind-up. I never saw anyone less satanic than Mick. He even wore a crucifix.'

The demonic tendency also showed on 'Stray Cat Blues', a paean to illicit sex recorded Velvet Underground-style. (Played an early version of 'Cat', Pallenberg uttered crisply, 'It's crap.' The song was re-mixed.) 'Salt of the Earth' was derived from 'All You Need Is Love'; 'Dear Doctor' (sung in mock drawl) from country blues. The title of the album itself, *Beggar's Banquet*, was suggested by Gibbs. Eventually released in America in November 1968 and Britain before Christmas, *Banquet* reached number five and number three respectively – modest for a record once described as Jagger's favourite. The critics concurred: 'The Stones come to terms with violence more explicitly than before and in so doing are forced to take up the subject of politics (*sic*),' wrote Jon Landau. 'The result is the most sophisticated and meaningful statement we can expect to hear concerning the two themes – violence and politics – that will probably dominate the rock of 1969.' According to *International Times*, the LP 'retained the cynicism and drive of earlier albums but replaced the roughness with intrinsic thematic simplicity'.

More pointedly, *Rolling Stone* noted, 'The Stones have returned and are bringing back rock and roll with them . . . Their new album will mark a point in the short history of rock: the formal end of all the pretentious, non-musical, boring, insignificant, self-conscious and worthless stuff that has been tolerated in the past year in the absence of any standards set by the several great figures in rock and roll. *Beggar's Banquet* should be the mark of this change, for it was *Their Satanic Majesties Request* which was the prototype of junk masquerading as meaningful.'

Banquet was mixed by Jagger, Richard and Jimmy Miller – a New Yorker previously involved with Spencer Davis and Traffic – in Hollywood. On 26 July 1968, his twenty-fifth birthday, Jagger appeared theatrically at Tony Sanchez's club in London. Among the guests were Lennon, McCartney and Paul Getty. *Banquet* was ceremonially played and received until, in Sanchez's words:

> McCartney discreetly handed me a record and told me, 'See what you think of it, Tony. It's our new one.' I stuck the record on the sound system, and the slow thundering build-up of 'Hey Jude' shook the club. I turned the record over, and we all heard John Lennon's nasal voice pumping out 'Revolution'. When it was over, I noticed that Mick looked peeved. The Beatles had upstaged him.

The evening ended, Sanchez adds, when Robert Fraser, newly rehabilitated from his drug habit, 'slipped a small polythene bag from the pocket of his velvet jacket' and suggested that Jagger inhale the contents.

Fraser's was one influence on Jagger. Away from it he still inhabited the world of Stewart, of Keylock, of Thorogood. He drank; he joked. He carried on. He was genuinely fond of 'characters' with their tough-guy patter and approvingly dubbed Keylock 'Mr Get-It-Together'. On his birthday he bought him cufflinks. At the King's Head in Cheyne Walk they drank vodka together. Keylock also introduced another factotum, Alan Dunn; at weekends they, Jagger and Faithfull drove to Redlands. There conditions deteriorated: Richard and Pallenberg existed in constant twilight, drapes hermetically drawn, Thorogood's wall precluding visitors. Cash lay in bundles on tables, in drawers, under kitchen appliances. Whereas Jagger, in Pallenberg's phrase, 'insisted on sheets' Richard slept, if at all, on the floor. Once he awoke to drive his Bentley at speed into the garden shed. Meals were chaotic, the food invariably surplus to requirements – whole steaks jettisoned or thrown to Richard's pet hound Syphillis. Sundays found Jagger driving – 'and very badly', notes Thorogood – to the relative sanity of Chelsea.

There he baffled visitors by appearing strident one instant, almost satisfied the next. Richard himself noted that '. . . because everybody has a different idea of what or who Mick is, he's confused himself'. One day Jagger watched football at Stamford Bridge. The next he took Jack Nitzsche to the ballet and instructed him to 'look pretty because you're going with me'. (Later, says Nitzsche, the party sat down in a restaurant, 'and then Mick left . . . I think he did it just to make an entrance'.) Later still he appeared alone, watching cricket in the members' stand at The Oval. While *International Times* urged him to join the revolution, Jagger joined the Country Gentlemen's Association.

He continued to act as a surrogate father. This was one area, all agreed, where Jagger consistently excelled. In June it was learned that Faithfull was pregnant. 'Groovy,' Jagger announced. 'I'm very happy about Marianne having our baby. We'll probably have another three. But marriage? Can't see it happening . . . We just don't believe in it.' The theme was echoed in a special edition of the *David Frost Programme* on 6 September. Confronted as before by the official opposition, now represented by the headmistress Mary Whitehouse, Jagger gave a summary defence – 'I don't see how you can talk about this bond [marriage] which is inseparable when the Christian Church accepts divorce' – while omitting to mention that he had asked Faithfull to marry him and been refused.

'Mick,' she noted later, 'had very little insight about himself. I often heard him say that he'd rather not know what he's like. "I am what I am," he used to say, "and everything just happens, doesn't it? So I let things happen to me and then react." That's just the way Mick was, but I can't complain ... I chose to live with Mick. I made that decision. And then I hated it and resented it. I hated so much being in the shadow of somebody like that. I really felt hunted and used. I felt that all my experiences were being drained as if by a vampire and used by him in his work, and it left nothing for me.' For this and other reasons the lovers remained just that; there were periodic suggestions of marriage, periodically declined and Faithfull, in fact, was divorced from Dunbar only in 1971. Keylock was surprised to see Jagger, notoriously reluctant to display his feelings, 'visibly knocked out' at the prospect of fatherhood. Others noted the obvious pleasure he took in children's company.

Jagger now reverted his attention to Jones. During the recording of *Banquet* the Stones' lead guitarist had been virtually invisible. On some nights he appeared only to fall asleep. 'What can I play?' he once asked. 'I don't know,' said Jagger. 'What *can* you play?' Legend maintains that at this stage, summer 1968, Jagger and Richard conspired to remove Jones from the group. He was, the theory goes, an embarrassment. No good. No use. *Non compos*. Nothing.

The truth, as so often with the Stones, is different. Jagger resented Jones, but he resented him on one level only: his failure to contribute. Shirley Arnold, the group's fan-club secretary, notes that 'there was this friction between them ... Mick was very creative and must have felt Brian was holding him back'. Korner, too, believed 'they kept quiet about the fact Brian wasn't really playing on the albums, which shows understanding. They were very creditable ... They tried to look after him as best they could.' Jagger today describes the whole episode as 'sad'.

It was his well-meaning idea that Jones spend the summer alternately at Stargroves and Redlands, away from the attentions of the Chelsea police. Jagger and Faithfull would visit periodically. Keylock remembers an evening in late August when Jones – enraged at Jagger characterizing him as 'paranoid' – struck out dementedly with his fists. (Contrary to folklore, there was no knife.) Other days the two would sit alone discussing Jones's trial. In private Jagger brooded about Faithfull's prognosis – 'Brian's in danger. He's going to die' – and as to whether to finally replace him in the group. Aloud he said nothing.

Jones's hearing was on 26 September. In the court autumn light fell on the green-and-white check walls – the check of schools or psychiatric wards. The judge was the same who had sentenced Jones the previous October. Keylock and Poitier sat in the gallery. In a high tremulous voice Jones said he had rented the flat while his new house was being decorated. He knew nothing of any cannabis. 'The first thing I heard was a loud banging at the door. I did not immediately become aware of what it was. A minute might have passed before I knew it was something very intent on entering the flat. I put on a caftan – kimono sort of thing – went to the door and looked through the spy hole.'

'What did you see?'

'Three large men.'

'Who did you think they were?'

'Police, perhaps, or' – Jones's voice fell dramatically – 'agents.'

'Of the police?'

'Yes. Since last year I seem to have had an inborn fear of the police.'

To his defence counsel Jones added: 'When the ball of wool was shown to me I was absolutely shattered. I felt everything swim. I don't knit. I don't darn socks. I don't have a girlfriend who darns socks. I did not have the slightest knowledge that the ball of wool was in the flat. It was such an important time in the group's life. We had not had a record out in a long time and we were just promoting one. We had the feeling that this new record was going to lead us on the road back to success. The trouble involving me and two other members of the group –'

As if on cue Jagger and Richard entered the court and sat in the public gallery surrounded by schoolgirls. The judge looked up through his pince-nez at Jagger's green velvet jacket, yellow scarf, his black hat. There was a pause. Jagger removed the hat. The judge finally addressed the jury, reminding them that the burden of proof rested not on Jones but the police – whose case was entirely circumstantial. No evidence of cannabis use had been found, no ash, no cigarette ends. 'If you think the prosecution has proved without a doubt that the defendant knew the cannabis was in his flat, you must find him guilty. Otherwise, he is innocent.'

'Groovy,' said Jagger.

Outside in the hall he and Richard signed autographs. Poitier beamed. Keylock timed the jury: forty-seven minutes. As the foreman announced 'guilty' Jones slumped to his seat, head in hands. Jagger's shoulders were heaving. After a pause the judge continued in his musical cackle: 'I think this was a lapse and I don't want to interfere with the probation order that already applies to this man. I am going to fine you according to your means.' (Fifty pounds with a hundred guineas costs.) 'You must keep clear of this stuff. For goodness' sake, don't get into trouble again.'

Outside Jones and Jagger danced.

The new house referred to was Cotchford Farm in Sussex, once the home of A. A. Milne. Jones moved in in November. The literary connection enchanted him; the garden was dotted with sundials and statues, under one of which the original manuscript of *Winnie The Pooh* was said to be buried. A swimming pool had been added. Jones promptly diverted Thorogood from Redlands with the brief to restore the farm exactly as Milne had known it, pool excepted. He announced his intention to live there for the remainder of his life.

When he bought Cotchford Jones practically ceased to function as a musician. He gave up even the pretence of recording. In late November he ad-libbed his way through the *David Frost Programme*; after that, nothing. Thorogood, with whom he shared a bottle of wine most evenings, states categorically that 'Brian's priority, bar none, was the house. When he talked about the Stones it was always in the third person. Not that he complained about Mick or Keith . . . It was just old friends growing apart.'

Jones continued to draw on the group's considerable resources. Shirley Arnold, Janey Perrin and Joan Keylock became used to the familiar late-night call demanding guitar strings, money or merely moral support. He invariably announced himself on the phone as 'Nuisance'. Not the least of Jones's qualities was his ability to analyse his own predicament: 'I wouldn't be in this mess,' he once told Keylock, 'if I'd lived with you.' Later Jones arrived for dinner at the Keylocks' wearing his stage clothes and make-up. He was told to come back dressed normally. Even his new housekeeper, Mary Hallett, became a mother figure. They used to read the Bible together.

All this exasperated Jagger. It irked him. He may have carped at Jones, but much of it was simply professional frustration. By late 1968 Jagger was bored and talking of touring. The group's immigration status, already precarious, was further threatened by Jones's conviction. (Keylock remembers Jagger assiduously courting Lord Harlech, former British Ambassador to Washington and Walter Annenberg, his opposite number in London.) There were other, practical, considerations: it became rare, says Thorogood, for Jones to leave Cotchford; reaching London was almost imperial status. As for touring – 'forget it'. All this was received by Jagger as he drafted the group's strategy.

The first step, manifestly, was releasing *Banquet*. Originally scheduled for July, it remained in cold storage three months later. The problem was the cover – a pastiche of a bathroom wall designed by Jagger and Richard. The graffiti ('Lyndon Loves Mao', 'I sit broken-hearted', 'God rolls his own') was one thing, the etching of a nude girl on a drainpipe another. What really distinguished it was the scrawled reference to a senior Decca executive. When Edward Lewis saw that he pulled *Banquet* forthwith. 'We don't find it offensive,' Jagger retaliated. 'Decca have put out a record [*Atomic Tom Jones*] with an atom bomb exploding on the cover – I find *that* more offensive than graffiti.'

Lewis insisted: no airbrush, no album. Jagger simmered. Klein flew in from New York. In November the Stones recorded a song aptly entitled 'You Can't Always Get What You Want'. Jagger, with much muttering and intimations as to the future, succumbed; *Banquet* was released with a white cover eerily reminiscent of *The Beatles* a month earlier.

Keylock was dispatched to arrange a suitable launch. He tried hiring the Tower of London. A small tremor passed at the name given. Several restaurants were sounded and found equally unwilling. Finally a booking was made at the Elizabethan Room of the Gore Hotel. On 4 December Jagger, Jones, Wyman and Watts (Richard was lost) appeared dressed as beggars for the seven-course banquet. Keylock had done his homework: wenches served boar's head in claret, as well as port and malmsey; clay pipes were smoked. Snuff was ingested. Even Jones looked animated. At this point Jagger stood up in his collarless shirt, top hat and frock coat, announcing: 'I hope you've had enough to eat and drink. We didn't ask you here to enjoy yourselves, did we?' He opened a cardboard box.

For ten minutes the place resembled a silent film set. Pies were thrown. With one creamy swoop Jagger wiped out Jones and Watts; Wyman followed. Keylock planted two on either side of Lord Harlech's head, which hung there like fluffy earmuffs. ('I'm here because Mick is a friend of mine,' Harlech said later – no one detecting the presence of irony.) The ensuing mêlée was replayed on *News at Ten*, as was 'Street Fighting Man'; 'great publicity,' said Jagger. Later he wrote and apologized to the Gore Hotel.

Faithfull, meanwhile, had experienced a complicated pregnancy in a rented mansion in Eire. At weekends Jagger appeared with a Harley Street doctor, Victor Bloom. In early November she flew to London; on the twenty-first she entered a nursing home in Avenue Road, St John's Wood, where, the following day, she miscarried. According to an interview, to the question 'Why did I lose the baby?' Faithfull's doctor reached across the desk, took her right arm at the wrist, and turned it slowly and dramatically until the inside of her elbow was face up: *My God, he thinks I'm a junkie*. The official explanation was that the baby was lost when Faithfull's waters broke due to her uterus being insufficiently strong. The child, had it lived, would have been a girl called Carina.

Faithfull's miscarriage proved a turning point. Both parties were affected, perhaps more markedly so Jagger. He had the newly delivered cot removed from Cheyne Walk. He bought Faithfull roses. He faced the press. Later the mood altered. Faithfull, according to Sanchez, sought refuge with a succession of lovers, himself included; Jagger, not averse to the same course of action, returned to *Beggar's Banquet*. In the New Year he met and bedded an American singer-actress, Marsha Hunt, an Afro-haired exotic of known intelligence. By spring 1969 Keylock was driving Jagger to Hunt's flat in Marlborough Place, St John's Wood. 'He came like a golden eagle with a broken wing, and I suppose he believed I had the willingness and capacity to bandage it up and help him soar,' she announced. 'She listens,' said Jagger.

Hunt brought at least partial relief from Jagger's continuing battle with Decca. Sanchez quotes him as promising, 'Those bastards won't get away with [the cover]. I've got one or two ideas how we can get our own back.' Keylock, too, remembers Jagger 'ranting' about his record company. 'Three more albums,' he muttered. 'Three . . . more . . . albums.' In public he adopted a different tone:

> 'What really worries me is the principle of being dictated to over our product by our distributors. I am opposed to all forms of censorship. The only censorship one can have is by the artists themselves, which we do subconsciously anyway.'

By that time Edward Lewis may have been one of Jagger's two least favourite people. Klein was the other. Before Christmas near-daily requests issued from Maddox Street for money. Jagger tried pleading, persuasion, he tried threatening. A typical message from the group's accountants read: 'I explained to you the absolute urgency of dealing with the outstanding information we require . . . Allen, I must stress that our clients' best interests are being prejudiced by failure to return this outstanding information which only you can provide . . . PS, we are still awaiting, also, funds in order to settle the £13,000 tax liability that is now overdue in respect of the past remuneration for Rolling Stones Ltd.'

To Keylock, Jagger continued to speak openly of 'dumping Fatso'. When, in January 1969, the Beatles requested a reference for Klein they were advised to proceed with caution. Jagger later vigorously denied having recommended his manager's services to Lennon; Jeff Griffin, a BBC producer, was told, 'I didn't foist Allen on John. Allen foisted himself.'

Jagger was never in serious danger of destitution. He continued to receive annual guarantees, while song-writing with Richard made them infinitely the wealthiest Stones. Even so, with two houses, a wardrobe and Faithfull to maintain he may have realized that, rich as he was, he could be richer. That was exactly how he put it, says Keylock, the Jagger of objectives, of strategy, of methods, ambitious Jagger. Because he was ambitious. The word might have been made for him.

In May 1968 Jagger finally found a film script he liked, Donald Cammell persuading him to play a parody of himself in *Performance*. While Jagger considered this a challenge, the studio viewed it on a different level – a sort of adult *Hard Day's Night*. Cammell even received a message enquiring if the 'other boys' would be available. (They weren't.) Jagger arrived for shooting in September briefed by Faithfull to 'play it like Brian – only more so'.

He himself had a contrasting view. Before filming he announced, 'It's not supposed to be a comedy, but James Fox and I are going to make it into a comedy. The cat I play is not really a pop musician . . . He's like me, he's a freak.' To Dunn or Keylock, who collected him from the set in Lowndes Square every evening, he rapidly confided, 'It's getting fucking heavy.' Some nights he fell asleep before even reaching Cheyne Walk.

Much of *Performance*'s tension centred around Pallenberg, a profusion of blonde zigzagging hair and green catlike eyes. Richard's girlfriend was cast as Jagger's lover. The script called for them to simulate sex – or, failing that, to do what came naturally. Such was the zeal of the resulting performance that it eventually won first prize in a Dutch blue movie festival.

Performance was basically the tale of Turner (Jagger), a professional recluse with only Pallenberg and an androgynous French girl (Michele Breton) as company. A fleeing hoodlum (Fox) takes sanctuary. In the course of the film he undergoes initiation into group sex, drugs and other rituals before emerging in full camp regalia and make-up. After filming Fox suffered a nervous breakdown and joined an obscure religious sect, the Navigators; '*Performance*', he told the *Daily Mail*, 'gave me doubts about my way of life . . . After that everything changed.' The film could only have been made in the sixties.

Jagger, too, spent much of *Performance* wearing female cosmetics. He also, to achieve the mood, smoked DMT – a drug so violently hallucinogenic it causes tiny haemorrhages around the brain. When he arrived on set (late, having visited the pregnant Faithfull in Ireland) there was almost palpable suspicion among the sixty-eight actors, technicians and crew variously present: Who does this wide-eyed, mumbling and likely moronic pop star think he is? The answer was immediate - Jagger was a professional. On the first day he rehearsed a scene with Fox a dozen times without complaint. When the cameraman Mike Molloy had wooden marks hammered into the floor Jagger ordered them removed and played the ensuing scene without flaw. Cammell and his co-director, Nic Roeg, considered this outstanding.

Richard, meanwhile, complained acidly about the evident realism of Jagger's and Pallenberg's love scenes. He retaliated by refusing to cooperate on the single required for the film's soundtrack, 'Memo From Turner'. According to an interview he gave in 1984, Cammell was compelled to take Jagger into a pub in Berwick Street and ask, ' "Mick, for God's sake, what about the *song*?" Standing there at the bar, he suddenly burst into tears. It was a thing he could always do for maximum effect – just like John Gielgud. "I'm sorry," he said. "I blew it." It was then that I realized he'd decided to get the song finished. From then on, after all that indecisiveness, the decisions were made like *lightning*.' Jagger also, in Keylock's hearing, apologized to Richard. 'We're all one big family,' he announced. Faithfull's comment was unrecorded.

Performance languished for two years, during which Jagger's mood grew less sanguine. 'As a film,' he noted, 'it really wasn't successful, so therefore I wasn't very successful in it . . . I wasn't portraying myself, and that's precisely what people thought I was – but then that's what acting is. Making people believe that's what you are.' A relay of editors went to work on the film, eventually spawning no fewer than five separate versions, none of them acceptable to Jagger and Cammell, who telegrammed Warner Brothers:

Re: *Performance*: This film is about the perverted love affair between Homo Sapiens and Lady Violence. In common with its subject, it is necessarily horrifying, paradoxical and absurd. To make such a film means accepting that the subject is loaded with every taboo in the book.

You seem to want to emasculate (1) the most savage and (2) the most affectionate scenes in our movie. If *Performance* does not upset audiences it is nothing. If this fact upsets you, the alternative is to sell it fast and no more bullshit. Your misguided censorship will ultimately diminish said audiences both in quality and quantity.

Performance was eventually screened in January 1971 and earned Jagger faint praise. It was never generally released.

He followed it by appearing in *Ned Kelly*, a yarn about the eponymous Australian outlaw. Jagger was hired by the director Tony Richardson, responsible both on stage and celluloid for a number of authentic successes. *Kelly* was not one of them. Laden with a never-delivered message, the film was Jagger's own *Girl On A Motorcycle*: an unadulterated flop that saw him deliver a series of inane one-liners in a vague Irish brogue. At one stage he was injured when a prop pistol exploded in his hand.

When *Kelly* premiered in June 1970 Jagger commented, 'That was a load of shit ... I only made it because I had nothing to do. I knew Tony Richardson was a reasonable director and I thought he'd make a reasonable film. The thing is, you never know until you do it whether a film will turn out to be a load of shit, and if it does all you can say is, "Well, that was a load of shit," and try to make sure you don't do anything like it again.'

So it proved. Other than concert films and videos *Kelly* was Jagger's last wide-screen performance for over twenty years. In the interim he was said to have considered *Ishtar* and *A Star Is Born*, in the roles made infamous by Warren Beatty and Kris Kristofferson respectively. Gore Vidal's *Kalki* was also plotted but never filmed. In January 1971 Jagger held discussions with William Burroughs and the director Anthony Balch about starring in the former's *Naked Lunch*. A decade later he was to fly to the Peruvian jungle to shoot *Fitzcarraldo*, Werner Herzog's allegory of a man hauling a river steamer over a mountain. For two months Jagger squatted in mud huts terrified of rats and afraid to eat. Jason Robards, his co-star, dropped out with dysentery. Jagger himself fell ill. In Paris, meanwhile, his girlfriend began to receive letters indicating he was lonely. On a whim she flew to Lima, then on to Pukalpa – 'no streets, just dirt, and no taxis, just buzzards in the road' – and finally Iquito, where 'as soon as we landed all these Indians – real Indians all painted with loincloths and stuff – came over and got my suitcase and put me in a canoe ... They rowed me down the river and I rowed up next to the steamer and there was Mick, sitting there in the sun playing backgammon with someone from the crew.'

In the end, due to the usual commitments, Jagger abandoned *Fitzcarraldo*. His part was written out. He was said to be 'disappointed', even 'devastated'; for eight weeks he had had the scrutiny of the cameras and accomplished nothing.

Other than a cameo in Hans Christian Andersen's *The Nightingale* on cable TV (Jagger in pigtail and silk kimono), that was all until 1992. In his search for the elusive role ('I like to do films, but I don't want to do the kind of films that people want me to do, which is to always play rock and roll singers') Jagger selected a futuristic thriller. *Freejack* – wherein healthy humans are catapulted through time to undergo mandatory brain transplants – earned mixed reviews. Jagger, a black-clad mercenary paid to encourage unwilling donors, was said to be 'the world's most unlikely hard man', 'not bad' and 'embarrassing' in a film described by the critic Barry Norman as 'urgently needing a brain transplant of its own'. There were inevitable rumours that he took the part only for money. Jagger's own interpretation was different: 'I loved watching Errol Flynn as a boy – all that swashbuckling.' ('Having a good time', without recourse to the demands of art or money, remains Jagger's stated intention to this day.) 'Now here I am in an action film and it's great, a bit like *Bladerunner*, and I get to have lots of fire-fights, shooting high-tech machine guns which is what boys like.' Critics agreed that Jagger exuded more strength and appeal of body than of soul. They directed his attention to television.

Television was Jagger's next project in 1968. On 10–12 December the Stones were joined by Lennon, Clapton, The Who, by jugglers, plate-spinners and midgets in *The Rock and Roll Circus*, a Christmas revue noted tartly by Wyman as 'conceived by Mick and financed by the band'. Filming took place at Wembley. In the resulting chaos a female trapeze artiste hung overhead as pianist Julius Katchen played Brahms. The midgets, freaks and clowns all plied their small concerns. A cowboy on horseback announced The Who, who proceeded to steal the show – *Tommy* was previewed with unequalled ferocity. A bouquet of flowers arrived at the group's office the next morning accompanied by a note: 'Thank you for working so hard on the television show – really. Mick.'

After an interval by a hastily arranged supergroup (Lennon, Clapton, Richard) the Stones themselves emerged at three a.m. Their set, a weird amalgam of the old ('Route 66') and new ('You Can't Always Get What You Want') climaxed with six separate takes of 'Sympathy', in the latter stages of which the audience was barely conscious. Jagger ripped off his scarlet T-shirt to reveal a leering tattooed Satan on his chest. The drums crashed, the house lights came up but the applause failed to occur.

Circus was never aired. According to Wyman, 'when Mick saw the rushes of the shoot, he insisted that our appearances were below standard, since we'd gone on so late and so tired; the audience, too, lacked spark in the film for the same reason. He had a re-shoot costed, but this came to £10,300 and nothing was done.' Keylock, characteristically, is more specific: 'He thought he'd been upstaged by The Who. I remember him moaning about it that night.' The group left Wembley at six a.m. drawn and depressed, the surreal aspects of the *Circus* reinforced by the presence of Elsa Smith, Jagger's relief teacher at primary school. She was found outside hectoring the few lingering fans about 'young Mike'. Keylock was delegated to quietly remove her.

'Roots,' writes Wyman, 'have always been essential to me, and to a lesser extent to Charlie. Mick, Keith and Brian were much more nomadic; to this day, Mick doesn't seem content to stay in one location for more than a couple of months.'

On 18 December Jagger, Richard, Pallenberg, Faithfull and Faithfull's son – a quintet impossible to envisage a month earlier – flew to Lima, among their other motives being an expressed interest in Inca mythology; they wanted to study the 'inner tension' of ancient cultures. Immediately on arrival there was evidence of tension at the Crillon Hotel where Jagger was barred from appearing bare-chested in the lobby. Declining the manager's request to dress more soberly the party moved to the adjacent Hotel Bolivar where Jagger and Richard wrote a song entitled 'Let It Bleed'. Later they sailed to Rio de Janeiro. Even there they were rumoured to be dabbling in drugs, Satanism, or worse. 'We're hoping to see this magician,' noted Richard cryptically.

The group spent Christmas in a wooden hut of military decor near Recife. Each morning Jagger and Faithfull's son walked alone on the beach. They sang. They swam. They hunted for sand crabs. According to a 1974 interview, Faithfull considered this 'a fantastic relationship for a grown man and a little boy . . . Except Mick is not quite grown in many ways – he's still a boy with high spirits.' She also admitted to being 'happier [than] in several years'. When Jagger returned in February he announced himself 'raring to go' to Keylock. Immediately he produced a single for Faithfull called 'Something Better'. Lest this be taken as evidence of more permanent stability, the B-side was entitled 'Sister Morphine'. The lyrics ('Here I lie in my hospital bed . . .') were Faithfull's own.

Jagger himself returned to the studio. The Stones convened to record *Let It Bleed*; they hired a sixty-strong choir to complete 'You Can't Always Get What You Want' and taped an authentic Delta blues, 'Love In Vain'. The first quarter of the new year was busy. In spring Richard took possession of 3 Cheyne Walk, a Queen Anne mansion two hundred yards from Jagger's, the idea being for them to collaborate more freely on songs. Keylock remembers a prototype of 'Honky Tonk Women' being played in

Jagger's conservatory, though Sanchez says the same number was 'bashed out on an old honky-tonk piano' in his nightclub; 'Gimme Shelter' and 'Midnight Rambler' also took shape in the unlikely setting of a Chelsea drawing room. By May Jagger and Richard were convinced the new album would equal, perhaps exceed, the level of *Banquet*. Richard began to talk about touring behind the LP. Jagger wanted the money. Nineteen sixty-nine, he repeatedly stated, would be the group's *annus mirabilis*. He announced the release of a greatest hits collection, *Through The Past Darkly*.

This seemingly simple project – another milestone down the road towards divorcing Decca – caused Jagger inordinate grief. Early in the year he wrote to the graphic designer M. C. Escher:

Dear Maurits,

For quite a time now I have had in my possession your book and it never ceases to amaze me ... In fact I think your work is quite incredible and it would make me very happy for a lot more people to see and know and understand exactly what you are doing. In March or April we have scheduled our next LP record for release, and I am most eager to reproduce one of your works on the cover-sleeve. Would you please consider either designing a 'picture' for it, or have you any unpublished works which you might think suitable?

A reply from Escher which Keylock saw read:

Some days ago I received a letter from Mr Jagger asking me either to design a picture or to place at his disposal unpublished work to reproduce on the cover-sleeve for a record. My answer to both questions must be no ... By the way, please tell Mr Jagger I am not Maurits to him, but very sincerely, [signed] M. C. Escher.

Next Jagger complained in a telex to Klein, 'Your inefficiency is a drag. What the fuck did you do with all the photographs [for *Darkly*]? They were supposed to be delivered to Andy Warhol. We await your reply.'

Finally, on 21 May the Stones assembled for a photoshoot at St Katharine's Dock. They were pictured with their faces leering through a shattered pane of glass. The ensuing octagonal cover caused further friction with the Decca art department. ('Two to go . . .' said Jagger.) The album was eventually released in September and promptly made number one.

Richard was delighted with *Darkly*. Jagger spoke exclusively of design costs and expenses. By mid-1969 his frustration at Klein's accounting system – at the group's finances generally – bordered on mania. He insisted that the Stones tour America and Europe forthwith, excluding Fatso from the arrangements. He also instituted personal economies; money, says Keylock, 'didn't exactly flow' to Jagger's employees. Even Faithfull was restricted to twenty-five pounds per week. Larger sums, meanwhile, not involving notes and coins, continued to change hands freely. Stargroves was bought on a whim for twenty-five thousand pounds. In late 1968 Jagger also purchased a cottage for Faithfull's mother. He freely gave money to old acquaintances, including Wentworth School. When, a decade later, Sid Vicious – not known as an admirer of the Stones – was charged with murder, Jagger spontaneously offered to pay for his defence.

'Mick,' said Stewart, 'could always sit down to dinner and remember three hours later who had the scampi and who had the prawn curry.' He exercised stringent personal control over the Stones' expenses. Keylock and Bergman were explicitly instructed to decline requests from political causes. Begging letters went unanswered. In the King's Head Jagger frequently omitted to buy a round. His sponsor might be rewarded weeks, sometimes years, later by an

Above Mike *(left)* and Chris Jagger on holiday in Marbella, 1953. The guitar stayed in the closet for the next ten years. *(Popperfoto)*

Right MJ at home with Wentworth County schoolfriends *(Gareth Bolton)*

Left 'A complete hair fetishist': MJ at the Ealing Jazz Club, 1962. *(Rex)*

Right Jagger at the time the Rolling Stones signed with Decca, 1963. *(Tom Keylock)*

Opposite MJ *(fourth row down, fourth from left)* in his Tommy Steele phase, Dartford Grammar, 1960. Clive Robson stands to his right. *(Anthony Smith)*

Left MJ leaving the Wolverhampton Traffic Court (complete with *Daily Telegraph*) in November 1964. His solicitor had assured the judge 'my client has no fleas'. *(PA)*

Below Jagger allowed, even encouraged, this shot in the BBC make-up department, 1966. *(Rex)*

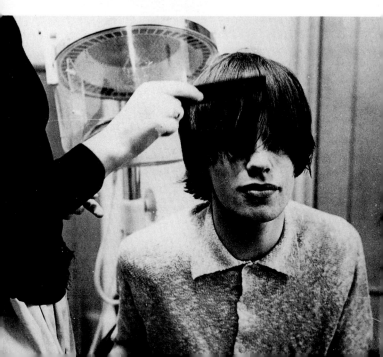

King of the Scene. *(Rex)*

Doing the frug with Cher; Michael Caine looks on. Meanwhile, Jagger's affair with Faithfull had become official. *(Rex)*

Left Performing on the Eamonn Andrews show, 5 February 1967 – the night Jagger announced he was suing the *News of the World*. (Hulton-Deutsch)

Below Keith rolls his own in Morocco. (Tom Keylock)

'The visually suggestive symbolism that sparks the mass orgy.'
(*Pictorial Press*)

Leaving the committal hearing in Chichester, 10 May 1967.
Jones was arrested the same day. *(Popperfoto)*

expensive painting. Another paradox: Jagger daily, dementedly, spoke of 'being skint' as he was chauffeured between Chelsea and his country mansion. Like all the then rich he affected to be poor. He had a morbid fear of losing his money.

Klein may have been a contributory factor. By mid-summer Jagger was unable to mention his manager's name calmly. Later he gave an interview in which he stated, 'Half the money I've made has been stolen. Most artists in show business suffer the same kind of thing . . . It's all the hangers-on and parasites. There are very few honest people in the profession.' By June relations between the Stones and New York were openly hostile. Jagger continually carped about living expenses; Richard brooded. 'About then,' said Stewart, 'Mick apparently decided to crack down. I don't think he particularly wanted to get involved in the business. Allen forced him.' Faithfull and Keylock concur: the Jagger of audits and accounts, the Jagger who scrutinized bills and sought ingenious shelters, cost-conscious Jagger, was born that summer. Someone, as he said, had to do it.

When in July Jagger met Rupert Loewenstein, descended, like Faithfull, from Austrian nobility and managing director of bankers Leopold Joseph, the reaction was immediate. Would he, Loewenstein, deliver them from Fatso? Could he undo what Klein had done? Or, in Loewenstein's words: 'He told me that the Stones had been in the grip of a character named Allen Klein who had done them in financially, and he asked whether I would take them as a client . . . I discussed taking on the group with my partners, but they were very much against any involvement, saying it would be bad for the image of the firm. It was very hard to win them over, but I finally prevailed.'

By then Jagger was committed to touring. He had additional plans: a group film was discussed, biographies mooted. Jagger himself accepted the role in *Ned Kelly*. He seemed full of schemes, relieved, so he said, to be working.

Some of this relief was communicated to the group. At weekends Jagger would ring Richard (W. Wittering 31508), Watts (Halland 215), or less frequently Wyman (Rattlesden 499) and Jones (Hartfield 536). To the first he talked constantly about performing. The others received details of recording sessions and dates. When Jones complained of a bad review of *Banquet* he was told not to worry – Jagger himself was 'going into publishing'.

Rolling Stone began life as a faintly subversive San Francisco news-sheet, its title a tribute to its editor Jann Wenner's musical idols. By 1969 the magazine was in danger of being taken seriously. Wenner was bored and talking of moving to Europe. In late March he appeared in London, where discussions took place with Jagger, who enthused about transplanting *Rolling Stone* to Britain with himself as chief executive. A name, Trans-Oceanic Comic Company, was registered and premises taken in Hanover Square. For four giddy weeks it actually seemed possible; the idea was to open a *Rolling Stone* bureau in London, reprinting features from the parent title but under independent editorial control. Jagger, whose capacity to drop projects passes the comprehension of any other dilettante, was said to be 'ecstatic', until it was pointed out that with *Bleed*, *Ned Kelly* and a likely tour his involvement would, at best, be indirect – direct involvement being what he specifically wanted. By Easter the idea had been quietly dropped, with Jagger an estimated ten thousand pounds poorer.

His fortunes fell further when on 28 May he was visited at Cheyne Walk by Sergeant Constable – the same Sergeant Constable who had arrested Jones – and half a dozen colleagues. Reports vary as to what happened next. According to Jagger, 'I didn't get the chance to say anything . . . One of them stuck his foot in the door and the rest came barging in', while in later court testimony he was said to have 'seen police in the street and dashed home through a window shouting, "Marianne, Marianne, don't open the door. They're after the weed."' In both versions Jagger was held in the dining room while Constable searched an antique desk in the study. He returned holding a small wooden box containing a quarter-ounce of cannabis. Jagger and Faithfull were taken to Chelsea police station and charged under the now-familiar Act. At Marlborough Street Court they were each released on fifty pounds bail. The trial hung over them until the following January (after a preliminary hearing on 19 December), when Jagger was fined two hundred pounds with fifty-two pounds costs; Faithfull was acquitted. On the same day the Home Secretary announced plans to 'crack down' on the drug problem generally.

There was a postscript. According to Sanchez's account Jagger was yet again a victim of conspiracy.

— * phoned Marianne to say he could let her have some very cheap heroin. He brought it to the house on Cheyne Walk in two small bags . . . Less than four hours later there was a ring at the door, and as soon as it was opened, the Detective Sergeant and his team burst in . . .

'I just don't know what the hell to do,' [Jagger] told me over the phone that evening. 'The guy who sold the stuff to Marianne says he can fix the forensic lab test on it for two thousand pounds, but I don't trust him. I think he'll take the money and scarper. You know how he ripped off Keith all those times.'

'Let me have a word with Marianne,' I said. 'You're sure it was smack, aren't you?' I asked her.

'No, I'm not sure at all,' she said. 'That's the funny

---

* In his book *Up and Down with the Rolling Stones*, Sanchez names the supplier as 'the man who was "looking after" Brian Jones' – in other words Keylock, who in fact spent a substantial part of his working life keeping drugs away from the group.

thing. I was just trying to tell Mick. It was like snorting talcum powder.'

'Yeah, well, I'll bet it *was* talcum powder,' I said. I surmised that the man had sold Marianne talcum powder, pretending it was heroin. Then he had tipped off the narcs there was heroin in the house, and now he was trying to collect two thousand pounds from Mick for bribing the police analyst.

'I'm certain that bloody bent Sergeant was in on it, too,' said Mick. 'He's probably collecting half the profit.'

Jagger repeated the allegation in print, claiming he had been asked to pay two thousand pounds in order for the police to 'keep their mouths shut'. Constable sued; Scotland Yard investigated; the criminal charges were reviewed. In a subsequent move Constable was transferred from Chelsea and left the Rolling Stones' lives forever. His libel action never came to court.

A further irony of Jagger's arrest was that it jeopardized the group's visa prospects at the very moment these were under debate. At a meeting with Richard at Redlands on 23 May it was agreed that, with two recent convictions, Jones would never be admitted to America. His days as a touring musician were over – and touring was just what the Stones intended. Keylock remembers a number of immediate suggestions as to a replacement: Clapton, Jimmy Page and Paul Kossoff were mentioned, as was Ron Wood, only for his colleague Ronnie Lane to intercept the call and decline it on Wood's behalf. Jagger also canvassed the veteran blues singer John Mayall who suggested a young protégé, Mick Taylor. Taylor was summoned on 30 May. He arrived at Olympic as the Stones were recording 'Honky Tonk Women'. 'I gave them a riff,' he said. 'It seemed to work . . . I still thought I was being auditioned to play just on one album. It wasn't until the end of the session that I realized they were asking me to join them.'

That left the question of Jones. At Cotchford he was living with Poitier and Frank Thorogood; he pottered; he grew plump. Visitors were surprised when they saw what the celebrated dandy now looked like. According to Thorogood, Jones liked nothing more than to tour the estate, suggesting an addition, offering an amendment, relishing the opportunity, previously denied him, to possess his own property. He was visited by Mayall and Alexis Korner. He became an habitué at the Dorset Arms. Later that spring he was joined by a new girlfriend, Anna Wohlin, a student with whom in her own deposition he was 'together nearly every minute of the day'. When Jagger, Richard and Watts appeared at Cotchford on 5 June Jones had every reason to be smiling. In fact he was smiling.

The subsequent interview lasted twenty minutes. According to Richard, 'the fact that he was expecting it made it easier . . . Even so, I don't think he took it all in.' In Jagger's view, 'We had to do it . . . It was either stand up or fall over. I elected to stand up. You can't let people hang you up that much.' Watts maintains that 'we took the one thing away from him – playing in a band'. After the car left Jones was said to have broken down at the kitchen table and cried.

Not according to Thorogood. He remembers the evening of 5 June well. Jones, he says, 'hardly registered' his sacking – it affected him like the death of a distant, elderly and alienated relative. Later the two drank wine by the pool. Jones was perfectly composed. His only comment was on the irony of Jagger citing the 'bust thing' when the only current such thing was his own.

Jones was also offered a settlement: a hundred thousand pounds in a typically intricate series of instalments. Jagger, with his lifelong aversion to confrontation, even suggested that Jones might, in a year or two, rejoin the group; Klein was telexed in New York to that effect. In London Keylock was told that Jones was henceforth to be regarded as on holiday.

The news was released on 8 June. According to Jagger, 'The only solution to our problem was for Brian to leave us. He wants to play music which is more his own rather than always playing ours. We have decided that it is best for him to be free to follow his own inclinations. We have parted on the best of terms. We will continue to be friends and we're certainly going to meet socially in future. There's no question of us breaking up a friendship. Friendships like ours just don't break up like that.'

Jones himself played along with the 'artistic differences' theme, adding: 'I have a desire to play my own brand of music rather than that of others, no matter how much I appreciate their concepts. We had a friendly meeting and agreed that an amicable termination, temporary or permanent, was the answer ... The only solution was to go our separate ways, but we shall remain friends. I love those fellows.'

That same weekend Jagger was among the 150,000 present at a free concert in Hyde Park starring Blind Faith. Restless and committed to touring, the Stones had recently planned to appear at the Coliseum in Rome. When the Mayor's office intervened Jagger suggested the park. (There was also, says Keylock, the question of competitiveness. 'We'll pull quarter of a million,' he explicitly remembers Jagger claiming.) Suddenly, in the space of a week, the group had announced both a new member and the date – Saturday 5 July – of their biggest ever concert. The Stones were back: official.

At this stage, according to Sanchez, 'Jagger was worried that the fans would realize that [Jones] had been mistreated, and he persuaded Keith, Charlie and several Stones employees to phone Brian asking him to come to Hyde Park ... Many of those close to him felt there was something slightly unpleasant in Jagger's egocentric desire to parade his vanquished rival before the world.'

Korner had a different understanding. 'Mick,' he said,

'was genuinely concerned. He asked me to go to Cotchford. There was no ulterior motive.' Keylock, too, was delegated to visit Jones; he delivered a piano and other instruments at Jagger's request. Thorogood confirms that 'Brian was "up" just before the end.'

On Tuesday 1 July the pollen count in East Sussex reached 355. In mid-morning the temperature was seventy-five degrees. Thorogood remembers Jones, wheezing and morbid with asthma, inside watching television. It was the Prince of Wales's Investiture. Later that afternoon Thorogood was joined by Janet Lawson, a local agency nurse, also a friend of Keylock's. According to Wohlin, 'We all had dinner together and then some drinks. After that Brian had a swim in the pool for a couple of hours. Frank, Janet and myself did not go in that evening ... While he was [swimming] Brian came to the edge and asked me for his squirter, which he used as a name for his inhaler. He often used it and I didn't think anything about it. He used the inhaler and went on swimming.' Later Jones had Thorogood raise the temperature in the pool from eighty degrees to ninety.

Next morning, as he did every Wednesday, Thorogood worked at David Bailey's house in Regent's Park. At noon Jones called, eager to discuss his latest plans. He also phoned Keylock, asking him to arrange a holiday for Wohlin and himself. According to both men Jones sounded happier than he had in years.

He spent the remainder of that afternoon watching Wimbledon on television. At six Thorogood returned. He found Jones supine on the living room sofa, the French windows open to the sun. 'Brian,' he says, 'was lying there with Anna, perfectly happy. He asked me to buy some drink.' Thorogood returned from the Dorset Arms with bottles of vodka, wine and a half-bottle apiece of brandy and whisky. He, Jones and Wohlin had a double each – no more. At eight Thorogood excused himself and went to the garage flat he shared with Lawson.

An hour later Jones knocked at the door. He wore the look of a happy man, if not a model of sobriety. Would they care to join Anna and himself for a nightcap? Thorogood looked at Lawson; they would. Jones led them inside with a torch, the garden full of insect noises in the gloom. In the living room he drank brandy, Thorogood vodka. They talked; they watched *Rowan and Martin's Laugh-In*. The programme was followed at nine fifty-five by Bobbie Gentry. The alternative was the news. It was then that Jones – in Lawson's words 'seeming anxious to be occupied' – suggested a swim. Immediately Thorogood turned on the garden lights, the water a now near-fluorescent blue. The four changed like suddenly excited children.

First they sat drinking at a garden table. Jones's pet spaniels Emily and Luther appeared on command. He adored playing with the dogs – their thrown tennis ball left a vapour trail in the lights. The mood became playful and disjointed; Jones, says Thorogood, was 'fairly drunk, though in a cheerful way'. He finished a fourth or fifth brandy. At exactly eleven – the moment a wrestling match, audible from the garden, came on television – he stood up, flexing his hands rigid above his head. His legs were exquisite. Above that all was creeping fat. Jones staggered on to the diving board. Thorogood steadied him. Wohlin, too, dived in. Lawson refused. 'I considered,' she later said, 'that Frank and Brian were in no condition to swim . . . I wanted to disassociate myself with the escapade and in order to keep an eye on the trio I partly hid myself in an effort to avoid their requests to join them.'

Jones, in subsequent testimony 'swimming quite normally', splashing, singing, flinging soggy leaves to the dogs, announced to Thorogood, 'I love this place.' His mood was one of distinct if drunken light-heartedness. When Wohlin left the pool he seemed instantly to miss her. 'Brian,' says Thorogood, 'always wanted you around.' Lawson too returned to the house.

The two men swam for twenty minutes. Gradually Jones grew more subdued. He floated distractedly at the deep end. When Thorogood announced he was going in Jones merely grunted. It was midnight.

By the time Thorogood walked the thirty yards to the house, dried, and lit a cigarette five minutes may have passed. As he reached the living room Lawson looked up in surprise. Where was Brian? Still in the pool. For a moment they froze there. A phone rang upstairs. Then Lawson was up and running into the garden.

'You shouldn't have left him.'

'Brian's all right.'

'Brian's drunk!' Lawson shouted.

Thorogood was the first to dive into the pool. He seized Jones by the arms, legs and finally by his spread hair. Lawson and Wohlin lifted him, face down, on to the grass. Instinctively Lawson ran to the house to ring the police. She picked up the phone and dialled three, four, half a dozen times (the upstairs receiver was later found off the hook); eventually Thorogood got through. Lawson returned to the now sobbing Wohlin and turned Jones over. Between them they applied mouth-to-mouth resuscitation and massage. For fifteen minutes they worked in unbearable silence. Then lights came on all around and dogs barked in the night as policemen stared down at Jones.

· VI ·

. . . AND THE WHEEL

At that moment Keylock was less than a dozen miles away. Earlier in the evening Richard had asked him to drive to Redlands to collect guitars. When Thorogood – now instantly sober – rang Keylock's number the phone was answered by Joan. 'Frank,' she recalls, 'was in a state. He kept babbling for Tom.' In his absence Joan rang Shirley Arnold, the group's fan club secretary, and also the studio. 'Brian,' she told Stewart, 'has gone.' Stewart told Jagger and Richard, then in the process of recording a song called 'I Don't Know Why'.

'There were a few visible tears,' said Richard, 'but it wasn't really unexpected.' Jagger's reaction was muted: 'I felt a bit shocked, but it was really inevitable . . . the guy was unbearable.' Three days later he amended, 'It all depends what you believe in . . . If you're an agnostic, he's dead and that's it . . . I don't believe in Western bereavement. I can't suddenly drape a long black veil and walk the hills.' He also spoke of Jones's 'shyness' in writing songs – 'It wasn't a question of forcefully stifling him.' Jagger summoned Thorogood ('Was it suicide?'), Perrin and Keylock, delegated the thankless job of handling the press. 'Mick,' says the last, 'was badly rattled . . . He was shaking.'

The Inquest opened on 7 July. Jones's autopsy revealed the presence of both alcohol and 'an amphetamine-like substance . . . suggesting ingestion of a fairly large quantity of a drug'. Two dense spots were attributed to 'diphenhydramine, present together with methaqualone in mandrax, which the deceased is known to have taken'. The theory that Jones had died following an asthma attack was refuted by the pathologist Albert Sachs: 'In [an attack] the bronchi are in spasm. This would tend to seal the lining tissue and prevent the entry of water while the spasm lasted. The viscid adherent mucus in the bronchi which is present in an asthmatic attack was not found . . . As the interval between his last being seen alive and found in the bottom of the pool face downwards was only five minutes, I feel it unlikely that he had an attack of asthma at the time of death.' The official verdict: Misadventure, specifically, 'Drowning whilst swimming under the influence of Alcohol and Drugs.'

None of which prevented the inevitable debate: was Jones murdered? *Was* it suicide? After a police enquiry not notable for its restraint, an autopsy, inquest, and at least one book aiming to prove otherwise, not one credible witness has been found to promote foul play. No evidence ever emerged that Jones was physically manhandled, let alone a motive. On the second question, the testimony of Thorogood, Lawson, Wohlin – and those who spoke to him, like Keylock and Korner – confirms that Jones was cheerful, even content, at the time of his death. He loved Cotchford. He was enamoured with Wohlin. Both Korner and Mayall heard him discussing plans for a new group. On the day he died he rang Keylock to ask him to arrange a holiday. 'If anything, he was happy,' says Thorogood. 'A year earlier, I wouldn't be so sure.'

Thorogood's version is simple: Jones, as the autopsy proved, was in an advanced state of physical decay. His liver 'showed dysfunction due to extensive fatty degeneration'; his heart, too, was swollen. By the time he flopped in the pool he was, by almost any clinical definition, drunk. He may have taken a sleeping pill. Submerged at midnight in warm water the mind is likely to wander; add the above and a state of disorientation, even deprivation, becomes possible. Significantly, when Wohlin left the pool Jones became quiet and subdued. For twenty minutes he barely acknowledged his companion. By then the garden was silent, head-high in mist, the clouds seeping in the pool like fluid, the surface of the water acting as a filter. After Thorogood left, Jones, he believes, did what anyone might have done: he fell asleep.

The funeral took place on 10 July. According to Korner and Thorogood, Jones had repeatedly asked to be buried at Cotchford or, failing that, nearby Hartfield. His parents insisted on Cheltenham. Keylock, in charge of arrangements, remembers one 'harrowing' interview with Lewis Jones in which the family views were pungently stated. Cheltenham it was.

More than five hundred mourners gathered outside the parish church where Jones had sung as a choirboy. Fleet Street was represented. The family appeared: Lewis and Louisa Jones, their daughter Barbara and Suki Poitier, turbaned like Pola Negri at Valentino's funeral cortège. Among others who attended were Watts, Wyman, Stewart, Keylock, Thorogood, Perrin and Linda Lawrence, holding Jones's illegitimate son Julian. Among those who didn't were Oldham, Klein, Richard – and Jagger, by then preoccupied with events in Australia.

Inside the church Canon Hugh Hopkins addressed the grubby, gawping and by implication Godless congregation: 'Brian had little patience with authority, convention and tradition. In this he was typical of many of his generation who have come to see in the Stones an expression of their whole attitude to life. Much that this ancient church has stood for in nine hundred years seems irrelevant to them.' The Canon then quoted from Luke 15, the Prodigal Son, and from a telegram Jones had sent his parents: 'Please don't judge me too harshly.'

Outside, in Priory Road, there was a wreath of red roses from Jagger and Faithfull. The bronze coffin, ordered by Keylock from New York, was lowered into plot V11393, on a turning of a lane in the cemetery next to Albert 'Bert' Trigg, beloved husband of Ethel. The sun was shining. The burial was watched by hordes of weeping fans, bunched like the hills that rose, narrowly separated, in the distance. Sweating photographers craned into the opening. A woman threw a single yellow rose as the gravediggers sent down their earth. A policeman saluted.

All this affected Jagger profoundly. In the week following Jones's death he hovered between the two worlds – business as usual and the certainty that, for the Stones, nothing would be usual again. On the afternoon of the third the group met at Maddox Street. According to Shirley Arnold, 'they all showed it in different ways ... Charlie actually cried, whereas I think Mick was too shocked. Charlie came up early, Mick arrived ... They started talking about Hyde Park and the first thing Mick said was "We'll cancel it," and then they [in fact, Watts alone] said, "No, we'll do it, we'll do it for Brian."'

Over and over that afternoon the office stereo played Tim Hardin's doleful 'Bird on a Wire'. 'Jagger,' said Arnold, 'wandered around, tripping over a dog bowl on the floor.' It says much for his resilience that at three o'clock, a dozen hours after the news, he was bawling the group's new single on a BBC sound stage. 'Honky Tonk Women' was released on 4 July. An early, unrecognizable country version of the song included Jones on lead; eventually it was re-recorded with Taylor. 'Women' featured magnetic rhythm (inspired, he insists, by Ry Cooder), hypnotic drums and a vocal slurped, not sung, by Jagger. It immediately reached number one in both Britain and America.

Jagger next appeared at Rupert Loewenstein's. He met Princess Margaret, also Peter Sellers and the fashion designer Hardy Amies. The last admired Jagger's white ruffled frock, eerily reminiscent of a teenager's party dress (actually inspired by Greek military uniforms). Next day, 4 July, the *Evening News* was told what the world wanted to hear: 'We will do the concert – for Brian,' Jagger stated. 'We have thought about it and feel he would have wanted it to go on. I understand how many people will feel, but we are doing it because of him.' That evening he rehearsed with the group at the Beatles' office in Savile Row. Faithfull was solicited for 'something good' to read; Keylock, mysteriously, for butterflies. As night fell thousands were already peacefully camping in the park.

Jagger's thoughts ('I'm never nervous usually, but I am a bit . . .') as he left Cheyne Walk the next afternoon were only partially centred on the concert. He and Faithfull were due to fly to Sydney in the morning. The pollen that had so plagued Jones the day before his death had returned and for the first time in a decade Jagger developed hay fever. His eyes reddened, his lips were chapped and he sneezed continually. He had laryngitis. Already United Artists had been asked whether *Kelly* could be delayed. Their reaction was negative. In Marlborough Court Marsha Hunt persistently queried his 'intentions': Klein also rang; Jones's body lay in the mortuary. When Jagger arrived at the Londonderry Hotel – pale, tremulous, clutching a volume of poetry – he looked, says Keylock, like 'the only straight person' in a party of revellers.

In the hotel Jagger revived, pronouncing happily on the 'beautiful vibes' and 'Englishness' of the occasion. Outside, Keylock, in charge of security, was briefing his stewards – Hell's Angels, benign suburban mimics of the outlaw Californian gangs, fidgeting nervously, their faces wreathed in compliant goodwill. 'No violence,' Keylock announced. 'Someone gets heavy, leave 'im to me.' In fact the day was eerily calm. Police made twelve arrests – one in twenty-five thousand. Four hundred fainted in the heat.

The concert's real tension occurred off stage with Klein. He sat in the Londonderry in his bulging T-shirt and Hush Puppies, continually buttonholing Jagger to discuss money. ('Typical of Allen', says Keylock, 'to choose the one time no one was thinking of it.') There were references to residuals, to low-yield returns. 'Not now,' Jagger rasped. 'Not *now*.' In the elevator, Keylock uttered the hissed aside, 'You've screwed this lot rotten.' 'It's a rotten business,' said Klein.

The Stones, Klein, Keylock, Sanchez and Michael Cooper were then conveyed by armoured truck around Hyde Park Corner, where they transferred to a makeshift dressing room. Richard and Taylor tuned up. Watts distributed apples to the arms that, trunklike, protruded through the open window. Wyman smirked. Only Jagger, his game face now replete with lipstick, mascara and eye-liner, pacing the aisle, seemed to recognize the significance of the event. 'Listen,' he instructed the compère, Sam Cutler, 'the first thing that's going to happen is I'm reading something for Brian . . . We all want to think about him today . . . I hope they all agree with what I say.'

'Bound to.'

'Can you say something so that they're prepared . . . yeah . . . 'cos otherwise, you know, it might be difficult for them to shut up.'

'It's a very nice crowd, Mick. I reckon it's 650,000.'

'No!'

Jagger's hands flew up as if to ward off the words. Cutler made the announcement. At the word 'STONES' Jagger, with a deep breath, flounced – no other word describes it – on stage. Over a T-shirt and bell-bottoms he wore his teenager's dress, frilly at the collar and cuffs, around his neck a brass-studded collar. It says volumes for Jagger's self-confidence that, in front of three hundred thousand fans and a TV audience of millions, he chose to come on like a thirteen-year-old at a school dance. Perhaps that was the

point: in an earlier era sex symbols were either unequivocally male (Elvis) or equally female (Monroe). Jagger occupied the ground in between. When he frugged on stage,
pouting, straightening his hem, even the Angels gaped. 'It
was like everyone froze,' says Keylock, a dozen feet away.
'Mick just smiled. He knew he had them.'

First there was the tribute to Jones. Jagger, shuffling in
his white shoes, blowing kisses from his fingertips, adjusted
the mike: 'Aawrite ... OK, now listen ... Will you just
cool it for a minute ... 'Cause I really would like to say
something for Brian ... And I'd really dig it if you'd be
with us for what I'm going to say. I really don't know how
to do this' – a conclusion much of the crowd had reached
already – 'but I'm going to try ... I hope you can just cool
it before we start ... I'd really appreciate it if I could just
say a few words about what I feel about Brian ... and I'm
sure you do ... what we feel about him just *going*' – here
Jagger's hand floated upwards – 'when we didn't expect him
to ... OK?'

Jagger then took a book in both hands, tossed back his
hair and read:

Peace, peace! He is not dead, he doth not sleep –
He hath awakened from the dream of life –
'Tis we, who, lost in stormy visions, keep
With phantoms an unprofitable strife,
And in mad trance, strike with our spirit's knife
Invulnerable nothings. – *We* decay
Like corpses in a charnel; fear and grief
Convulse us and consume us day by day,
And cold hopes swarm like worms within our living clay.

Shelley's *Adonaïs*. Neglecting, perhaps for the only time in
his career, to assume an accent Jagger proceeded like a
Dartford sixth-former on Speech Day:

The One remains, the many change and pass
Heaven's light forever shines, Earth's shadows fly;
Life, like a dome of many-coloured glass,
Stains the white radiance of Eternity,
Until Death tramples it to fragments – Die,
If thou wouldst be with that which thou dost seek
Follow where all is fled!

At that Keylock and his crew shook three thousand white butterflies into the sky from cardboard boxes. The crowd cheered, Jagger jackknifed, the band worked. After a manic, off-key 'I'm Yours, She's Mine' a single lepidoptera still swooped, dived, hovering playfully just beyond the reach or range of Jagger's grasp as he announced a number whose very title seemed ironic: 'I'm Free'.

From there things deteriorated. Musically, Hyde Park was a mess: missed intros, rambling solos, atonal chords. 'Perhaps,' says Wyman, 'the sheer weight of the occasion got to us.' At times Jagger could be seen rolling his eyes imploringly at Richard: 'Tempo! Tempo!' As a finale African dancers wheeled on stage for an extended 'Sympathy'. Jagger shimmied, strutted, touching Taylor once, twice, four times on the arm ('Smile, damnit. *Smile*'), nodded, winked at Keylock, assured everyone they'd had a good time – and left. Afterwards there was a party at the hotel. Jagger, Keylock remembers, left early, loudly announcing his intention to 'kip' prior to flying to Australia. What he failed to add was that it was with Marsha Hunt.

Mid-morning of Sunday 6 July found Jagger groggily leaving Marlborough Court, kissing the woman known affectionately as Fuzzy-Wuzzy before joining Faithfull in Chelsea. At the airport more reporters asked, as they had all week: How are you? How do you *feel*, Mick? ('Devastated.') After two stop-overs the couple landed in Sydney on 8 July to placards demonstrating against Jagger's arrival.

'POOFTER,' read one: 'GIVE IT TO CHIPS.' Reporters pondered the presence of the famous singer dressed in maxi-coat and white Isadora scarf. After a customs inspection notable for its diligence Jagger was said to be 'down', 'drawn' – 'distraught', even – by recent events. There were, the press noted, 'only four fans' at the airport to greet him.

Immediately he and Faithfull made for the Chevron Hotel. On the thirteenth floor Jagger flopped on to the antique bed and fell asleep with his boots on. Faithfull rang room service and ordered hot chocolate. She reached in her handbag for a bottle of Tuinals, a legally pre-scribed barbiturate. She took one. Seven or eight pills had already been swallowed before she slipped into a dream (actually the prelude to a coma) about Jones, with whom Faithfull 'walked through this great big, weatherless place,' her companion at length announcing, 'I have to go on alone.'

'COLLAPSE! DRUG SQUAD AT HOSPITAL.' The Sydney *Mirror* first alerted the world to the news: Jagger, implausibly, had woken only minutes after his lover had drifted into unconsciousness. Faithfull was rushed to St Vincent's Hospital, whose first bulletin informed the press of a collapse 'possibly related to fatigue'.

The truth was more dramatic: within hours Faithfull was in critical condition. Reports grew less encouraging. By the early hours of 10 July her life, a spokesman admitted, was despaired of. For six days Jagger – at times accompanied by the director, Tony Richardson – waited at Faithfull's bed. (His first words when she recovered, 'Wild horses wouldn't drag me away', later became the basis of a song.) Alan Dunn also arrived; 'the public,' he said later, 'believe Mick to be callous, but he's quite sensitive . . . He was in tears when we got back from the hospital.' Perrin flew in to handle the press, prone to such questions as, 'What does Marianne

· 210 ·

mean to you?' and 'She gone yet?' When an agency photo-grapher tricked his way into Faithfull's room Jagger had to be restrained from assaulting him.

Eventually the crisis receded. On the twentieth Eva Faithfull flew to her daughter's bedside. Slowly, not with-out protest and prevarication, Jagger was persuaded to start work on *Ned Kelly*. Faithfull's part was taken by her under-study. Inevitably the drugs squad appeared, Jagger and Faithfull being questioned until a report – whose very word-ing hinted at official disappointment – admitted that the Tuinal was 'evidently' legal and no further action would be taken. In London the press visited Faithfull's doctor, her father, even her estranged husband, the *Sketch* observing that 'no matter how well Jagger behaves' – and he did, bringing Faithfull flowers, squeezing her hand – she was the second woman in less than three years to 'apparently attempt suicide' on his behalf.

Or was she? Faithfull's own version was given to A. E. Hotchner.

I phoned room service and had them send up some hot chocolate, which I slowly drank while swallowing some of my sleeping pills ... When I started to take them I only intended to take a few, enough to get me to sleep, but watching myself in the mirror of the vanity table, sipping the hot chocolate and carefully placing each pill on my tongue before swallowing it, I somehow couldn't restrain myself, and I kept putting pill after pill on my tongue. I saw Brian appear in the mirror looking directly at me, and I became Ophelia, the part I'd played at the [Royal Court] theatre. As the number of pills I swallowed mounted, so my desire, as Ophelia, to commit suicide as I had in the play, increased.

As a footnote, Ben Brierley (who later married Faithfull) adds: 'Marianne was always prone to that sort of theatrical gesture. In Sydney it misfired. I wouldn't attach any blame to Jagger.'

———

In September, filming complete, they holidayed in Singapore. Jagger's next – long overdue – priority was to arrange the American tour. Klein, the Stones unanimously agreed, was out. For more than a year Jagger had avoided his manager as a werewolf avoids the dawn. In his place the group hired Ronnie Schneider (Klein's nephew, but more sympathetic) to negotiate a fourteen-city itinerary, eighteen shows, tickets a staggering $7.50. The money, Jagger ordered, was to be paid not to the booking agency but into the group's own off-the-shelf company, Stones Promotions. As further proof of their resolve to end Klein's, and William Morris's, control the Stones personally selected their own support acts: B. B. King, Chuck Berry, Terry Reid, Ike and Tina Turner. They hired a stage manager, Edward 'Chip' Monck, 'the wizard of Woodstock', and the Hyde Park MC, Sam Cutler. Jagger, notes Keylock, was 'dead serious' about his comeback. In October the journalist Stanley Booth and film-makers David and Albert Maysles were commissioned to record it.

'The whole thing,' said Jagger later, 'became much more professional. We had our own lights, our own crew . . . Up until then rock and roll tours had been pretty ramshackle . . . You'd be playing every kind of place, which is a bit disorientating for a performer. It's much easier if you play the same place, same stage, same configuration – it becomes like your second home.'

The tour began with two weeks of rehearsals and illicit recording in Los Angeles. Jagger, Stanley Booth observed, was by now a kind of modern Renaissance figure, holding forth on politics, money, the world ('We'll blow it up eventually') – even, less frequently, on music. After conducting a rehearsal of the group's set he was heard to mutter,

'It doesn't matter what we decide to do – once we get on stage all the plans go by the board anyway.' Booth came away impressed by Jagger's ability to exist between the two roles: sober, even scholarly, entertainer and authentic rebel. He granted interviews to the *New Yorker*, *Esquire*, a bushy-haired ABC News ('You can't tell by looking any more, can you?'), *Ramparts* and *Rolling Stone*. He negotiated; he haggled with Schneider. He charmed. When a young blonde fan appeared as the group were being photographed she was invited to 'get your clothes off and get into the picture'. She did.

The first concert was at Fort Collins on 7 November. Terry Reid was followed by B. B. King; after a delay – extended, some felt, to generate tension – Cutler's voice blared through the gloom: 'Now ... The greatest rock 'n' roll band in the world* ... the ROLLING STONES.' Jagger leapt on, black suede trousers with silver buttons, scoop-neck sweater, long red Isadora scarf and – incredible touch – a foot-high Uncle Sam hat: Jumpin' Jack Flash. 'Has it really been three years?' In 'Midnight Rambler' Jagger flogged the stage with his belt, in 'Sympathy' spun the scarf like a stripper. 'I wish I could see you,' he cooed; 'you're probably even more beautiful than I am.' On cue the lights came up, the crowd flared, Jagger sang 'Street Fighting Man', dotting the stage with rose petals. In front stood Klein, beating back fans with a broom handle.

Defying both insult and innuendo the group's manager dogged them through America. In New York Jagger sat at a banquet table as a riot of press struggled to interview him.

'What you think of the war?'

'What you think of America?'

'What you – ' (Here Klein's clenched hand fell like a mallet.) 'Ah ... are you any more *satisfied* now?'

---

* Although Jagger later disowned the title, it is certain that, on the twenty-three times he used it, Cutler was never dissuaded.

'Sexually, d'you mean, or philosophically?'

'Both.'

'Sexually – more satisfied, financially – dissatisfied. Philosophically – trying.'

'Are you sadder but wiser?'

'Wiser.'

Also older: at twenty-six Jagger had become a kind of senior statesman; in America Little Richard, Hendrix, even Chuck Berry sought him out. He attracted Morrison and Joplin, also a young, soon-to-be-lionized country musician, Gram Parsons. ('The Stones,' said Parsons' friend Roger McGuinn, 'ripped him off for all he knew.') It was Parsons who advised Jagger before going on stage, 'Don't expect them to scream.' No bad advice: the crowds in Los Angeles, Detroit, Baltimore – even New York – had all too obviously come to listen. Songs were greeted with polite if prolonged applause. ('Suddenly,' says Richard, 'there was an audience listening, instead of screaming chicks.') Parsons also alerted Jagger to Manson Fever, a condition prevalent among the American rich since the slaughter that August of Sharon Tate. According to Stewart, 'Mick's one great fear became being physically hassled.' In New York he hired a bodyguard.

Another change: the radical trend previewed in 1966 had become a tendency. On 3 November, as the Stones rehearsed in Los Angeles, Richard Nixon had appealed publicly to the 'great silent majority of Americans' to support escalation in Vietnam, prompting mass demonstrations in Washington. One sign read, 'Tyranny has always depended on a silent majority', another proclaiming, 'I'm an effete intellectual snob for peace.' When, a week later, news broke of the massacre of South Vietnamese civilians in My Lai – Nixon maintaining that protesters had 'remained noticeably uncritical of Vietcong atrocities' – a virtual state of political civil war existed. In Oakland Jagger was greeted with manifestoes: 'We play your music in rock 'n' roll marching bands

as we tear down the jails and free the prisoners, as we tattoo
"BURN BABY BURN!" on the bellies of the wardens and
generals and create a new society from the ashes of our fires.'
In Dallas students picketed his hotel. At the University of
Chicago Jagger sent for Abbie Hoffman, the radical charged
with conspiring to riot at the 1968 Democratic Convention.
'We're in the same business,' Hoffman informed him. 'Your
thing is sex, mine's violence.'

'Yeah, I love a good fight.'

'Say, do you know where you are, what happened here,
the demo — ?'

'I know,' said Jagger.

'Why don't you give us some bread?'

'For what?'

'The trial. The Chicago Eight.'

'I got my own trials.'

In the San Francisco *Chronicle*, meanwhile, Ralph Gleason
berated Jagger for setting 'unreal' ticket prices: 'Are the
Rolling Stones really able to use all that money? How much
can they take back to England? How much profit do the
British manager, the American manager and the Agency
have to make?' Gleason might have been surprised. Jagger
took personal interest in the financial aspects of the tour.
('I figure,' said Schneider, 'you'll each take home a hundred
Gs.' 'Ninety,' said Jagger immediately.) Encouraged by
Loewenstein, he was thinking of emigrating from England
and needed all the capital he could get. 'I made a ridiculous
amount last year,' he admitted to Booth. 'I got paid for two
films in the same fortnight. I don't know where to live.
England is so small-town.' He also confessed to needing,
rather than wanting, a hit record.

Let It Bleed was released on 5 December. It reached
number one in Britain, number three in America. 'They
invite us into the fantasy of the opener ("Gimme Shelter"),'
said *Melody Maker*, 'and conclude with "You Can't Always

Get What You Want", where there is a lot of blood, drugs and desolation, but very little sympathy. The Stones rarely worry about contradicting themselves.' 'A classic,' said *Creem*. The critics were particularly drawn to 'Shelter', a modified version of 'Under My Thumb' with ice-cream harmonies by Merry Clayton and 'Live With Me', an impertinent rocker that parodied Jagger's jet-set excess and included a reference to his best friend shooting water rats, one of Richard's known habits. Richard himself sang 'You Got The Silver', included by Antonioni on the soundtrack of *Zabriskie Point*, after an engineer erased Jagger's version. 'Country Honk' was inspired by Parsons, the title track by parlour games (references to coke, sympathy and 'parking lots' – Faithfull's euphemism for her vagina) at Cheyne Walk. In 'Monkey Man' Jagger playfully alluded to the group's reputation – coupling 'messianic' with 'satanic' – before concluding

'We love to play the blues'

– sung, for once, wholly without irony. Jagger really meant it. He had the blues.

For more than a year things had gone downhill with Faithfull. First there was *Performance*. Faithfull's miscarriage. Hunt. The suicide bid. Now, in Dallas, Jagger was drawn aside by a reporter and asked had he heard 'the news'? He hadn't. Faithfull, his informant stated, had left him and moved in with a new lover, the film-maker Mario Schifano, in his apartment in Rome.

Jagger exploded. To be publicly cuckolded flouted his own long-standing convention: maximum discretion, no fuss, no performance and above all no *press*. When Faithfull was quoted by the *Daily Mail* ('I love Mario. I am happy with him. People can help me by just forgetting me'), Jagger immediately demanded Schifano's number. He rang it repeatedly. ('I can only say what's in my heart . . .' Booth overheard him.) When a reporter asked, 'How's Marianne Faithfull?' she was answered tartly, 'Fine. How are *you*?' He also rang Hunt.

Then there were the groupies. Since 1966 a virtual cottage industry had sprung up to service the needs of touring musicians. In Los Angeles Jagger was attended by such luminaries as the Butter Queen and Suzie Creamcheese. Most tenaciously was he pursued by the Plaster Casters. Of Kathy (half of Kathy and Mary, the Dynamic Duo) Booth wrote:

> She gave us a long list including the Beatles, Led Zeppelin and Terry Reid, but for two years they had wanted Mick Jagger. They'd be with a guy and then split and say, 'He was cool, but he's no Mick Jagger.' When they finally got picked up by the Stones and were at the house, Mick went upstairs to bed, then came back down throwing Floris Sandalwood perfume on Kathy and Mary and asked Kathy, 'Want to come upstairs?'
>
> 'My girlfriend has to come too.'
>
> 'OK.'
>
> 'We were really disappointed,' Kathy said. 'He was so bad. When he's being himself, he can get it on. Fair. But we were just laughing at him. He tried to come on like Mick Jagger, all sexy – when he's himself, he's fair. When we came downstairs from Mick's room, we said, "Well, he was cool, but he's no Mick Jagger."'

Jagger earned more favourable reviews from Pamela Des Barres – 'those lips'. He was also seen with one of Turner's back-up singers, the Ikettes. As Stewart said, 'He was no angel, but considering what was on offer . . .' (Here Stewart would shrug, indicating a deluge.)

Late November found the group in the studio in Muscle Shoals, Alabama. They recorded 'Brown Sugar', 'You Gotta Move' and a song, Richard said, 'I wrote because I was doing good at home with my old lady . . . and I gave it to Mick, and Marianne just ran off with this guy and he changed it all round': 'Wild Horses'. They advanced plans for a free concert eventually held at the Altamont Speedway, San Francisco, on 6 December.

Altamont began as a well-intentioned reply to Gleason's strictures on ticket prices. Jagger was also thought to require a suitably dramatic finale to the Maysles' film; there may even have been an element of genuine charity. The experience of Hyde Park (and the simultaneous Woodstock) had lent credence to the Californian ideal of 'be-in's, to the requirement for periodic demonstrations of 'togetherness'. In July Jagger had told Keylock to 'imagine this in San Francisco'. Keylock imagined it: 'At least,' he said, 'don't hire the bloody Angels.'

But hire them Jagger did. As negotiations veered between New York, Muscle Shoals and California one Rock Scully, manager of the Grateful Dead, proposed Sonny Barger and his motorcycle gang as a sort of Praetorian guard – the idea being to have the Angels work with the event, not against it. Jagger immediately acquiesced. That left the question of a venue. Golden Gate Park was suggested, and just as readily rejected by the mayor. In late November Craig Murray, director of Sears Point Raceway, offered his site gratis, only for his employer, Filmways Inc, to intervene two days before the event. The Stones were invited to cede all distribution rights to the Maysles' film or, failing that, pay a hundred thousand dollar fee. When this was reported to Jagger in Alabama he hired the lawyer Melvin Belli. Belli in turn located Dick Carter, operator of Altamont Speedway, Livermore, fifty miles south-east of San Francisco. Carter's only conditions were that the concert be free and that the site be scrubbed down afterwards.

When Jagger arrived on inspection at two a.m. he declared the scene 'groovy'. He walked among the slumbering shapes, smiling and laughing, smoking a cigarette of dubious legality. In the Huntington Hotel he changed into burgundy suede boots, velvet trousers and a cape. A helicopter returned him to Livermore, where immediately there was a display of violence: a boy, no more than sixteen, rushed forward and punched Jagger in the face screaming, 'I hate you, I hate you!' By then the Jefferson Airplane had been and gone, their set truncated when Hell's Angels bludgeoned the singer Marty Balin unconscious. Parsons' group, the Buritos, followed. There was naked anarchy on, in front of and behind stage as Angels abused, spat on and finally clubbed spectators. A teenage girl was stabbed repeatedly with a sharpened pool cue. Jagger's bodyguard Tony Fuches broke his wrists in a brawl. Crosby, Stills, Nash – and a new recruit, Neil Young – gave half their scheduled performance. They ran for their helicopter like fugitives from an invasion. The Angels, drunk, drooling, some riding the tools of their trade through the crowd, were the next act. For an hour they flailed, fought, belched, spewed and spat; the concentration was excessive. Darkness fell. Bonfires were lit. Another girl was manhandled off stage. The medical tent swelled; by 6 o'clock there were two hundred reported injuries. The rest of the crowd, estimated at four hundred thousand, waited. 'The reason we can't start,' announced Cutler, 'is that the stage is loaded with people . . . I've done all I can.' Then the ultimate deterrent: 'The Stones won't come out until everybody gets off. *Everybody*.'

When Jagger finally appeared he was flanked on stage by Cutler, Schneider, Booth, Monck, David and Albert Maysles, a dozen Angels and at least one comatose fan. 'Fellows,' he kept muttering. 'Will you give me some room? Will you move back, *please*?' Somehow he got through two numbers. 'Whoo, whoo! Ah, yeah!' Jagger swigged from a bottle of Jack Daniel's on the amplifier. As the group played 'Sympathy' there was an explosion and a hole opened in the crowd. 'Keith – Keith – *Keith*!' Jagger's voice rose in counterpoint to the music. 'Will you cool it and I'll try and stop it.' Richard unstrapped his guitar. 'Sisters,' said Jagger. 'Brothers and sisters . . . Come *on*, now . . . That means everybody cool *out*. Just be cool now, come on . . .'

'Somebody's bike blew up, man.'

'I know. I'm hip. Everybody be cool now, come on . . . Can everybody just . . . I don't know what happened, I couldn't see . . . Everyone just cool down . . . Is there anyone who's hurt? . . . Good . . . We can groove . . . Something very funny happens when we start that number.'

Next a two-hundred-pound naked girl, pinned in the red and green spots, tripped as if pushed on stage. 'Fellows,' Jagger enquired, 'surely *one* of you can handle her?' An Angel duly rendered the girl senseless. More nervous delay. 'Who . . . who . . . I mean, like people, who's fighting and what for? Hey, people . . . I mean, who's fighting and what for? Why are we fighting? I mean, like . . . every other scene has been cool . . . Like we've – '

'Either those cats cool it,' Richard snapped. 'Or we don't play.'

Things calmed down after that. One of the Angels ('You wanna all go home, or what?') took the mike. Stewart appealed for help. 'Can you let the doctor go through, please? . . . We have also . . . lost in the front here a little girl who's five years old.' 'Play cool-out music,' Richard instructed Jagger.

For five minutes the crowd was treated to the Stones, for the first and then only time in their career, playing authentic Muzak. Richard and Taylor fingered their guitars. Wyman hummed. Jagger stood there mumbling lyrics. 'We all dressed up, we got no place to go.' He recovered after a hasty 'Stray Cat Blues'. 'Baby . . . all along a hillside . . .

hey, everybody, ah . . . we gonna do, we gonna do, uh . . . *what* we gonna do?'

' "Love In Vain",' Richard snarled. 'Aw yeah,' Jagger said as the song ended. 'Hey, I think . . . there was one good idea came out of that number . . . which was . . . I really think the only way you're gonna keep yourself cool is to *sit down*. If you can make it . . . So when you're sitting comfortably . . . Now, boys and girls . . . are you sitting comfortably? When we get to really, like . . . the end . . . and we all want to go absolutely crazy and jump on each other, we'll . . . stand up again . . . d'you know what I mean? But we can't seem to keep it together standing up. OK?'

Jagger then sang the first line of 'Under My Thumb' before an aisle formed in the audience and a black man in a green suit rose, arm aloft, as Angels fell on him like maggots on a carcass. They were twenty feet from stage. The crowd parted, the music ebbed and Jagger, cupping an ear, shielding his eyes in the lights, pleaded: 'Now there's one thing we need . . . Sam, an ambulance . . . a doctor by that scaffold there, if there's a doctor can he go there. OK, we gonna, we gonna do . . . I don't know what the fuck we gonna do. Everybody just sit down. Keep cool. Let's just relax . . . get into a groove . . . Come on . . . We can get it together. Come *on*.'

The man in the green suit, Meredith Hunter, died later of multiple stab wounds. According to an eye-witness, Paul Cox, 'An Angel kept looking over at me and I tried to ignore him, because I was scared after seeing what they were doing all day and because he kept trying to cause a fight . . . Next thing I know he's hassling this Negro boy beside me . . . He reached over and shook him by the side of the head, thinking it was fun, laughing, and I noticed something was going to happen . . . The boy yanked away, and when he yanked away, next thing I know he was flying in the air, right on the ground, just like all the other people it happened to. He scrambled to his feet, backing up and trying to run from the Angels . . . and his girlfriend was screaming at him not to shoot, because he pulled out his gun . . . And then some Angel snuck up from right out of the crowd and leaped up and brought this knife down in his back.' According to Cox, Hunter's last audible words were, 'I wasn't going to shoot you.'

After that the group played on. Jagger sang 'Gimme Shelter' (with its refrain 'Rape – Murder – It's just a shot away'), 'Little Queenie', even 'Satisfaction'. According to Kathy Ward, a seventeen-year-old high school senior, 'It was actually a good concert. There was no trouble except in front.' By 'Honky Tonk Women' Jagger was up and dancing again. 'Well, there's been a few hangups . . . yes . . . but generally . . . I mean, you've been beautiful . . . groovy.' He even sang 'Street Fighting Man' as scheduled. 'We're gonna kiss you goodbye,' Jagger trilled. 'Bye bye. Bye-by-y-y-y-e-bye.' The drums crashed, the rose petals fell, the Stones fled. In the helicopter Jagger was gruesome, gushing, sweaty, tense. 'How could anybody think those people are good, that they're people you should have around?' he said.

'Some people just aren't ready,' said Richard.

'I'd rather have had cops.'

He entirely missed the irony. Unnerved as Jagger was he still failed to grasp the significance. Next morning's *Chronicle* compared the event favourably to Woodstock. In London the *Daily Express* led with the impish 'STONED'. Only on 8 December did *The Times* break cover: 'At least four (*sic*) people were killed and many more injured when a crowd estimated at between 200,000 and 500,000 turned up to a free concert given by the Rolling Stones . . . It was a chaotic afternoon and evening, with some 40 miles of traffic jams, caused largely by a late change in the concert's venue.' In San Francisco, meanwhile, Sonny Barger freely imparted his version on Radio KSAN: 'In the process of it there was . . . quite a large girl that was going around topless and kept trying to climb up on stage. And, like, this Mick

Jagger, he used us for dupes, you know.' (According to Barger 'the whole scene' developed when a number of motorcycles were kicked over and set on fire.) Within a week the Angel's lament had become a chorus. David Crosby believed 'the major mistake was taking what was essentially a party and turning it into an ego game . . . I think [the Stones] have an exaggerated view of their own importance, especially the two leaders.' The promoter Bill Graham enquired, 'What right had you, Mr Jagger . . . in going through with this free festival? What right to leave the way you did, thanking everyone for a wonderful time? . . . What did he leave behind throughout the country? Every gig, he was late. Every fucking gig he made the promoter and the people bleed. What right does this god have to descend on this country this way?'

Graham's remarks were included in a book-length feature in *Rolling Stone* the following January. The magazine placed the blame for Altamont squarely on their namesakes. 'Jagger's performing style is a form of aggression . . .' wrote Pauline Kael. 'Not just against the straight world but against his own young audience, and this appeals to them, because it proves he hasn't sold out and gone soft. But when all this aggression is released, who can handle it?' *Rolling Stone*'s reviewer Lester Bangs described Altamont as 'the product of diabolical egotism, hype, ineptitude, money manipulation and, at base, a fundamental lack of concern for humanity', a charge also levelled at the Stones personally. 'We don't need to hear from [the group] via a middle-aged jet-set attorney. We need to hear them directly. Some display – however restrained – of compassion hardly seems too much to expect. A man died before their eyes. Do they give a shit? Yes or no?'

Predictably, Altamont also revived the Satanic innuendo. Another correspondent wrote of Jagger 'with his full consort of demons, the Hell's Angels . . . just a few days before the Winter Solstice when the forces of darkness are at their most powerful'. Even the less imaginative Ralph Gleason believed 'some beast was out in the open ... [Altamont] was, perhaps, the end of rock's innocence, a warning that the vast amount of energy contained in the music and its immense worldwide audience had elements of danger ... And it seemed significant that all this was presided over by the greatest live entertainer in rock history, Mick Jagger.'

He was certainly great; critics agreed on that – though they entirely missed his sense of levity. While *Rolling Stone*, *Ramparts* and *Crawdaddy* ran articles depicting Altamont as a diabolic orgy, while the Chicago Eight, Black Panthers, White Panthers, CORE and the NAACP extolled the Stones as the marching band of the revolution, Jagger himself was admitting in print: 'I think back on a demonstration in London where people were chanting "Ho Chi Minh" through the streets. At that time I was a participant. Today I find the whole thing simply ridiculous. Young people are just so naïve.' Altamont to him had no more significance than 'one gig that went really wrong'.

Did he care? *Did* Jagger give a shit? According to Pamela Des Barres he spent the night of 6 December sobbing and talking of retirement. On the phone to KSAN he said, 'I thought the scene here was supposed to be so groovy. I don't know what happened. It was terrible.' Over and over Jagger stressed his own helplessness in the teeth of the giant forces that overwhelmed him: 'You expected everyone in San Francisco ... because they were so mellow and nice and organized, that it was going to be all those things ... But of course it wasn't.' It also, he said, 'taught me never to do anything I wasn't on top of'. The Jagger emerging from Altamont would stress that virtue above all others: control. Henceforth his performances would be more guardedly ironic – mass funny entertainment. To his credit he allowed and even encouraged the Maysles' film depicting the actual transformation; when *Gimme Shelter* was released in 1970 Jagger donated the profits to charity.

On 7 December, Pearl Harbor Day, Jagger flew to Geneva to bank the tour receipts. From there he moved to Nice, where he searched for a house with Marsha Hunt. In private he discussed plans to perform in the New Year in Moscow, Tokyo and New York, none of which happened. In public he admitted, 'I don't really like singing very much. I'm not really a good enough singer to enjoy it . . . I know that if I keep on playing guitar I can get better, whereas I can't improve much as a singer.'

Faithfull, meanwhile, was living at her mother's cottage with Schifano and the long-suffering Nicholas. Jagger had met his lover at the airport only to be told – another public indignity – 'It's over.' He returned alone to Cheyne Walk, where Hunt had the impression that 'he missed family life, the child and the dog more than the woman'.

A week before Christmas Jagger tried again. He appeared at the cottage and (so Faithfull told Hotchner) 'was on the verge of physically attacking' Schifano. What Jagger did next is unknown. What is known is that Schifano left overnight. Jagger climbed into bed with Faithfull who, she said, 'knew in my heart that the real purpose of the confrontation was to restore his ego and that once back in London we would settle back into the deadly routine'. He accompanied her to court; he bought her a mink coat. He played her 'Wild Horses'.

A free man, Jagger gave two concerts at the Savile Theatre followed by two at the Lyceum – the atmosphere, noted the *Guardian*, as 'decorous as a Festival Hall gathering'. Jagger restricted himself to plain, old-time rock and roll: no clenched fists, no V-signs, just a spring-heeled figure who skipped smartly to the footlights and, just as quickly, pulled back.

· VII ·

TROPICAL DISEASE

The brakes were relined, the tyres retrod, the engine tuned and a number of other refinements added as the Stones entered the seventies. The first priority obviously was money. The American tour had earned Jagger a hundred thousand dollars and he continued to receive royalties. *Performance* and *Ned Kelly* were in the bank. Even so, rich as Jagger was, as he put it to Keylock, he could always be richer.

Early in January it was learned that an illicit tape of the Stones' Oakland concert, *Liver Than You'll Ever Be*, was on sale in America. Jagger was piqued. He had London Records file for damages in the High Court and enlisted the Copyright Protection Society to prevent its sale in England. That got him thinking: if a demand existed for an authentic on-the-road Stones LP, why not meet it? This seemingly straightforward project occupied the group for the remainder of February. The engineer Glyn Johns was instructed to mix tracks from their performances in New York. The tapes were heavily edited. Silences, sometimes extending to a minute, were deleted. Guitars were overdubbed. The result was *Get Yer Ya Ya's Out!* (derived from voodoo) in which, prefaced by Cutler's nightly announcement, a more-or-less typical concert was compressed into forty-seven minutes. It was a classic. 'Sympathy' was a throwback to the days when the Stones were, in Stewart's words, 'a two-handed guitar band' – Richard and Taylor played solos like bolts of static. 'Rambler' was extended to eight and a half minutes. There was even a version of the unreleased 'Little Queenie', 'one of those rare instances', wrote Lester Bangs, 'where they cut Chuck Berry with one of his own songs.' *Ya Ya's* was issued in September; it went to number one in Britain and, competing alongside the Oakland bootleg, number six in America.

As with any Stones project, there were inevitable complications. Jagger had intended *Ya Ya's* to be a double album, featuring the tour's support acts. A master tape was produced including B. B. King and Chuck Berry; pressings were made. At the last minute Decca intervened with objections about costs. For the second time in as many years Jagger, the man of talent, struggled unavailingly with lawyers and accountants. In June Edward Lewis was heard to observe, 'It goes out as a single – if it's the last Stones record we do.' It was.

The contract with Decca formally expired on 31 July. For six months every major label (Decca included) paid homage at the court of Rupert Loewenstein. In September, when they toured Europe, the group's hotel resembled a world trade fair: sales executives soared in elevators, chattering madly. Jagger, not for the last time, enjoyed the prestige of significant controversy – there were reports of 'serious bribes . . . and inducements' even as he interviewed EMI, CBS, RCA. He sent Decca a staggering expenses claim to test their sincerity. (They paid it.) Finally Jagger settled on a distribution deal with Kinney Group, parent company of Atlantic, known for its widespread support of blues and soul artists. (The LPs would actually be released on Rolling Stones Records.) Atlantic's president, the Armenian-born Ahmet Ertegün, had courted Jagger in New York. He appeared in his designer blazer and wing-tips, a bald man with a goatee, cracking jokes about Ray Charles, bearing a six-album, four-year package deal. That was good enough for Jagger, who appointed as president of his new label Marshall Chess, scion of the very family from which a decade earlier he habitually bought Jimmy Reed LPs, calling the Blue Boys for one more rehearsal in the back bedroom: We can make it.

Controversy was anticipated over the firing of Klein. Since returning from America Jagger had run down his manager in earnest; he was excluded from record company negotiations; references to Fatso increased. Keylock remembers at least one night when the five Stones and Loewenstein conferred in the studio – Lewis Jones was also represented. According to Wyman:

> Our decision to quit Klein was swift and unanimous. The problem was a monumental: *how?* His contracts with us were watertight in his favour. Who would take on the Herculean job of extracting the poverty-stricken Stones from the jaws of such a plausible, street-wise accountant who knew all the angles and appeared to have locked us up for years?

Jagger would. On 30 July he formally announced that the Stones had terminated their agreement with Klein, who therefore had 'no authority to negotiate' on their behalf. Two years of litigation followed. In 1971 the group filed suit for twenty-nine million dollars in New York, claiming Klein had exploited his position for 'his own personal profit and advantage'. There was an additional dispute concerning a compilation LP, *Hot Rocks*, Klein claiming the tracks were his, the Stones theirs. The whole thing, says Wyman, was 'very ugly . . . The signs were that the suit would be lengthy and exhausting . . . We had two options – of taking Klein to court and spending two years in litigation with enormous legal costs and having our money frozen – or settling with him for what I thought was a ridiculously low figure.'

Eventually the Stones, to whom Wyman believed 'Klein owed a minimum of seventeen million dollars', agreed on two million. On 9 May 1972 they announced 'settlement of all outstanding difficulties' after thirty-six hours of continuous negotiation in a New York lawyer's office.

Except, of course, difficulties remained. Later in 1972 a live LP was thwarted when Klein exercised his claim to all pre-1970 material. 'Klein and Decca,' observed Richard, 'are grabbing all they can ... Being a live album, it has three old songs to which they have the rights.' As late as 1984 Jagger sued Klein for back royalties, prompting the *Daily Express* to report: 'The two men have been personal enemies for years and have not spoken since Klein accused Jagger of insulting his daughter by pulling a face at her.' Jagger also told the court that he feared Klein would damage the Stones' reputation by releasing sub-standard material. 'The group are upset as this stuff is rubbish ... I do not want him in my life. It's like dealing with the Russians.'

Klein and Decca were only two of a series of departures in the new decade. Keylock, Thorogood and Sanchez also left, replaced by men like Dunn and later the tour manager Peter Rudge. Employees were rarely formally fired. Jagger eschewed confrontation. Slowly, over a period of weeks, associates would find their presence no longer required; locks would be changed, phone calls unanswered, the reasons, if any, remaining obscure. 'With Mick,' says Keylock (whose own departure followed a difference of opinion concerning his availability for extracurricular work), 'you had the impression he periodically wanted to change. Anyone who reminded him of the past went too.'

The list included Faithfull. After the reconciliation with Jagger she 'found it difficult to organize myself enough to act on what my mind told me to do ... The heroin kept me off balance, and I often did weird things ... There were times in restaurants when I would pass out in the middle of dinner, my head in my food.' Eventually in mid-June

Faithfull left 'with Nicholas under one arm and a Persian rug under the other . . . I didn't take anything, out of pride – it gives me an edge on Mick, because he really feels that women are terrible grasping creatures.' Faithfull's first move was back to her mother. When Jagger continued to visit she did the only thing she could to prevent him: she grew fat. 'The shape of a woman's body,' she reasoned, being 'of extreme importance to Mick . . . I stuffed myself with gobs of fattening food, and on the day that Mick finally showed up and saw this thing that had once been the lovely Marianne Faithfull, he left abruptly, as I knew he would. That was the end.'

During the three and a half years of their relationship Faithfull had suffered a nervous breakdown, miscarriage, heroin addiction, arrest and attempted suicide. In October 1970 she was finally sued for divorce by John Dunbar who belatedly named Jagger as co-respondent. Two years later Faithfull was admitted to a drug dependency unit at Bexley Hospital. She returned to the stage. There were two broken engagements before she married the guitarist Ben Brierley in 1979, the groom, twenty-seven, smoking a hand-rolled cigarette, Faithfull, thirty-two, in straw hat and sandals. 'Ben is a very good fellow. I expect to be with him for the rest of my life,' she announced. They were divorced in 1986. Faithfull also made a creditable comeback LP, *Broken English*, and appeared riotously on *Saturday Night Live*, before which Jagger visited her backstage. Her friend Barry Fantoni describes her as 'like a beautiful Afghan hound who has been mistreated by a succession of masters'. Faithfull herself defines happiness as 'something that happens to other people'.

On 24 June 1970 *Ned Kelly* was premiered at the London Pavilion. Jagger, sensing the enormity of the ordeal, stayed away. Later that night Glyn Johns brought a blonde Californian itinerant, Janice Kenner, to the studio. According to an interview Kenner gave in 1974 the dialogue ran as follows:

'You want a job?' asked Jagger.

'Yes. I don't want to go home just yet.'

'What can you do?'

'Anything.'

'Can you cook?'

'Sure.'

'So – where do you like to wake up? The country or the city?'

Despite considering him a 'pretentious bastard', Kenner accompanied Jagger to Stargroves, where they remained in the guest cottage for three days. (In the ten years he owned it the main house was almost constantly under repair. At various times Jagger installed his parents, brother, and a hairdresser named Maldwin Thomas as caretakers.) He also bedded a second Californian, Catherine James, briefly installed as chatelaine of Cheyne Walk. According to Sanchez, 'Mick's ménage à trois came to a stormy close when he announced in August that the Stones were off on a tour of Europe and that Catherine would not be coming . . . When the final explosion came she lashed out at Jagger, kicking, spitting, scratching and trying to tear his hair out by the roots.' James left that night.

Jagger also had an affair with the girl both Keylock and Thorogood describe as 'the best thing that ever happened to Brian Jones', Suki Poitier. Poitier was the last in a series of women to sleep with serial Stones, a list including among others Pallenberg (Jagger, Richard, Jones), Faithfull (Jagger, Richard), the model Uschi Obermeir (Richard, Jagger), Pat Andrews (Jagger, Jones), Astrid Lundstrom (Jagger, Wyman) and Linda Keith (Richard, Jones). More pertinently, he continued to see Marsha Hunt. Dunn assumed Keylock's job of chauffeuring the lovers either to Marlborough Court or to Stargroves, where Hunt told Jagger the news that April: she was pregnant. Their daughter Karis was born at St Mary's Hospital, Paddington, on 4 November 1970. Paternity was concealed from the press. 'He's no longer involved with us,' said Hunt. 'At first I thought I cared for him a lot, but I found out afterwards I didn't really know him at all.' Eventually in June 1973 Hunt filed an application order in Marylebone Magistrates Court naming Jagger as father. Perrin retaliated. 'This allegation is not admitted ... There are discussions between the parties about the merits of the allegation.' After terms were reached Hunt returned to the offensive in 1978, freezing Jagger's proceeds from a concert in Los Angeles pending settlement of her claim for maintenance. In January 1979 she was awarded seventy-eight thousand dollars a year and Jagger was formally named as father. On 29 February 1984 he made a statutory declaration to the Registrar-General in London, where a new birth certificate was entered. By then Jagger, though not having custody, bore sole financial responsibility for the child. He visited Karis at Bedales School and Yale, paying her tuition; he attended her graduation. Karis stayed with him in New York. She was later employed as a researcher on group projects, including the retrospective video 25×5 in 1990. 'I do think a neglected child is a terrible thing,' said Jagger. 'If, for instance, the parents are separated and live in different towns ...' On balance his treatment of Karis, if not always her mother, was considered upright, even upstanding. Keylock believed 'Mick had all the attributes to be a father, not least his being childlike himself'. Jagger confirms it: 'I love kids.'

At the time of Faithfull's departure Jagger was recording at Olympic and the new mobile studio at Stargroves. He wrote a song entitled 'Bitch', also 'I Got The Blues'. Jimmy Miller, Nicky Hopkins, Billy Preston, the horn players Jim Price and Bobby Keyes were contracted as session musicians and Paul Buckmaster hired to add strings. Buckmaster's touch was most evident on 'Moonlight Mile' (a.k.a. 'The Japanese

Thing'), an acoustic ballad modulating between keys in a crescendo. 'Mile' was one of Jagger's more elaborate works. It was also the source of a contractual dispute with Taylor, who felt his contribution sufficient to merit a credit: Jagger–Richard–Taylor, if not Richard–Taylor. The accompanying album, *Sticky Fingers*, was released in April 1971. Nine of the ten songs were attributed to Jagger–Richard, the tenth to the Mississippi blues guitarist Fred McDowell. Years later, after he left the group, Taylor noted 'it was a Jagger–Richard mafia when it came to songwriting . . . Charlie, Bill and I all made our contribution.'

On 2 September the Stones began their first European tour in three years. Bobby Keyes accompanied them. 'I'd never played gigs on that large a scale before,' he admitted. 'It established a whole new set of standards.'* Off stage Jagger was pursued throughout by fans, by press, by paparazzi (one of whom he punched to the ground in Rome); on stage he came on like a cartoon, bumping and grinding like Danny La Rue – a man whose birthday he shares. He continued, even so, to defy caricature. While Jagger interviewed record executives, weighing warranties and advances, while Loewenstein was instructed to negotiate with Paris's leading tax lawyer, Maître Michard-Pellisier, about the Stones' possible migration, even as he manoeuvred Decca into paying a multi-thousand-pound bill at the George V, Jagger was granting an audience reported in his bête noire, the San Francisco *Chronicle*:

> The Rolling Stones plan to give money to the Black Panthers, according to an interview with group leader Mike (*sic*) Jagger in the Copenhagen paper 'Politiken' yesterday, at the start of their first European tour in

* 'The crowds were totally freaked out,' said the tour's lighting engineer, John Dunbar. 'They'd see Mick and they were going, "Mick! Mick!" Guys weeping – it was like the holy virgin.'

three and one-half years. The tour opened officially with a concert in Helsinki last night.

'I want to earn money on our new records, not for the sake of the money but to invest it in other things, such as the Black Panther breakfast program for ghetto children. We have already set money aside for that,' Jagger was quoted as saying.

He said the Stones were planning a company to distribute the group's records outside the usual distribution channels. He claimed the profits of the big American recording companies went to buy arms and support right-wing organizations. 'I want the money to fight this with,' he said.

– a cutting that quickly found its way into Jagger's voluminous FBI file. (Edgar Hoover, then in his forty-sixth year as Director, once wrote of alien subversives: 'Out of the sly and crafty eyes of many leap cupidity, cruelty, insanity and crime.' They were 'moral rats', 'borers from within', 'the unmistakable criminal type'. Gordon Liddy, once an associate of Hoover, says 'he had a special place in his heart for pop stars. He hated them.')

The tour ended in Munich on 11 October and Jagger returned to Chelsea. On his last visit to the house Keylock arrived at Cheyne Walk, knocked and saw the rear view of a slim, red-suited figure standing in the hall. He put out his hand – 'Mick' – and froze there like a statue. Slowly the figure turned. It was a woman.

Bianca (christened Blanca) Pérez Morena de Macias was born in Managua on 2 May 1944. Her age, as with other aspects of her life, was widely misquoted; in 1970 most sources reported her to be twenty-one. Her father was a Nicaraguan financier who separated from his wife, Dora, in 1957. Bianca and her brother Carlos were subsequently brought up in some hardship. Dora ran a small pavement café in which both children worked. In repressed, corrupt Managua women were rarely encouraged to assert themselves. 'I was brought up in a terrible way,' said Bianca. 'Brainwashed by sexual repression. I was taught that virginity was the biggest asset in life, and I believed it.' At seventeen, encouraged by Dora, she applied for a scholarship at the Institute of Political Science at the Sorbonne. She arrived in October 1961, the same month in which two Dartford teenagers met on a suburban railway platform.

In Paris Bianca discovered fashion. She became a confidante of Yves Klein, though not one of his models. She met Michael Caine, as well as the record executive Eddie Barclay. (Press reports later described her as Barclay's fiancée, despite the fact he was already married.) In 1967 she made a brief foray to England, being photographed in a sheathlike dress and feather boa at the Dorchester. For six months she was a minor courtier of the London scene, though never meeting its king. She returned to Paris. On 22 September 1970 Donald Cammell took her to the Stones concert at the Olympia, afterwards introducing her to his friend at the George V with, legend insists, the words, 'You were made for each other.' An hour later Jagger and Bianca left together.

She joined the tour. In Rome Jagger sent a limousine to meet her. They were photographed lunching together in Vienna. All parties were agreed that Jagger was smitten by the olive-skinned Latin looks, invariably described as haughty – a description many also applied to Bianca's personality. At Heathrow she assured reporters the couple were 'just good friends', adding 'I have no name. I do not speak English.' Bianca was installed at Cheyne Walk where, according to Sanchez, summoned to converse with her in her native Spanish,

I chopped [cocaine] crystals up on a small mirror, set out two thin lines, and Bianca rolled up a five-pound note to snort one line through each nostril. 'Ambrosia', she said at last. And Mick grinned one of those grins that split his face in half like a shattered coconut. She laughed, too, and suddenly it hit me: they were twins. Mick could love this woman because she was he. She looked the same, thought the same, and making it with her was the closest he would possibly get to his ideal: making love to himself.

Elsewhere opinion of Bianca varied. Pallenberg was openly hostile, while even Richard felt the chill of shifting allegiances: 'I think she had a bigger negative influence on Mick than anyone would have thought possible,' he told Barbara Charone. 'Bianca stopped certain possibilities of us writing together because it happens in bursts; it's not a steady thing. It made it a lot more difficult to write together and a lot more difficult to hang out.' When sessions resumed for *Sticky Fingers* observers noted Bianca's distracting effect on Jagger. 'Suddenly,' said Stewart, 'there were days when Mick disappeared.'

November saw the couple living together at Stargroves. On the fourth Jagger was telephoned with news of his daughter Karis's birth. He continued to visit Hunt. According to an interview she gave to Frankie McGowan, 'For a long time afterwards we were friends . . . If Bianca was giving him a hard time, he would come and tell me. In fact it was Mick and Bianca who baby-sat for me when I went to audition for a part in a musical . . . I never married Mick because I knew it wouldn't work. I just couldn't be married to someone who didn't get up till two in the afternoon.'

At Thanksgiving Jagger and Bianca flew to Nassau. He introduced her to Loewenstein and also to Ahmet Ertegün. Slowly but deliberately (the manner by which all such conclusions were reached), over a period of weeks two decisions were arrived at: the Stones would within the term of the current tax year sign for Atlantic and move to France.

Secondly, Jagger would marry Bianca. The group were informed of one, only Richard of the other. Whatever reservations he had he artfully concealed them from Jagger. 'Good luck,' he said in Sanchez's hearing. 'If you love her, that's all that matters.' Aloud Pallenberg said nothing.

A farewell British tour was announced in February. Even the hint of retirement – though Jagger avoided the word studiously – was enough to generate box-office mayhem in Manchester and Coventry. At the Liverpool Empire police were called in to control the crowd. In the course of the previous year the Beatles had acrimoniously disbanded and on 1 January 1971 McCartney sued the remaining trio. Now, in *The Times*'s phrase, 'the second icons' of sixties culture were on the point of dispersal. Background interest in the tour was high. On opening night, 4 March, Jagger appeared wearing a satin suit, belt, choker and, incongruously, a cheap watch. *The Times*, *Telegraph* and *Guardian* sent their arts correspondents – the Stones, with their mass migration, their new label, new single, above all with Bianca, had become what they never were before: acceptable. That spring Jagger exchanged cheek for chic. On the tour bus he travelled in a beret and suede coat, talking in French as Bianca dealt cards. She stung Marshall Chess for ten thousand dollars at gin rummy. The focus of attention shifted to Loewenstein's successful negotiation with Michard-Pellisier, the *Telegraph* reporting on the fortunes of the group for whom 'personal taxation advantage' appeared to be the only motivating factor. Jagger retaliated with a full-page advertisement: 'Comment, I feel, should be made on reports which estimate the Rolling Stones' fortune from recordings at £83,000,000 . . . The sum mentioned is ludicrous.' In Leeds students flooded the concert hall with leaflets demanding the Stones 'own up' about their finances. In Brighton an actual demonstration preceded the concert, slogans like 'Sell Out' and 'Strolling Bones' brandished by tense, aquiline teenagers, like elongated animals, prowling the Big Apple foyer. One girl made it backstage ranting, 'Forget me! You and all your Rolling Stones!' before being ushered out. 'Boring, isn't it?' sniffed Jagger. He sat in front of a mirror applying his eye-liner and rouge before donning his satin jacket and necklace. That month *Tailor and Cutter* voted him one of the world's hundred best-dressed men.

The tour ended with a televised concert at the Marquee, the same Marquee as in 1962, the same manager uttering the same misgivings about Richard's playing. It was perhaps tactless of Harold Pendleton to insist on installing a lurid neon sign, 'MARQUEE CLUB', immediately above the Stones; more so to mutter audibly, 'Still useless' behind their backs. The upshot was a fracas climaxing in Richard swinging his guitar at Pendleton's head and being dragged backwards by Jagger and Dunn, still seething with cumulative rage. At the group's farewell party in Maidenhead it was Jagger's turn; he circulated for four hours before, in Kenneth Anger's words, 'at about two a.m. the sound system went dead . . . Mick asked why this had happened, and was told that a village ordinance forbade music after then. Mick promptly picked up the table and threw it through an enormous plate-glass window that overlooked the Thames. The piece of glass must have cost twenty thousand . . . That was *his* gesture toward having the music turned off.'

By 1 April the Stones, their families, Perrin, Dunn and Bergman were installed on the Riviera. Jagger and his fiancée lived at Bastide du Roy, between Biot and Antibes, in a style Stewart described as 'surprisingly near the middle of the deck'. Jagger was seen in St Tropez and spent weekends with Richard at Cap Ferrat or even Wyman in Grasse. In the first month of exile the group were closer than at any time since 1967. Years later Jagger insisted the move had been remedial: 'When the band left England, then we only had the band. If we'd stayed I probably would have quit and retired.' On 6 April the Stones arrived by yacht at

Port Pierre, Cannes, for a party to announce their new label, Jagger treading the gangway in a cloak and calfskin shoes as fans bayed and reporters brawled behind barricades. George Trow contributed the following to the *New Yorker*:

> Although the party took no coherent direction, it was interesting in that it marked the first time that Ahmet [Ertegün] and Jagger paced out together the territory they held in common. The exact boundaries of this territory were yet to be determined but it was clear that there would be room enough for Prince Loewenstein, Mica Ertegün and a number of other more or less well-known figures from the international café society, including a striking American (*sic*) girl named Bianca Pérez Morena de Macias … It was clear, in fact, that in the territory in which Mick Jagger was now to be based, he would have a certain amount to learn from Ahmet – more, perhaps, than Ahmet had to learn from him.
>
> Control was what Ahmet and Loewenstein had to offer the Stones. Both offered access to productive adult modes – financial and social – that could prolong a career built on non-adult principles … Andy Warhol, who understood almost perfectly the social temper of his time, had successfully made the move by effecting the most minimal compromise, and Mick Jagger was offered the same chance.

He accepted with alacrity.

The same month the Stones released 'Brown Sugar', initially recorded in an era of almost archaic remoteness in Alabama. It reached number two in Britain, number one in America. 'Sugar' was a quintessential rocker, driven by Richard and the saxophonist Keyes, much in the mould of 'Live With Me'. Jagger's avowed belief in self-censorship (and common sense) led him to veto the original title, 'Black Pussy'. In later years he also changed a number of the song's lyrics relating to 'tasting' and 'whipping' women. Immediately there was speculation that 'Sugar' referred to Hunt, to the soul singer Claudia Lennear – at least to *someone*, presumably black, probably female. The very logo of the new label – Jagger's own lips and tongue slavering in a cunnilingual leer – made the point. It was reinforced when, a week later, *Sticky Fingers* was launched in a sleeve no less alarming than its contents. Warhol's design showed a jean-clad crotch (Jagger's) replete with zip: the fusion between fashion and rock. *Fingers* opened with 'Brown Sugar', then 'Sway', in which Taylor for the first time was encouraged to lead on guitar; 'Wild Horses'; 'Can't You Hear Me Knocking', three minutes of raw chords and a further four of improvised sparring between saxophone, organ and percussion (not dissimilar in structure to *Aftermath*'s 'Goin' Home'). 'You Gotta Move' was in gospel-blues idiom, 'Bitch' in the style of 'Brown Sugar', whose B-side it was; the self-evident Stax pastiche 'I Got The Blues' and 'Sister Morphine', for which Faithfull was sometimes credited, sometimes not (in the end it was Richard who formally insisted she receive a royalty). 'Dead Flowers' was a country rock burlesque heavily influenced by Parsons, as was 'Moonlight Mile' by Taylor. The album came replete with drug references – 'cocaine eyes', 'speed freak jive', 'head full of snow', 'needle and a spoon' – quite apart from the harrowing implications of 'Morphine' ('trying to score' . . . 'cousin cocaine' . . . 'in the morning I'll be dead'). Jagger himself later adopted the elegant defensive: 'None of our songs want to encourage drug use. I don't particularly want to encourage drug use. Not encourage it – I mean, you can write about it but you don't have to encourage it.'

Before leaving London Jagger and Bianca had appeared at Thea Porter's boutique in Soho. 'I looked out of my office,' she said, 'and saw Mick, standing in the doorway, posing. Bianca was doing her usual impenetrable mask, and he said, "We've come to see whether you can make Bianca a wedding dress." I was feeling tired and jaded, so I just said, "Not until she's paid me for the last one." Mick shrieked with laughter and said, "I'll do anything for Bianca's honour," got out his cheque book and paid me. They looked at various things, but Bianca got more and more bad-tempered. Perhaps she didn't like being reminded of her debt.' On 2 May, Bianca's birthday, Jagger presented her with a diamond bracelet; a week later he collected two wedding rings from a Paris jeweller. At this point Don Short of the *Mirror* made the not illogical assumption that 'Pop star Mick Jagger is planning a secret wedding . . . He has applied for a special dispensation to marry without having his banns posted.' Short, not for the first time, was spot on. At the very moment Bianca was stating 'There's not going to be a wedding this week, next week or ever,' Jagger was taking instruction from a Jesuit priest in a remote white-washed chapel on a hill.

'I only did it for something to do,' Jagger said later. 'I've never been madly, deeply in love. I'm not an emotional person.'

Those who knew Jagger best detected the presence of irony. Bianca herself was adamant that 'as far as marriage is concerned, I was frightened of the whole idea. It's Mick who is the bourgeois sort . . . He insisted on having a proper ceremony and becoming man and wife in the conventional sense.' Certainly Jagger agreed to a series of briefings with Abbé Lucien Baud, whom he impressed with his intelligence and evident sincerity. Undoubtedly he phoned his parents in Wilmington insisting he wanted to do 'everything right'. Assuredly he saw his wedding as a commitment ('Getting married's really nice, as long as you don't get divorced afterwards. It's very important that you shouldn't get married if you think that you could get divorced . . . I think marriage is groovy'). Even as late as 1973 he informed Jeff Griffin of the BBC: 'Important? Of course it's important.' 'He really meant it,' says Griffin.

In April Jagger had been offered the chance to prolong a non-adult career into adulthood. He followed it by the next logical progression. Intimates of Jagger saw the old man within the young one. He, alone of the Stones, spoke in Loewenstein's terms – trust, exemptions, securities. Even in the sixties Keylock remembers him speculating about the future. However exotic the fringes of his life, Jagger was forever striving to stabilize it at the centre. The marriages to Ertegün and Bianca were both of them part of the process – as was a third component, parenthood. By early May Bianca was four months pregnant.

On the tenth, a Monday morning, word reached Shirley Arnold in London: Jagger would marry on Wednesday. Arnold was given a guest list including Joe and Eva, Chris Jagger, Lord Lichfield, Paul and Linda McCartney, Ringo Starr, Eric Clapton and Keith Moon. On the eleventh a charter jet took off from Heathrow with, said Perrin's wife, 'all the musicians smoking drugs – even on that short journey'. In St Tropez they transferred to the Hotel Byblos, where already reporters skulked and squatted in laundry hampers like something out of *A Hard Day's Night*. ('Quite nostalgic,' said Ringo.) In the lobby Perrin kept a straight face – 'there'll be no wedding' – as half the world's rock stars gathered overhead. The press descended on the more forthcoming Abbé Baud who admitted, 'I only realized [Jagger] was a celebrity of some sort when the commissioner at the town hall called on me and said that I should not say anything about him because he was arranging for a quiet wedding.' *The Times* duly copied on its front page.

Meanwhile, according to Tony Sanchez, Jagger was ringing him to discuss the matter of wedding presents.

'You know what I'd really like,' he asked. 'Don't you?'

'It might be just a little tricky,' I told him. 'But give me an hour or so, and I'll phone around and see what I can do.'

'I'd be very grateful, Tony. A guy needs a little C-O-K-E to get him through his wedding day.'

Sanchez's account ends with his arriving at the hotel, where he found Jagger pacing the floor and discoursing gloomily about marriage. 'The whole fucking thing is more hassle than it's worth.'

A different version is supplied by Jagger's mother, who remembers the family spending the previous evening together 'with everyone in high spirits'. Mick, she insists, was 'ecstatic' at the prospect of marriage, if not the ensuing publicity. 'Boring as it is,' says Eva, 'we all sat in Mick's room laughing and chatting together. The only sour note was the press – and the fact that I had a splitting headache.'

The next morning began with a dispute over money. Under French law, it was learned, a couple must sign one of two pre-nuptial agreements: either property is held separately or together. A heated discussion – 'incredible pressure' as she later described it – preceded Bianca agreeing to the former. An hour later there was another unforeseen development: both the civil ceremony and blessing, Perrin explained nervously, remained open to the public. Even as Jagger was donning a cream three-piece suit, floral shirt and sneakers, a small swarm of press, photographers and bystanders – including his old adversaries the *News of the World* – were waiting in the council chamber of the Hôtel de Ville.

'You kidding?' Jagger screamed. Immediately he whirled back in and slammed the door. Perrin informed the mayor that his client was locked in his room '*et il refuse absolument de descendre*'. Jagger refusing absolutely to descend was enough for Mayor Estezan to postpone the wedding for an hour. More flash bulbs went off in the crowded chamber.

It grew hot. Eva's headache returned. Finally, ninety minutes after the appointed time, bride and groom entered together. Bianca wore a white St Laurent suit, braless, under an orbital white hat ringed with roses. Jagger seemed to eye the exit but finally arrived, scowling, at the mayor's table. The civil ceremony took place, witnessed by Roger Vadim and the actress Nathalie Delon. Behind them Richard argued furiously with Pallenberg. 'We were shocked,' says Wyman, 'that apart from Keith, none of the Stones were invited to the wedding.'

The party then proceeded by convoy to the church of St Anne. Whatever impression Abbé Baud had formed of the bridegroom's character, nothing could have prepared him for the riot of rock stars, fans, demonstrators and *Paris Match* reporters descending on his vestry now. Perrin, first inside, bolted the chapel door. When the newly-weds emerged from their hired Bentley they had to knock to get in. Jagger shouted with sensational volume. He beat his palm on the heavy oak a dozen times. Eventually an usher anxiously lifted the beam sealing the door, looked out and swung it open. Furious, Jagger took his place at the altar. The bride was given away by Lord Lichfield; at Bianca's request the organist played snatches of Bach's 'Wedding March' and the theme from *Love Story*. The abbé flinched visibly when a musician fell senseless in the aisle, but recovered to tell Jagger:

'You have said that you believe youth seeks happiness and a certain ideal and faith. I think you are seeking it too, and I hope it arrives today with your marriage.' Taking a breath, he added, 'But when you are a personality like Mick Jagger it is too much to hope for privacy.'

The reception took place in a disused theatre at the Café des Arts. Celebrities embraced and grew ecstatic at the sight of each other as Terry Reid sang. Later Jagger himself joined in a session with Steve Stills and Doris Troy. (Richard, in Nazi uniform, had blacked out.) Bianca, changed into a skirt, low-cut blouse and turban, danced once with Joe Jagger in his business suit and protruding top-pocket pencil, then left alone. Years later she gave it as her opinion that her marriage had ended on her wedding day.

The event, like Ertegün's reception, absorbed the press and altered their perception of Jagger for ever. Just when, after years of effort, it became possible to appreciate the quintessential sixties phenomenon, the Pop Star – an obligingly insolent, insurgent and preferably insensate figure – Jagger amended the rules by marrying a hopeless exotic in scenes more redolent of a Hollywood opening. Clearly what was needed was a new appreciation of the phenomenon altogether: henceforth, in the seventies, the established views of pop – patronized by the 'serious' press, eulogized by others – would change. Immediately, in St Tropez, there were signs that the traditional allegiances were shifting.

Mick Jagger [stated *The Times*] married Senorita Bianca Pérez Morena de Macias at St Tropez town hall. The civil ceremony started 90 minutes late after arguments between Mr Jagger's impresario and the police, over the number of reporters and photographers in the wedding chamber . . .
    . . . A coincidence that the many prominent guests noted was that the bride's signature in the register was immediately next to that of her former husband (*sic*) Mr Edward Barclay, who remarried here a few weeks ago.

The paper chose to feature the announcement on its front page.
    A different tone was adopted by Richard Neville, then awaiting trial on obscenity charges, in *Oz*:

The wedding was stark public confirmation of the growing suspicion that Mick Jagger has firmly repudiated the possibilities of a counterculture of which his music is a part . . . Street Fighting Man found Satisfaction in every pitiable cliché of la dolce capitalism, from snacks in the Café des Arts to the 75ft yacht hired for £3000; the kilos of caviar washed down with champagne, two gold wedding rings from the exclusive Parisian jeweller, a charter flight laden with celebrities and sycophants, all immortalized on film by good friend and Queen's cousin, Patrick Lichfield . . . The Jagger myth, epitomizing multi-level protest for nearly a decade, finally exploded with the champagne corks.

Elsewhere headlines ranged from 'ROLLING STONE GATHERS LITTLE NOTICE', 'MICK WEDS IN HIPPIE CHAOS' and – inevitably – 'SATISFACTION'. As so often the case with Jagger, the reports reflected the writers' own perspective on the cultural revolution in society (*Oz*'s 'la dolce capitalism' being the *Mail*'s 'hippie chaos') rather than anything he specifically said or did. There was even a postscript from Michael Caine: 'I was with Bianca for quite a long time,' he stated. 'We enjoyed the relationship very much, and I was a bit upset when I read about her marrying Mick Jagger . . . She'll argue about everything until you feel you're going mad. I bet they're fighting like cats and dogs already.'

Not according to Jagger. The first year of marriage was always the one he referred to nostalgically. On 13 May he was pictured outside the hotel, grinning, the flared trousers of his suit almost covering the heels of his Cuban shoes. Neville's diatribe entirely missed the irony of Jagger's perspective. Previously entertainers had been either professionally cheerful or morose; happy or sad. Jagger's role included elements of both. His intelligence allowed him to hold apparently contrary views and still function. If the media were more inflexible in outlook, he implied, that was their look out. Henceforth Jagger's attitude to the press would be in classic English radical tradition: the lust for success vying with contempt for those who bestow it. Already in St Tropez punches were exchanged with reporters.

The aforementioned yacht deposited the newly-weds at Micinaggio. They honeymooned there, in Venice and New York. Any doubts Bianca may have had regarding the future direction of her life were removed by the sight of Keith Moon, naked, abseiling into her hotel room. Jagger later described this as a singular moment in his marriage, though less so than the occasion in 1975 when Led Zeppelin's John Bonham pulled a gun on him. Bianca herself developed a kind of New York *hauteur* – 'High Yellow', Warhol called it – seemingly caustic, arrogant, once allegedly dismissing a long-time Stones employee because he omitted to tip his hat to her. Early in the marriage she seems to have bridled at what she referred to as the 'Nazi state', the elaborate court of agents, advisers, accountants, chauffeurs, bodyguards and occasional musicians surrounding her husband. Perrin's wife remembered her once ringing to complain vehemently of feeling 'peesed off'. Nor was the pregnancy without complications ('I hated it. It was horrible ... Mick was difficult about the whole thing'). On 30 July the couple admitted what by then was self-evident; Bianca would, within three months, give birth. While his wife settled uncomfortably in Paris Jagger returned to work.

It was Richard's idea to record an LP not in Paris, Nice or the Montreux Casino but – by means of the mobile unit – in the basement of his own house. In early July Nellcôte, a mock-Roman villa in Villefranche-sur-Mer received two lorry loads of equipment, musicians and musicians' friends. At a time when other groups were experimenting with synthesizers, with choirs, with full-blown orchestration, the Stones elected to record a double album in their guitarist's kitchen. *Exile on Main Street* began life as 'Tropical Disease'. 'It was crazy,' said Andy Johns; 'someone would be overdubbing guitar, with people sitting at the table talking, knives, forks, plates clanking.' For Richard it was a return to the primal, two-track recording techniques of original rock and roll; 'basic', he approvingly called it. Jagger was less convinced: he 'hated the basement where we did it . . . It sounded bad.' Keylock remembers him stating, as early as 1965, his preference for 'big buildings to work in'; one of his or Stewart's jobs had been to arrange the studio's partitions to afford Jagger maximum room. Stewart himself detected 'definite friction' between Jagger and Richard concerning not only *Exile* but the future direction of the group. 'Tense' is Wyman's description of the ensuing sessions.

Further hostility greeted Jagger's frequent departures to Paris. 'Mick spent most of his time during *Exile* away,' Richard told Barbara Charone, 'because Bianca was pregnant . . . you know, royalty is having a baby.' Jimmy Miller remembered 'many mornings after great nights of recording, coming over to Keith's for lunch, and within a few minutes of seeing him, realizing something was wrong. He'd say, "Mick's pissed off to Paris again." I sensed resentment in his voice because he felt we were starting to get something and when Mick returned the magic might be gone.'

Drugs, never far from the reaches of the Rolling Stones, circulated freely. According to an interview a group employee, Sally Arnold, gave Hotchner: 'When I was nannying for Mick and Bianca, Mick was most certainly taking cocaine and smoking grass. And I suspect they were taking amyl nitrate, because the evidence was all over their bedroom . . . Another time, Mick asked one of his friends to carry some hash through customs for him. The friend never used drugs, had never even been around drug people, so as he approached customs he got so worried that he swallowed the whole lot.' Wyman recalled the recording of *Exile* as 'immensely damaging to the band and everyone close to us . . . Practically everyone dabbled in drugs at that time, including Keith and Anita, Mick Jagger and Mick Taylor, Jimmy Miller, Bobby Keyes and Keith's friend Gram Parsons.' Parsons accidentally, and the photographer Michael Cooper deliberately, died from drugs overdoses in 1973. According to Wyman, the only people to remain 'regularly straight' were Watts, Stewart, Nicky Hopkins and himself.

Expatriation itself extended Jagger's options. For all their protestations ('The Stones like France tremendously'), the group never intended to emigrate permanently. Both Thorogood and Keylock remember Jagger talking in 1969 of a 'year off'. Other friends were assured of his return after the statutory twelve months required by tax law. The behaviour of the most confirmed hedonist is governed by certain domestic constraints: by family, by friends, by the presence of parents and children forever associating him with the past. Supposing he then eliminates the past by moving to a foreign country: the first result is a doubling of the hedonistic instinct. Freed from the past, the émigré lives exclusively for the present. He re-invents himself without feeling the embarrassment of appearing unhistorical, illogical or inconsistent. He admits to certain indulgences; he experiments. Jagger, in 1971, was doing no more than a million expatriates before him and a million who would follow. If, as Arnold, Wyman and others claim, he extended his drug use and ingrained it, there is no evidence to suggest he intended doing so permanently. Or, in Keylock's words, 'The thing about Mick is that he could take it or leave it . . . He's never going to be hooked on anything.' While others at Nellcôte succumbed to heroin addiction Jagger presented himself most Friday evenings for the shuttle to Paris, beaming and clutching flowers for his confined wife.

The couple's daughter was born at the Rue de Bélvèdere Nursing Home on 21 October 1971. After prolonged discussion she was christened Jade (because, said her father, 'she's very precious and quite, quite perfect') Sheena (in deference to Bianca) Jezebel (in consultation with Paul Getty, who later gave his yacht the same name). Jagger, all parties agreed, was overwhelmed. He immediately phoned his parents in Wilmington. Richard was told not to expect him at Nellcôte for a month. He wrote personally to the British vice-consul on 16 November registering the birth. 'I've always been a good father,' Jagger informed the press, 'and this kid makes it easy to be . . . I really feel now as though I might be able to settle down just a bit. We want to have loads more kids – at least four,' an unconscious echo of his sentiment ('I'm very happy about Marianne having our baby . . . We'll probably have another three') on an earlier occasion.

Recording ended in November, when Jagger immediately announced plans to tour America. He summoned the promoter John Morris, assuring him, 'I want to do small places and get back in touch with the audience, like in the old days before the economics of it got out of hand.' Jagger then proceeded to discuss 'the economics' like the business student he once was. At a subsequent meeting Morris raised the question of security. 'Yeah,' said Jagger; 'you read what just happened to Jethro Tull in Denver? People all coked up, throwing bottles at the band . . . Anything can happen on this tour.'

'We have to make sure it doesn't.'

'But I want to perform,' said Jagger. 'I must perform.'

Morris was later discarded in favour of Peter Rudge, a twenty-five-year-old hyperactive Cambridge graduate much given to phrases like 'far out', 'heavy' and, referring to Jagger, 'the principal' (as in 'The principal requires . . .'). Preparations for the tour were elaborate: in every city an advance guard inspected dressing rooms, scrutinized stages, supervised getaways and block-booked hotels. (In 1969 there were still occasions when, after finishing a show, the Stones would be driven downtown looking for rooms.)

Jagger was to be accompanied throughout by a bodyguard, Leroy Leonard. The stage manager was again Chip Monck, who engaged the first all-union rock and roll crew, pony-tailed carpenters working alongside unsmiling family men. Gary Stromberg was hired to publicize the tour, Ethan Russell to photograph it. Marshall Chess was included to promote *Exile*. At the last minute Jagger agreed to a film-maker, Robert Frank, and author, Robert Greenfield (with both of whom he later fell out), to record the event, just as he had in 1969. Greenfield endeared himself by noting that in the interim the Stones had become démodé:

> Rock stars were working half-naked with snakes twined around their midriffs. Their hair was dyed burnt sienna and they were flaunting their omnisexual-ity as helicopters dive-bombed their audiences with skyloads of paper panties. The Stones played straight, English, white, second-generation rock . . . There was the slim, but very real, possibility that this time around in the American rockbiz drugstore, where new, amphetamine-charged inputs were plentiful, the Stones would prove to be no more than a placebo.

In the nearly three years since Altamont the music industry had changed as much as in the three that preceded it. In 1969 Jagger had come on like a caricature, shimmying in a stovepipe hat and wiggling his rear; he was a sensation. Since then David Bowie had performed in front of twenty thousand fans wearing a dress. Hendrix and Morrison, both dead, had set new standards of public ribaldry. A third generation of British acts (the Faces, Deep Purple, Led Zeppelin), all with prominent singers, had effectively broken the Stones' monopoly. Why, in the face of all the above, would a married, millionaire, father-of-two with everything to lose voluntarily tour America in election year, in *summer*, facing derision, disparagement and likely physical jeopardy? Why?

'Insecurity,' says Greenfield.

Three months before the tour began Jagger was driving to Sunset Sound studios in Hollywood to mix *Exile*, arranging the eighteen tracks to give each its optimum overall effect. He drew his car into the parking lot outside the building; immediately a fan, a teenage girl with a look of open and terrible disclosure, came forward. 'Oh, Mick. We heard today you're going to tour. That's . . . great!'

'Yeah.'

'Mick' – here the girl's voice fell an octave – 'aren't you afraid of . . . being shot?'

He actually was. As preparation for the tour continued, a small army of managers, accountants, accountants' assistants, publicists and bodyguards attaching itself to the principal, as *Time*, *Life* and *Newsweek* jockeyed for position, the same question would be asked over and over, with persistence notable even in journalists: 'Are you scared? *Are* you afraid?' To which, in Greenfield's idiom, Jagger would bring forth a 'total schoolboy sincerity and say, "Well . . . ai mean . . . it's more or less wha ai do, inn't it? So I've got to do it. Ai mean, either I do it or . . . I don't do it. If I don't do it . . . what am I going to do? Do ya know wha ai mean?"'

Or as Jagger himself would admit later, 'Don't say I wasn't scared. I was scared shitless.'

Mixing took place in the early weeks of 1972. Each evening Jagger would angle his rented Cadillac down Sunset Boulevard, diligently stopping for pedestrians (an erratic driver in his youth, he improved with age), signing autographs at the studio door before joining Richard, Miller and Andy and Glyn Johns inside. Slowly, over the space of months, *Exile* was edited to fifteen usable basic tracks and two more, 'Loving Cup' and 'All Down The Line', were added from the *Let It Bleed* sessions; a third, 'Tumbling Dice' (a.k.a. 'Good Time Woman') dated from *Sticky Fingers*. Stewart, who attended a number of the Sunset sessions, noted that 'Mick really committed to the production . . . whatever he missed in the recording he made up for later'.

Between December 1971 and March 1972 Jagger, a known socializer, was seen at exactly one Hollywood function – a Chuck Berry concert at which he and Richard were ejected from the stage. 'It developed into a little ego thing . . .' said the latter; 'people were paying more attention to [Berry's] backing band than they were to him.' Berry's own version is even stranger: 'I didn't know who they were.'

The world checked in with Jagger periodically – there were meetings, near-military strategy sessions, with Ertegün and Chess, elaborate reports from Rudge, but for a hundred consecutive days he stayed with his wife and daughter, dutifully driving home – to Marion Davies's former mansion in Beverly Hills – each morning, against the traffic. None of the novelty of fatherhood had worn off. He was extravagantly proud of his daughter, bathing and feeding her, holding her babbling on the telephone to her grandparents. He had a terrible weakness for family, for roots, for belonging. In February 1972 Clive Robson, Jagger's Dartford schoolfriend, was attending a law symposium in Los Angeles. The phone rang in his hotel room and a voice enquired if he were free that evening. Robson was; he found himself in a roomful of 'strange, on the whole distasteful people, hangers-on, jesters and flunkies, at the centre of which stood Mick wearing a velvet suit and make-up'. Immediately Jagger saw Robson he drew him into a corner. For an hour they talked about school, about cricket, about A Levels and Eric Brandon, Jagger slipping through a series of accents before engaging Dartford 1961 – a voice, says Robson, quite distinct to the one he used elsewhere. He came away with the impression that under it all – the accent, the velvet suit, the mascara – it was the same Jagger. 'I got the feeling it was all a sort of game, nothing terribly serious. I'm not saying he didn't wink.'

A new single was released on 14 April. 'Tumbling Dice' was driven by a typical rhythm guitar and vocals comprising Jagger, Richard, Clydie King and Vanetta Fields. It may be the best song the Stones ever recorded. The essence of 'Dice' is basic: three chords, drums and a chorus. As a rock song it had everything – rhythm, pace, wit ('Women think I'm tasty/But they're always trying to waste me'); even melody. The single reached number five in Britain, number seven in America. It was followed a month later by the release of *Exile*.

Critics to this day are divided by the record. Some held it to be an unfinished epic, others that it was merely unfinished. Reviews invariably use the words 'rough' and 'raw'. Because it was: despite the gloss applied in Los Angeles, whatever the labours of Jagger, Richard, Miller and the Johns brothers, even today, transferred to CD, *Exile* retains its primitive basement appeal. After the relative urbanity of *Sticky Fingers*, and in face of a trend towards studio sophistry, the record perplexed its numerous critics. 'It was like four single-sided albums,' said Jagger; 'something for everyone. It wasn't really meant to be played all at once. But people didn't understand, especially the English reviewers ... They seem to have this weird idea of the Rolling Stones as being this band and we've never been that band, but they imagine we are.' Among the notices was one describing it as 'the group's first LP without a standard out-and-out rocker'.

Exile in fact began with two such standards: 'Rocks Off', four and a half minutes of abject, unadulterated sleaze, and 'Rip This Joint', faithful to the original Nellcôte recording – scything guitar, pounding piano and a lyric that somehow embraces the Butter Queen, immigration men, ying-yang, Alabama, Little Rock and Richard Nixon in just over two minutes. After that things calmed down. 'Shake Your Hips' was played exclusively for laughs, in rockabilly style; 'Casino Boogie' recalled the blues; 'Tumbling Dice'; 'Sweet Virginia', another song influenced by Parsons, received saturation airplay despite Jagger's reference to removing excrement from his footwear. It was followed by 'Torn And Frayed', more country blues wherein the guitar player portrayed as 'damaged' in 'Jigsaw Puzzle' (*Beggar's Banquet*) returned as merely restless, amid allusions to codeine, bordellos and 'dressing-rooms filled with parasites'. At this stage, halfway through the album, Jagger insinuated the first political note: 'Sweet Black Angel', a paean to the black activist Angela Davis, then awaiting trial on murder, kidnap and conspiracy charges in California. Side two ended with 'Loving Cup', basically a vehicle for Watts and Hopkins, originally recorded in 1969 and previewed at Hyde Park.

If *Exile* had ended there it might have remained a curiosity, a mere anthology of rock, blues, country and even calypso. Suddenly, on side three, Jagger's aloofness ended. After 'Happy', Richard's euphoric rocker, the group offered four songs as brilliantly eccentric as any in their career: 'Turd On The Run' (whose very title sent Mary Whitehouse into print) detailed the privations of *Exile*'s recording, Jagger – as he would so often – analysing his own predicament with wry detachment. 'Ventilator Blues' (Taylor's first and only song-writing credit) was a classic return to the idiom, segueing into 'I Just Want To See His Face', three minutes of atonal gospel apparently recorded on a primitive cassette over the telephone. The backing singers returned on 'Let It Loose', more choral blues in which Jagger, to his eternal credit, actually sounded soulful. In yet another reversal, the album closed with three consummate rockers, 'All Down The Line', 'Stop Breaking Down' and 'Soul Survivor', and a gospel-reggae anthem, 'Shine A Light', featuring Billy Preston. The overall impression was of a sixty-six minute blindfolded roller-coaster ride. *Exile* was heralded by the San Francisco *Chronicle* as 'one of the seminal moments in [Jagger's] career'. Even this was too conservative: it was *the* seminal moment, the point at which his and Richard's talents simultaneously found expression. If ever there was a statement of musical beliefs *Exile* was it.

As the album was released the Stones were in rehearsal in Switzerland. The exact cause of this costly, disruptive and elaborate detour may never be known, though Sanchez observes 'it was easier for [the group] to go to Keith [staying in the Montreux Metropole hotel] than Keith to go to them'. There were rumours of drug clinics and even of wholesale blood transfusions in order to obtain the necessary medical clearance to enter America. Whatever the cause the result was that all five Stones were issued work permits at the US Embassy and all five proceeded to miss their plane to Los Angeles. Rehearsals eventually continued on a sound stage at Warner Brothers (Jagger's theory being that, if the group were to play in large halls, they should practise in one). At the far reaches of the room Monck could be seen assembling his stage: a vast plywood dais, painted white and lubricated, at Jagger's orders, in warm water and Seven-Up to render it danceable. The stage, speakers, amplifiers, lights and the forty-by-sixteen-foot mirror designed to reflect the principal from all angles were transported in two bulging theatrical haulage vans; the group itself travelled by private DC-7, its fuselage daubed with Jagger's outsize lips – The Lapping Tongue, he christened it.

Press interest in the tour, primarily in Jagger, was not merely intense – it was feverish. With five telephone calls Stromberg secured an equal number of cover stories: *Life*, *Time*, *Newsweek*, *Esquire* and *Rolling Stone*. The jockeying, says Greenfield, was brutal. Names were bid on like a stock auction. Every major title vied to interview Jagger, the more enterprising suggesting 'celebrity writers' of their own. The *Saturday Review* proposed William Burroughs (one of the few people to refuse an invitation to Jagger's wedding; he

In Memoriam Brian Jones:

Right Jagger reading 'Adonais' in Hyde Park, 5 July 1969. The outfit, designed by Michael Fish, was based on Greek military uniform. *(Topham)*

Below The funeral: Canon Hopkins, Louisa and Lewis Jones, Barbara Jones, Suki Poitier, Tom Keylock. 'Don't judge me too harshly,' Jones had asked his parents. *(SI)*

Above Raising the curtain at the University of Illinois, November 1969. *(Rex)*

Left The Roundhouse, 1971. Farewell concert following the Stones' decision to emigrate. *(Popperfoto)*

Joe and Eva Jagger, denying wedding rumours, en route to St Tropez. *(PA)*

Wedded bliss. *(Topham)*

Above Jagger bearding his younger brother, 1979. *(Rex)*

Left Jagger performing with Tina Turner at 1985's major musical event, Live Aid. At one stage he ripped her dress off. *(Topham)*

Arriving in New York after Jerry Hall's drugs trial with their daughter Elizabeth, February 1987. 'Mick and Jerry to wed' ran the next day's headlines. *(Topham)*

Downe House, Richmond, overlooking the Station Hotel where the Stones played thirty years ago. *(Peter Barnes)*

The Rock and Roll Hall of Fame, January 1989. Jagger
quoted Cocteau while Richards studied his nails.
(Richard Young/Rex)

Celebrating National Music Day with Jerry Hall. They separated a month later. *(Topham)*

Primitive Cool, 1992 style. *(Pictorial Press)*

also declined the tour) before settling on Terry Southern. *Rolling Stone* commissioned Truman Capote, then the most celebrated non-fiction author in America. There is evidence that Jagger was instinctively and often expressly 'highbrow' in his personal tastes – at a meeting with Stromberg he expressed an interest in inviting Gore Vidal 'and the other one' (Norman Mailer) to cover the tour. There was no shortage of willing applicants: merely performing in America for the first time since Altamont afforded Jagger status. By hinting it could be the 'last tour ... ever' he raised his profile from merely sky-high to celestial. There was also the recurring theme of security – or, as Ethan Russell put it, 'It could have been Mick that got it at Altamont ... and that's why they all want to be around this time.' Years later the novelist John Cheever would recall being removed from the Guardsman's Bar in New York and flown to California for a story conference 'with editors almost baying for Jagger's blood'. The very week in which rehearsals began George Wallace was gunned down while campaigning for President.

The tour opened on 3 June in Vancouver. Jagger cavorted in a rhinestone jumpsuit while two thousand non-ticket-holders rioted outside. Two teenagers charged the stage as the group played 'Brown Sugar'; they were intercepted at the very microphone by Jagger's bodyguard. Bottles dotted the stage. Next the Stones played twice in Seattle. That same afternoon Angela Davis was acquitted of murder, prompting Jagger to introduce 'Sweet Black Angel', '*Great ... fucking great*,' over and over, to the obvious bemusement of the white, weary and mainly indifferent audience. ('One half of me wants to make a lot of money,' Jagger would say, 'but the other half is jivey enough to really want to see it all happen.') The mutual suspicion with which the Stones and middle-America still viewed one another was conveyed in the Seattle *Post-Intelligencer*: 'You might call the concert organized frenzy ... At the fringes of the main-floor

throng, many young persons bobbed up and down to the
music. On stage, Jagger bounced up and down to whatever
motivates him ... Some of the vulgarity was missing,
although a four-letter word was used and some of Jagger's
gestures are of the bump and grind variety ...' At one a.m.
the group arrived by Cadillac at the nearby Edgwater Inn on
Elliott Bay. A dozen local teenagers, predominantly female,
ascended with them in the elevator. What happened next is
described by Greenfield:

> At the first post-gig party there's a bit of smoking, a
> little music from the cassette player, and a lot of people
> watching each other, waiting for something to happen
> ... There are some young kids and one pulls an envel-
> ope out of his pocket and snorts out of it and passes
> it down. The next kid snorts out of it, too, and hands
> it to Marshall Chess ... when the Stones' bodyguard
> vaults into the room and says 'Let's go' to Mick and
> Keith, Marshall doesn't have much of a chance to
> think about it. The hotel manager, disturbed at the
> noise emanating from the room, has called in the local
> police to investigate.

Twenty years later Ryan Grice, then an Edgwater Inn bell-
boy, recalled appearing in Jagger's room. 'It was surprisingly
neat, considering ... Mick was sitting there watching TV
with the sound down, playing a tape ... It was tense ...
You got the feeling you weren't wanted. There was a dusky,
Spanish-looking woman lying with her eyes closed on one
of the beds. No, it wasn't his wife.'
So it went: San Francisco, Los Angeles, San Diego,
Tucson, Albuquerque; the fifty-strong party advancing like
an army, unlike 1969 the concerts impeccably organized,
policed ('I'd rather have had cops') and punctual. 'It wasn't
fun,' Jo Bergman said later. 'And it wasn't supposed to be.
Be efficient, make money, and don't hurt anyone; that

was the given system.' There was even a friendly word for Bill Graham. From the moment Jagger appeared in San Francisco, hand outstretched, teasing the promoter, 'What's doing? Is there some good black music on somewhere?', it was as though Altamont had never happened. 'The thing about Mick,' Graham said later, 'is that he could always apologize. I admired that.'

Lest Jagger's remorse be misconstrued he was involved in an incident that very night at the airport. As the Lapping Tongue taxied on the runway a young woman in hotpants approached Dunn. Could she ask the group for their autographs? For her daughter? The Stones' vaunted aloofness from their audience and snide remarks about groupies notwithstanding, they rarely declined convivial meetings with attractive fans wearing, as this woman was, a tour T-shirt. Escorted by Stewart she stepped down the aisle of the plane, leant over a seat and said, 'Mick Jagger?' He nodded; so she went on: 'I am hereby serving you, Michael Philip Jagger . . .' and began reading off a list of charges relating to Altamont. The next thing anyone knew, said Greenfield, 'this sweet lady came rocketing unsteadily down the airplane stairway screaming, "He hit me, he hit me", followed through the door by Keith Richard, silhouetted by the light from within, swinging an armful of papers up to the sky.'

The woman, a process server named Vivian Manuel, later told a court in Alameda, California, that Jagger had struck her 'several times'. Jagger admitted doing so because 'she threw the papers at me . . . I reacted quickly. I was sorry later.' He successfully petitioned that a judgement awarding damages to farm owners adjoining Altamont be quashed on the grounds of 'improper service'. The suit was eventually settled out of court.

A month later, en route to Pittsburgh, two female fans equally afforded access, provided in-flight entertainment witnessed by Greenfield:

A few minutes after takeoff, Margo goes to the doctor's seat and says, 'Doc, I've got a heart murmur, wanna hear it?'

Of course he does. She's wearing a little sweater that she's got to take off and naturally she's not wearing anything underneath. Someone comes back and lifts Mary up on to his head and pulls off all her clothes . . .

Everyone comes to the back of the plane to watch. Mick Taylor is playing bongoes, Keith's shaking a tambourine, Jagger is wailing away, doing his 'Oh don't do that – Oh don't do that' rhythm. Bill Wyman's young son happens to be on the flight and Bill takes him up to the front end and interests him in looking out the nearest window.

In Chicago Jagger economized on overheads by staying with a man whose very name embodied upper-echelon American celebrity: Hugh Hefner. For three days the Playboy mansion with its colour-coded rooms replete with cosmetics, Jacuzzis, TVs, stereos, food and drink, with its swimming pool, steam room and underwater bar, its frock-coated butlers and Bunnies, played host to the Stones touring party. When the group performed at the International Amphitheatre Jagger was attacked on stage by wild-eyed fans, girls crawling on to the amplifiers like insects; almost a throwback. 'They were famous,' noted the Chicago *Sunday Times*; 'now they are a legend.' That same week *Exile* reached number one in the US.

On Midsummer Day the Lapping Tongue set down in Kansas. Waiting in the bar of the Muehlenback Hotel were the photographer Peter Beard, Lee Radziwill (sister of Jacqueline Kennedy) and Truman Capote. Capote had briefly met Jagger in New York, describing him as a 'scared little boy very much off his turf' – mild compared to his later strictures. After the concert at the Municipal Auditorium Jagger greeted the author backstage.

'Hey.'

'Hey,' said Capote.

'What are you doing in a dump like this?'

An unpromising start. For six years, 1959 to 1965, Capote virtually lived in Kansas. After reading a one-column story in the *New York Times* ('Wealthy Farmer, Three of Family Slain') he began a lengthy investigation into the deaths of the Clutter family and the motivation of their killers, Richard Hickock and Perry Smith, eventually entitled *In Cold Blood*. He criss-crossed the state, wintering there twice. He lectured at Kansas State University. He even attended the killers' execution at the State Penitentiary. While all the above may not have qualified Kansas as Capote's favourite resort he instinctively resented Jagger's attitude. 'Arrogant' he later called it, a description Jagger himself admitted applied to his stage persona: 'When I go on the road I just go crazy. I become a total monster. I don't recognize anybody,' a remark he later amended by adding, 'I'd like to see someone else do what it is I do.'

In Houston Bianca appeared. She arrived theatrically at the hotel in a khaki suit, hat and walking stick while on stage Jagger bumped, shook, frugged and shimmied in 110 degree heat. After a merely melodramatic 'Brown Sugar' he went caterwauling downstage in 'Bitch', hands flapping, lips pursed, jumpsuit ajar, his heels skidding on the watery stage. 'All Down The Line' followed, then Richard singing 'Happy'. Jagger was back and frugging again in 'Tumbling Dice', strutting like James Brown, arms pumping, shaking, akimbo, legs braided rather than crossed, before dropping Brown-like to his knees for 'Midnight Rambler'. Some of the songs from *Exile* were not so much seized on as accepted: 'Sweet Black Angel', 'Sweet Virginia', Jagger's elaborate introduction cut short by the eruption of 'Honky Tonk Women'. The song ended with the singer leaning forward and, doglike, extending his leg. Richard's and Taylor's guitars merged into 'Street Fighting Man', the drums crashed, the lights flared, Jagger threw roses. The cheering began and increased in volume. The noise seemed literally to detonate, wave after wave, breaking in a single drumroll like the sound of cracking bones, Jagger grinning, sweating, stooping to wink at the eye of the camera recording him (*Ladies and Gentlemen, the Rolling Stones*), running down-stairs, backslapped, a shrug, another show to prepare for – and who *could* do what it was he did?

In St Louis Jagger ran straight off stage, into a car, down-town. 'When we walked in [to the restaurant] everyone looked like the Stones,' said Stromberg. 'Completely dis-hevelled. The ratio was one waiter per guest.' After the preliminary cajoleries Jagger was handed the extensive wine list. Waiters stood behind him with their tasselled books. After fifteen minutes studying the options Jagger finally selected a 1939 Mouton Rothschild. When the steward returned, blowing the dust from the bottle, Richard asked to taste it. 'He brought it over to Keith, who started drinking it straight from the bottle,' said Stromberg. 'Keith turned to the steward and casually said "It's very good" and put the bottle down. The steward literally had tears in his eyes.' Jagger himself blinked.

'It's completely wrong,' he stated later, 'to get fucked up and go out and play. I disagree fundamentally. The thing for me is to be as straight as possible . . . Not that I wouldn't take a beer or get a bit drunk, but I never went on stage loaded. That is, out of control. How could I?' In America, as throughout his career, he continued to attract the degenerate and the dissolute while not associating himself with either. Given the constant proximity of drink, drugs and other inducements – many of them offered gratis in the hope of securing Jagger's endorsement – his restraint was remarkable. ('He was no angel, but considering . . .') Early in the tour Jagger insisted that the crew accompanying the Stones remain 'clean'. He was rarely pictured holding a drink, much less anything more exotic. At the hotel he invariably made for his suite and locked the door. While Richard dropped his television from a tenth floor window in Denver Jagger was inside reading *The Rise and Fall of the Third Reich*. In Detroit he arbitrated a dispute between a friend of Richard's and the group's bodyguard. Everything he did, on and off stage, was characterized by a sense of intense personal control. Not until Boston was he arrested.

The problem began when, diverted by fog, the Lapping Tongue was compelled to land in Warwick, Rhode Island. The Stones were already late, tired and irascible when an agency photographer, Andy Dyckerman, arrived at the terminal. Immediately there was a confrontation with Stromberg ('I have a perfect legal right to take pictures...' '...And I've got one to stay with you and make sure you don't'); Rudge appeared; finally the police. Things might have gone on indefinitely had Richard not floored the photographer as he ran past him on the tarmac. That was enough for Dyckerman. He complained; Richard was arrested, Jagger running alongside shouting, 'Look, man. What are you *doing*? We got a show tonight.' (The actual words were more colourful.) After the third or fourth 'fucking stupid' Jagger joined his guitarist in the paddy-wagon. For good measure the police also arrested Chess, Robert Frank and Richard's bodyguard. While the remaining musicians were bussed to Boston, Rudge engaged a lawyer. On stage Stevie Wonder, the Stones' support act, played for two hours.

A combination of the Mayor of Boston, the Governor of Rhode Island, F. Lee Bailey, assorted lawyers, Rudge and Ertegün finally freed Jagger at midnight. Out on bail, charged with obstructing a police officer (an offence that never came to court) he was driven at wild speed north to Boston, coincidentally suffering its worst outbreak of civil disorder in a decade. From the window of his Cadillac Jagger could see the glow of smouldering rubble. He then performed for two and a half hours, singing, stretching, flexing his wirelike trunk, repeating as if only just sensing the enormity of the achievement, *'We made it.'* The concert finished at three a.m.

The tour ended in New York, at Madison Square Garden amidst scenes not witnessed since the Beatles. 'MICK IS LOVE TO 20,000 AT STONES BASH' headlined the *Daily News*. 'Mick Jagger touches the isolated sense of togetherness that many young people came to feel about themselves in the sixties,' noted its elder sister, the *Times*, Bill Graham adding with typical restraint, 'Jagger is the biggest draw in the history of Mankind. Only one other guy ever came close – Gandhi.'

Whatever the fiction the fact was that, on 26 July 1972, New York society experienced something approaching a collective breakdown. Normal protocol was suspended in the rapacity to obtain tickets (up to five hundred dollars for a thirteen-dollar pair) for Jagger's final performance or, better still, the party following it. Of the former the *Times* wrote,

> One could not help realizing that [Jagger's] appeal to young people reaches beyond music, beyond theater and into symbolic expression of generational independence … His songs symbolize sexual independence, emotional liberation, and a kind of simplistic political realism … Couched in rudimentary rhythms, whiplash sound and drawling melodies, glittering with fancy dress costumes and flashily choreographed, it is a message that has almost inevitable appeal.

Not least when Jagger was presented on stage with a cake and, *Banquet*-like, custard pies to celebrate his birthday. The subsequent reception was attended by Capote, George Plimpton and Tennessee Williams, by Oscar de la Renta and Woody Allen; Dylan sat posing for pictures with Zsa Zsa Gabor. Warhol took polaroids. 'Everyone', as the

Post put it, was there: Lord Hesketh, Isabel and Freddie Eberstadt, Count Vega del Ren, Gianni Bulgari – even the mandatory naked girl in a cake. Jagger himself perched at a table laden with champagne, with tequila, with Triple Sec and Tanqueray, bent as if by the very weight of his head towards Ertegün. On his right sat Bianca, having appeared, disappeared and reappeared in the space of a week. Somewhere in the background Muddy Waters, engaged for the evening, played 'Rollin' Stone'.

'It was a pretty wild tour,' states Jagger; 'girls, drink, you name it . . .' (his eyebrows arch); the one confirming him, undoubtedly rich, unequivocally famous, as yet still a threat to American society. The point was echoed by Capote in his account of the tour entitled 'It Will Soon Be Here', inspired by a nineteenth-century painting of Midwestern farmers rushing to save their crops from an oncoming storm. Later, in a long interview outlining his refusal to publish the piece, Capote spoke of the 'manufactured' excitement generated by the Stones and their management. 'Since there was nothing to "find out",' he noted, 'I just couldn't be bothered writing it.' In his handwritten notes for the story he described the group as 'evanescent people who are not important . . . complete idiots', seeing 'no correlation at all between Jagger and a Sinatra . . . Jagger can't sing, his voice is not in the least charming, he can't dance . . . he has no talent save for a kind of fly-eyed wonder. He will never be a star (*sic*). That unisex thing is a no-sex thing. Believe me, he's about as sexy as a pissing toad.' In more sober vein Capote admitted that Jagger 'could, I suppose, be a businessman. He has that faculty of being able to focus in on the receipts in the middle of "Midnight Rambler", while he's beating away with that whip. Maybe it's his financial adviser that he's whipping.'

Southern was more complimentary, informing *Esquire* that 'it has become apparent to certain persons who did not previously recognize it (critics and the like) that Mick Jagger has perhaps the single greatest talent for "putting a song across" of anyone in the history of the performing arts . . . This is all the more remarkable when it is realized that there is virtually *no connection* between the public, midnight rambler image of Jagger and the man himself. On the contrary, he is its antithesis – quiet, generous and sensitive.' Southern predicted a career in acting.

The tour's PR man, Gary Stromberg, described Jagger as 'invulnerable . . . He knows instinctively how never to give an audience enough. Because they'll take as much as you give and chew you up if they can. Jagger will give you a glimmer. The way he works on stage makes him seem vulnerable, but he has a tremendous sense of himself. He knows what works for him. He's got great instincts' – then, slipping into the vernacular of his profession, 'He ain't finished yet. He has a lot of mindfucking left to do.'

The question of when, if ever, Jagger would 'finish' was constantly aired. In New York he was widely noted to be twenty-nine, the age at which Nijinsky performed in public for the last time. Backstage Jagger was asked by Dick Cavett if he could picture himself at sixty, 'doing what it is you do now'.

'Easily.'

'Really? Going on stage with a cane, moving the way you do . . . ?'

'There's a lot of people that do it at sixty. I think it's a bit weird . . . you know . . . but they seem to still get their rocks off at it. Marlene Dietrich still does it, and she's more than sixty.'

A month later Jagger would state that 'when I'm thirty-three, I'll quit . . . I couldn't bear to end up as an Elvis Presley and singing in Las Vegas. It's sick.'

That left the question of money. During the tour the Stones played to 462,000 fans, each paying $6.50: three million dollars. Of this the group (via their holding company Promo Tours) received two million minus thirty per cent withheld for tax. Each of the Stones and Rudge, via *his* company, Sound Image, thus earned $233,333. Having arrived in America at the end of May and departed in the last week of July, Jagger made $3,888 a day, $27,222 a week, or (for purposes of comparison) $1,419,000 p.a. – 120 times more than the average white-collar worker. The tour also saw *Exile* reach number one, selling more than a million copies, each netting Jagger ten cents as well as his song-writing royalty, perhaps totalling $250,000 overall. Although he insisted during the tour, and at periodic intervals thereafter, 'I'm not interested in money. A businessman wants to be rich . . . I don't', Robert Frank, for one, was 'amazed' by the way Jagger allocated his attention, holding financial conferences with Rudge before sprinting on stage to perform. Others were equally impressed by his ability to simulate near-anarchy while maintaining rigid control over details of his own life. As to when Jagger might eventually retire Greenfield offered the simple response: 'When he can afford it.'

'It was never really good,' Jagger would admit later; 'not after the first year.' Certainly as early as 1972 there were indications that his marriage seemed not to be working. That September, when Shirley Arnold retired from the group's office, Jagger and Bianca arrived separately at the leaving party each bearing a present 'from both of us'. There was then a public dispute as to which – the topaz cross or the designer scent – was the official gift. Arnold herself noted, 'It used to get us down, the way they were always arguing, right from the beginning,' adding, 'Mick didn't seem to love her as he'd loved Marianne.' Donald Cammell recalled a holiday in Spain in which the couple fought and 'permanently . . . threw mud at each other'; a BBC reporter remembers having to 'referee, rather than interview' them. Among the obvious causes of Bianca's disenchantment was her continued subjection to the 'Nazi state' wherein, no less than other subjects, she was forced to compete for Jagger's attention; that and her husband's persistent refusal to commit himself to political protest, specifically against the Somoza regime in Nicaragua. Bianca's repeated avowal – 'I have nothing to do with them' – if anything understated the breach between herself and, in particular, Richard and Pallenberg. Relations with the last bordered on zero. According to Sanchez, Pallenberg was convinced Bianca would 'break the Stones up just like Linda Eastman broke up the Beatles'.

'I like her.'

'She won't be around much longer,' said Pallenberg. 'I've put a curse on her.'

Richard's reaction was more guardedly critical. He blamed Bianca for a number of Jagger's more conventional traits (most of which preceded her by decades): 'Mick always says he wants an office with a secretary . . . a real bourgeois hang-up – to have a secretary and all that "I'm at the office, darling."' More pertinently he detected Bianca's influence at work on the music. Jimmy Miller believed that 'the basic material for songs used to come out of a collusion between Mick and Keith' whereas after *Exile* 'it became Mick's song or Keith's'. Miller was also present in December 1972 during the recording of the song 'Winter'. 'The phone rang and it was Bianca. Mick said he'd ring her back after the take. Jagger did the vocal, which was good. Before doing another he called Bianca back . . . ten minutes later he did another and it was *gone*.' To the press, having recently rediscovered the gossip column as a substitute for immortality, Bianca became a near-daily fixture: in and out of Tramp, on Concorde, at the Ritz, tea at the Palace. She developed an extensive original wardrobe – forties' ballgowns, shoes from Manolo Blahnik, hair by Ricci and the silver swagger canes that became her hallmark, none of which appeared to conspicuously gratify her. While Jagger wrote songs for the new album Bianca was winning the Hat of the Year award in London; even then she omitted to smile because, as she told the journalist Ross Benson, it would make her 'look silly'. In January 1973 she was voted one of the World's Best Dressed Women by American fashion editors. She appeared at a charity gala at the Grosvenor House Hotel wearing a U-neck sweater and pearls. She also, according to Benson, berated Jagger for the 'frivolity' of his life compared to her own. His response was to write a song entitled 'It's Only Rock 'n Roll (But I Like It)'.

Bianca's main proclivities were towards modelling and its logical extension, acting. Like Jagger she found the transition to film – with its demand for greater intimacy than either was willing to give – frustrating. She appeared in two fringe projects, *The Ringer* and *Flesh Color*, but others failed to occur. Throughout her marriage Bianca continued to insist on (if not always assert) her independence. 'I've never been Mrs Jagger,' she stated. 'Always Bianca Jagger . . . We are two very strong-willed people. Maybe each of us should have married somebody different.' A glimpse of the couple's domestic *usage* was provided to *The Sunday Times*: 'Mick sleeps with many women but rarely has affairs with them. They are all trying to use him – they are all nobodies trying to become somebodies.' Among them was apparently Faithfull, who admits to a tryst with Jagger in the Montcalm Hotel. 'It's weird,' she said . . . 'We've slipped back into a relationship. I think we'll always be connected, no matter what.' He also saw Shrimpton, with whom he exchanged baby stories.

From an early age Jagger had relished the opportunity to travel. In the seventies, furnished for the first time with the time and money to do so, he became a virtual itinerant. For a year he flitted constantly between London, New York, Los Angeles, Gore Vidal's villa in Ravello, Ireland, France and, finally, Jamaica, where the Stones convened at Dynamic Studios to record the LP *Goat's Head Soup*. Even this proved impermanent. On 2 December 1972

French police issued a warrant for the arrest of Richard and Pallenberg on charges of heroin use whilst at Nellcôte. The remaining Stones were required to attend the hearing in Nice. (They arrived, loudly protesting their innocence, on Richard's yacht *Mandrax*.) On 6 December Jagger issued a statement: 'Charlie Watts, Bill Wyman, Mick Taylor and myself deny categorically that we have been charged by the French police with the buying and use of heroin. The four of us were not freed on "provisional liberty" because we have never been arrested on any charge . . . at no time did we hold drug parties in our houses.' Sergeant Maurey of the Sûreté was less convinced: 'We have been investigating the case in secret for the past thirteen months and three arrests have been made in connection with drugs.' Eventually, in October 1973, Richard, Pallenberg and Bobby Keyes were each fined five hundred pounds and given a twelve-month suspended sentence. The case against the others collapsed when prosecution witnesses, one of whom suffered an apparent seizure while giving evidence, were found to have been coached by the police. A free man, Jagger returned to Jamaica, indicating that the Stones' tax exile could now be regarded as at an end. 'I don't like the people or the weather [in France],' he said. 'The food's greasy and they're all thieves.' Despite Jagger's repeated denial, reports circulated that one, more or all of the group had been imprisoned and in the space of a week both Japan and Australia refused them entry visas. It says much for Jagger's reputation that while elements of the press berated him for 'selling out' on the Riviera – and while he himself had married and had children – at least two governments continued to regard him as unsafe. In Jamaica, too, he was followed by armed police. After a week they abandoned the attempt to record his 'subversive' activities. Where were they? They found no evidence. Most evenings Jagger sat on the terrace of the Hotel Terra Nova sipping Red Stripe and occasionally playing a guitar. He rediscovered an interest in cricket and was seen in the crowd at Sabina Park. Winston Stagers, then a security guard at Dynamic, remembers him as 'either amazingly friendly or totally ignoring you, usually the former'. Rudge, too, told Barbara Charone: 'Mick can be nice one day and treat you as if he's never seen you in his life the next ... That's how he keeps people on edge.' A profile of Jagger in *Melody Maker* that Christmas hailed him as 'a great example of a confusing myth. He can destroy what you want, what you thought of him, but on the other hand, the next time you meet him he can make up for it.' When in June 1973 Mike Oldfield performed his seminal work *Tubular Bells* at Queen Elizabeth Hall Jagger appeared backstage. 'He was charming,' says Oldfield. 'I remember him sitting holding my hand before I went on.' When they met years later Jagger appeared not to recognize him.

As for security, the shadow of Jagger's life, he knew he could expect to be threatened at any time. One morning in Jamaica a letter arrived from California. In polite, surprisingly plausible tones Jagger was informed that, based on a series of elaborate astrological data and the coincidence of his surname beginning with the same letter as 'Jones' and 'Joplin', he was about to die; a date was given. Stagers was briefed to be extra vigilant that day and discouraged the few idle sightseers at the studio door. When Jagger appeared, according to the guard 'making a great joke of the whole thing', he walked in as if nothing were wrong; he even insisted on buying Stagers a drink in a public bar. Two British tourists on holiday in Jamaica also saw Jagger by the pool of the Terra Nova and found him 'polite' and 'unassuming' when approached. One of Jagger's strengths, and not the least of his weaknesses, was to give impressions faster than people could absorb them. The same week he was charming holidaymakers in Kingston he guested on Carly Simon's 'You're So Vain', a song of which critics claimed – and Simon never denied – he was the subject.

Yet another side of Jagger was revealed at Christmas. On 23 December 1972 an earthquake devastated western Nicaragua, killing seven thousand people and severing communications with the outside world. Bianca, unable to reach her mother, was distraught. Suddenly, on Boxing Day, Jagger's indifference ended: Perrin was instructed to arrange an airlift of anti-typhoid serum and other medicine. The Jaggers themselves flew to Managua two days later. The city was in bedlam: according to the Reuters' correspondent 'few modern catastrophes, not excluding war' could have exceeded it. For forty-eight hours Bianca searched in the ruins for her parents. At one stage Jagger himself made a public appeal, in fluent Spanish, over the radio. Eventually Dora and other members of her family were found safe in neighbouring León. Jagger, visibly unnerved by the experience, left for California promising to 'do something' for Nicaragua. On 18 January the Stones gave a benefit concert at the Los Angeles Forum. A decade before other musicians became enamoured of charity, Jagger unostentatiously, unhesitatingly and efficiently raised five hundred thousand dollars. A Hollywood radio station auctioned memorabilia (Jagger's jacket, Richard's guitar) for additional cash. In the end close to a million dollars, administered by a trust beyond the Nicaraguan government's control, was collected. Even then some suggested the presence of an ulterior motive; in his autobiography Wyman notes that 'Mick favoured a Los Angeles venue, since this could help our status with the (American) government'. In May 1973 the Jaggers were presented with a Golden Key by the US Senate, an award Wyman thought 'odd . . . since the other Stones didn't get a letter or a word of thanks'.

Another curiosity: the very week of the benefit the Australian Immigration Ministry lifted its ban on the group. Jagger promptly announced plans to tour there. On 21 January the Stones gave the first of two preliminary concerts at the International Sports Centre, Honolulu, Jagger brandishing a rhinestone mask and flouncing in a parody of David Bowie. (Among Jagger's qualities remains the ability to influence and be influenced in equal measure.) In Australia he sported newly cropped hair – 'I'd begun to feel an old tart' – and even appeared wearing a tie. On stage he seemed overwhelmed in make-up. This was the tour in which Richard berated Jagger for 'slapping paint all over his face to an absurd Japanese theatre degree', adding to Barbara Charone, 'Mick is getting older and he's got to find a way to mature ... He's got to stop running around the stage and getting himself out of breath in the first ten minutes.' A disinclination to 'mature' led sections of the Australian press to describe Jagger variously as 'demented', 'dated' and 'refusing to grow up', critics noting that what had once been 'youthful bad manners' was now merely mannered, 'the element of spontaneity,' trumpeted the *Herald*, 'replaced by a highly contrived package of excess.' Jagger further endeared himself to the *Herald* by attending a news conference dressed in pink satin tails and black sequins and filming the assembled press. Shortly after the tour ended on 27 February Jagger announced his intention to become 'a musician, not just a singer'. He arranged for guitar lessons with Richard.

As with other anticipated events, Jagger's maturity failed to occur exactly as predicted. There was never a moment when he irrevocably 'grew up'. Elements of the old, unreconstructed Jagger, Jagger ascendant, were already surprisingly adult – in time they merely increased. As early as 1967 Keylock believed him to be 'orthodox, if anything old-fashioned' with children; he restricted Faithfull's son's television and sweets. His attitude to his own parents was notably respectful. In Australia he contacted Eva's family and invited them to dinner. He wrote regularly to Wilmington and visited his father when the latter was invited to lecture at George Washington and Purdue universities. In public Joe was conciliatory: 'The rebellious thing was put on Mick by promoters . . . He's a little against the establishment, if the establishment is wrong, and so am I. In many ways I agree with Mick.' Despite initial reservations – 'I was disgusted with the way Mike was wriggling his body about and gyrating' – even Eva relented. 'You can't argue against success, can you?'

Jagger was present that April when his parents turned sixty. He also attended a reception at the Ritz to launch a new label, G&M Records, one of whose first signings was Chris Jagger. His career as a musician remained frustratingly in chrysalis. Over the years Jagger's brother variously fronted a rhythm and blues band, decorated, gardened and became a working freelance journalist. Intrigued from an early age with Kathmandu, many of his pieces concerned travel on the sub-continent ('The high peaks are literally breathtaking as we continue climbing and then pass over a ridge to a wide valley where mountains sweep off in the dusty distance in shades of pink and brown under a bright blue sky.'). He also organized his own cricket team, for which his elder brother occasionally – unsuccessfully – turned out.

In April 1973 the BBC aired the first of six weekly instalments of *The Rolling Stones Story*. The Corporation sent Jeff Griffin to Los Angeles to conduct interviews. He found Jagger in a suite at the Beverly Wilshire Hotel, agreeable and willing to talk on condition that the group's presence in America, to mix *Goat's Head Soup*, not be revealed ('No work permits'). Jagger spoke fluently for two hours about his roots. He paid tribute to Oldham and Easton – the latter of whom, when approached, refused to contribute to the programme – mentioned Gomelski and admitted in private, 'On stage, Keith runs the show.' He struck Griffin as a man wholly at ease with his past; he even spoke nostalgically of Dartford. At one stage, says Griffin, Jagger fixed him with a look of almost mortifying sincerity. 'You want to know what music I really like? Truly?' Griffin indicated polite interest. 'Marching bands,' said Jagger. Nothing about his expression suggested the presence of irony. Jagger also admitted to difficulties in writing original blues material. 'I'd love to do that, but' (here his shoulders arched) 'I can't.' Today Bob Beckwith cites 'abandoning the idiom' as his only criticism of how his former singer turned out.

At some stage in the interview Griffin asked Jagger about marriage. Speculation was rife. What were the couple's beliefs? Was it – Griffin asked in delicate, well-rounded terms – an 'open' arrangement? For ten minutes Jagger spoke persuasively of commitment. He confirmed that marriage was 'serious'. He mentioned Jade. 'The whole thing,' says Griffin, 'was like an advertisement for old-fashioned values with mild libertarian leanings.' Anyone listening would have come away thinking Jagger to be a civilized and rational adult with a conservative outlook on life, the whole hierarchy of being; it was a marvellous performance. No one would have guessed there was a famous female singer lying on the bed next to him.

Jagger's relations with the press generally were ambivalent. Early in his marriage he detected interest in his 'fantasy' life – the fashions, the socializing, the trips to Barbados and Mustique – and acted to mobilize Perrin on his behalf. 'Someone asked me if I minded bad reviews, and I said no. As long as my picture is on the front page I don't care what they say about me on page ninety-six,' he said. To Barbara Charone he spoke of the 'soap opera' aspects of being Mick Jagger, then added, 'It's all essential to the band. It makes them talked about every week.' His intuitive sense of public relations led him to admit, 'I'm not important. It was just an invention of journalists . . . I never spoke for a generation. I did things that were taken to represent others just because I wanted to do them.' Alan Freeman calls him 'about the shrewdest person ever in terms of knowing how to project himself'. Griffin agrees: 'Every interview has the sub-text of promoting the group. No one does that like Jagger.' He also recalls that 'stupid questions' would be dismissed as such without compunction.

Jagger, in the midst of life, encountered such questions daily. In July 1973 he was asked to comment on rumours of having 'warned' David Bowie against seeing Bianca. Jagger himself had kept company with Bowie's wife Angie and, coincidentally or not, released a single that summer with the same name. A week later the two singers, Lou Reed, Jeff Beck and Mick Ronson were seen hobnobbing at dinner. More speculation followed Jagger's announcement on 7 July of a forthcoming European tour. Would Bianca accompany him? ('Never.') That summer the couple were pictured in Positano holidaying with Andy Warhol and his partners Fred Hughes and Jed Johnson. (In later years Jagger engaged Hughes as an art supplier and Johnson to decorate his homes.) Bianca was fascinated with Warhol. His clothes, voice, wigs, his stories of growing up among the coal and steel dust of Pittsburgh, intrigued her. Already by 1973, Bianca's circle – Liza Minnelli, Victor Hugo, Halston – differed from her husband's. Strongly attracted to New York she spent the remainder of the summer at Warhol's Factory patronizing his work. The following year she became a paid assistant and in 1975 arranged to *Interview* the President's son Jack Ford, cavorting in the Lincoln Bedroom and sparking rumours of an international romance. A colleague of Ford's press secretary, Jerry terHorst, calls this 'about the most damaging single event of the Presidency'. The ennui with which Jagger greeted such antics and his later critique of Warhol – 'He had virtually no sex life, so he lived vicariously through others . . . Boring . . . All he'd ever say was "Wooww, I'll have a vodka" and then talk to his dachshund' – suggest that, early on, his tastes and Bianca's diverged. When in July a reporter asked if the couple would travel together the reply was instantaneous: 'You wouldn't take your wife to the office, would you?'

When the tour began, in Vienna on 1 September 1973, critics noted that Jagger's performance had become inflated, exaggerated almost to a caricature of the original. The rhinestone jumpsuit no longer became a singer approaching, in professional terms, late middle age. That summer, at home in Chelsea, Jagger had turned thirty. On stage his movements consisted of a series of stylized kicks, jabs and karate-inspired chops, eerily suggestive of the declining Elvis. The Stones also succumbed to amnesiac neglect of their audience; of the sixteen songs performed not one predated 1968. Off stage Jagger responded bluntly when asked by Perrin how best to publicize *Goat's Head Soup*: 'Hire Blenheim Palace.' Simple. The launch party took place on 6 September and, in Sanchez's words, reveals the following about the internal dynamics of the group:

Keith and I set off with Marlon. As soon as we arrived, we bumped into Bobby Keyes, saxophonist and junkie. I was still only snorting dope then, but Keith and Bobby both fixed. They went into a back room that had been set aside for the Stones to shoot one another up. I was left outside on sentry duty. Ten minutes later Mick skipped past me, and I could hear him pleading with Keith, 'Come on, man, you've got to show your face . . .'

A short while later some primitive instinct made me glance towards the door, where Anita was storming in like a harridan . . . Bianca could only mutter, 'What's the matter? Where have you been?'

'Where have I been?' Anita screamed so that all heads turned. 'It's nothing to do with you where I've been, you stupid bitch. Come on, Keith, we're going.'

Mick heard the commotion and hurried over to Keith to whisper, 'Just grab her and get out of here'.

Later, according to Sanchez, 'all hell broke loose' in the group's car, Richard and Pallenberg punching each other while their four-year-old son looked out of the window.

The tour touched London, then reached Austria, Switzerland, West Germany, Denmark and the Low Countries. Every night, as *Paris Match* put it, Jagger 'delivered the goods' – the problem being his perception of what the goods were. In Berlin he came on like a nightclub act, sitting straddling a chair like Liza Minnelli. He wore three, four, even half a dozen bracelets. His sheer inability to structure a song made some wonder how he could ever have been taken seriously. The obvious tension with Richard diminished the group, not the reverse. While Jagger insisted on rigid control over aspects of his own life his guitarist entered an era of epic disorder: arrested for possession of cannabis and firearms; Redlands burnt to the ground; fined by the French courts; another fire ravaging his hotel room. Throughout the summer and autumn of 1973 a large part of both his and Jagger's attention would be directed inwards and not enough, it seemed, on the group; or as Pete Townshend put it, 'If a band goes along without accelerating its talent, it is inevitable that they either split up or go into cabaret.'

· VIII ·

MORE CIRCUITS THAN
JASCHA HEIFETZ

The new single was released in August. Critics were divided into those who were shocked by the song and liked it and others, shocked by it, who detested it. 'Angie'* was a straightforward, middle-of-the-road ballad of which Stewart once noted, 'You could imagine Andy Williams doing it.' It later won an Ivor Novello Award. The group mimed the song on video, Jagger in white flared trousers and waistcoat, rose petals falling, Watts dropping asleep. Although parallels were drawn with 'Back Street Girl', with 'Lady Jane' and other primitive Stones dirges, 'Angie' and its accompanying album were received coolly in the wake of *Exile*. 'You can't play or write outside the mood of the times,' Jagger observed – and admittedly the singles charts that summer were dominated by the likes of Gilbert O'Sullivan, the Carpenters and Donny Osmond. Even so, to release 'Angie' in the same musical breath as 'Tumbling Dice' or 'Brown Sugar' – not to say 'Honky Tonk Women' or 'Jumpin' Jack Flash' – took nerve that must have tested even Jagger's ample self-confidence. In America pundits reserved judgement on the song, suspecting the presence of an elaborate joke: it promptly reached number one.

* While the title was generally thought to refer to Angela Bowie, a more likely candidate would be Richard's daughter, born 17 April 1972.

Goat's Head Soup followed suit. Years later Jagger gave an interview in which he admitted to having thought, 'It's 1972. Fuck it. We've done it,' adding, 'Looking back, I can accept the fact that we were coasting.' In so doing he was disparaging a number of albums starting with *Goat's Head*. Others noted that the somnolent, Caribbean locale of its recording appeared to have affected the album itself. At times the playing was so loose it was disjointed.

Goat's Head began with a startlingly inept effort to reprise 'Sympathy for the Devil': 'Dancing With Mr D', a laughable pastiche of 'demonic' allusions and failed rhymes ('City' with 'Virginia') underscored by merely mundane guitar. '100 Years Ago' was better; basically a vehicle for Taylor, the song was first written by Jagger in 1969. Keylock remembers a version of it being rehearsed that summer and also recalls the lines referring to the 'wisdom' of 'not growing up' being penned at Cheyne Walk; even at twenty-six Jagger was sensitive to ageing. 'Coming Down Again' was another mock-country blues, sung by Richard; it was followed by 'Heartbreaker', a neatly structured rocker combining brass, keyboards, a chorus, wah-wah guitar and 'meaningful' lyrics about teenage drug addiction and heavy-handed police. Then 'Angie'.

Side two opened with 'Silver Train'; originally recorded in 1970 before being sold to the blues guitarist Johnny Winter, it was later overhauled and remodelled to include Jagger on guitar, demonstrating the point about being 'a musician, not just a singer'. (If a musician is someone not merely adept but inventive with his instrument, then Jagger in 1973 remained just a singer.) Things went further downhill with 'Hide Your Love', four minutes of improvised lyrics and pounding piano (Jagger's) which even a Taylor solo failed to revive. At this stage, with his stock for the album alarmingly low, Jagger played guitar on and sang a song of breathtaking originality: 'Winter'. Words like 'evocative' and 'soulful', invariably used to describe the track, only partially convey its sense of atmosphere; in five minutes of rhythm, melody, mood and intelligence Jagger summarized the basis of his talent – the talent to express adult themes in a non-adult format. 'Winter' anticipated the era when rock songs would become almost compulsorily 'serious', dealing, as did Jagger, with a sense of foreboding, of life closing down.

Goat's Head's penultimate track was 'Can You Hear The Music?' an unsettling psychedelic throwback again salvaged by Taylor. The album ended, aptly, with the last song recorded – to which there was, anyway, no answer. When he first heard 'Star Star' (a.k.a. 'Starfucker') even the urbane Ertegün paled: not merely was the chorus slaveringly repeated sixty times, but the lyrics further included references to 'pussy' ('Bad', an Atlantic memo noted) and Steve McQueen (worse). Eventually one was deleted – the other signed a waiver. Songsheets were altered implying the chorus to be 'You're a Starbucker, Starbucker . . .', among the most implausible expedients with which even the Stones were ever associated. 'I'm not saying all women are star fuckers, but I see an awful lot of them,' said Jagger, whereupon the BBC, finally grasping the significance of the song, banned it for ever.

'A marking-time album' was how Richard subsequently described *Goat's Head Soup*. The critics agreed, ranging from 'insipid' (*Melody Maker*) to 'an almost criminal waste of vinyl' (*Creem*). The LP divided into four strong tracks, five notably weak ones and a tenth, 'Angie', that was both. As much on promise as performance, *Goat's Head* reached number one in Britain and America, trading on the Stones' reputation as fascinating, absorbing and dramatic beyond anything the industry had known before. It sold a million copies. Later there were reservations, among them the belief that Jagger had ceased to be 'deep' (a word used by the San Francisco *Chronicle*) and become merely decadent; that much of the posturing of *Goat's Head*, 'Star Star' included, concerned antics of interest only to himself and his immediate clique. The charge of depravity was underlined that December when Jagger was mentioned by name in a parliamentary debate concerning the Independent Displays Bill. Immediately the National Council for Civil Liberties came to his defence: 'I'm sure Mick Jagger offends the modesty of the average man at certain points in his act . . . Even so . . . The implications for freedom of expression are great.' It was noted by some that the official poster for the group's European tour comprised a caricature of a naked woman, while Sanchez recalls that at the final-night party in Berlin on 19 October 'a senior record executive waltzed around the crowded dance floor with a blond Fräulein who was naked but for a pair of high-heeled shoes'.

A month later Jagger returned to Germany to record. (Of his former colleague's qualities, Taylor nominates 'still insisting on working, even though he doesn't have to' as paramount.) The group took up residence in Musicland Studios, Munich, where they recorded the Dobie Gray hit 'Drift Away' and a version of Whitfield-Holland's 'Ain't Too Proud To Beg', both suggesting a return to basics. In December Jagger went back to Cheyne Walk, where he learned the following: the couple's cook, with sensational violence, had quit, leaving Bianca at home alone with a Christmas turkey. A teenager named Bridget Matthey was recruited – as was her father, coincidentally head of the bullion dealers Johnson Matthey, allowing him to boast later of being the 'only chairman of a public company to have stuffed Mick Jagger's bird'.

As Jagger was only in a state of transition, not yet a full initiate, he declined to answer questions on 'getting old' or (once, in Germany), whether 'the art form has hope in the heart (*sic*) of the middle-aged'. He restricted himself to the group: they were touring, they were recording – what more did people want? On a rare note of candour Jagger added, 'Maybe the reason why the Stones are still going is because we've always been sufficiently aware of what's going on to be influenced, but not so that we slavishly follow trends,' omitting to mention that the group themselves were notably influential – witness the advent of Bowie (whose 'Rebel Rebel', released that February, was a carbon of 'Satisfaction'), Slade, Queen, T. Rex, Alice Cooper and, most blatantly, the New York Dolls, among others.

At the very moment he wrote 'Star Star', while his name was pronounced in Parliament like a rare and acutely contagious disease – even as he was characterized as 'odious' by one Labour MP – Jagger continued to lead a life of, at times, almost ludicrous orthodoxy. In early 1974 he was seen at the West Indies–England Test match in Trinidad. He was present when, at the end of a day's play, Tony Greig broke Alvin Kallicharran's wicket as the batsman wandered absent-mindedly towards the pavilion. This, while within the letter of the law, was widely considered outside its spirit and a heated debate – inflamed by segments of the local press – resulted in Kallicharran being reinstated. As Greig went in to lunch the next day he was stopped on the pavilion steps by a man in a tailored white suit. 'Good work,' said Jagger. 'I don't blame you.' Greig believed him.

The same week, in Washington, Gerald Ford admitted on television, 'Mick Jagger? . . . Never heard of him', an oversight to be dramatically corrected in 1975. Ford may have been disingenuous; he may have been genuinely ignorant of Jagger's FBI file, which shows him to have been under constant official surveillance since 1964. If so, the Vice-President was virtually alone of American society; that spring and summer, merely by doing nothing, Jagger provoked even wilder speculation: he was rumoured to be dead (again); a recluse; even collaborating on a musical with Elvis Presley (whom he never met). In retail terms Jagger now joined the junk food of celebrity, vying with Taylor, Onassis, cancer cures and Soviet psychic phenomena. 'STRIP ROW AT STONES PARTY' and 'NAMES JAGGER OVER LOVE CHILD' ran two headlines in the *Enquirer*. Even

Jones staged a tabloid comeback: 'MODEL WHO PRAC-
TICES DEVIL WORSHIP CLAIMS DEAD ROCK STAR IS
FATHER OF ILLEGITIMATE SON.' While Jagger (and
indisputably Oldham) had once coveted such coverage, by
the mid-1970s it became increasingly trying. 'Once in,' as
he noted, 'it's impossible to get out.' That summer, which
saw the publication of no less than three books critical of
himself, Jagger inserted a verse indicating his willingness to
'stick my pen in my heart', illustrated by a lurid caricature,
in his new single. Again the classic radical's dilemma: Jagger
enjoyed being rich; he relished being famous. ('Doors are
opened for me that are closed to a lot of people.') What
surprised, even angered, him was the assumption of a matching responsibility to the media – elements of whom, weary
of mere reporting, increasingly reverted to invention. Or,
as he put it: 'It's all lies . . . They're all stupid and people
believe what they read because it's there in black and white.'
(Here Jagger would shrug, indicating the hopelessness of
his dilemma.) 'But if that's what people want, fine.'

If the tabloids were most susceptible to Jagger, other sections of the press followed suit. In March he attended the
Oscar ceremonies in Los Angeles, earning himself a review
in *Variety*. *Guitar Player* featured him in Jamaica, the cricket
magazines in Trinidad. Even, at the other end of the media
totem, the *New Yorker*: 'Thousands and thousands of people
go into a room and focus energy on one point, and something happens . . . The [Stones'] musicianship is of a high
order, but listening to Mick Jagger is not like listening to
Jascha Heifetz. Mick Jagger is coming in on more circuits
than Jascha Heifetz. He is dealing in total, undefined sensual
experience of the most ecstatic sort. It is compelling and it
is satisfying.'

By now Jagger was a musical migrant. In 1974 alone he
was seen with Bowie, Clapton and Dylan – with the last of
whom he drank champagne, and seriously proposed playing
the drums, during the recording of *Blood on the Tracks* in

New York. He sang with Lennon and Harry Nilsson. More significantly he collaborated with Ron Wood, then in the process of recording his first solo LP in the basement of his home in London. According to Wood he became 'very close with Mick on a social level'; they wrote a song together, 'I Can Feel The Fire', on which Jagger played rhythm guitar as well as suggesting the LP's title, *I've Got My Own Album To Do*. Wood, reciprocally, helped with the recording of 'It's Only Rock 'n Roll'. That July a pick-up group comprising himself, Richard, Rod Stewart, Andy Newmark and Willie Weeks performed two – largely undistinguished – concerts in London; Jagger, while rumoured to be backstage, never appeared. He, alone of the Stones, continued to mix the group's new album in Los Angeles.

In July, the fifth anniversary of his death, *New Musical Express* published an open letter from a fan of Brian Jones. 'We were so saddened when we went up to Cheltenham last Wednesday ... Although [Jones's] grave was covered with flowers, the founder of the greatest rock and roll band in the world had been forgotten by Mick Jagger, Bill Wyman, Charlie Watts, Keith Richard and Anita ...' Perrin was briefed to issue a denial: 'I think I should elucidate concerning the attitude of other members of the Rolling Stones in connection with the death of Brian Jones ... Brian is not forgotten by Mick, Bill, Charlie, Keith or Anita ... The reverse is the case and considerable thought was given to sending a floral tribute. After much heartsearching it was decided that, rather than the ephemeral salutation of flowers, a donation to charity should be made. Knowing as the boys did of Brian's personal contributions to children (q.v.), it was decided to donate money to the United Nations Children's Fund. Normally this matter would not be mentioned.' That same month Jagger told Roy Carr in *Creem*: 'Wanting to be leader ... That's what messed Brian up. He was desperate for attention.'

Jagger had other reasons for remaining in Los Angeles.

In February 1973 a jet carrying Richard and himself to Jamaica was denied landing permission in California. He was later plainly and positively told that the Stones would never – 'under any foreseeable circumstances' – be allowed to work, let alone tour in America again. Jeff Griffin, who interviewed him in Los Angeles, remembers Jagger being 'paranoid' of the authorities. Amazing to relate, even as Jagger was receiving a Golden Key from the US Senate, other elements of the government persuaded the Immigration Service to exclude him on the grounds of (a) his and Richard's history of arrests; (b) incidents relating to the 1972 tour (riots, assault, general debauchery); (c) Altamont (ditto). When, in 1974, Jagger was pondering this ban – with its concomitant loss of earnings – he was introduced to a former Secret Service agent-turned-attorney, Bill Carter. Carter was employed to negotiate with the FBI, CIA, INS and any other competent agency on Jagger's behalf. He discovered that the government's prime objection to admitting the Stones was their 'inability to guarantee the safety of concert-goers', in short, Altamont, and the pervasive reputation of their singer. In late August and September Carter lobbied his contacts in Washington. He held meetings, some formal, others less explicit. He even persuaded Jagger – dressed in a jacket and tie – to visit the Department of Justice. The end result was that by November the Stones, with a new LP climbing the American charts, were given permission to tour in 1975. The presidency had by then been resigned by Nixon – whose Domestic Subversives and Other Enemies list bracketed Jagger with Bill Cosby, Paul Newman and Joe Namath – in favour of Gerald Ford, still professing to have 'never heard of him'. Jagger was given the news at a group meeting in Switzerland where Richard, in an effort to enhance his own prospects of touring, was again resident in a private clinic. According to Stewart Jagger was ecstatic: 'First the album,' he said, 'then the tour. A gas-out.'

It's Only Rock 'n Roll was released in October and

improved on the standard of *Goat's Head* – no inordinate improvement. 'If You Can't Rock Me' was a trite but satisfying opener; it preceded a competent cover of the Temptations' 'Ain't Too Proud To Beg', largely distinguished by Richard's guitar (described by *New Musical Express* as 'apparently being slammed into a brick wall – but in tune'); the title track; a throwaway ballad; then the extended cantata, sometimes referred to as 'an epic', 'Time Waits For No One', underscored by Latin guitar. Jagger's point about the Stones 'covering the whole gamut' was illustrated on side two: an authentic Jamaican reggae, 'Luxury', with lyrics derisive of the idle rich, was followed by a typical Richard rocker; a blues love ballad; 'Short and Curlies', a rehearsal number apparently included in error and finally 'Fingerprint File', a slab of brooding melodrama wherein Jagger catalogued the perils of celebrity (eavesdropping, wire-tapping, harassment by the FBI) in rap idiom over mass synthesizers and drums. The album, generally favourably received, reached number one in America and number two in Britain. The accompanying single, despite a chaotic video and a graffiti campaign orchestrated by Jagger, fared less well. *It's Only Rock 'n Roll* was the first in a series of productions credited to the 'Glimmer Twins' – a pseudonym dating from 1968 when, en route to Rio, Jagger and Richard were repeatedly approached by a fellow passenger asking, 'Who *are* you? Give us a glimmer.' Coincidentally it was also the first on which the vocals were fully audible.

A week after the album's release Jagger received Carter's report in Geneva. He flew to New York, where he attended the premiere of the animated film *Sergeant Pepper*, posing with Lennon and mugging like one of the Monkees. He then left for Managua where he monitored the progress of relief work financed by his charity performance in 1973. While at a reception he received a phone call from Taylor: 'About the recording dates in Munich. I won't be there.' As the whole party rocked with delight, shouting with laughter,

Jagger went pale. At the very moment, his battles with the Immigration Service over, he was proposing to tour, he was confronted with mutiny from behind his own lines. Why?

The story came out only by degrees. Even in calmer conditions Taylor wasn't a natural communicator. A retiring, unobtrusive figure, he met Jagger on his return to London in December; they attended a Clapton concert together. Afterwards, at a party given by Robert Stigwood, Taylor confirmed it: 'I'm out.' Immediately Jagger turned to Ron Wood, hovering alongside. In Wood's words Mick was '... beating about the bush, sending out all these feelers. "Let's say Mick Taylor left the band. If it became possible for you to join the Stones, would you?" I said, "Sure, but I've got the Faces, and I'd never want to mess that up." Mick understood. "Oh, no," he went. "I wouldn't want you to split up the Faces. But if you can work it out, it'd be great, huh?" So I told him, "Look, if you ever get desperate, give me a call." A few months later the phone rings, and it's Mick: "I'm desperate."'

The announcement was made by Jagger on 12 December 1974. 'After five and a half years, Mick wishes a change of scene and wants the opportunity to try out new ventures, new endeavours. While we are all most sorry that he is going, we wish him great success and much happiness.' Officially Taylor left citing the traditional 'musical differences' and did, briefly, join a group led by Jack Bruce. Unofficially there were rumours that Taylor considered himself inadequately rewarded by the Stones. There were darker rumblings about drugs. One of Taylor's few public appearances with Bruce was at a Cambridge May Ball in 1975. He seemed to doze off on stage while students catcalled from the shadows. Later he recorded an indifferent solo LP and sold his gold discs at auction. 'Problems,' Jagger said later. 'He had a lot of personal problems.' Later still he admitted that 'people objected to Mick Taylor because there was too much just solo/rhythm. Keith got lazy', adding witheringly, 'He was never very well dressed. I could never get him to wear the right clothes on stage.' Even Taylor's depiction of himself as 'the only man to leave the Rolling Stones and live' proved hollow. In fact he was the second person to do so with the same surname.

Taylor's departure illustrated the consistently high casualty rate around the Stones. Over the years 'keeping up' with Jagger and Richard became a compulsion among those vying for attention. Oldham was an early victim. Both Faithfull and Pallenberg succumbed to heroin addiction arguably sustained by the drug's constant proximity to the group. At different times and of varying causes Jagger's friends Michael Cooper, Gram Parsons and Talitha Getty died sudden deaths. After a weekend at Redlands Stanley Booth concluded that 'if Keith and I kept dipping into the same bag, there would be no book, and we would both be dead'. On a professional note both Jimmy Miller and the Johns brothers fell away; Bobby Keyes, according to Dunn, 'wound up broke in mind, body and pocket', but emerged to appear on the Stones' 1989–90 world tour. Of other employees Dunn himself survived, while Arnold, Bergman and Sanchez left, the last for a drug rehabilitation clinic. Even Keylock, after twenty years, recalls the tendency to 'crack up' by people around the Stones. 'They were the ones eating caviare all day, not Mick and Keith.' Frank Thorogood, who saw the process at first hand, believes that 'Jagger always let people have their head – drink, women, the lot – to see how they managed. The idea was to prove you could still cope. It was a test.'

In the long years of his fame Jagger had learned to contain his own excesses. A member of a (still) celebrated group was present at the very party at which Taylor resigned. 'Mick was talking to me about touring in eastern Europe, wanting to do it but worried about visas and concerned about "giving a bad impression". He actually said that. Standing there with a glass of wine he looked like someone from the

Foreign Office.' Jeff Griffin also remembers Jagger as 'if anything, restrained ... constantly wrong-footing people by being the exact opposite of what they expected'. When, that Christmas, a party including Bowie, Wood and Gary Glitter descended on Cheyne Walk, Glitter, anticipating a night of heavyweight debauchery, was merely shown Jagger's wine cellar.

Early in the new year the Stones returned to Munich to record. A guest list of guitarists including Clapton, Jimmy Page, Jeff Beck, Steve Marriott (who later complained in private of being insufficiently remunerated) and the Americans Wayne Perkins and Harvey Mandel joined them. Jagger auditioned Peter Frampton, Rory Gallagher and even Geoff Bradford, an original group member in 1962. At times the lobby of the Munich Hilton looked like a scene from *A Chorus Line* as musicians swarmed and mingled, awaiting the call to perform. Finally in March Ron Wood appeared. 'After just one number,' said Richard, 'we thought, "That's it. It's obvious."' Wyman agreed: Wood 'brought musical vitality and a powerful, likeable personality into our ranks'. Jagger was less convinced. He envisaged the process as taking months ('As far as finding a permanent guy ... I really don't know'), if not years to complete. His lifelong tendency was to hedge, ad lib and procrastinate. Had Richard not intervened the Stones might even now be functioning as a quartet.

Throughout April sensationally loud music welled through the windows, into the ruts and hollows, over the tangled crab-grass of an estate in Montauk, Long Island. Residents of the Ditch Plains trailer park were woken in the night – yapping dogs, even wolves, the loud grief of coyotes. From East Hampton to New York the word spread with the ferocity of a brush fire: the Rolling Stones were rehearsing. The only question was: for what?

PAUL WASSERMAN INVITES YOU TO A PRESS ANNOUNCEMENT AT 11.30 A.M., THURSDAY, MAY 1st, AT THE ROOM ADJOINING FEATHERS IN THE FIFTH AVENUE HOTEL, 24 FIFTH AVENUE AND NINTH STREET, NYC. TV CREWS SHOULD BRING PORTABLE EQUIPMENT ONLY.

So ran the single-spaced telex. Wasserman, a bald, bulky publicist whose clients included Linda Ronstadt and Dylan arrived early, clutching a manila file marked cryptically 'EYES ONLY'. By noon a crowd of ninety TV technicians, reporters and onlookers, some with deadlines to meet, had grown restless. At one Wasserman took the podium and, as the cameras rolled, theatrically introduced 'a man who needs no introduction' ... Professor Irwin Corey, a local comedian of dubious repute. Corey entertained the crowd for ten minutes, then ten more. Protests overlapped among the press and became the same protest. The first journalists had left the hotel when, through the great bowed panes, the old Village reflected in the windows of rising new construction, a bass note sounded with startling volume. The press arrived, ragged, on Fifth Avenue, in time to glimpse a flatbed truck, the Stones atop, 'Brown Sugar' blaring through a portable amplifier. The drums crashed, Jagger waved, the group dropped into cars. Wasserman beamed. 'Brilliant,' he said over and over; and again, 'The man's a genius.' Later still he admitted that Jagger had 'borrowed' the idea from travelling jazz groups publicizing their appearances in the 1930s.

A fortnight later, in Rudge's office, Jagger addressed the problem of organizing – for the first time – a tour of predominantly outdoor arenas. 'Those kids are all on downs, aren't they? They take some Quaaludes and then some more downs and smoke pot and then heroin and then some cocaine and some Ripple wine, right? Maybe we should all get together in here and take all of that and see what would entertain us . . .' Moments later he grew serious. 'I never wanted to be a rock and roll star. I've never been into singing teenage lyrics . . . When I started I did songs written by old people . . . "You Gotta Move" was written by a seventy-year-old man. What does it matter?' 'Nothing,' said Rudge, truthfully enough. Recruiting Wood meant that the Rolling Stones would continue to perform at least a parody of themselves on and on, for ever, as in a dream. It meant, too, that the performance took a perceptible turn for the ornate, with added touches of the circus and vaudeville. Where once was brooding antipathy was now merely an old-fashioned double act: 'Mick,' wrote Wood, 'needed someone like me to fool around with. He wouldn't dare fuck with Keith.' On opening night, 1 June, Jagger appeared to the strains of 'Fanfare for the Common Man', cavorting on the hydraulic, six-pointed stage in his baseball uniform and jacket, shaking, strutting, goosing Wood, straddling an inflatable balloon of suggestive aspect in 'Star Star', blithely handing the microphone to Billy Preston ('Hey, Billy, what you want to do?' 'Uh . . . Like to do one from my new album'), retrieving it for 'Street Fighting Man', lashing the stage in a climactic 'Midnight Rambler'.

Two shows later, 3 June, the group's rented 707 – Mylar mirrors, bars and bathtubs – landed at San Antonio. Immediately Jagger crossed the scorched asphalt to greet the waiting fans, beaming like a campaigning politician while the other musicians skulked in cars. At the Hilton he was all smiles, posing for photographs, preening that night in a Giorgio Saint Angelo jumpsuit, red with a reversible yellow and black jacket, green stretch trousers and ballet shoes. On subsequent nights Jagger appeared in a lavender jacket, Lycra bodysuit and even a white kimono. In Buffalo he sported an Indian headdress. 'Stagecraft,' noted the *New York Times*, 'tending to supplant invention.' Before leaving San Antonio the group (for a consideration of four thousand pounds from the *Daily Mirror*) attended a photocall at The Alamo, leading to the following in *Time*:

> Although they will play to 1.5 million fans during their three-month tour of the Americas, Mick Jagger and the Rolling Stones are only tourists in some places ... As they gathered near a wooden door, it suddenly opened and a woman in her sixties emerged. 'Would you mind not leaning against the door?' she snapped. 'You're blocking our way to The Alamo –'

– or, as the journalist Chet Flippo saw it: 'Ugly Brits abroad ... rich rock stars being paid to cavort in front of an American shrine. They set back Anglo-American relations by a hundred years.'

'I don't have that many problems,' Jagger stated in Boston. 'Not day-to-day ones, because I have people to look after me ... I'm very lucky, I don't have to pack my bags, I don't have to worry about my aeroplane, I don't have to worry about my cars. But then you have a lot of people who have emotional problems, and I don't.' Even so, 'when you're on a big tour, and people expect a lot from you, there's pressure ... You have to learn to relax ... You have to be calm and effective and [ensure] all your judgements are balanced, because after a while the pressure gets so much that a lot of bands just freak out on the road. Which has always been a thing of humour for us ... if you can keep the humour, it's all right.' Later in the tour he admitted to Flippo that 'adulation of the masses' still mattered:

> 'That must be why most of those people never give up performing. Because they just can't go on without that sort of rush.'

'Is that, do you think, the most intense sort of feeling?'

'I suppose,' said Jagger, 'it's a bit like having an orgasm. Sometimes an orgasm is better than being on stage; sometimes being on stage is better than an orgasm.'

Throughout the ten weeks of the tour, attended by fans, by writers, critics and psychopaths, by groupies and commentators attempting to 'explain' his significance, Jagger continued to display the polar opposites of his character: crude, frantic, flamboyant on stage, almost morbidly withdrawn off. The very week he was reviled in the *National Star* under the headline, 'IT'S TIME WE EXORCISED THIS DEMONIC INFLUENCE (Where have we failed that this simple-faced disciple of dirt is a hero to our teenage kids?)' Jagger was quietly arranging for his parents to move to a retirement bungalow in Westgate-on-Sea. He continued to write home, rarely omitting to mention cricket scores and the weather. He negotiated with Garden House and Bedales schools on behalf of Jade and Karis respectively. He dined in expensive, though not ostentatious, restaurants with his wife. In Washington he entertained the Soviet commercial attaché who asked what Jagger would do to 'improve cultural standards' among eastern youth. 'Nothing,' he replied. 'They can improve their own standards without me.' Later, while Richard and Wood were arrested in Arkansas for reckless driving and illegal possession, Jagger was being discussed – at length and in terms worthy of a minor conglomerate – in the *Wall Street Journal*.

The tour encompassed forty-five concerts in twenty-seven cities, 1,300,000 fans paying ten dollars each. After ten million dollars expenses (stage, lights, travel, security, wardrobe, catering, back-up musicians and support groups) and thirty per cent withheld for tax, the Stones and Rudge shared $2.1 million, $350,000 each. Apart from Wood, who was on a fixed wage, each of the original members earned

$400,000, or just less than ten thousand dollars for every two-hour show.

The tour also increased sales of *Made In The Shade*, the compilation LP comprised of songs from *Sticky Fingers*, *Exile*, *Goat's Head Soup* and *It's Only Rock 'n Roll*, released in June and, less agreeably, of *Metamorphosis*, a collection of out-takes, doodles and rehearsal numbers issued by Decca. *Metamorphosis* was one of Jagger's numerous complaints when he met Jeff Griffin on 26 July, his thirty-second birthday, celebrated, implausibly, at the Indiana University Assembly Center. Jagger was in better humour four days later in Atlanta. After an ecstatically received concert he was approached backstage by a wide-eyed Southern blonde who invited him, without apparent irony, to view her etchings. They were seen by Griffin leaving the stadium together. In Jacksonville Jagger admitted to the journalist Lisa Robinson, 'I *am* inhibited on stage, to an extent . . . There are certain things you wouldn't do. I wouldn't throw myself into the crowd . . . I have to play within a musical reference.' He also confirmed his dislike of wives on the road: 'It would be different if they did everything for you, like answer the phones, make the breakfast, look after your clothes and your packing, see if the car was ready, and fuck. Sort of a combination of what Alan Dunn does and a beautiful chick.' Later still in Florida there was a knock at Griffin's door. Jagger-the-celebrity yearning to be Jagger-the-common-man stood there, grinning inanely. Would Griffin care to talk? He would. For an hour Jagger held forth on the tour, on performing ('There is a perpetual adolescent thing'), on music, on America. He sat in his white bathrobe sipping beer and smoking Gitanes. After the formal interview Jagger fixed Griffin with a look of startling openness and asked, 'What's the score?' For half an hour more they discussed the England–Australia cricket series. Even then Jagger seemed reluctant to leave. 'Look,' he said finally. 'There's someone in my room' (the film producer Julia Phillips attempting to interest him in, yet again, playing a parody of himself) 'I don't want to see. Can I hang out here?' Griffin came away impressed at how alert, how urbane and how vulnerable Jagger was. The next afternoon he found him in his room singing folk songs with Faye Dunaway – 'and very passably, too'.

The tour ended on 8 August. Plans to extend it to Mexico and South America were abandoned, as was Jagger's burning ambition to tour Russia; his interview with the Soviet attaché had proved fruitless. A contemporaneous memo drafted by the British Commercial Secretary in Moscow noted 'the feeling, shared by others in the Ministry, that Mr Jagger represents an unacceptable influence' – this despite Jagger's 'obvious sincerity' and 'willingness to compromise'. Even in post-Nixon, post-Vietnam, libertine America, Jagger continued to give offence, though the principal opposition had shifted from the government to individual pressure groups. That August the Coalition Against Macho-Sexist Music, lobbying every Congressman in the Union, accused the Stones of 'perpetuating sexual stereotypes', a charge later repeated by Men Struggling to Smash Sexism: 'The Stones are tough men ... In Vietnam our brothers have killed and raped millions in the name of this ideal. Is this the kind of person you want to be?' More pertinently, in 1976 the feminist lobby objected to the group's LP *Black and Blue*, promoted by a poster of a bruised, scantily clad blonde, roped, trussed and pouting. Two years later it was Jesse Jackson's turn, railing at Jagger's lyrics ('Black girls just want to get fucked all night . . .'), described as 'an insult to our race and degrading to our women'. ('But they *do*', protested the singer.) As late as 1989 Jagger was still writing lines ('Get out of my face/Get out of the sack/Don't give me no lip/Don't give me no crap' from *Steel Wheels*) of doubtful appeal. Throughout it he remained defiantly unapologetic; he might be charming to women, he might like them, he might love them, but – 'if you can't take a joke, it's too fucking bad'. In public he continued to insist that the only form of censorship was self-censorship.

Jagger's liking for Ireland, as so many of his tastes, was acquired from Faithfull. As early as August 1968 the two had holidayed with the brewery heir Desmond Guinness in Leixlip. They reappeared to find not one of the eighty-odd taxis waiting at Heathrow willing to take them. That autumn, 1975, after appearing in New York, Jagger and his wife returned to Eire.

While there he read; he visited the Irish Georgian Society; he sang a 'surprisingly good' version of 'Danny Boy'. On 21 September he attended Circasia 75, a charity event in Dublin featuring Sean Connery, John Huston and Milo O'Shea. Folk songs were sung as Jagger, in loon pants and bowler hat, jigged with Shirley MacLaine. He even attended a Johnny Cash concert. Later, the days shortening with October speed, the couple returned to London where Jagger, in now familiar vein, spent the next months recording before flying to Montreux and Munich. Another repeat performance: the family spent Christmas in Recife. In the new year, having been voted 'best dressed musician' by *New Musical Express*, Jagger summoned the group to New York, where he stated that (a) the tour would reconvene in Europe that spring, at which time (b) *Black and Blue* would be released, and (c) the Faces having finally imploded, Wood could now be regarded as a permanent fixture. The album was mixed at Atlantic Studios that January at the very moment Wood's predecessor was selling his memorabilia (£75 for a gold disc) at auction in London.

For Jagger's first British concerts in three years, more than a million postal applications were received. Fourth and fifth nights were added at Earl's Court, then a sixth. At a time when the album charts were dominated by Demis Roussos, by Abba and John Denver, when even Perry Como reached number one, the Stones proved that they no longer existed solely on the basis of their music. Their appeal lay not only in the allure of their name, but in their (unprecedented, for a rock group) longevity: the Stones knew Muddy Waters, who knew Willie Dixon, who virtually invented the format. The million who applied for tickets applauded not only the supreme showman Jagger was but the huge attainments he brought with him. When he sang he expressed not merely the lyric but the memory of other songs. It took you back.

At Easter the group returned to the Riviera. They appeared in Nice; they practised; they ate at the Moulin de Mougins. 'Charming,' said the owner, Roger Vergé; 'the singer was *un peu plus chic* than the rest.' Reviews of the American tour – the music, as opposed to the staging – had been mixed and Jagger promised 'refinements' in Europe. Rehearsals were elaborate, publicity intense. Throughout the spring there was a conscious effort to promote not only the group but *Black and Blue*, released that April.

It is important to understand what kudos the album brought to Jagger's career: none. Where *It's Only Rock 'n Roll* was sloppy, *Black and Blue* was unstructured. Tracks ranged from the quasi-disco 'Hot Stuff' (which wasn't) to 'Melody', in pseudo-jazz idiom. Only 'Hand of Fate' was authentic, *Exile*-style rock. 'Cherry Oh Baby' was loosely played reggae; 'Crazy Mama' merely loose. There was even an 'Angie'-like single wherein Jagger sang, straightfaced, of fatherly love ('I put my daughter on my knee . . .'), 'Fool To Cry'. *Black and Blue* led *Creem* to describe the Stones as finally passé: 'It's all over, they really don't matter any more or stand for anything . . . This is the first meaningless Stones album.' *New Musical Express* compared the LP – unfavourably – to the Ohio Players; Richard later described *Black and Blue* as 'rehearsing guitar players'; Jagger himself as 'not very good – certainly nowhere as good as *Let It Bleed*', created under similar conditions. The album nonetheless reached number two in Britain and number one in America.

Black and Blue also contained a track, 'Memory Motel', with which Jagger elucidated on his song-writing technique with Richard: 'I wrote the first part, the piano part, which I played . . . So I go "mmmmmmmmm, a-mmmmmmm", and Keith goes "hmmmmmggghhh . . . uhhh . . . that sounds awright . . ." and I say, "Well, I only just started it" . . . I like to get everything finished, done, typed up, all written out . . . But he doesn't like that so he says, "I've got a middle bit here", and he sits down at the other piano and plays the middle bit. Then I learn that and he learns my part, and then we make the track. Boring, isn't it?' (The word certainly applied to 'Memory Motel', a lengthy, life-on-the-road lament apparently dedicated to the photographer Annie Leibovitz.)

In more coherent mood Jagger noted, 'When we first started, Keith and I used to be very separate and I used to just write the words. Now we mix it up a lot and I write quite a lot of music and Keith writes some words . . . A song can start off anywhere. You meet a chick and she's got a beautiful name, and you get an idea, a lyric idea about a chick with a beautiful name . . . Sometimes it works the other way around. You get an idea for a melody, and you just start playing it – and suddenly the words come . . . they fit, they're right, they tumble into place. Those are always the best songs.' Stewart himself believed that 'Mick always wanted a number written, ready and rehearsed before recording', whereas Richard trusted to improvisation. A number of the group's early hits derived from no more than a basic chord structure – 'I go in there with a germ, the smaller the better, feed it to them, and see what happens.' Both partners agreed that the group (or, as with 'Honky Tonk Women', the session guitarist Ry Cooder) invariably advanced the concept into the finished product. While Watts – off whom Jagger perpetually bounced ideas – acquiesced, Taylor, who believed 'the best songs were only two-thirds written when we heard them', and to a greater extent Wyman bridled: 'They'd bring in a song,' says the latter, 'suggest a style and what the bass line and drums might do, and then we'd play around with it and throw in our own ideas.' While Wyman notes factually that 'input by me or Brian or Charlie was never recognized financially', it was equally true that the overall Stones sound – blues and soul welded to lyrics enabling a young white audience to identify with the message – was exclusively Jagger's and Richard's. Keylock, who attended every British recording session from 1965 to 1970, states bluntly: 'The songs were Mick and Keith's. The others just went along. End of story.'

The European tour opened on 28 April 1976 in Frankfurt. Again Jagger came on dressed by Giorgio Saint Angelo; again streaming in make-up; again there were touches of self-parody. According to the critic Charles Shaar Murray:

> Jagger prowls and struts and minces and flounces like a faggot chimpanzee, his whole body one big pout. His moves are athletic/gymnastic rather than balletic, like a calisthenics programme designed by the Royal Canadian Air Force.

And:

> He shoulders into Ronnie Wood, limpwrists so extravagantly that the movement spreads right up his arm to his shoulder, and niggers outrageously between numbers, going 'All *right!*' and '*Yeah!*' and 'Ssssssssu-*guh!*' like he was Isaac Hayes.

Finally:

> The trouble is that Jagger's cosmic inflation of spoiled brattishness has been so crudely exaggerated that it's

stylized itself up its own ass. It's a good show, but he comes on so strong that it just degenerates into hamming.

Later, in the group's hotel, Murray was prevented from interviewing Wood by a sound '. . . exactly like Mick Jagger saying in his proletarian voice, "Oi fort your review [of *Black and Blue*] was bahluddy stoopid."' After repeating the assertion Jagger spoke briefly to Wasserman and the record executive Dave Walters, who informed Murray, 'Paul's just told me that Jagger said that if you're not out in thirty seconds, he'll get the heavies to throw you out.'

From Frankfurt the tour touched Munster, Kiel, Berlin, Bremen and Brussels; the Stones reached London on 21 May. While tens of thousands queued for tickets in Warwick Road, squatting and freezing in doorways in Eardley Crescent, a stretch Mercedes pulled up and Jagger himself, in white flannel suit, distributed passes. On his order, money-off coupons for *Black and Blue* were provided to unsuccessful applicants. On the morning of the first concert he became godfather to five-month-old Jean-Paul Menzies, son of the Stones' assistant Anna Menzies, at a service in south London. He was telephoned by Princess Margaret, whom he arranged to be introduced to the group backstage, the Stones shuffling up like a Cup Final team at Wembley. He had his parents driven in from Westgate. He even invited Dick Taylor, who found him 'subdued', as his guest. 'There was a feeling,' said Stewart, 'that everything depended on how things went in London.'

They went abysmally. The sound at Earl's Court was likened to a railway platform tannoy. Jagger himself seemed lost among the props of his new mania for mass entertainment, which included pails of water, confetti, even a trapeze for 'Jumpin' Jack Flash'. There was a sense that the stage, the balloons, the Italian designer suits were no more than substitutes for what the Stones once were: raw, unadorned energy. After the show a visibly demoralized Jagger described Earl's Court as 'the worst toilet I've played in – and I've seen toilets'. His comment to the *Daily Mirror* – 'People overestimate us, we're not as good as people think' – for once failed to convey irony.

One plausible explanation is provided by Sally Arnold. Speaking in 1990 to A. E. Hotchner, she recalled:

> I made coke and heroin available during the performances . . . We had a walkway on each side of the stage, which Mick and Billy Preston would mount and then dance on the platform that connected them . . . The entire structure was covered with drapes, and hidden underneath the drapes were the amps . . . That's where I put lines of cocaine and heroin . . . While the show was going on, all of us would sneak back behind the drapes and have a quick line whenever we needed a fix, and that included Mick.*

Then again, the 'distance' separating Jagger and Richard, noted by Taylor in 1961, was all too evident to the same observer at Earl's Court. In London Richard came on stage like a man recently exhumed. Shadows that might have been cast by Bela Lugosi flickered over him. He was a heroin addict and alcoholic. Leaving a concert at Stafford on 18 May Richard nodded off at the wheel of the Blue Lena: the Bentley veered, left the road and came to rest in a field outside Newport Pagnell. A police search of the contents revealed traces of LSD and cocaine. A fortnight later Richard's and Pallenberg's ten-week-old-son Tara died of a 'flu virus in Geneva. When Taylor saw his old art school

---

* The journalist Nick Kent, present at Earl's Court, also noted that 'Jagger, Wood, and Richard were all going off and doing vast amounts of drugs. By that time the heroin abuse had got so bad even the roadies would come in and score . . . it was heroin city.'

friend backstage he had an overpowering urge to shout 'Help.'

Jagger's problems were of a different vein. For years his marriage had existed only in name. Bianca modelled exotic clothes and shouted at servants – that was her style. She derided Jagger for his primitive instincts; how long was he going to exhibit himself, foul-mouthed and full of obsolete tendencies? she asked. When would he *grow up*? Backstage at Earl's Court Taylor found Richard, for all his crises, at least ready to discuss them; Jagger's were incommunicable, and becoming more so all the time.

Jerry Faye Hall was born in Gonzalez, Texas, on 2 July 1956. She was one of five daughters of a truck-driver father and a woman who saw *Gone With The Wind* sixteen times. At fourteen Hall worked in the local Dairy Queen; the same year she discovered sex. She rode horses; she graduated from Mesquite High School. In May 1973, with an eight-hundred-dollar compensation payment following an accident, Hall arrived in Paris. She had tea with King Vidor and Jean-Paul Sartre. She modelled for Helmut Newton. In September 1974 *Newsweek* ran an article wherein 'languid, leggy Jerry' was said to be taking Paris by storm. She signed to the Eileen Ford agency in New York and was featured in *Vogue*, from which pages the singer Bryan Ferry chose her to appear on the cover of his album *Siren*; it was with Ferry that she attended the Earl's Court concert on 22 May. What happened next is described in Hall's autobiography:

We went backstage and Mick was sitting there in his dressing gown and he was so much smaller than I'd imagined . . .

After we went out to dinner, we all got in the limousine and that's when Mick really got to me. He pressed his knee next to mine and I could feel the electricity . . .

Mick came back to the house with us and he was so much fun, jumping around and joking ... Bryan was getting sort of freaked out about the whole thing. I'd go into the kitchen to fix some more tea and Mick would follow me and Bryan would follow *him*. He was real jealous that Mick was flirting with me. And I tried to behave myself. But finally Bryan got really upset and said, 'I'm going to bed.' He stomped off and everyone started to leave. Mick tried to kiss me when he was going out the door but I didn't let him.

There was a second, unexpected result of the débâcle at Earl's Court. It lead directly to the acceleration of a stripped-down, atavistic and frequently atonal musical style previously existing in embryo: punk. (Or, as the Sex Pistols said: 'It was Mick Jagger and the Princess that did it.') By mid-1976 a wave of these bands – the Pistols, the Clash, Damned, Stranglers, Subway Sect, Eddie and the Hot Rods, the Buzzcocks – had emerged in direct opposition to the kind of theatrical rock purveyed by the Stones. The essence of the groups' protest was pithily summarized at the 100 Club Punk Festival that September: after railing for some time at 'poofs', 'ponces' and Jagger in particular and pausing only to be violently ill, the Pistols' Sid Vicious hurled a bottle off stage, blinding a female fan in one eye. The resulting publicity – no less than the Pistols' appearance on Bill Grundy's *Today* programme that December – crystallized opinion: either you were appalled by punk and loathed it or you were appalled by it and admired it – though even the latter may have admitted to a sense of *déjà vu*. When Nick Mobbs, A & R Manager of EMI, said of the Pistols, 'Here at last is a band with a bit of guts for younger people to identify with; a band that parents actually won't tolerate,' he omitted only to add, 'They aren't just a group, they're a way of life.' Because, whatever the merits of their case, the Pistols in general and their manager Malcolm

McLaren in particular did nothing not already done by the Stones and Andrew Oldham.

One of the persistent legends of punk is that Jagger had appeared – alone, white-faced and tremulous – outside the Pistols' headquarters, waited indefinitely, then fled. He denied it: 'Total fantasy ... Nobody ever slams the door on me in the King's Road.' A year later Jagger was interviewed by the critic Chet Flippo:

'Johnny Rotten says you should have retired in 1965.'

'Well, then he should definitely retire next year. He was on *Top of the Pops* in England and that was a cop-out for the Sex Pistols ... It's aimed at a real teeny market, people with clean hair and all that.'

'People who buy records.'

'Yeah, who buy singles. And when the Sex Pistols went on *Top of the Pops* they copped out. Now they're on the front of *Rolling Stone*. That's a real cop-out. If I was Johnny Rotten, I wouldn't do either. I wouldn't do *Top of the Pops* and I'd tell *Rolling Stone* to go fuck themselves ... I don't care what Johnny Rotten says. Everything Johnny Rotten says about me is only 'cause he loves me 'cause I'm so good. It's true.'

Later in the same interview Jagger assured Flippo, 'I'm, along with the Queen, you know, one of the best things England's got. Me and the Queen.'

In the end, if nothing else, punk served to give expression to the British propensity for irreverence and buffoonery at the expense of the very elements (the rich and famous) so revered in America. Jagger himself, speaking from New York, acknowledged the point. 'I think in England it's much more of a real thing than it is here ... here it's a kind of association. In London you get all these kids that are really out of work ... you know, nothing else to do but play in rock groups.' Despite consistently denying any 'overt' influence and maintaining, *'We're* a punk band ... It's the attitude that counts,' Jagger, says Wood, 'got along quite well' with Rotten. Significantly, the next Stones album included an authentic new-wave number, while by 1978 Jagger's stage act was noticeably pared down. He even sported a torn T-shirt.

There were other changes. That spring Marshall Chess resigned as president of Rolling Stones Records and was replaced by Earl McGrath. Although this was attributed to the ennui of managing a single-act label, Richard was blunter: 'Marshall got totally disenchanted [with Atlantic] because Mick had blown any leverage Marshall had with it ... Mick got involved hobnobbing and drinking with the record people. Mick socialized with Ahmet Ertegün so the mystique was gone.' Ertegün himself was negotiating, and would partially lose, a new contract to distribute the Stones. After nine years Jagger also replaced Les Perrin, ill from hepatitis, with the former music critic Keith Altham.

After London the tour returned to Europe – Holland, France, Spain and Switzerland. On 21 June the Stones played Zagreb where Jagger swung from ropes and shouted, *'Zivjeli! Ovo je* Starfucker!' in a variety of dialects while in London Bianca, in Dior suit and sunglasses, attended Paul Getty's memorial service with Getty Jnr, who wore tennis shoes. The tour ended two nights later in Vienna, after which Ertegün was foolish enough to accuse Jagger of having 'quieted down'. Jagger responded by destroying Earl McGrath's hotel room, splintering the chandelier and over-flowing the bath: eight thousand dollars' damage. After that he flew to his summer home in Montauk where, on 26 July, at a party attended by Warhol and his major domo Fred Hughes, he turned thirty-three. A month later Jagger was in England again, playing to an audience of two hundred thousand at Knebworth – the Stones' first festival appearance since Altamont; they gave a performance described by

The Times as a 'shambling parody'. (A film crew, returning to London, was surprised to be stopped by Bianca, standing by the roadside, thumbing a lift.) In New York – again – Jagger stood backstage at a Marvin Gaye concert, after which, in Wood's words, 'Mick unknowingly went up [to Gaye] and started laying on all this advice ... "Oh, you should have done this song, you should have done this, done that." All that Jagger wisdom spewing forth, and then ... "Hey, man, that's all well and good, but I'm Marvin's brother. Marvin will be back soon."' He also attended the Montreal Olympics, sitting mute with Bianca in matching tracksuits while reporters noted their 'sullen' expressions. 'I got married for something to do,' he informed *Woman's Own*.

On 29 August, while Jagger was in Los Angeles editing 150 hours of concert material for a live album, his childhood hero died in Oakland. For some years Jimmy Reed had been increasingly afflicted by epilepsy, compounded by alcohol. His friend John Lee Hooker remembers 'hiding bottles left and right around JR' – and this from a man who enjoyed a drink himself. That same month, Jagger's political mentor Tom Driberg died in London.

While in Hollywood Jagger met Mike Maitland, president of MCA, to discuss a new record contract. He had lunch with Walter Yetnikoff of CBS and dinner with Ertegün. As in 1970 high-powered executives soared in jets and arrived at Jagger's hotel in convoy. Certain film stars and presidential candidates enjoy similar treatment. Candidates and film stars were exactly the company he was keeping: on 30 October Jagger was at Wood's house in Los Angeles with, among others, Governor Jerry Brown and Warren Beatty. When Wood's wife went into labour Jagger accompanied the couple to hospital. On the second floor of Cedars Sinai the two musicians slept in moulded plastic chairs. 'Mick,' says Wood, 'was great ... he went in a few times to hold Krissie's hand. Then he helped me fill out some papers to allow a Caesarean section.' When fans arrived at the hospital door Jagger went outside, calming them with two lowered hands, and chatted affably for an hour.

In New York work continued to produce a saleable live album edited from over eighty performances. Early in the process Jagger and Richard concentrated on the three concerts at the Paris Abattoir. They were consistently good arena rock – but they *were* arena rock. Richard then had the idea to include material performed in a club or bar, a throwback to the Crawdaddy days. The only problem was: *which* club or bar? And how would the Stones ever perform there? While he was pondering that Jagger commuted between Los Angeles, Montauk and the St Pierre Hotel in Manhattan. On 23 December 1976 he took possession of a four-bedroom townhouse on 73rd Street; John Lennon was a near neighbour. On Christmas Eve the Jaggers had dinner at Fred Hughes' house where, according to Warhol's *Diaries*, 'Mick was asking for coke.' The next day, said Warhol, 'Mick sat down next to Bob Colacello and put his arm around him and offered him a pick-me-up and Bob said, "Why, yes, I am rather tired" and just as he was about to get it, Yoko and John Lennon walked in and Mick was so excited to see them that he ran over with the spoon that he was about to put under Bob's nose and put it under John Lennon's.'

In the new year Jagger appeared unexpectedly at Aylesbury Crown Court (as he had once appeared at Jones's trials) to lend moral support to Richard. He sat in the public gallery in a check jacket and muffler while the guitarist deadpanned a series of one-liners ('What do I do? Make the most noise') provided by his barrister. On 12 January Richard was found guilty of possession of cocaine but cleared of possessing LSD: fined £750. 'Keith,' says Wyman, 'invariably emerged from his crises with incredible luck.' For a month the Glimmer Twins remained in situ: Richard in the rebuilt Redlands, Jagger in Cheyne Walk and Stargroves.

They were together at Redlands on 12 February, the tenth anniversary of the raid on the same house. Apprised of this Jagger threw back his head and laughed; Richard seemed slower to comprehend.* After that it was Paris, Los Angeles, New York. Warhol's *Diaries* record that on 20 February Jagger and Bianca 'had had a fight ... she'd accused him of having an affair with Linda Ronstadt'. From there Jagger met the group in his idea of an 'ideal, out-of-the-way spot' in which to play a small club: Toronto.

Jagger's choice was based on the city's being large enough (but small enough) to accommodate the Stones; its adjacency to New York; and the availability of El Mocambo, a bare-boarded tavern of dubious mock-tropical decor deemed perfect for recording. The plan, as Jagger had it, was to assemble in the Harbour Castle Hotel, eat well, drink well, continue to interview supplicant executives, perform one or perhaps two concerts and leave.

That was the plan. The precision with which Rudge and Dunn, in particular, arranged the excursion was immediately rendered void at the airport: Pallenberg was arrested. While his common-law wife was charged with possession of hashish (fined four hundred dollars) Richard and their seven-year-old son were driven to the hotel. A notably morbid-looking Jagger flew in from New York. Three days later, 27 February, Richard was woken by five plainclothes Mounties to be relieved of the following: passport; work permit; hypodermic needle cover; plastic bag with traces of white powder; red-coloured pills; hotel sugar bag containing two grams of resin material (believed to be hashish); gold foil paper with traces of white powder; five grams of cocaine; razor blade with traces of white powder; switchblade knife with traces of white powder; hypodermic needle with liquid;

* Jagger's autograph that night took up seven-eighths of an A4 sheet of paper; there was just room for Richard (styling himself 'The Rolling Stones') and Watts to add their signatures in the margin.

brass lighter with traces of white powder; silver bowl with traces of white powder; teaspoon with traces of white powder; purple pouch with traces of white powder; plastic bag containing twenty-two grams of heroin. ('And *that*,' said a Stones employee, 'was only his weekend stash.') Later that night Richard was charged with possession of cocaine and heroin for the purpose of trafficking.

On 1 March, Jagger discovered the need to fly to New York, citing his daughter's bout of appendicitis. On his return to Toronto he was greeted by an Associated Press flash: 'Keith Richard, lead guitarist with the Rolling Stones, has been charged . . .' The Toronto *Star*: 'WILL STONES GET ANY SATISFACTION?' And the *Globe*: 'COULD *THIS* BE THE LAST TIME?' Immediately Jagger summoned Wasserman and Bill Carter; he retreated to his hotel suite with Dunn and Rudge. He chaired a group meeting – the agenda of which can only be conjectured – as a spokesman for RSO Records revealed, 'On 2 March 1977 [we] withdrew a seven-million-dollar offer to the Rolling Stones for their recording rights to the USA after protracted negotiations . . .' Reporters barricaded the hotel and swooped in helicopters outside Jagger's window while fans fought in the street. The ideal, out-of-the-way spot had become *Metropolis*.

Compounding the problem was the presence in Toronto of Margaret Trudeau. She appeared at the hotel on 4 March (her wedding anniversary), registering under her maiden name in Suite 3219, adjacent to Jagger's. That night the Stones played – brilliantly – at El Mocambo, Jagger in a green and white striped jumpsuit, red socks and buckskin shoes, singing 'Little Red Rooster', 'Route 66', even 'Around and Around'. The Stones, said the *New York Times*, were 'going back to their roots, knocking out raunchy British rhythm and blues. The only nagging fear was that it might have been the completion of a circle . . . Mr Richard, the band's co-leader and song-writer with Mr

Jagger, was arrested last Sunday.' There was a noticeable kink in Jagger's voice as he announced the inevitable 'Star Star'. Next night he spelt it out: 'All right, Margaret?'

The press exploded. Among the saner headlines were 'PREMIER'S WIFE OGLES POP IDOL', 'MRS TRUDEAU'S ROCK FOLLY' and, from the Toronto *Sun*, 'C'MON, MAGGIE':

> Ever since Margaret Trudeau went to hospital with emotional problems, the country has been understanding of her periodic eccentricities. But there's a limit ... When Mrs Trudeau behaves erratically and inappropriately in a public place, someone has to say something ... It is not only reprehensible, it is unacceptable for the wife of the Prime Minister to be cavorting with a group like the Rolling Stones.

In Ottawa the Premier himself issued a statement indicating his wife's activities were her own affair: 'I have no intention of suggesting she come home.' What none of the media realized was that Jagger had politely suggested just that and, just as politely, been refused; that and the fact that, yet again, he wasn't the 'pop idol' in question. It was Wood.

On 8 March, as Richard appeared in Old City Hall Court, Jagger packed and left. Immediately in Manhattan he issued a statement: 'Margaret Trudeau is a very attractive and nice person, but we are not having an affair.' Encouraged by Wasserman and Carter, Jagger also telephoned the New York *Post*. 'FROM AN "INSULTED" MICK' the headline read.

> Rock star Mick Jagger has called the *Post* to say he and Margaret Trudeau have no romantic ties, just a 'passing acquaintance for two nights'. Hints to the contrary are 'insulting to me and insulting to her', the lead singer of the Rolling Stones declared with an

injured air . . . 'Princess Margaret wanted to be introduced to the group in London. Lee Radziwill followed us. All these ladies are very charming to have around and there is no suggestion of anything other than that' . . . Chatting briefly with the *Post* outside their townhouse yesterday, the willing Mrs Jagger said the couple had been deluged with calls about Mrs Trudeau and Jagger. 'We laughed about it. We thought it was very funny.'

In fact Toronto was the beginning of the end for Jagger and Bianca, as it would be for Richard and Pallenberg; the Trudeaus, too, divorced. For the rest of March Jagger remained in New York, 'catching hell', said Flippo, from his wife, socializing with Bowie and Iggy Pop, with Dylan and Stevie Wonder. In April he found the ideal venue in Studio 54, a disused theatre hurriedly converted by Warhol, Capote and Bianca into the Oz of discos. Though derided by Jagger as 'somewhere to pick up girls' he nonetheless hastened to join the nightly gathering in the club's private gallery, embracing what Warhol called the 'social disease' whose symptoms included an obsessive need to socialize, the preference for exhilaration over conversation and the judging of an event's success by the number of celebrities in attendance. It was at Studio 54 that Jagger again met Jerry Hall on 21 May. At five o'clock the following morning he suggested 'a cup of tea' at 73rd Street; Hall accepted.

We went in and started making tea in the kitchen and I wouldn't let him kiss me. I was saying, 'No, no . . .' I was very nervous.
And he said, 'Let's just have tea in here . . .'

Later, Hall relates, flowers arrived at her apartment. Jagger invited her to dinner at a Thai restaurant; he serenaded her; more flowers were delivered. When, shortly afterwards,

Hall's father died there was a message from Ferry indicating he was too busy to see her. 'Mick,' Hall states, 'was there when I needed someone.'

Although immense effort was made to ensure the affair's secrecy, the habitués at Studio 54, Xenon and Elaine's – whose business it was to know such things – realized by midsummer that Jagger's allegiance had shifted. On 28 June he appeared in the 21 Club with Hall. According to Warhol, 'I thought things were fishy with Mick and Jerry and then the plot started to thicken. Mick was so out of it that I could tell the waiters were scared he'd pass out. His head was so far back and he was singing to himself.' Later that same week there was a knock at the door of the home dressing room at a cricket Test match in Nottingham. It was opened by one of the England selectors, John Murray, who beheld a man in a violent green suit 'behind whom were half a dozen chattering groupies, indicating the captain had invited them in'. Once the groupies dispersed Jagger was admitted to the players' balcony, where he sat for an hour with Murray and his fellow selector Alec Bedser. They found him subdued, respectful and deferential; he asked for their autographs. Later there was a siren-like gulping and whooping noise at the door; it was the groupies. Jagger disappeared with an apologetic grin – a shy, unobtrusive figure beneath a façade designed to convey the reverse, thought Murray. As the door closed Bedser was asking him the identity of the man he assumed to be an actor.

Later in the summer there was a final effort to reconcile with Bianca. They flew to the Greek island of Hydra where, at a local discotheque, the Jaggers were seen dining at separate tables. A photographer friend, Nick Karantilion, reported: 'They both seemed very unhappy. Mick was in a very distressed mood. After spending the evening with them I am convinced they are busting up.' Jagger was in Turkey when, on 16 August, Elvis Presley died. 'They started playing all his records one after the other and eventually I sussed the logical thing – he's snuffed it.' Hall, meanwhile, returned to Ferry in Los Angeles.

Almost lost in the imbroglio was the question of Jagger and Bianca's daughter. Jade attended Garden House School in London and stayed with her parents in Chelsea or with Joe and Eva in Westgate. In June she met Hall, who quickly adopted a worldly elder sister's role – 'I told her what my mother told me about Karma.' Whatever the defects of his marriage, Jagger unquestionably doted on his children. He visited both schools on parents' days, not forgetting to question their teachers about discipline. He wrote frequently from abroad and bought presents. Both daughters visited New York. In 73rd Street they were received like guests at a luxury hotel of which Jagger was proprietor. Outside interests were encouraged. 'My father,' says Jade, 'was keen I was not too sheltered.'

Another aspect of celebrity: that summer Jagger attempted to stop publication of *The Man Who Killed Mick Jagger*, a novel by David Littlejohn, Associate Dean of the University of California, on the reasonable grounds that someone might convert the theory into practice. According to press reports the author was advised by Jann Wenner, 'I know Jagger . . . He's continually fantasizing and in dread of being shot and killed by some nut at a rock concert.'

The shadow of violence – one arguably cast by his own image – had fallen on Jagger since 9 August 1969, the day on which Sharon Tate and four others were slaughtered in Los Angeles. Keylock remembers his employer 'sheet white' at the security implications of that winter's tour. In 1972 Jagger was said to have travelled with a loaded .38 revolver. In Montreal that July a terrorist planted dynamite in one of the Stones' equipment trucks; later there were threats that Jagger's meals had been poisoned. On 8 December 1980 John Lennon was assassinated; immediately security arrangements, already elaborate, were tightened. According to Wood, Jagger 'would come over to my house in New York and I'd have to escort him back home in the middle of the night' – and this only three blocks away. On 15 October 1981 a woman named Carol J. Tostenrude was arrested in Seattle for threatening to kill Jagger on stage. As late as March 1984 he and Hall were forced to hire armed guards to escort them and their newborn daughter from hospital after threats against the family; through all of which Jagger continued to insist that aspects of normal life be maintained, archly comparing his own 'ordinary' existence to Lennon's, 'Shut up in all those apartments for four years.' Even on tour – when insurance policies insisted he be protected – Jagger would periodically appear, alone or with Hall, in public. Much of his later work was influenced by his experience and understanding of New York – experience, as Jagger said, 'you can only have by getting out there'. To his credit, even after 1980 he continued to do so.

Meanwhile in the autumn of 1977 he returned to work with Richard editing the live album. By now Jagger's relations with his partner were a composite; into the equation went anger, frustration, disparagement, guidance and anxiety. He willingly travelled to Philadelphia, the only city falling within the court-imposed restriction on Richard's movements. For the second time in a decade Jagger was confronted with a colleague apparently hellbent on self-destruction, and for the second time he responded with a mixture of irritation, impatience and genuine concern. When the resulting album, *Love You Live*, was released it was noted that the songs were formally credited to 'Richard–Jagger', not vice versa. Since Jagger retained personal control over the LP's design, packaging and artwork – 'ruining' the cover, according to Warhol, by his outsize handwriting – it can be assumed that he made the concession as a show of support. In a further gesture the album was dedicated to

Keith Harwood, the group's sound engineer who was killed that summer in a car crash.

Love You Live's first two sides were a reasonable facsimile of the concerts in Paris. The highlights were the introductory 'Honky Tonk Women', a medley including 'Get Off Of My Cloud' and a manic 'Star Star' – lacking nothing short of the visuals. After a version of 'You Can't Always Get What You Want' so slow it seemed in danger of stalling, the group accelerated into side three – the El Mocambo dates. If ever there was evidence that Jagger could still, at thirty-four, deliver his message, this was it. 'Mannish Boy' and 'Crackin' Up' were merely brilliant. 'Little Red Rooster' was genius. Even that paled compared to 'Around and Around', the Chuck Berry number so beloved of the Blue Boys. (Alan Etherington believes Jagger's vocal was as good as – better than – the 1961 version.) After that the group subsided into side four – more competently performed covers of their recent past. *Love You Live* reached number five in America, number three in Britain. It was released in the former by Atlantic, winners of the door-prize rumoured to value the Stones at twenty-one million dollars for six albums. Worldwide, meanwhile, the group signed to EMI, allowing Jagger to deadpan: 'In this jubilee year, I think it is only fitting that we work with a British company.' His motives may not have been entirely patriotic: Jagger was also prompted to ask EMI, 'If I go on the telly and do worse things and say more swear words than the Sex Pistols, will you sack us? Because there's no way you're going to get your money back.' The response was in the negative. Rumours of a million-pound minimum guarantee per album were dismissed by all parties.

On 14 September Jagger was in the audience at the 'Crickets' concert at the Kilburn Gaumont, London, to mark the forty-first anniversary of Buddy Holly's birth. Afterwards he informed the *Evening Standard*, 'Rock and roll is for adolescents ... It's a dead end ... My whole life isn't rock and roll. It's an absurd idea that it should be.' He also described Richard, cryptically, as 'the original punk rocker'. Eight days later, at David K's restaurant in New York, he assured Chet Flippo: 'I'm not interested in the public's image of me . . . I just try and make the best music I can. Without being rude to any member of the record-buying public that's not what pushes me to write songs.' He retracted his quote in the *Evening Standard* – 'I object to journalists regurgitating my last week's answers to the gutter press' – and derided the current vogue for New Age pop (Barry Manilow, Andy Gibb): 'Silly . . . I hate it . . . I don't even really like white music, anyway – it's never been my inspiration. Not even Elvis.' That same week he was informed by the artist Victor Hugo: 'You look very much like [Bianca]. Every year you look more like her.' 'Maybe next year's going to be different,' snapped Jagger.

In fact, within a month he was living with Hall in the George V, Paris. In November the couple flew clandestinely to Morocco. Their luggage having been lost at the airport (as Jagger's would be surprisingly often throughout his career), for three days they wandered through Agadir in Berber caftans and hoods. Hall wrote later, 'I could see we were really in love. I knew I was going to stick with Mick . . . I called Bryan and said it was over.' Her emotions were unaffected by the knowledge that Jagger had spent 21 October, Jade's sixth birthday, at his Cheyne Walk home – the last time, according to later testimony, he made love to his wife. At Christmas he bought Hall a bracelet and earrings (which she lost on the Paris metro), adding to the pair he presented her with on her twenty-first birthday. Jagger himself put his money where his mouth was, having a tiny diamond set into his right upper front tooth. On New Year's Eve, after detouring via London, the couple flew to Barbados under the names 'J. Beaton' and 'J. Hall Beaton' (Jagger's other aliases including Mercedes, Waxley, Wexler,

Kent, Shelley, Spade and, most frequently, Michael and Philip).

The precautions were well taken. Leaving the Paris Elysée Matignon on 25 January, the couple were approached by an agency photographer. Jagger threw a punch; it was returned; the singer sprawled on the pavement, legs thrashing like an upended insect. In New York the same week, Bianca was seen with Warren Beatty and Ryan O'Neal, and also with Bjorn Borg. In February she issued a statement concerning her marriage: 'There is no disagreement between us and we are tired of the harassment.' As she spoke Jagger was backing his rented blue Renault into the parking lot of Pathé Marconi Studios with Hall at his side. The latter quickly adapted to the peculiar demands of life with the Rolling Stones: asleep all day, dinner at midnight, recording until dawn, the schedule of a normal day inverted. Throughout the spring Hall continued to model – Chicago, Boston, Dallas, Los Angeles, preferring, she says, 'the idea of having my own money' – a preference all too eagerly endorsed by Jagger. In Paris she contributed to living expenses, even paying her own hotel bill. This impressed Jagger; it intrigued him. By March 1978 he was speaking openly of the woman whose penchant for steer-roping and leg-wrestling, whose hallmark Texas drawl so differed from Bianca's glacial hauteur. In New York tongues wagged about the woman described as 'The Girl Who Came In From the Cows'. 'Nobody likes Jerry, they think she's plastic,' noted Warhol. 'I like her. She's so cute.'

Recording ended in March. Immediately Jagger returned to the playground on 54th Street where, on 3 April, he attended an Academy Awards dinner with Hall, Warhol, Capote and – incredibly – Margaret Trudeau. Abandoning the St Pierre (where the desk clerk's 'Good morning, *Miss* Hall' was thought deficient in warmth) they took up residence in the Hotel Carlyle, a crumbling but elegant façade, where the pianist Bobby Short played Cole Porter numbers in the lounge, on East 76th Street. Later in April Jagger flew to Jamaica, where he attended the One Love Peace Concert and signed the reggae artist Peter Tosh to Rolling Stones Records (having refused Wyman's suggestion of Eddy Grant). The first insight into his domestic life with Hall was supplied in an interview with *Hit Parader*: 'If you're with a woman and the sexual relationship is working like a Rolls Royce or a Mercedes Benz, everything smooths out. The other things aren't important.' Jagger was missing from his wife's thirty-fourth birthday party on 2 May at which she was presented with a white horse mounted by a naked man led by a naked woman. Instead he rented Todd Rundgren's home in Woodstock, New York, living openly with Hall for the first time as man and wife. 'The Queen Bee,' noted Capote, 'will be furious.'

If anything this underestimated Bianca's reaction. For some months – since her husband had flown to Paris – Jagger's wife had been consulting a lawyer. Now, on 14 May, she filed papers for divorce. Citing 'irreconcilable differences' she opened the long campaign with a warning shot: Jagger was never formally served, because, according to Marvin Mitchelson, 'she hoped for a reconciliation – especially since they have a little daughter'. At the house in Woodstock private detectives mingled with curious bystanders, fans and armed guards, while inside a third presence entered the picture – Richard, undergoing heroin withdrawal by neuro-electric acupuncture, the 'black box' pioneered by Dr Meg Patterson. According to Hall:

> He was lying there wearing these things that looked like headphones ... Mick and I would feed him. And every time the hooks would fall off we'd clip them back on ... We'd cover him up with a blanket at night. It gave Mick a very good feeling to be able to help Keith.

As with Jones, so with Richard: Jagger acted with genuine and affecting concern.* Throughout May and early June the guitarist gradually recuperated. His colour was white and yellow, the hollows of his eyes glared, his stubble grew randomly in clumps, nonetheless Richard, within his own harrowing parameters, was improving. On 13 May Jagger made the announcement: the Stones, as they had every third year since 1966, would tour America. So the press asked the next question: would there be an album?

There would. *Some Girls* was released on 9 June. Hailed immediately as a classic, the record underlined the Stones' eerie ability to survive and even prosper from their crises. Because they did prosper: at a time when Richard was, at best, in limbo, when Wyman spoke openly of leaving, when Jagger himself faced divorce and possible financial jeopardy, the group delivered their finest work since *Exile*.

Some Girls, originally entitled *More Fast Numbers* and *Don't Steal My Girlfriend*, was a return to the basics. There were additional touches of country, of disco, even of punk, but the underlying influence was the blues. By means of repeating and omitting stanzas, by personalizing and localizing lyrics, in some cases by outright mimicry, Jagger adapted the Southern boogie tradition of Muddy Waters and Jimmy Reed to late-seventies New York. In doing so – bringing a style once stigmatized as 'race' or 'speciality' music to a largely white, predominantly urban audience – the Stones reverted to doing what they did best: affectionate imitation with traces of gratuitous lewdness and wit. It was *Some Girls* whose lyrics so affronted Jesse Jackson. There were obvious

* Despite the evidence of Rundgren's recording engineer, Tom Edmonds, that 'Keith stayed with Mick and Jerry for a total of (only) three days', there was no doubt Jagger took his job seriously: that spring he approached John Phillips, formerly of the Mamas and the Papas, to obtain four hundred methadone-like Dolophine tablets to see Richard through the summer.

gibes at Bianca. Even the cover caused offence – a collage of a Frederick's of Hollywood lingerie display (suggested by Hall) over which Raquel Welch and Lucille Ball threatened to sue.

Some Girls opened with 'Miss You', a disco pastiche in which Jagger cooed and croaked the street-level lyrics. ('Why should it provoke such emotion?' he asked. Because 'Miss You' gave regal endorsement to the idiom.) Released as a single it reached number three in Britain, number one in America; both Hall and Jagger's wife claimed to have inspired it.

Bianca's influence was most evident on 'Respectable', a derisive self-portrait in the style of 'Live With Me' (where the joke had at least been intentional), in which references to 'Rag trade girl', 'easiest lay on the White House lawn' and, climactically, 'Get out of my life – don't come back' could only have had one subject. 'Just My Imagination (Running Away With Me)' was a superior cover of the Temptations' hit; the title track; then 'Lies', a frantic punk-like thrash with undertones of Slade and Status Quo. Side two opened with 'Far Away Eyes' (a.k.a. 'Truck Driver Blues'), a country-rock frolic whose lyrics, 'Driving home . . . Early Sunday morning . . . Listening to gospel music on the coloured radio station', Richard, the Roy Rogers aficionado, found affected. (Relations between the two generally were strained during the recording of *Some Girls*: 'Anything I do, he's got to negate,' Richard told Barbara Charone. 'He's very dictatorial lately, whereas before the studio was run on a much more co-operative basis.') 'When The Whip Comes Down' was pure Jagger, a paean to the homosexual demi-monde in New York; 'Before They Make Me Run' was equally palpably his partner's; the title referred to his impending trial. The two combined on 'Beast of Burden', an extraordinary blues ballad whose chorus, a series of derogatory questions, recalled Howlin' Wolf's 1954 hit 'Baby, How Long'; it also revived the charge of misogyny periodically levelled at Jagger since 'Under My Thumb'. Finally 'Shattered', a shouted Baedeker tour of New York laboriously recorded in, like the bulk of Jagger's songs, the key of F – was utterly original and later described by Jagger as an all-time favourite. *Some Girls* reached number two in Britain, number one in America. It earned euphoric reviews. Background interest in the tour intensified.

It opened in Florida on 10 June. For seven weeks the Stones played a novel mix of arenas and more intimate auditoriums, clubs and even theatres. Jagger, too, approached the tour more modestly: gone were the designer suits in favour of primary-colour trousers, T-shirts and golf caps; make-up was reduced. At the Rupp Arena, Lexington, a fan was shot and others plunged through a sheet of plate-glass in a dispute about tickets; in Orchard Park the crowd turned irate when the Stones refused to play an encore. In Arizona a marquee reading, 'Welcome Mick Jagger ... and the Rolling Stones' brought a reaction from Richard. Those were exceptions: generally the mood was one of hardened professionalism. Jagger was accompanied throughout by Hall, Rudge, Loewenstein, Carter and Dunn and by a bodyguard, James Harrington, later arrested for burgling him. On stage, too, he seemed subdued – shorn of the previous tour's theatrics he concentrated on singing and, increasingly, on rhythm guitar – in anticipation, some said, of Richard's imprisonment. He saved his more frantic performances for Los Angeles, Chicago, New Orleans and New York – the last of which caused Lennon to dub him for ever 'the Charlie Chaplin of rock'. In Fort Worth on 18 July, Jagger hosted a birthday party for Ian Stewart. As the festivities began in the Fairmont Hotel, music blaring, Jack Daniel's, B_{12} ampoules and other substances soiling the floor, he took Chet Flippo aside and announced, 'Solzhenitsyn's right in a lot of ways. About America. When we were in France, we were cut off from the media and no one wrote about us ... Solzhenitsyn said everyone in the US is subject to this terrible TV and radio. I agree.' Later Flippo was forcibly ejected when Jagger's attention was drawn to an unfavourable article in *Rolling Stone*: 'I'm fucking pissed off . . . I get real mad at this vicious shit . . . This is the end. No more interviews. I don't mind criticism – real criticism – but I don't expect the kind of bitchiness in these reviews.' He was also introduced to Hall's mother and sisters who, unsurprisingly, found him 'charming'.

As in 1972 the tour ended on Jagger's birthday. The group's accountant Bill Zysblat estimated gross receipts of ten million dollars, minus expenses, minus tax: $4.5 million divided by six, three-quarters of a million dollars for each Stone for forty-seven days' work. Sales of *Some Girls* reached eight million. In May Jagger was a gossip-column exotic associated with glamour and style, yet whose achievements lay exclusively in the past. In July he enjoyed the prestige of near heroic attainment. August found him in reflective mood, it being characteristic of Jagger that the greater his successes, the less he pronounced on them, living in San Francisco with Hall, Jade and, surprisingly, Bill Graham, later being joined by Jones's eldest son Julian. Jagger sent flowers when Les Perrin died in London on the seventh. Later in the month the family moved to Los Angeles – a sense of the past reiterated by Jagger's choice of recording studio: RCA Hollywood, last employed in 1966.

In October the group appeared on *Saturday Night Live*, their first US television appearance since Ed Sullivan. On the day before filming Jagger came down with laryngitis. He mugged his way through 'Respectable', then a sketch with Dan Akroyd ('Why Jagger? Because it's my name . . . my father's name') before returning to croak 'Beast of Burden'. At this stage a nationwide television audience was treated to the sight of Jagger French-kissing his lead guitarist. Says Wood: 'There we were on stage . . . I had my eyes closed for a few seconds and suddenly I felt this wet warm thing slurping on my face. It was Mick's tongue. I tried to kick him, but he was too fast. He loves putting people on the spot.'

A fortnight later, 23 October, Richards, finally restoring his legal surname, appeared in court in Toronto. Wearing a tan three-piece suit he denied having popularized narcotics in his songs: 'That's a misconception ... About one per cent glorify the use of drugs, and Mick Jagger wrote them, not me.' His lawyer admitted that Richards had used heroin since 1969 to combat exhaustion, ingesting at least two and a half grams a day 'just to keep normal'. He indicated that art was historically created from fragments of the tortured soul – Plath, Huxley, Van Gogh. An affidavit from Loewenstein advised that Richards' casual spending had totalled $175,000 in 1975, $300,000 in 1976 and $350,000 in 1977. This was to establish that he was sufficiently wealthy not to commit crimes in order to obtain drugs. Finally, on 24 October, Judge Lloyd Graburn delivered his verdict: 'Maybe the Rolling Stones have encouraged drug use in their songs. Still, [Richards'] efforts have been to move himself away from the drug culture and can only encourage those who emulate him ... No jail or fine is appropriate.' He was sentenced to probation and to perform a benefit concert on behalf of the blind. Immediately the Crown Prosecution Service gave notice of appeal.

In London Jagger faced problems of his own. On 26 October his wife's lawyer attempted to serve him with divorce papers. The morning the bailiff arrived at his hotel Jagger flew to Jamaica. 'I think he left as soon as he heard they were after him,' said Mitchelson. 'He has a feeling about these sort of things.' To the journalist Ross Benson, Bianca added that Jagger would 'fight like a tiger' to avoid the case being heard in alimony-conscious California. To Benson, with whom she formed a social relationship, Bianca also complained of Jagger's 'hollowness' as a radical spokesman, comparing him unfavourably to Dylan or

Lennon; of his 'artificial' stage persona which, like Shrimpton and Faithfull before her, she found contrived and condescending; and, most pointedly, of having been turned away from her husband's dressing room on the grounds of possessing the 'wrong badge'.

After appearing with Hall at the Kennedy Awards Gala in Washington, Jagger again confronted the shadow of his own past: in Hong Kong he was greeted with dogs and cocked machine guns and denied permission to enter. The couple flew on to Singapore, thence to Bali, where on 31 December Hall, a member of the Try Everything Once Club, insisted they sample a hallucinogenic omelette. She spent the remainder of the year comatose in bed ('I've never liked drugs,' she says).

In Manhattan Jagger and Hall occupied an apartment with four bare-beamed rooms on Central Park West. At the back was an alley, and the bedroom contained a massive humidifier. All the furniture looked as though it had been rented. Jagger spent the early spring there with Hall, Jade and occasionally with Karis. He carped at his extended family but with underlying affection. Hall's rapport with his daughters surprised and delighted him. The family flew together to England where, after twelve years, less than one of which he spent under its roof, Jagger sold Stargroves. Before leaving it Hall catalogued the carved antique bed, the Moroccan furniture, the tapestries, swords and wall-hangings. ('It was like Brighton Pavilion.') She also read a chestful of Jagger's love letters from Faithfull: 'I felt a bit of jealousy . . . I think of all the girlfriends he's had he loved her the most.' Stargroves, which cost twenty-five thousand pounds, was sold for two hundred thousand. Later Jagger was granted an eviction order against the estate's elderly caretakers who felt, after a decade, deserving of more than the statutory twenty-eight days' notice. At the court hearing Jagger waived costs against the couple, prompting an aside from the judge: 'I'm glad to hear it, in all the circumstances.'

Immediately Jagger left for Compass Point Studios, Nassau, to begin work on a new album, arriving each night in a decrepit rented jeep. On 5 February, as the group worked on a song entitled 'Emotional Rescue', Bianca named her price: $12.5 million or half the total amount her husband allegedly earned during their marriage. As an interim measure she demanded $13,400 a month living expenses (rent $4,000, clothes $2,000, transportation $2,000, chauffeur, nanny and live-in maid $1,500, food $1,200, entertainment $1,000, travel expenses $500, incidentals $500, telephone $300, laundry and cleaning $200, utilities $200). Jagger's response was instantly to cut off Bianca's credit cards. He also had the interior of Cheyne Walk, where his wife and daughter still lived, painted violent red. In her Los Angeles lawsuit Bianca noted that Jagger had 'bragged that he's never given any woman anything and never would, no matter what the circumstances'.

On 5 April lawyers acting for Bianca finally served papers on Jagger in New York. That same week Chet Flippo was summoned to Central Park West; he was greeted by an apparently conciliatory Jagger in stockinged feet, jeans and glasses, slicing a razor through a 'glittering pile of white powder', inhaling the contents and rolling an outsize cigarette. 'We want,' he stated under a covering cloud of smoke, 'to go to China.'

A protracted silence followed this. Jagger squinted through the haze, the glasses, the smoke. 'What we need,' he added, 'is a concise, detailed history of the band to present to the Chinese government. Something that explains to China why China needs us.'

A detailed history?

Jagger nodded.

Including Altamont?

At this point Jagger looked away and laughed. 'Why do you have to mention Altamont?'

For most of that night and the next Flippo sat typing the required document. He sent it to Jagger, who paid him five hundred dollars, and in turn to the Chinese ambassador who relayed it to Peking. By October the London *Evening News* was reporting the tour as a fait accompli: 'It's a great opportunity,' said Jagger. 'We're all looking forward to playing to people who haven't to any large degree been exposed to rock music.' Later in 1979 Jagger was invited to Washington for an interview with the ambassador to discuss the logistics of such a tour. According to Flippo, 'The meeting was a mess and the Chinese were horrified by some of Mick's remarks ... The opinion within the Stones camp was that Mick blew it.'

Also in April Jagger returned to Toronto. Richards' sentence was fulfilled by two concerts at the Oshawa Civic Auditorium ostensibly staged by the New Barbarians, a pick-up group comprising Richards, Wood, Keyes, the pianist Ian McLagan and session musicians Stanley Clarke and Ziggy Modeliste. The audience – less than a third of whom were legally blind – were filing home when John Belushi emerged on stage: 'I'm a sleazy actor on a late-night TV show, but here are some real musicians'; the Stones appeared on cue. 'If it'd been a matter of charity, of providing money,' Jagger said later, 'we'd have written them a cheque. But the judge told Keith to play for disabled people. We put on a *show*.' 'The Stones weren't merely solid,' opined the *Star*; 'they were sensational.'

While the Barbarians extended their tour to America Jagger returned to divorce hearings in London. On 3 May – the day on which Margaret Thatcher, a woman he was known to admire, was elected – he argued for four hours at the High Court. In a parallel move in Los Angeles, his lawyers were assuring Judge Harry Shafer that 'while the Jaggers made love as recently as October 1977 ... their marriage was over in every true sense in 1973'. The judge ordered Jagger to maintain his wife in the 'sumptuous style' to which she had since become accustomed. 'She should not,' he added, 'be starved into submission.'

When Jagger heard the above he was splenetic. For days he ranted at Bianca's avidity and extravagance, her short-comings as a wife and mother. 'How is she?' shouted reporters outside the High Court. 'Terrible,' mouthed Jagger. A guest at Eric Clapton's wedding, which Jagger attended, remembers him 'muttering madly at the bar, not looking like an entirely happy man'. At the same party, at which Hall fell asleep on the newly-weds' bed, a Radio Luxembourg employee recalls 'Mick . . . communicating in a series of groans, grunts and non sequiturs. Interviewing him was like going three rounds with a flyweight trained by Warhol and managed by Harold Pinter.' Later that summer, symbolically if not actually to evade detection, Jagger grew a beard. He returned to the studio just as in London Justice Eastham ruled that 'proceedings should, in all conscience, be heard in England' but that prohibiting action in California would be 'discourteous' to the American judiciary. Bianca herself flew to Nicaragua to rescue relatives embroiled in the civil war, noting tartly, 'I can do nothing to help them . . . Although Mick was told by a judge in the United States to pay me money, he hasn't. After the divorce hearing, I intend to fly back to Nicaragua to work for the Red Cross, although it will be a very stiff task to raise my fare.'

As Jagger's marriage entered its final phase, so Richards separated from Pallenberg. On 20 July a seventeen-year-old neighbour, Scott Cantrell, was found shot dead in the couple's upstate New York estate. According to Pallenberg the boy had been playing with the gun and talking of Russian roulette. The New York *Post* reported that the first police to arrive at the scene were staggered by the sheer filth and air of decay: 'There was a powerful, unpleasant smell, as if there was a dead cat somewhere.' Although subsequently cleared by a grand jury of involvement in

Cantrell's death, Pallenberg quickly left. 'Mick and I never hit it off,' she informed Hotchner. 'He'd always put me down, make snide remarks, criticize the way I dressed ... He envied Keith and was jealous of me.' Later that year Richards met the model Patti Hansen whom he would marry.

Richards also heard on 17 September that the Ontario court had denied the Crown's appeal and, despite the prosecutor's assertion that 'this calls our very system into disrepute', avoided jail. The verdict was relayed to Jagger in Paris, in tandem with similar good news from London: the divorce would, after all, be heard in the High Court. (Bianca later admitted that it had been 'unwise' to employ so aggressive a lawyer as Mitchelson, who, she confided to Benson, had been counter-productive. Jagger's opinion of the man who represented both his wife and on an earlier occasion Marsha Hunt can only be conjectured.) On 2 November 1979, after eight and a half years of marriage, Bianca was given a decree nisi and awarded custody of Jade.

Hall was now seen repeatedly and in public with Jagger. They appeared in London at Biba's and Stringfellow's, at Langan's and Mr Chow's. Hall's ways intrigued Jagger. Her humour diverted him: the stories about Gonzalez and Mesquite, of Hall's aunt and sisters, their mother in her Neiman-Marcus underwear (Jagger was shocked). Hall insisted on her own career. She maintained her influence on Jagger to be 'subtle', adding 'I never [want] to become Yoko Ono' and, most winningly, 'I love the Stones. They're great and they make a lot of money. Why should I try to ruin a good thing?' – the very assurance lacking from Bianca. In December the couple returned to New York, where Jagger attended the *Rolling Stone* Christmas party, singing beerily alongside Jann Wenner and resembling, like Richards, a man narrowly escaping jail. When, on New Year's Eve, he and Hall met Bianca at Woody Allen's party all three behaved with becoming grace.

· IX ·

'I'M FINE. THERE IS
NO TOMORROW'

Inquisitive, well-read, susceptible to ideas, Jagger was notably reticent in political sayings. As early as 1967 his weekly lunches with Driberg – the MP invariably holding forth while Jagger scowled and scanned the menu – indicated his interest in government to fall short of personal involvement. Keylock confirms that a number of Jagger's overtly 'political' songs – 'Street Fighting Man', 'Salt of the Earth' – were the subject of inordinate studio ribaldry: 'Mick never took them half as seriously as the press did.' Later Jagger's wife was heard to complain that his work studiously avoided any reference to 'real' issues, a charge also made by, among others, Abbie Hoffman. Throughout the 1970s liberal and left-wing causes on both sides of the Atlantic vied in vain for Jagger's endorsement. Towards the end of the decade he spoke approvingly of Margaret Thatcher, whom he described as 'Iron knickers'; Hall informed the world he was impressed by her sense of destiny. Finally, in February 1980, Jagger appeared at a presidential campaign soirée for Edward Kennedy in New York. He stood drinking Pouilly-Fuissé and eating smoked salmon as women in ballgowns collected his autograph. Norman Dicks, a US Congressman from Tacoma, was at the party: 'Mick was charming in a sort of vague, non-committal way. All efforts to have him specifically endorse the Senator failed.' Later in the year

Jagger was also seen with Jerry Brown, whom he first met at Linda Ronstadt's house.

Evidence of his real interests followed in Manhattan, where Jagger was buttonholed by an English journalist on the doorstep of his Central Park apartment. Immediately the conversation turned to cricket. What was the score in the Jubilee Test in India? Informed that the match had ended in an England victory, Jagger's whole face seemed to brighten. His eyebrows arched, his forehead wrinkled, his tongue drooped out like a scarf. 'Gra-ate.' He paused for several minutes discussing bowling averages and pitch conditions. That summer he attended the England–West Indies Test match at Lord's and familiarized Paul Getty with the game, thus introducing English cricket to its major single benefactor.

The spring and early summer were spent in New York, completing videos to accompany the new album and remixing tracks. On 18 June Jagger flew to Paris where he attended Nelson Seabra's Red-and-White Ball at the Pré Catelan – he and Hall, Bianca with Andy Warhol. Immediately Jagger returned to England, where *Emotional Rescue* was released on the twenty-second. It reached number one both there and in America.

The LP opened with 'Dance', a vague, mid-paced loosener with hopelessly improvised lyrics; 'Summer Romance' followed, an insipid rocker wherein Jagger portrayed himself as 'a serious man with serious lusts' – that in contrast to the 'spotty' object of his desire; in the ersatz reggae 'Send It To Me' Jagger reprised the theme of 'Some Girls': 'She could be Rumanian, she could be Bulgarian, she could be . . .' Things improved on 'Let Me Go', a typical Richards belter, later an on-stage favourite; then 'Indian Girl', a country ballad in which Jagger sang, none too convincingly, of 'fighting the war', of M16s and Che Guevara to the refrain 'life just goes on getting harder and harder' – an assertion immediately refuted in 'Where The Boys

Go', a leftover from the session that produced 'Respectable', which it strangely resembled, Jagger snarling the Cockney vocal. 'Down in the Hole' was a relatively rare effort to write the blues – derivative of sound, adaptive of lyric, the Deep South transported to post-war Berlin. The title track followed, a disco pastiche in 'Miss You' mould written on electric piano by Jagger, whose vehicle it was: '[It's] about some girl that's in some sort of manhood problems . . . I'm the one who's doing the saving.' In yet another *volte-face* Jagger then bawled 'She's So Cold', leaving Richards to croon 'All About You', a parting salvo at Pallenberg.

Emotional Rescue, Jagger admitted, suffered by comparison to *Some Girls*, commenting, 'I don't think anyone can expect a new album necessarily to be as good as the last one . . . You can't expect them to be all of the same standard and to please the same people'. The critics Jimmy Guterman and Owen O'Donnell went one further in their book *The Worst Rock and Roll Records of All Time*: '*Emotional Rescue* was a depressing return to middling seventies form after the welcome aberration of *Some Girls*. There was little that was flat-out awful, but much of it was filled with lazy throwaways – elemental jams that shouldn't have been considered worthy of release on a Rolling Stones record. They didn't care; why should we?' Others noted that a number of the sessions' strongest songs – among them the country rocker 'Claudine' and 'Lonely at the Top' – were omitted, either for legal reasons or, in the latter's case, to resurface on Jagger's subsequent solo album.

Then again, *Emotional Rescue* was the first public outing of the new-look Rolling Stones, a look that saw an apparently rejuvenated Richards aligning with Wood against Jagger. According to an interview he later gave *Rolling Stone*, Richards got the impression he was 'horning in' and 'trying to take control' against Jagger's wishes. 'In the seventies, when I was on dope and I would do nothing but put the songs together and turn up and not deal with any of the business of the Stones, Mick took all of that work on his shoulders ... When I cleaned up and *Emotional Rescue* time came around – "Hey I'm back, I'm clean, I'm ready; I'm back to help and take some of the weight off your shoulders" – immediately I got a sense of resentment.' 'Mick was the one person who never stopped believing in Keith,' says Richards' manager Jane Rose. 'He went out of his way to make sure Keith got everything he needed to get well ... Only I don't think Mick intended for him to get *this* well.' Richards also felt the ironic edge of Jagger's tongue: discussions in the studio were invariably oblique, with Jagger showing a marked tendency to withdraw. 'Mick has got to be more real with people,' jibed Richards. Stewart, present for most of the *Emotional Rescue* sessions, described them as 'again, either Mick or Keith with a backing band ... There was less debate than before.' When one such debate occurred – over whether or not to record 'Dance' as an instrumental – Richards irritably walked out. Jagger insisted on lyrics.

More of which he continued to provide to the world's press. To *New Musical Express* Jagger declared, 'No one has security for life ... Security doesn't lie in money.' (That summer, to Richards' chagrin, he turned down a multi-million dollar offer to tour America.) Asked by *Melody Maker* 'How long do you want to be in rock and roll?' he replied, 'For ever?', a position immediately reversed in *Rolling Stone*: 'I'm afraid rock and roll has no future ... It's only recycled past.' To Nick Kent he admitted surprisingly frankly, 'I enjoy changing personalities ... I've got to be very chameleon-like just to preserve my own identity.' 'Doesn't that,' Kent asked, 'reach a point where you lose contact with yourself?' On 26 June Jagger appeared at a reception for the album's release in a New York club where, according to the writer Victor Bockris, 'he took [his bodyguard] into the toilet and proceeded to snort half a gram of coke, smoke a big joint and bolt half a bottle of whisky in order to become "Mick Jagger" for forty-five minutes.' He also hosted a launch party at the Duke of York's Barracks, London, where he arrived by bicycle.

His thirty-seventh birthday saw Jagger on holiday with Hall in Morocco. They slept on carpets on the roof of Christopher Gibbs' house in Marrakesh. ('Ah,' thought Hall, 'the *sixties*.') When she purchased a four-hundred-acre ranch at Lone Oak, east of Dallas, Jagger bought a smaller property nearby. In Texas Hall rode quarterhorses and thoroughbreds; she exercised; she worked out. Jagger, though less physically active, joined in the spirit; for Christmas he bought Hall a Ford Bronco. In September they jointly paid two million francs for Château de la Fourchette, north of Amboise in the Loire Valley. Fourchette came equipped with ten bedrooms, a garden landscaped by Alvide Lees-Milne (beneath which was said to be buried a seventeenth-century golden horse) and picnic tables on which Hall served afternoon tea. In due course Jagger arranged for much of the furniture from Stargroves – the tapestries, the ornate wall hangings and swords – to be transferred. He installed a satellite television dish. According to Hall: 'We watch[ed] videos of old movies and [did] a lot of reading . . . It's wonderful. No one bothers us.'

Along with the videos, the books, the Scrabble, the backgammon and charades went Saturday night cross-dressing parties: 'Everybody loves it,' a guest informed *Vanity Fair*. 'You're staying with Mick and Jerry in France, and everyone comes down to dinner in drag, and it's just huge fun. Masses of people sort of screaming, running in and out of each other's bedrooms, applying make-up . . . Mick was terribly dashing one night in a tight black shift and a ratty silver-fox fur. He was so chic, he looked like Coco Chanel.'

It was only natural, then, for Jagger to reconvene the Stones that October in Paris. They recorded material for a new album, also updating numbers from their capacious vaults, one of which, 'Tops', dated as far back as the

Jamaican sessions that produced *Goat's Head Soup*, and caused a contractual dispute with Taylor. Jagger was in the studio when on 2 November he was summoned to London to hear the terms of his final settlement with Bianca in the High Court. Although the figure was never made public, it was quoted to Ross Benson as 'not more than a million pounds'. Bianca also told Benson that the money, payable in increments, was 'always late' and that attempting to communicate with Jagger was impossible. The couple were also ordered to return to court to confirm custody arrangements for Jade, to whom – even Bianca agreed – Jagger remained a doting father.

Any resentment he may have felt at the terms of the settlement were mitigated by the evident intensity of his relationship with Hall. On 1 December she told the *Daily Star*: 'I can't believe how weird and dirty Mick Jagger is. When I have to be sexy in front of the camera, I think of Mick Jagger and it always does the trick. Mick is one of the sexiest men in the world and the best lover I've ever had ... He's a genius.' She made a similar comment to *Rolling Stone*. A week later John Lennon was shot dead in New York, causing Jagger to 'remember all the good times we had together ... When a friend of yours dies, that's what you think of – the good times.' He and Richards jointly sent a telegram to Yoko Ono.

Jagger was himself in New York for Christmas. On 27 December he flew to Lima to begin work on *Fitzcarraldo*. The director Werner Herzog later praised the 'beauty' of Jagger's acting, declaring it 'impossible' to replace him once the decision had been taken to withdraw. Wyman, in *Melody Maker*, was less certain: 'Mick Jagger is a fantastic performer, and no other band has a Mick Jagger. He's no good without the band and the band would be a little dull without him; however, we could go on stage without him, while he couldn't go on stage without us.' In Barbados, meanwhile, Jagger recuperated from *Fitzcarraldo* with Hall, Richards and Patti Hansen. He watched the Test Match at Bridgetown; he arranged the release of a compilation album, *Sucking In The Seventies*, later banned by a number of American stores. He met the promoter Bill Graham to discuss touring.

Much was later made of Jagger's reluctance to continue the tradition of three-yearly progresses through America. Stewart remembered 'Mick's face going white' at the mere mention of another performance. Early in 1981 Jagger confirmed in private that he cared nothing for touring. Elements of the press, public and, more pertinently, Richards and Wood,* on the other hand, cared for little else. They began an elaborate campaign to return the Rolling Stones – the stage managers, the carpenters, the caterers, the truckers, the accountants, the *group* – to the stage, a campaign later characterized by Jagger as 'walking down the street and people saying, "Hey, Mick, when're you playing next? When're you playing New York next?" On and on and on . . . Until you say, "OK. Let's do it."' Jagger's assent was also secured with the help of projected gross box-office receipts of fifty million dollars – in addition to proceeds from T-shirts, sweat shirts, buttons, badges and posters, TV and video rights and four million dollars from an agreement with Jovan Perfumes to allow their name to be printed on concert tickets. In the end the most persuasive voice in Jagger's ear may have been Loewenstein's.

After Easter in Mustique – an otherwise bleak outpost of the Grenadines developed in the sixties by Colin Tennant and his friend Princess Margaret – Jagger returned to the studio in April. The other Stones and seventy employees variously engaged on their behalf were told to prepare to tour in September. Jagger gave a series of interviews teasing

---

* Jagger himself had doubts about Wood, who had been deported from St Marteen the previous February for cocaine possession. Throughout the 1980s there were rumours, never fulfilled, that the Stones would hire yet another guitarist.

the press into the familiar state of nervous expectation. Asked in one if he was 'too old to rock', Jagger pursed his lips, promising to be 'totally candid' in his answer, which turned out to be no. He was also at pains to stress the 'normalcy' of his life, his dedication to work – even, most winningly, his mocking self-portrait as a 'dilettante Englishman abroad'. Critics came away genuinely impressed. Instead of a pasty-faced inebriate they encountered a razor-suited executive drinking tea and discussing art. In June, dressed in the athletic clothes he now favoured, Jagger supervised the shooting of a video to promote a new single, 'Start Me Up'. On 2 July, barely seven months since Lennon's death, he was walking the streets of Greenwich Village for another film, *Waiting On A Friend*. That night, still dressed in his luminous white trousers, check shirt and hat, he hosted a birthday party for Hall at Mr Chow's. Luciano Amore, a waiter at the celebrated restaurant, remembers Jagger 'slumped at a table with Jerry and Andy Warhol, drinking a lot of Heineken and generally carrying on. You could say he was in a good mood.' Jagger's own birthday was spent at home in New York.

Mid-August found the Stones secluded in the hamlet of Brookfield, Massachusetts. Every day Jagger woke at Longview Farm before noon. He exercised; he practised karate; he rehearsed. He continued to give interviews and even allowed *Life* to photograph him dutifully jogging through the neighbouring woods. On 26 August Jagger was driven to JFK Stadium in Philadelphia where, flashing his diamond smile, he made the announcement: the Stones would, within a month, tour – official. Within twenty-four hours three and a half million applications had been received for tickets. Jagger also tirelessly plugged the upcoming album, declaring it 'great', 'a gas' and 'the best thing we've done in years'.

It proved to be. *Tattoo You*, released on 31 August, exceeded even the standard of *Some Girls*. 'Start Me Up', originally recorded in 1977, was arguably the group's most commercial single since 'Brown Sugar'; it reached number seven in Britain, number two in America. Based around yet another Richards guitar hook, the song was largely distinguished – as was the LP generally – by the jewel-sharp sound engineered by Chris Kimsey and Bob Clearmountain. Even the vocals were audible. 'Hang Fire' followed – an uncertain, free-form rocker whose assessment of Britain as the country 'where nothing gets done' was rendered obsolete by the fact that it, too, dated from 1977. The song segued into 'Slave', a rhythmic filler from the *Black and Blue* sessions; 'Little T & A', sung – gasped – by Richards; 'Black Limousine', yet another from the archives; and 'Neighbours', an original Jagger composition concerning Richards' eviction from his Manhattan apartment for unsociable behaviour. Side two opened with 'Worried About You', a bass-inspired ballad also dating from *Black and Blue*, as did 'Tops' from *Goat's Head*; 'Heaven' was a vague psychedelic throwback; 'No Use In Crying' a warm-up for the *Emotional Rescue* sessions and, finally, 'Waiting On A Friend', a sublime guitar-saxophone ballad eagerly seized on as evidence of a new, reconstructed attitude ('It's about not just wanting to have a woman for a sexual reason'), carefully overlooking the unreconstructed, defiantly old-world sneer of 'Little T & A'. *Tattoo You* reached number two in the UK, number one in the US, where it sold a million copies in the first week of release.

The fourteenth of September was a typical autumn day in Worcester, Massachusetts. The announcement board outside the timber roadhouse known as Sir Morgan's Cove read, 'Tonight: One Performance Only: Little Boy Blue and the Cockroaches'. It was the Stones. An hour before the scheduled start a crowd of eleven thousand brawling fans surrounded the three-hundred-seat club. Jagger gave a vintage performance, superior to the El Mocambo, superior even to the Station Hotel, while outside crowds rioted and police horses charged in the gravel forecourt. Immediately the Mayor of Boston banned the Stones from any future public rehearsals. 'The appearance here of Mr Jagger,' he noted, 'is not necessarily in the public interest.' Jagger himself was tired, effusive, and happy at the Longview retreat: 'Within three or four years I won't be able to do what I do now.' He admitted to hesitating to tour after Lennon's death – 'but you can't spend your life being paranoid. There'll always be nutters and you have to watch out for them.'

The tour itself opened in Philadelphia on 25 September. Introduced by 'Take The "A" Train' the Stones slouched on the pink-tinted stage, flanked by twin promontories extending into the crowd, under a rear canopy painted yellow and blue incorporating a car, the American flag and Jagger's lips in vaguely Oriental design, topped by five thousand balloons. The first – gloriously unreconstructed – song was 'Under My Thumb', Jagger jumping, mincing, strutting and snarling in his red T-shirt and white football pants while overhead a circling plane buzzed its trailing message: 'ROLLING STONES UNFAIR TO WOMEN'. Then 'Let's Spend The Night Together' ... 'Shattered' ... 'Neighbours' ... 'Beast of Burden' ... 'Tumbling Dice' ... finally a clutch of vicious, three-minute classics: 'Start Me Up', 'Honky Tonk Women', 'Brown Sugar', 'Jumpin' Jack Flash' (Jagger rising in a mechanical cherry-picker – a source of continual disagreement with Richards – over the straining heads), 'Satisfaction'. More balloons, fireworks. For some time Jagger's amplified voice, *'Yeahhh! Aaawrite!'* echoed around the field, indicative not of his desire to return but just the reverse: the sentiments were expressed by way of a radio microphone as he sat demurely in a speeding van between Hall and Jade. When it became apparent that there would, in fact, be no encore elements of the ninety thousand crowd tore down barriers and rushed the stage.

'It's weird,' Jagger announced. 'Last time we toured people came to the shows but there was a kind of "So what?"

about the whole thing. This time they're going crazy. Why?'
(He seemed genuinely bemused.) Three reasons suggest
themselves: that, in the interim, the Stones had passed from
musical has-beens, their achievements lying wholly in the
past, into the realm of Living Legends, their original Baby
Boomer fans holding to them as a palliative against ageing;
that Richards' very presence gave the group a kind of morbid appeal; and that, since 1978, Lennon, Keith Moon and
John Bonham having died, three rival or potentially rival
icons, the Beatles, Who and Led Zeppelin had been reduced
or removed, while a fourth and fifth, Dylan and the Beach
Boys, had cheapened themselves to almost risible levels. In
short Jagger, at thirty-eight, was a figure of nostalgia, a
monument appreciated not merely for himself but for having survived so long. That and the fact that for sixteen
dollars – the price of an indifferent meal – the Stones
delivered two hours of nonpareil rock.

In Los Angeles the group were preceded on stage by
Prince. The predominantly white, predominantly middle-
class audience became indignant and pelted the singer with
bottles. Afterwards he approached Jagger in tears asking to
be removed from the tour. According to Stewart, Prince was
advised to 'quote, shape up': 'Bottles,' said Jagger. 'You're
worried about *bottles*?' The pressures to which the Stones
themselves remained subject were demonstrated the following week in Seattle. A woman was arrested for informing
the crowd she intended to kill 'that son of a bitch Mick
Jagger'. Later a second woman, Pamela Lynn Melville, fell
to her death from an outside balcony at the stadium; Jagger
sent flowers. The concert itself was described by the Seattle
Post-Intelligencer as 'Wonderful . . . [Jagger] prancing across
the center of the stage and out onto its long wingways, with
his elfin, androgynously erotic grace . . .' He was 'as raw,
raunchy and full of juice as ever', 'a walking, writhing grace
note', a 'lovely'. Elsewhere the press concurred: for a man
widely believed to have 'wasted' much of the seventies, the

eighties found Jagger profoundly rejuvenated: dressed down, minimally made-up, eager to please, with none of the arrogant loathing of his earlier work characteristic of other performers. He even sang 'Time Is On My Side'. The critics agreed: if greatness consisted of the taking of infinite pains, then Jagger, in middle age, remained a great entertainer.

In San Francisco he joined Mayor Dianne Feinstein in a televised 'Save the Cable Cars' appeal. He had dinner with Jacqueline Onassis, also, on 17 October, with Richards – the twentieth anniversary of their meeting at Dartford Station. An understanding of their relationship is central to understanding Jagger as a performer. Notwithstanding the tension, notwithstanding the jealousy, Jagger admired Richards; he respected him. Stewart went one further in stating that 'Keith [was] the one person, bar none, Mick ever listened to.' On stage, as Hal Ashby's film of the tour confirms, Jagger deferred to Richards in matters of musical procedure; songs began, ended or expired on the guitarist's whim. Once, during an extended introduction, Jagger was cut short by the opening chords of 'Miss You', glancing back with the look of a man surprised in the shower. In Virginia a fan evaded the presidential-level security and rushed Jagger on stage. He was a foot away when Richards swung at him with his guitar, nodded at the – obviously shaken – singer and continued playing. Nineteen eighty-one was the year in which the 'Human Riff' belatedly received credit not only as the group's abiding genius but as the closest to the spirit of what they once were.

The distance separating Jagger from the others – from the popular perception of the Stones as irreparable morons – was confirmed in an interview with Rona Barrett in Michigan. Subjects ranged from the Pope ('Glad he got over it') to Dylan ('a religious maniac') to Ronald Reagan ('I'd like to have some influence to get him and Brezhnev talking'). To Barrett's question, 'Are you aware of the great influence

you have . . . that you can turn it into something positive?'
Jagger responded archly: 'You mean set a good example?
I'll *try*.' In New York he, Richards and Watts heaped ful-
some praise on the city elders before appearing anony-
mously at the employees' entrance of Madison Square
Garden and enquiring politely if they might be let in. (The
man who did so remembers 'almost tangible relief' when
Jagger later left through the same door; there was a sense
of indulging an admittedly gifted but temperamental child.)
The concert that followed was extolled in the *New York
Times* as 'spectacularly musical and overwhelmingly physical', as embodied by Richards and Jagger respectively. 'Mick
. . . was *singing* – hitting the notes, finding new ones, phrasing carefully and often inventively.' Backstage, flanked by
Dunn, the group's security supervisor and divers electricians
and engineers, a cast including Peter O'Toole, Jack Nichol-
son, Robert Redford, Tony Curtis, Ryan O'Neal, Robert de
Niro, Paul McCartney and John McEnroe vied for Jagger's
attention. Bianca was also present. She left without greeting
her ex-husband, after allowing diplomatically: 'It was
superb. They seem to get better as the years go on.'

As if to refute all this Jagger then gave his most abject
performance of the tour. It was to an audience of two hundred at the Checkerboard Lounge, Chicago; Muddy Waters
sat in his grey suit and tie while, stage-left, Jagger minced,
shuffled and swaggered his way through 'Mannish Boy' with
apparently no sense of the altered acoustics of his surroundings. There was also, one of the audience believed, something ghoulish about Jagger's insistence on filming the
event, 'as if he wanted a souvenir before the old man died'.
If anything he was more at home in the hockey stadia and
ballparks that constituted the bulk of the itinerary – as
Richards said, 'Exaggerating a façade without letting anybody know anything about you.' To eighty thousand at the
Sun Devil Stadium, Phoenix, Jagger announced 'One for *les
girls*'; as Richards ground out 'Honky Tonk Women' the

curtain flared and Hall flounced on: 'We danced around and he hit me on the bottom ... It was thrilling.' The next night, in Kansas, Mick Taylor appeared. The reunion overexcited him – according to Wood, 'He shocked us with how loud he was blasting it ... bulldozing through parts of songs that should have been subtle, ignoring breaks and taking uninvited solos.' Jagger's comment was unrecorded.

The tour ended on 19 December. During it the Stones and Graham were said to have earned twenty-two million dollars after expenses: $3.6 million each for eighty-five days' work. On the whole Jagger's reputation was enhanced. Critics detected traces of self-parody; certain concerts seemed heavy with a never-delivered message (in Los Angeles Jagger was still assuring the crowd, 'We're going to have a good time' as Richards signalled the closing number); there were mutterings about the firmament of stars occupying, as if by divine right, front-row seats. Fifteen million dollars, expressed as an annual figure, *was* a lot of money. Even so, the *New York Times* concluded, Jagger was worth it: he was associated with flair, with style and with certain other values. When he sang he expressed not merely the song but the mood behind it. In an era lacking enduring musical direction of its own – punk having divided into Two-Tone and the no less anaemic New Romantics – Jagger constituted a figure of belonging, of continuity and even, it now seemed, of permanence.

A sense of belonging may have led Jagger to his next acquisition, a five-bedroom brownstone on West 81st Street – described by Warhol as 'just a regular house' – giving visitors the impression of having been designed for a family; that and the subsequent building of a home on Mustique. The latter consisted of a three-room cottage, dismissed by Jagger as 'literally a shack on the beach', eventually surrounded by a series of adjoining Japanese pavilions, a bath-house with hot tub, children's cottage and outlying games room, the whole connected by polished hardwood walkways and bamboo railings. Decorated, as was the New York home, by Jed Johnson, the theme was unostentatiously oriental: artefacts, Kabuki masks, sushi prawn chaise longues. Jagger named the property Stargroves.

After eight weeks away he returned to New York in March, edited concert tapes and worked with Hal Ashby on the accompanying film, belatedly entitled *Let's Spend The Night Together* ('Twenty-five songs spanning twenty years of the greatest on-going act in Rock and Roll'; it was panned by critics). In the *Rolling Stone* Readers' Awards Jagger was voted best male vocalist, the Stones best group, *Tattoo You* best album and 'Start Me Up' best single. Buoyed by this and by further inducements from Loewenstein, Jagger flew to London on 28 April; at Le Beat Route he announced European concerts in May, June and July. Graham was again tour director, Dunn again handled logistics. The only significant change was Jagger's replacement of his British publicist Keith Altham by twenty-six-year-old Alan Edwards, a man duly impressed by the different poses his employer adopted for the press – 'a bit of sex for the *Sun*, quiet intelligence for *The Sunday Times*, camp bitchiness for *Time Out*'. To promote the European tour Jagger agreed to speak exclusively to courtly, urbane John Mortimer, author of *Rumpole of the Bailey*, a man not previously known for his love of rock and roll.

The opening night was in Aberdeen on 26 May. In the *Daily Mirror* John Millar noted, 'They're back ... From the first electric moment the Stones stepped on stage until the final sounds of "Satisfaction" died away, fans in the Capitol Theatre were gripped by that old Mick Jagger magic.' Critics were less inclined to the American concert album released on 1 June, duly earning the group a second entry in *The Worst Rock and Roll Records Of All Time*: 'The Rolling Stones' *Still Life* is a perfectly descriptive title for a live album as energetic as a plastic-fruit centrepiece.'

Jagger's sole on stage comments varied from the mundane ('Welcome, Virginia . . . Welcome, Hampton . . . All right, Chicago . . . Thank you very much, Phoenix') to the mildly mischievous ('Hope you're having a good time . . . drinking a few beers, smoking a few joints'). The LP, which critics agreed failed to do justice to the live event, reached number four in Britain and number five in America.

By this time the United Kingdom was at war with Argentina. Asked to comment by the French weekly *Libération*, Jagger announced he was sending videos – 'for moral support' – to British troops. He declined to comment on the war itself, lapsing into the elegant defensive – 'It's really none of my business' – as he would again in 1991, when he created a furore by releasing a single appearing to undermine both parties' positions at the exact moment the Western allies attacked Iraq. Again he avoided personal commitment: 'Sometimes war's right . . . sometimes it's not.' In 'Highwire' Jagger's only audible criticism was of the arms dealers (providing him with the opportunity to rhyme 'tank' with 'bank'), openly supplying both sides.

Early June saw the Stones in Holland, West Germany and France. On the fifteenth the Spanish soccer authorities withdrew permission for the group to appear in Barcelona for security reasons. 'The combination of the World Cup, the heat and Mick Jagger is too great,' noted a spokesman. Jagger himself assured the BBC: 'The [London] shows mean a lot to us and they better be good as well . . . We'll get our share of attention unless Princess Di has another baby.' The two sold-out performances at Wembley on 25 and 26 June were, in fact, perfect illustrations of the cross-culture the group now represented: Jagger, in striped breeches and pink jacket minced, kneeled, strutted, shouted and swaggered, kicking and screaming, as backstage Joe and Eva drank wine with Lord Linley. In Austria on 2 July Jagger hosted a vaguely Viennese celebration of Hall's twenty-sixth birthday. A symphony orchestra played waltzes while Jagger and Peter Wolf provided off-key harmonies. Later the group appeared at a local brothel where an Oriental transvestite crooned 'As Tears Go By'.

The highlight of the tour was reached in Turin. Wearing an Italian soccer jersey Jagger assured the crowd at the Communal Stadium, *'Tre-uno . . . Tre-uno'*, a prediction regarding that night's World Cup Final with West Germany. He was right. The crowd responded in kind, *'Grande, grande'*, as Jagger, flapping like a displaced fish, flailed once, twice, three times with his strangely outsize hands. '"Satisfaction", *bene*?' By the time, on 13 July, *La Stampa* was reiterating his power 'to shock . . . to intensely surprise', Jagger was dining with Roman Polanski at his villa in Ramatuelle. In Naples he was visited by Antonioni.

In Nice something almost nostalgic happened, when Hell's Angels snarled and swooped with billiard cues at the Parc des Sports de l'Ouest, putting the concert in jeopardy. Memories were revived of Altamont – the difference being that, in 1982, the Stones travelled with their own executive security. The situation was saved, says Wood, by 'Jim Callahan's super-tough strongmen . . . cracking the key troublemakers' bones'. As the inquest began that night Jagger was dancing at Regine's in Monte Carlo.

The tour ended in Leeds on 25 July. Again, as they had every closing night since 1966, the press engaged in a frenzy of speculation: 'STONES – IT'S ALL OVER NOW' . . . 'COULD THIS BE THE LAST TIME?' Jagger, as he had every closing night since 1966, merely shrugged. On the twenty-sixth, his thirty-ninth birthday, he celebrated in the upstairs room at Langan's Brasserie. According to the manager Harry McHugh, 'Mick and Jerry stayed until everyone had gone home. Then I saw Jerry struggling down with him because he was plastered . . . I grabbed Mick who, to my horror, turned out to be a bag of bones. Suddenly Jerry said nervously: "Be careful. Don't drop him. You're carrying forty million pounds' worth of pop star like a sack of potatoes."' Jagger recuperated at Château de la Fourchette. He returned to New York and, on 25 September, arrived by helicopter to see The Who open their farewell tour in Philadelphia. Backstage he sympathized with Pete Townshend about the rigours of playing America; the guitarist spoke of *angst* and alienation while Jagger addressed himself to haulage distances and logistics. Later there was a party which Jagger attended with his daughter. Observers found him to be nervous and distracted. By the month's end gossip columnists on both sides of the Atlantic were reporting that Hall had left him.

'I won't marry anyone again,' Jagger had informed *Woman's World* that April. 'If you're not successful at it, it isn't a case of try, try again.' Of Bianca he noted: 'Since the divorce we're not even friends. She's been so difficult and devious that I'll never be friends with her again.' Others remarked on the fact that, so far from being 'reconstructed', Jagger's attitude to women that spring and summer bordered on misogyny. In Hall's account: 'After we'd been together for five years, in 1982, he decided to start taking advantage of the way girls are . . . He seemed to want to go back to living the image of the famous rock star. Every time I'd leave town on a job he'd be in the papers with this girl or that girl and I was getting hurt feelings . . . It was so seedy.' An employee who accompanied the Stones on both the American and European tours equally thought 'Mick went a little bit back to the sixties . . . Ian Stewart even used the words déjà vu.' The qualities that first distinguished Jagger – efficiency, enterprise, opportunism, substantial laissez-faire and egoism – were all revived in the 1980s, as was his abiding fear of commitment, the attribute on which Hall squarely blamed his behaviour. 'Our relationship had speeded up so much I think it frightened him.'

Gered Mankowitz, last involved with the Stones in 1967, was made vividly aware of Jagger's capriciousness when invited to photograph him that May in London. After a series of phone calls from the group's office ('Mick's just got up, and he's in the bath – we'll call you right back' . . . 'Mick's still in the bath, but Keith's up now, and says he's looking forward to seeing you' . . . 'Mick's out of the bath now, it's definitely on for tonight') he arrived at the rehearsal studio to be confronted with a 'really friendly' Jagger suggesting a second session two nights later. Mankowitz returned to a perceptibly cooler reception. 'Keith said, "Ah, you're back again." I said, "Yeah, we're going to do this session," and he said, "I don't think we are." I asked why, and he said, "Well, you remind us of really bad times. Whenever we look at you we think of one point five million dollars." I assumed he meant the money owed them by Klein, or whoever, and I just said, "Well, that was nothing to do with me . . ."' Jagger finally arrived at three-thirty a.m., 'really drunk and aggressive – he had that blinkered, "don't fuck with me" expression of his, pacing up and down. [Alan] Edwards asked him about doing some pictures and he said "Yeah, all right, let's do it. Don't take too long about it." I did some black and white shots, gave the film to them and left.' Mankowitz later informed his assistant, '*That's* why I don't want to deal with this any more . . . you just can't relate to that level of schizophrenia.' Today he adds that 'the whole group, especially Mick, were going through a bad phase . . . His ugly side really came out.' Other sources indicate that among the causes of his irritation was Wood's continuing drug addiction. Even at his favoured Lord's that August Jagger snarled at requests for autographs in the press bar. Peter Smith of the *Daily Mail* remembered him 'strutting past in a red T-shirt, flicking his hand at us like King Tut. Whatever it meant, it came across as monumentally arrogant.'

Meanwhile Hall, returning from modelling assignments to the Carlyle or West 81st, would 'find things next to the bed like earrings or a ring . . . It [became] impossible to pick up the phone without some girl on the line. Finally I decided to move out until he could figure out what he wanted – to date other girls or to be with me . . . Mick and I decided that we'd still see each other. We'd make a date. I'd get dressed up and wait for him and he wouldn't come. He'd stand me up. Then he'd say, "I was out with some eighteen-year-old debutantes" – rubbing it in.' In October Jagger was accompanied to a party at Regine's by the social-ite Cornelia Guest. Later he was seen at Xenon with Valerie Perrine, with whom he was immediately rumoured to be having an affair; in Paris it was the Venezuelan model Victoria Vicuna.

Events might have proceeded indefinitely but for the appearance of millionaire racehorse owner Robert Sangster. Sangster arrived in New York that October. He had dinner at the Carlyle; he consoled Hall; he comforted her. Later that month they moved (to separate hotels) in Los Angeles, Hall on assignment, Sangster to the races. It was at this point that elements of the British press caught up with them, promptly labelling Hall a 'gold-digger' and 'femme fatale'. Jagger, about to board a plane to Paris, was stopped by a reporter from the New York *Post*: had he heard the news? Just as he had in 1969, he shook his head. Hall, his informant stated, had left him and was living openly with Sangster in either the Beverly Wilshire or Hilton – full details to follow. Meanwhile Sangster and his friend Charles Benson of the *Express* merely aggravated matters ('I realize our current situation might set tongues wagging') in a press release.

On 5 November, under the tortuous headline 'SANGS-TER HALLMARKED AND MICK DON'T GET NO SATISFACTION', Nigel Dempster quoted Hall in the *Daily Mail*: 'Who knows what any of us will be doing in future?' She was further reported to have noted, 'Robert could buy Mick out ten times over' – a comment later ascribed to a third party. On the eleventh Dempster changed tack: 'The closest friends of Texan model Jerry

Hall, who has set her stetson at pools heir Robert Sangster, forty-six, have rallied round to deny that she is a gold-digger, interested in the chubby racehorse owner only for his estimated five hundred million pound fortune.' Hall herself was already having second thoughts – 'It seemed like Robert's life was going out every night with a whole entourage' – when Jagger rang from Paris 'really upset, proposing marriage, saying he was going to be good', whereupon she flew to New York, changed planes and left for Europe.

Immediately at the airport there was evidence of tension. Jagger met Hall in a sort of sweating scrum – the man of talent grappling with the *Paris Match* reporter and the stringer from *People*. After the formalities had been observed the couple returned to the hotel where the recriminations began. According to Dempster, 'far from the meeting being joyful, as described by ill-informed newspapers, Mick started at Jerry as soon as he met her at the airport . . . She really doesn't want to see him again.' In Hall's own account, 'I was having the closest to a nervous breakdown I've ever had . . . I just ran like a kid would run.' Dempster again: 'She couldn't take his abuse any longer.'

Neglecting to appear at the studio, Jagger organized a door-to-door search of neighbouring hotels. Stewart and Dunn were delegated to visit every club, café and *retraite* known to Hall since 1973. Jagger himself made a number of calls. At dawn on 16 November, according to the *Mail*, he was 'still doing his "Jumpin' Jack Flash" imitation, after a night on the town with two dusky ladies and a seventy m.p.h. car chase down the Champs Elysées . . . "I'm fine. I'm fine. There is no tomorrow," [Jagger] muttered as he was delivered to a seedy apartment block near the Opéra.'

It was at this stage that Hall surfaced. According to her, Jagger's first words were 'Come home – everything will be OK.' Despite giving Dempster the impression Jagger had 'physically twisted her arm' and her own admission that 'Mick was upset' she discovered him to be 'really sweet'.

The couple immediately left for Fourchette, Jagger assuring Hall, 'We're going to get married, we're going to have babies, we're going to be so happy . . .' By the time *People* featured the story on 22 November (' "For any relationship to last, there has to be a bit of playing about," said Mick Jagger last month. If that's the case, he and Jerry Hall should be together for ever') they were already walking hand in hand, shopping and pausing for *eau de vie* in the market square in Amboise. 'I was thrilled,' says Hall. 'I'd gotten him back and we were going to have children . . . Plus, when you've had a really serious fight with someone you know each other better. You know what the other would do when a bad situation came up. To have survived all that really makes love stronger.' Or, in Jagger's words: 'We just broke up for a while. That's all.'

One aspect at least of middle age, as the condition asserts itself, is worth stating: things thought never to happen happen daily; sometimes the very efforts to arrest them are notable. Whatever the cause – the banking of his American receipts assuring him of serious, not merely substantial wealth, the purchase of homes rather than glorified dressing rooms, the continuing relationship with Hall – it is hard to avoid the conclusion that Jagger, approaching his fortieth birthday, underwent something akin to a male menopause. The pique, the spleen, the womanizing, the public diatribes all suggest a man motivated by intimations of ageing. One had only to mention the word 'marriage' to receive negative impressions. The obvious target of these outbursts was Hall. In 1982 she risked (as had Shrimpton, Faithfull and Bianca) being minimalized to the fringes of Jagger's life; she resisted as Shrimpton, Faithfull and Bianca had not. In her autobiography Hall concludes her version of events by stating, 'Women have come up to me and said, "You were so brave the way you carried that off . . . So many men treat women so awful and the women just stay because they don't know what to do."' Or, as a journalist who knew both, who followed events at first hand and was present when Hall flew to Los Angeles with Sangster puts it: 'Mick never wanted Bianca near him except when it was vital to have her attend a dinner or babysit Jade. All that changed with Jerry. I think for the first time in his life he looked on a woman as a partner, equal or even stronger than himself – and it scared the shit out of him.'

Reconciled, the couple retreated to Mustique in December. Work began in earnest on Stargroves; Jed Johnson and his partner Alan Wanzenberg were briefed, in the former's words, to 'create a serene and uncomplicated environment. Mick's concept was East meets West . . . He liked the Japanese influence, but he didn't want to be a purist.' Johnson also believed the house to be 'rejuvenating' of its occupants. Refinements were subsequently made to the home on West 81st Street. Exotic plants and tapestries, personal computers, tape decks and VCRs were installed, and the unflattering references to Hall scrawled nightly across the bay windows removed. Jagger himself was in convivial mood; he threw a party for his immediate neighbours, in which, according to one, Rosalynn Corby, 'he was the epitome of British charm', even apologizing for the excessive sensitivity of the house's burglar alarms. In the *Sun* he spoke perceptively of the inevitable demise of the Stones: 'It will disintegrate very slowly . . . The band has done what it set out to do,' and he referred affectionately to Joe and Eva, then approaching their seventieth birthdays. In April, nearing his fortieth, he began work on his autobiography.

This typically Byzantine project began when, in July 1982, Jagger personally accepted a million-pound-plus advance from George Weidenfeld of Weidenfeld & Nicolson. A 'technical writer', John Ryle, deputy literary editor of *The Sunday Times* (and authority on Molière), was hired for fifty thousand pounds. Simultaneously a researcher,

Brooke Hayward, visited Jagger's parents, his brother, Korner, Shrimpton, Faithfull, even Bianca; notes were conveyed to Ryle in London or New York and thence to Jagger in Mustique. Early reports indicated the latter was experiencing 'difficulty' recalling major events of his life.

Eventually, in spring 1984, a manuscript was delivered to Weidenfeld and, by purposefully theatrical means, to a number of British paperback houses – most of whom promptly rejected it. On 10 May a spokesman for Futura was quoted in the *Daily Express*: 'No sex. No rock and roll. It's just boring stuff about his ordinary parents, his ordinary upbringing. I was surprised at the poor quality.' Ryle, the *Express* stated, was 'hard at work in New York' bringing the book up to scratch. A senior Weidenfeld editor, still associated with the firm, confirms, 'It was a shambles . . . The problem seemed to be a complete breakdown between Jagger and his ghost. The excerpts we saw weren't publishable.' A year later the *Mirror* reported that, as a last resort, Jagger had approached Wyman for help in recalling episodes from the group's past and been told, 'Get stuffed.' Wyman was writing his own book.

In April 1985 Jagger, his notoriously short attention now centred on LPs as a way of maintaining his name before the public, finally abandoned the project. Most if not all the advance was returned. Ryle was thanked and paid, after signing the confidentiality clause demanded of all Jagger's employees. (His sole public comment was to speak disparagingly of the 'exotic substances' smoked in editorial conferences.) In September 1989 Jagger informed *20/20*: 'I scrapped it . . . I just got sick of talking about the past and thought I'd leave all that book-signing caper till later.'

The road of excess leading to the palace of wisdom, Jagger in 1983 continued to exude copious public charm, speaking of himself with wry objectivity – literally as an object of praise and affection. ('You can't help laughing at the funny way people behave ... You just don't know how they're going to treat you until you reach the level you thought you wanted to reach.') In *Penthouse* he invited members of the public to 'shoot the breeze' with him at his office – though no record exists of any outsider having done so. To the *Star* he admitted, 'When you get to my age you really have to work at staying young ... Once I led the typical dissipated life of a rock star, full of drugs, booze and chaos. These days my health is my most treasured possession.' Ever the man in the irony mask, Jagger advised readers to get as much sleep as possible – 'Myself, I don't go to clubs or discos except to pick up girls.'

He continued to court Hall with renewed intensity. On 2 July he furnished Mr Chow's with bouquets of white roses for her twenty-seventh birthday. The couple rented a summer house in Vermont, where on 26 July Jagger himself turned forty. 'If anyone else asks me about it, I'll punch them in the mouth,' he announced, grinning broadly. Among the panegyrics was Pete Townshend's in *The Times*. Jagger, he revealed, was 'a complete exhibitionist', 'a name-dropper', someone 'whose beauty is its owner's greatest joy'; a person, on the other hand, 'who will still be beautiful when he's fifty ... [whose] talent will still be as strong at fifty because his ambition is not dependent on his youth, his song-writing is not dependent on his own suffering and his desire to be popular and loved not dependent on his personal insecurity.' Townshend concluded by stating, 'Jagger was into rock and roll before me but, unlike me, he still lives for it' – a point made repeatedly by Lennon in the 1970s.

In his fifth decade Jagger still invested confidence in the future, with good reason. In France he, Richards and Loewenstein met Walter Yetnikoff, president of CBS ('I know I have the reputation of having a big mouth ... In this business, you play your own ego'), a fractious, obese figure not wholly dissimilar to Allen Klein. On 20 August, at the Paris Ritz, the group signed a contract valued at twenty-eight million dollars, six million each for four albums, four million for publicity. It was the richest in rock music history. The agreement was widely seen as a loss-leader for CBS and prompted Sheldon Vogue of Atlantic to admit, 'We hated losing them, but the numbers they were asking just didn't make sense.' Even then Richards, again recalling the Klein débâcle, had reservations: 'Mick's not as good at business as people think. He's not as good as *he* thinks.' The *Wall Street Journal* duly noted.

Gratified, in the thick of life, Jagger returned to New York. There was a reception at the Black Rock, CBS head-quarters, rivalling in excitement that for Paul McCartney. No longer merely moneyed, he joined McCartney, Elton John and Lloyd Webber in a quartet immune to the vagaries of style or success – the fabulously rich. There were additional causes for satisfaction: the group's album, released that autumn, was a revival of the standard of *Tattoo You*, or better; Jagger, in a parallel move, negotiated the release of a solo LP; there was talk of a tour, of a career separate from or even surpassing the Stones.

In Vermont, Hall was three months pregnant.

· X ·

AN ENGLISHMAN ABROAD

Undercover, released on 7 November 1983, confirmed the group's ability to offend and upset. Of three accompanying videos two were banned while a third, wherein Richards and Wood buzzed Jagger with chainsaws, was suppressed for a year. Of the title track the BBC said, 'It is exceedingly violent and we couldn't consider it for *Top of the Pops*.' As if in celebration the song was an international hit.

'Undercover', a drums, guitar and electric organ mêlée was essentially a lament for political *disparus* in Argentina (where the song was banned in perpetuity); the attendant video showed Jagger, in seersucker suit and moustache, being bound, gagged and, inevitably, shot. This, he stated, was not trying to 'glamorize violence', but 'say something interesting' about conditions in Latin America. Somehow a discussion on Channel Four's *The Tube* became animated when Jagger was asked if he accordingly gave money to political causes. 'None of your business,' he snapped, ('repeatedly asking, "What can I do?"' says an acquaintance, 'without accepting responsibility for the answer'). The single reached number eleven in Britain, number nine in America.

It was followed by 'She Was Hot', a Richards rocker released with a film suggestive of the Jayne Mansfield epic *The Girl Can't Help It*; 'Tie You Up', in which Jagger addressed himself to the pain of love (including the need to lie, cry, cheat and 'forget about the past'); 'Wanna Hold You', a straight reworking of 'Happy', as was 'It Must Be Hell' of 'Soul Survivor'. 'Too Much Blood' was like nothing at all: an extraordinary fusion of funk, rap and *agitato* phrasing, it dealt with the case of Issei Sagawa, a Japanese literature student at the Sorbonne who in 1981 murdered his girlfriend, dissected her body, ate the flesh – some raw, some fried – before surrendering to the police; he spent three years in prison and a fourth in psychiatric hospital. (While Sagawa has variously been the subject of plays, novels and at least one PhD thesis, Jagger remains the only musician to have committed him to vinyl.) 'Pretty Beat Up' continued the tradition – as did 'Too Tough', a louring echo of 'Play With Fire' with overtones of 'Under My Thumb' (the title referring to the singer himself); finally 'All The Way Down', in which Jagger invoked his ironic edge on the subject of ageing: 'I was King, Mr Cool/Just a snobby little fool/Like kids are now' before concluding '. . . Still I play the fool and strut.' The title track aside, *Undercover*, with its references to 'hard labour', 'fifty lashes', *The Texas Chain Saw Massacre*, 'too much blood', tension, razors, battered babies, kitchen knives and prison – its cover of a naked, sectioned woman – marked a return to the basics, the jungle. The lyrics were the most atavistic since *Exile*, which it frequently resembled. The critics were fulsome. *Undercover* reached number three in Britain, number four in America, its every play, says Jeff Griffin, who interviewed him that autumn, monitored by Jagger, 'forever harrying, calling, complaining, comparing, checking . . . If ever there was a control freak, he was it.'

At year's end Jagger was seen in the company of the nascent Madonna, in whom he detected 'central dumbness', and Bette Midler, who recorded a version of 'Beast of Burden'. He flew to Cabo San Lucas, Mexico, where on 18 December, his fortieth birthday, Richards married Patti Hansen – the best man in white shirt and sunglasses, clapping, mugging along, giggling. He returned to domestic duties of his own: a baby shower for Hall, Christmas and, on 27 December, an electric blues festival to which he tried and failed to gain entry on the basis of being Mick Jagger. ('Sure you are,' said the brute, burly and glowering guard. 'Tell me about it.') On New Year's Day Alexis Korner died in London.

Except for professional excursions – video shoots, recording, a tax meeting or interview – Jagger now settled in Manhattan. His routine rarely varied: up at noon, tea ('I make it myself'), scanning or shredding the paper-chase of offers and demands, the invitations, solicitations and requests dropped daily on his mat, then bicycling the streets, frequently on some elaborate errand to acquire ingredients for dinner, a meeting with CBS on 52nd Street, accompanied by Loewenstein, Yetnikoff or Richards, a few moments in Shakespeare's or skimming cricket videos from England, dinner – the highlight and focus of Jagger's day – a nightclub, concert or disco not infrequently in the company of a Guinness or Rothschild, the Marquis of Bristol or Lord Lampton, the 'toffs' whom, says Anthony Haden-Guest, 'Mick finds so amusing, and vice-versa', the dawn arrival at 81st Street, the beery rendition of 'Stop Breaking Down' (designated by Hall 'our song'; with Ferry it had been 'Let's Stay Together'), the sleep after which all things were possible – or as Richards put it: 'Have you ever seen Mick after he's stayed up for a night? Forget it.'

Another restraining influence: by January, according to Hall, 'it dawned [on Jagger] he was having a child . . . He got excited and sweet. He was protective of me' – notwithstanding which Hall's requests for additional security were refused. 'You're just being neurotic and paranoid. Who do you think you are – Princess Di?' asked Jagger. 'They might write something in the English press but it's not going to be a big deal. I've dealt with it all my life.'

The couple's daughter was born in Lenox Hills Hospital,

adjacent to the Carlyle, in the early hours of 2 March 1984. It was a complicated delivery and some time elapsed before the baby was considered out of danger. Jagger, says Hall, was at first 'scared', then 'astonished' . . . 'I'd never seen him quite like that. He couldn't believe it.' His incredulity mounted when, on 5 March, the family left hospital – photographers swarmed and brawled as Hall's sister, holding the baby, arrived at 81st Street. In June the child was christened in St Mary Abbot's Church, London – Elizabeth ('It's a really pretty classic name') Scarlett (suggested by Jade). Jagger stood in a sports jacket and open-neck shirt while Joe and Eva, Chris Jagger, a clutch of uncles and aunts, Hall's mother and Charlie and Shirley Watts – the baby's godmother – collected at the antique font, the sun shedding chopped-up light through the medieval stained glass. Despite Eva's repeated references to 'Mick and Jerry's wedding . . . I mean, christening', the ceremony passed without incident. Jagger's cousin Herbert Scutts remembers 'Mick being somewhat wide-eyed and serious. He wanted everything done in, as he put it, a proper English fashion.' Jagger's renewed sense of tradition was confirmed as the party assembled later in a rented house in Holland Park (Cheyne Walk having been vacated by Bianca, then let, then sold, Jagger found himself without private property in England until 1991). Hall's mother circulated in her Nieman-Marcus hat and pearls as butlers in full regalia served tea. 'I was so excited,' says Hall; the following week, her twenty-eighth birthday, Jagger bought her an antique ring.

(In the very month Elizabeth was born Jagger had formally acknowledged paternity of his eldest child Karis, officially registered on 23 March. Both she and Jade attended the christening and the subsequent reception in Holland Park, where a photograph was taken of an apparently delirious Jagger with his three daughters.)

Jagger's focus now reverted briefly to the Stones: having

toured, recorded and released an album, what were the plans for the future? Evidently there were none. In March Wyman was quoted in the *Sun*: 'I've lost touch with whoever Mick is now . . . I'm sure he has as well. Seven or eight years ago I could still talk with Mick about books, films and intelligent things, but now I just talk to him in asides. Mick is a very difficult person to know.' Gradually over the spring and early summer it became apparent that Jagger's immediate priority was the recording of the solo LP encouraged by Yetnikoff, a man whose greatest joy lay in the promotion of stand-alone artists like Springsteen and Michael Jackson, and such freelance activities as duetting with Jackson on the soundtrack *State of Shock*. In May Jagger arrived at Compass Point Studios, Nassau, where a troupe of musicians including Jeff Beck, Chuck Leavell, Robbie Shakespeare, Sly Dunbar, Eddie Martinez and, more sporadically, Pete Townshend and Herbie Hancock recorded the basic tracks, later mixed in New York, that became *She's The Boss*. At a meeting at the group's new office in Munro Terrace, London, on 26 June Jagger informed the three original Stones (Wood being absent) that most if not all the coming year could be regarded as spoken for. Immediately there was speculation that the Stones would disband. Jagger denied it. 'Rumours like this come up regularly and have done since the sixties . . . The truth is we're very much together.' At a further meeting on 2 November Jagger vetoed the recording of a new album proposed by Richards. 'He wants to show everyone what he's capable of without the support of the group,' one source announced in the press. 'He wants the ego trip.'

In replacing Richards with Jeff Beck Jagger had asked for trouble. Rod Stewart, since reconciled with his former employer, once called Beck 'about three sandwiches short of a picnic'. Wood also had reservations. On 27 July the *Evening Standard* reported an incident between Jagger and his lead guitarist in Nassau.

Jeff insisted that Mick left the studio so he could concentrate on a solo . . . Jagger returned, listened to the tape and, stone-faced, ordered the engineer to erase it. Beck was furious and, after telling Mick where he could put his album, stormed towards the door. The engineer protested but Jagger was emphatic. 'Wipe it,' he repeated. Beck stormed out, whereupon Jagger, a schoolboy grin on his face, turned to the engineer and said he had simply been testing the guitarist's well-known short temper. 'Too late,' wailed the hapless flunkey. 'You told me to wipe it and I have.'

Recording occupied most of that summer and autumn. Jagger's sole group contribution was to authorize the release of a compilation album, *Rewind*, on 2 July and to co-host with Wyman the accompanying video. The latter, issued on 14 November, was a minor curiosity: the Stones' least likely duo hammered through sixty minutes of disjointed patter, variable accents and boffo Monty Python humour, Jagger dressed throughout in his shredded 1972 jumpsuit (it still fitted). The tape's only serious moment came when, asked to explain the group's longevity, Richards and Wood answered as one: 'Charlie Watts.'

She's The Boss – the very irony of which bore scrutiny – was mixed at the Power Station in New York, at which Jagger arrived each afternoon by taxi or bicycle. ('Mick,' notes Hall, 'likes to keep a feeling of normality'.) Between takes Jagger would relax at David K's, Mortimer's or the Kamikaze Klub, a venue frequented by New Wave musicians where a garrulous, unshaven figure known as 'Bruno' tended bar: Bruce Willis. Whatever the cause of this activity – whether, as Jagger puts it, he was feeling 'stultified' or for more egotistic reasons – the result was yet again to inhibit the Stones. At a meeting in Amsterdam Jagger – to protests from Richards and merely mute acceptance from Wyman and Watts – reiterated his plans and the following week flew with Hall and the director Julien Temple to Brazil to shoot videos for *She's The Boss*. While in Rio Hall, in what she referred to as 'planned parenthood', again became pregnant. The couple returned to Mustique at Christmas. Another child, an album in embryo, their four properties furnished and functioning, Jagger's substantial guarantees securely in the bank – or, some said, more exotic locales. That winter he turned down a million dollars to play a cameo of himself in *Dallas*.

An indication of the group's internal tensions was provided on 2 January 1985. Wood married Jo Karslake at St Mary's Church, Denham. Richards was best man, Stewart, Clapton, Beck and Peter Frampton attended, as did Watts and Wyman – almost every British rock luminary except Jagger. Where was he? Overseeing the installation of a desalinization pump at Stargroves. He, Hall, their child and nanny remained for a month in Mustique, where his only meetings were with Jed Johnson, Loewenstein and his new assistant Miranda Guinness (of the Rundell banking branch). He also gave an interview to *Rolling Stone* in which he spoke predominantly of himself and his own album.

She's The Boss was released by CBS on 4 March. It reached number eight in America, number six in Britain. The critics, as they will, divided. There was praise for the opening single 'Just Another Night', a drum and synthesizer mêlée with reggae undertones (which the Jamaican singer Patrick Alley later contended in court was plagiarized). A second single, 'Lucky in Love', fared less well. With no fewer than four keyboardists, two drummers, percussion and backing vocals there was a suspicion that Jagger had confused congestion for invention; the result was the opposite of the primal, back-to-mono approach favoured by Richards. Jagger and his co-producer's hopes that the album might somehow endear him to a younger club audience were sadly misplaced. 'Lonely At The Top', co-written by Richards, was orthodox pop wherein Jagger addressed the theme of female ambition ('It leads small-town girls astray') previously broached in 'Tops'; there and on 'Running Out of Luck' the day was saved by Beck's seismic guitar. In 'Hard Woman' Jagger returned to the blues idiom of 'Beast of Burden' (he even sounded vulnerable); there were additional touches of 'Love In Vain' – whose title recurred in the chorus – and 'Moonlight Mile'; strings were added by Paul Buckmaster as they had been on *Sticky Fingers*.

Lest this be taken as evidence of a new, sensitive Jagger, Jagger reconstructed, in 'Secrets' he was back to doing what he did best – disparagement, irony and put-down. By the song's final stanza its subject, variously described as 'rude', 'nasty', 'mean' and 'doing it for the money' was instructed to step forward and take her punishment – the climactic *Bad, bad, bad!* simulating a whip or belt. The theme was reiterated in the title track in which Jagger, having fallen for a 'stay-home' woman, saw the kitchen table turned: *she's the boss*. Like others on the album, the song was a synthesizer percussion medley which Jagger sang *giosco* with touches of rap and falsetto warbling. Like others it was promptly impugned by feminists. Jagger retaliated: 'It's her – *she*'s the boss.' The man was the one being pursued. Benny Hill used to make the same argument.

She's The Boss also saw Jagger in a small deluge of press activity. To the *Mirror* he admitted, 'The other [Stones] might think it's possible that if the album did well it might be the end' – a thought that had, in fact, occurred to at least three of them. In *Melody Maker* he reflected on the group's origins. 'It wasn't just a pose in the first place. In that period we were very angry and violent. But a lot of that disappeared when we achieved success. If it hadn't been for the drug busts . . . that changed our attitude to everything.' Finally, asked by *Rolling Stone* if he minded his children reading about the 'seamier side' of the group's activities, he replied, verbatim, 'You're throwing the question at me kinda as a bit of a curve. Hmm, I really haven't thought about it. I guess they know most of it, and I think it's not particularly – I don't think it's very good for them. Umm, I mean that's one of the things I have to put up with. I mean, they have to put up with.'

There were those who considered a Jagger solo album a contradiction in terms, his whole persona existing in being one of a group; others felt a rhythm section consisting of, among others, Dunbar, Shakespeare, Bill Laswell, Bernard Edwards, Michael Shrieve, Colin Hodgekinson, Tony Thompson, Ray Cooper and Anton Fig to lack the simple appeal of Watts and Wyman. In Paris they, Richards and Wood were joined by Jagger in the studio. Gradually over the spring and early summer tracks were eked out for a new album, the group's first for CBS. Observers at Pathé Marconi noted the sessions to have been 'blatantly controlled . . . arranged and conducted' by Richards. Of the eventual ten songs exactly three were written by Jagger and himself. Equally blatantly, recording took place at the very moment *She's The Boss* entered the charts; Jagger could have been excused his divided loyalties. This was a time when, said Stewart, 'Mick, to put it mildly, didn't see eye-to-eye with Keith' – whose sole public comment on *Boss* ('He could've at least recorded an album of Irish folk songs') was negative. After one particularly pungent exchange Richards spontaneously wrote a song aptly called 'Fight'.

In early June the Stones were invited, and declined, to appear at the year's primary musical event, Live Aid. Rumours surrounding the decision, averred by Wyman to have been unanimous, included the apparent reluctance of Jagger and Richards to appear simultaneously on stage – that and the intimidating presence of other artists. Immediately Jagger was reported to be planning a transatlantic duet with David Bowie, though this was later scrapped in favour of a re-recording of 'Dancing In The Street'. Next he announced plans to appear in the American segment of the concert, backed by Tina Turner. At the last minute Richards and Wood also agreed to support Bob Dylan.

While the last made fools of themselves in front of a television audience of millions Jagger gave a startling performance in Philadelphia. He performed with Hall and Oates; on cue Turner appeared for a medley of 'State of Shock' and 'It's Only Rock 'n Roll'. At one stage Jagger ripped her dress off. It was his first official performance outside the Stones. 'Dancing In The Street', meanwhile, released in August, reached number seven in America and number one in Britain. The video, wherein Jagger and Bowie primped, preened and projected sex remarkably plausibly for men of their combined age (eighty) was also a bestseller. Five thousand theatres aired it across America. The video for 'Hard Woman', also released that summer, was less successful; by July *She's The Boss* had peaked. Jagger returned to the studio in New York to mix tracks from the Paris sessions; he also attended a photo shoot with Annie Leibovitz for the new album, sprawling on the floor in his yellow trousers, his bare foot apparently cocked behind Richards' back.

In London Jagger found time to indulge his renewed love of cricket, watching portions of the England–Australia Test series. The former wicketkeeper Godfrey Evans remembers sponsoring Jagger at an official Test lunch at Lord's. 'He was no trouble,' he said. 'If anything he looked overawed at meeting his childhood heroes.' (Evans himself had been the outstanding man of Kent cricket in the 1950s.) Denis Compton also recalls Jagger as 'polite and even subdued' around famous cricketers. The only divergent note is struck by Colin Ingleby-Mackenzie, captain of Hampshire in the late 1950s and early 1960s. He, too, was impressed by Jagger's 'niceness' and 'complete lack of superstar behaviour' at a day's cricket. Afterwards Ingleby-Mackenzie invited Jagger and others to a party at his nearby home.

There things deteriorated: Jagger began drinking and then, at the same rate of speed, became obnoxious. A guest complained. The evening ended with Jagger insisting that the Ingleby-Mackenzies' son, over his parents' objections, accompany him home on his motorbike.

Jagger's own family was extended when on 28 August 1985 Hall gave birth to their second child, James Leroy Augustine, in New York. The delivery was less complicated, though for a time the boy's health was despaired of. Mother and son recovered in time for Hall to appear on BBC's *Wogan* on 30 September, when she revealed that Jagger was in the habit of singing 'Jumpin' Jack Flash' to lull the infant to sleep. The child was baptized at St Mary Abbot's on 8 November; the godparents were the actress Anjelica Huston, Loewenstein and Dunn. Speculation arose in the press as to when – if ever – Jagger would marry Hall, one report claiming that Eva had 'disowned' her son for failing to do so. She denies it: by 1985 the family, Joe, Eva, their two sons and sundry grandchildren, were fully reconciled. Mick and Chris Jagger spent part of that autumn pony-trekking together in India.

The Stones, a virtually academic concept since 1983, were brought into relief on 12 December: Ian Stewart died in London. All five members attended the funeral. Shrunken, pale, almost theatrically haggard, Jagger arrived at the last moment from Mustique, crying as Stewart's favourite record, 'Boogie-Woogie Dream', was played in the crematorium chapel. 'It's hard to remember when he wasn't there . . . [Stewart] was different from us because he was so straight,' he said admiringly. 'That funeral,' says Shirley Arnold. 'Mick with tears in his eyes . . . I'm sure if Stu had seen it he would have found it all quite amusing.'

Stewart's death had another, more material effect: it deprived the Stones of their common denominator – the one man able to mediate between Jagger and Richards – at the time they needed him most. According to his friend and neighbour Jeff Griffin, 'Stu was unique in that both Mick and Keith listened to him . . . He was the one person capable of knocking heads together,' a point echoed by Watts' lugubrious comment at the funeral: 'Who's going to tell us off now?' Richards later described Stewart's death as the moment 'the glue holding the Rolling Stones together came unstuck'. Wood, in 1987, added tartly, 'The Stones would certainly be working as a unit far more if he were still with us.' The group even played a private memorial concert on 23 February – their first official outing in nearly four years. Mankowitz, invited to the event by Stewart's widow, remembers Richards and Jagger, who greeted the photographer coolly, 'despite what you read in the papers, barely acknowledging each other'.

Jagger spent the ensuing months in the Caribbean. He oversaw building work on Stargroves. He was present in Barbados when, in mid-March, the West Indies overwhelmed the England cricket tourists, one of whom notes that Jagger's extensive eve-of-Test hospitality may have had a deleterious effect on the players' fitness. He had meetings with Bill Graham concerning a summer tour. He also received notice he was being sued over the recording of 'Just Another Night'. The suit, filed by Patrick Alley in White Plains, New York, demanded seven million dollars damages. Finally, in April, Jagger flew to London to promote the album virtually devised in his absence by Richards and Wood, *Dirty Work*.

The LP was prefaced by a single, 'Harlem Shuffle', previously a minor American hit in 1969; Chuck Leavell's keyboards replaced the horn arrangements of the original. The song was enhanced by a video shot at the Kool Kat Club in New York in which the group performed among animated cut-out characters, some of whom disturbingly resembled themselves. (Even as shooting continued the entire set was being offered for sale by a Loewenstein employee – 'It's not the Rolling Stones being tight with a buck,' said Jagger; 'it's the accountant being careful because I probably told him that he's spent too much on promotion.') 'Harlem Shuffle', the Stones' first non-original studio single since 1964, reached number seven in Britain and number five in America.

Dirty Work opened with 'One Hit' and 'Fight', both of which pursued the atavistic theme of *Undercover*: the lyrics alluded to flesh, blood, pulp, bruises, holes, splatter and putting the boot in. The former was also accompanied by a video in which Richards all too convincingly karate-chopped and lunged at Jagger. 'We'd got to the end of our tether . . . It was a fairly good portrayal of the relationship at the time,' he states. While the director Russell Mulcahy believed the film 'parodied' the couple's differences, Wyman was less convinced. 'An unwritten law of the band has always been that, whatever any player's other interests, private or professional, *the Stones takes priority*. The rest of the band believed Mick broke that bond.'

Wyman specifies the ensuing 'Had It With You', with its reference to 'Singing for your supper' and, climactically, 'It's such a sad thing . . . to see a good love die', as evidence of Richards' attitude. On 'Hold Back' Jagger himself reprised the elder statesman role adopted in 'All The Way Down': 'I've been climbing this tree of promises for over forty years,' he snarled over a track rendered vertebrate by Richards and Watts. Side one ended with 'Too Rude', a reggae standard salvaged by Jimmy Cliff and the producer Steve Lillywhite. He might have been Phil Spector, there was so much echo. He might have been Andrew Oldham.

'Winning Ugly' was yet another Richards rocker, whose lyrics – 'I was brought up to cheat/So long as the referee wasn't looking' – might have surprised the author of *Basketball: Coaching and Playing*. It lapsed into 'Back To Zero', a rhythm and synthesizer track in the style of *She's The Boss*. Jagger, whose last recorded comment on the subject ('We'll blow it up eventually') had been in 1969, again addressed himself to the arms race, admitting, with less irony than he might have cared to impart, to 'worrying about [his] great grandchildren'. ('As a parent,' he once said, 'all you can teach a child is what you've learned yourself' – and undoubtedly it was Jagger's generation, coming to maturity at the time of the Bay of Pigs, the Berlin Wall and the Cuban Missile Crisis, to say nothing of Vietnam, for whom the Cold War had most meaning.) 'Dirty Work' itself followed, a vaguely derivative rocker in which guitars predominated; 'Had It With You'; then the closing 'Sleep Tonight', a country-rock ballad sung by Richards and Tom Waits.

Dirty Work continued the tradition, begun in 1972, of releasing one superior album followed by one débâcle. The revival foretold by *Undercover* proved illusory. Much of the record appeared to be contrived by Richards and Wood – an impression confirmed by Wyman, who writes, 'Mick seemed preoccupied with finishing and promoting *She's The Boss* and Keith became resentful.' The total of three original Jagger–Richards compositions was the lowest of any album since *Out Of Our Heads*. The critics were unimpressed: the differences between the group's principals were seized on to explain the lacklustre product. 'There's bound to be rivalry . . . there's always been a bit of to-ing and fro-ing,' Jagger admitted later, adding, 'It's not just a question of keeping Keith happy, everyone's such a prima donna.' *Dirty Work* reached number three in Britain, number four in America. It was dedicated to Stewart.

The only surprising aspect of Jagger's falling-out with Richards is that it should have occurred so late in their long relationship. As early as 1960 Dick Taylor had omitted to introduce the two on the basis that 'the idea of Keith in a group was incredible', adding that Jagger and Richards 'had virtually nothing in common, apart from the music' – and even that from different perspectives. As Korner had said,

'There are compulsive players who have *got* to play ... and there are people who think, "Ah, this is how I'm going to make it."' For years Richards expressed himself on Jagger's behalf, drinking, debauching, satisfying his longings – a kind of surrogate delinquent. Jagger himself went along with this; he developed his own instincts, primarily remote and abstract, a doctrinaire who thought in fixed principles and moved cautiously in the rarefied atmosphere of his own fame, yet with a sharp intuitive knowledge of popular feeling. On stage Richards was often withdrawn to the point of moroseness. Jagger could say, 'Having a good time?' in eleven languages. He gave himself credit for co-existing with Richards and the more mundane souls – the lawyers, advisers, agents and accountants – surrounding the Stones. He stressed the need to communicate on their level. In Jagger's view he was compelled by the events of 1967 – his arrest, imprisonment, the real prospect of insolvency – to advance his more conventional traits. Someone had to do it. Richards believes Jagger was never anything *but* conventional: 'Mick might *think* there was something different about him before the bust ... in fact there's no difference at all. He hates that part of himself.' After spending much of the next decade chemically insulated, Richards emerged in 1978 to sense 'resentment' at his offers to help. Not only that – by then Jagger had career plans of his own. In October 1983 he informed his guitarist that, over the next five years, he intended to pursue his solo projects in tandem with the Stones. Exactly half that time later Richards was at the end of his long tether with him.

In the interim the power axis within the group had shifted so that, at times, Jagger was opposed by all four other members. Wyman notes that in 1986 'Mick ... committed the cardinal sin of putting another project ahead of a band effort'. Wood too remembers the release of *Dirty Work* as 'a very frustrating time, and I let [Jagger] know it'. Even Watts was heard to ruminate about resigning to join a jazz group. While the rest of the Stones maintained the one-for-all tradition embodied by Richards, Jagger's own priorities increasingly turned inwards to his solo career, his family. Or, as a journalist friend put it, 'By then the only people Mick was listening to were Loewenstein, Walter Yetnikoff and Hall.'

The result was that, in April 1986, each of the four Stones received a telex stating Jagger's refusal to tour.

Initially there was sympathy for this: Richards had long advised his partner to 'stop trying to be like Peter Pan' and concentrate on singing, as opposed to performing, on stage. Wood, too, understood 'the physical strain a tour put [on Jagger]'. There was even grudging acceptance of the lost income arising from such a decision. What most offended the Stones was Jagger's dispatch of deliberately formal, identical messages, later described by Richards, who destroyed his, as 'one hell of a way to treat us'; that and the fact that, within two years, Jagger would undertake world-wide concerts of his own – 'a supposedly solo tour,' says Wyman, 'totally dominated by Stones songs.'

Jagger's own perspective was different. He saw the decision to jeopardize the Stones as inevitable, even as a function of reality. 'The difficulty in growing up is that you start with this gang of people . . . [which] simply can't last for ever. It's very childish to think you can remain in the gang all the time.' Jagger also declared himself 'surprised' at the group's reaction. 'Everyone made too much of a fuss about it . . . Everyone should have been a bit more indulgent.' He referred to Richards' extracurricular activities, Wood's and Wyman's solo LPs, to Watts' frequent sorties into the jazz world: 'Why not me?' Jagger's endorsement of private enterprise was followed by a break with his creative partner and a complete change in the orientation of the Stones. By the time of *Dirty Work* they were hardly functioning as a group. Ingeniously, Jagger saw this as a cause, not the effect, of his own activities. 'I didn't think the time was right [to tour],' he told *20/20*. 'I didn't think the band were getting on.'*

In late career the Stones were abruptly caught short. *Dirty Work*, an album that might otherwise have rivalled *Emotional Rescue* or *Still Life*'s eighteen weeks in the charts, vanished after ten; the summer tour, proposed by Bill Graham, was cancelled. Other projects were quietly abandoned. In April 1986 *USA Today* began a three-part report on the group by John Milward headlined 'The Stones at a Standoff'. It chronicled the creative, personal and professional divisions between the group among whom 'physical contention' was said to be possible. Jagger promptly recorded a single entitled 'Ruthless People'. 'If Mick tours without us,' said Richards, 'I'll slit his throat.' Later in the year the guitarist was rumoured to have menaced Jagger at gunpoint with the words, 'I'll give you thirty-eight reasons to get out of the room – now.'

While Richards played with Junior Wells, with Etta James, Aretha Franklin and Chuck Berry, serving as musical director of two sixtieth birthday concerts in St Louis released as *Hail! Hail! Rock 'n' Roll*; while Wood appeared with Fats Domino, with Ray Charles and even a hurriedly re-formed Faces; while Watts' own thirty-three-piece orchestra toured the US; and while Wyman was exposed in the *News of the World* for his relationship with a teenage girl ('Bill knew the risk he was taking, but it didn't occur to me'), Jagger went tensely and tersely about the business of advancing his career. In June he performed without evident pleasure at a Prince's Trust concert in London, duetting with David Bowie. Afterwards Jagger and Hall stood exchanging quips with the heir to the throne. In July he was at Lord's; in August, France; finally, in Los Angeles, he

---

* In a later interview Jagger added that 'the relationships were terrible. Health was diabolical. The rest of the Stones couldn't walk across the Champs Elysées, much less go on the road.'

began work on a second album. Such was the air of paranoia surrounding the project – not dissimilar to the occasions when Jagger had courted Bianca and Hall – that a fight ensued with a photographer, just as it had then. His wooing of outside musicians had all the characteristics of an illicit affair. Jagger used the analogy himself: '[It's] strange working without the others . . . like having a wife and a mistress.'

In November a group consisting of Jagger, Beck, the drummer Simon Phillips, bassist Doug Wimbish and keyboardists Phil Ashley and Richard Cottle arrived at Wisseloord Studios in Hilversum. The Eurythmics' Dave Stewart was also present, as were Dunn, Chris Jagger and Miranda Guinness. Ten songs were finally recorded: seven by Jagger, three by Jagger and Stewart. Press speculation centred on the 'more mature' lyrics supposedly indicating ' Jagger [had] finally grown up' (the *Post*), and the melodic arrangements supplied by Stewart; those and Jeff Beck.

When, the following August, solo concerts were first mooted, a spokesman for Jagger was quoted in the *Sun*: 'Jeff is well known for being difficult to work with and tempers finally snapped . . . The tour has been postponed.' On 4 November the guitarist responded: 'I quit because Mick only offered me peanuts to play with him. It was laughable . . . an insult. I wanted to teach him a lesson because I believe if you want the best you have to pay for it . . . Mick's problem is that he's a meanie. He counts every single penny. For someone with his money, I can't believe how tight he is.' Beck nonetheless agreed to appear in the video for the LP's first single, 'Throwaway', which he largely underwrote on guitar.

In mid-December 1986 Jagger returned to Mustique. A sense of the distance then separating the Stones is provided by Wyman. After four months of lubricious comment on his affair with Mandy Smith, of near-daily tabloid agitation, of possible criminal action, even, 'There was hardly a word from any of the Stones.' Wyman, among others, thought the period 1986–7 'was really the end for the band – and what a terrible way to go'. On Christmas Eve a London public relations executive, Nick Miles, attended the carol service in Mustique's Anglican church. 'There were forty or fifty people there, nearly half the island . . . At the very last minute, as the door was closing, Jagger walked in with David Bowie. They both seemed to get into the hang of it . . . and, yes, they both sang.' Later that night Jagger also rang Richards in Jamaica – a conversation the latter described in the *Sun* as 'very polite – very formal. He said that we must have a drink when both of us were back in New York.'

Recording resumed at Blue Wave Studios, Barbados. In addition to its Englishness, and matching mania for cricket, Jagger enjoyed the island as 'a good place to work because there are few distractions . . . you don't get people dropping past every five minutes'. It was in Barbados, on 21 January, that Hall drove to Grantley Adams Airport to collect clothes and make-up forwarded from Mustique. At the desk there was evidence of confusion: no parcel was found for Miss Hall, but another – unlabelled – box was awaiting collection. Would she care to inspect it? She would. Inside was twenty pounds of marijuana.

Hall was seized, charged, held in jail overnight and eventually released on bail of five thousand dollars paid by Jagger. Even then she was ordered to surrender her passport and report to Holetown police station daily. Jagger – who later earned plaudits from the *Daily Mail* for his 'supportive' attitude – suspended work on his album. Overnight the press descended on the couple's hotel: the *Sun*, *Mirror*, *Star*, *The Times* and the *Telegraph*; even the *Independent* gave them a double-column spread. For a month Jagger appeared cheerfully each morning, smiling and joking, waving, shielding Hall from the prying eye of the media; he *was* supportive. He also engaged a senior Barbadian criminal lawyer, Elliot

Mottley, accompanied by an assistant with the name of Henry Ford.

After a second postponement Hall's trial opened on 16 February. Within minutes the prosecution's case had been discredited as customs supervisor Caspar Walcott admitted having twice lied under oath. For seven hours witness after all-too-plausible witness testified to Hall's innocence until finally Judge King, dilating his cheeks, adjusting his abundant hair under his wig, sent down his gavel. 'Complicated legal arguments' had to be considered – case adjourned. (In London, ITN reported that at this stage Walcott had privately approached the judge in an effort to have him drop the case – a claim later denied by both parties.) Hall, in tears, returned to the hotel. On the twentieth King gave a rambling, ten-minute summation before delivering his verdict: innocent on all charges. While Jagger grinned Hall sank to her knees in relief. 'I have been through a nightmare,' she stated, 'but I want to tell you that we must never forget the presumption of innocence. Ninety-nine out of a hundred people who are charged and sentenced are guilty people . . . I am happy to be one of the innocent ones.' Immediately she left for New York with Jagger, his record of being subject or party to a major drugs trial every tenth February uncannily preserved.

In New York Hall emotionally re-enacted the ordeal: she insisted events in Barbados had 'devastated' her; her lost modelling fees were estimated at two hundred thousand dollars. On the twenty-second, in the course of a harrowing diatribe on the trial and Barbados generally, she revealed that she and Jagger would marry – soon. The next day's *New York Post* carried the headline, 'JUBILANT JAGGER 'N' JERRY SET THE DATE' – although no date was given – under the lead: 'ANDY WARHOL DEAD AT 58.' Jagger himself returned to the studio.

The focus of his life having shifted to his family and his own activities, it was inevitable that Jagger would ignore the Stones. He did ignore them. On 3 March Richards was quoted by the journalists Richard Ellis and Craig Mackenzie: 'Up till this time last year there was still a chance Mick could have said: "Let's do it" and it would have happened ...' After learning of Jagger's refusal Richards admitted having considered Roger Daltrey as a replacement. He continued: '[Jagger] has told me to my face that he cannot work with me but he can't say why. I don't think he knows himself ... You can't sit down with a bottle of whisky with Mick and talk it over, thrash things out until you know what is really bothering him. He just reacts in a juvenile way, changing the subject or retaliating with some counter charge. That's very easy with me – you just call me a junkie. He's done that.'

A fortnight later Wyman added his views on the satellite TV programme *Music Box*. 'Mick is the guilty one. He has decided to do his own thing and be famous in his own right ... It's a pity we didn't go out with a big bang ... I don't know if we'll ever go back on the road. That depends on the glamour twins becoming friendly again. They're the problem.' In London press speculation continued and grew in intensity. There was talk of a legal dissolution.

Jagger again spent Easter in Mustique; again the spring and summer in France and London. He was in the former when, to his evident pleasure, Margaret Thatcher was re-elected on 11 June; the latter when, a week later, England drew with the touring Pakistanis at Lord's in conditions even cricket can rarely have witnessed – overnight three thousand gallons of water were drained from the outfield. Early July saw Jagger commuting between his homes in New York and Texas and his rented mansion in Kensington. He recorded videos for two singles from his new album.

He also, by late summer, adopted a more openly sympathetic – and, by his own admission, 'protective' – attitude towards Richards. In *Rolling Stone* both parties spoke repeatedly of a fresh start, of renewal, of the Stones being merely at the halfway stage in their career. Truly it must have seemed that the old lovers pined to reconcile. There was even talk that the estrangement had been deliberately contrived, in the manner of a trial separation, to allow the group breathing space. 'I felt I had to go and work with some other people to get revitalized,' said Jagger, unconsciously echoing his earlier comment, 'For any relationship to last, there has to be a bit of playing about.' 'We both grew up a lot,' said Richards. 'The press kept it going,' adds Jagger's mother, 'long after Mick forgot about it.'

Except, of course, he didn't forget about it. To *You* magazine in September Jagger admitted, 'We've had a very rocky time these last few years. And making music is not like any other job – you have to be in harmony.' In the same interview he described Richards as seeing the Stones 'very much as a conservative rock and roll band with strong traditions ... and as he gets older his ideas have become more conservative. I used to tell people that I would never need to make a solo album because I could do whatever I wanted to do within the band, but I think it started to get narrower so I no longer felt that. I like to be a bit more open-minded about things' – the man of talent, susceptible to influence, to punk, to two-tone, to acid house, rap and hip-hop saddled with a hopeless reactionary – a guitarist who in his spare time played openly with *Chuck Berry*. Despite the many pressures he was under Jagger felt himself to be progressing culturally; he invested both time and ingenuity, confident of its success, in his second album – the very title of which conveyed his amended view of himself.

Primitive Cool was released on 14 September 1987. It opened, as had *She's The Boss*, with a track entirely distinguished by Beck, 'Throwaway', the confession of a one-time Lothario finally in love – or, as Jagger said, 'I can imagine it being about Jerry ... but it might not be'. It was followed by 'Let's Work', an extraordinary panegyric on the ethic first extolled in 'Hang Fire': amid references to 'no sitting down', to standing tall, to being proud, drums were augmented almost to marching-band level; the track, written by Jagger and Dave Stewart, could have been a battle hymn of the Conservatives. 'Possessions are important,' Jagger told *You*, 'but there are more important things . . . Men and women like work. A lot of human grasping seems illusory – but that's what drives people on.' It was an almost perfect depiction of his own career. 'Let's Work', accompanied by a surreal video, was even released as a single; it reached number thirty-five.

'Radio Control' followed, another drums-guitar medley in which Jagger, the put-upon star, wryly probed his relations with the media. The melodic arrangements foretold in Holland were most evident on 'Say You Will', the 'more mature' lyrics on 'Primitive Cool'. The latter took as its premiss a series of questions – 'Did you walk cool in the sixties, Daddy?' – put to Jagger by his children, questions which, typically, he declined to answer. This, he later admitted, was an artifice ('My children don't ask me that . . . they'd probably be too bored') to conceal the real parties involved: Jagger and his father. He was forever asking Joe about the 'psyche' of the 1930s.

Side two opened with 'Kow Tow', a pneumatic rocker said to contain references to Richards – as, more plausibly, did 'Shoot Off Your Mouth'. ('Mick is very bitter about the row. He's had a real go at Keith and hopes he listens to the album and realizes the significance,' an anonymous spokesman told the *News of the World*.) 'Peace For The Wicked' was more artfully contrived pop; 'Party Doll' a vaguely Gaelic lament replete with fiddle; finally 'War Baby', as near as Jagger, in twenty-five years, came to outright protest. After stating 'I was born in a war . . . And it don't make me war crazy', that 'the arms race is on', 'the guns all in place', Jagger climaxed with the plea,

> Why can't we run this road together,
> Why can't we hope to find a cure?

– a startling conclusion from one whose fortune had derived from ambiguity.

Primitive Cool reached number forty-one in America and number eighteen in Britain; perversely it sold less well than the inferior *She's The Boss*. Had the album succeeded its values – maturity, perspective, the work ethic and pacifism – might have been those Jagger brought forward into the nineties; he might have become a Lou Reed or Van Morrison. An appreciation of the album's failure is central to appreciating Jagger's subsequent strategy: immediately he contacted Richards and discussed the prospect of a tour. The guitarist, engaged in recording his own LP, *Talk Is Cheap*, was non-committal. In a phone-in interview on the *David Letterman Show* Jagger failed to scotch the rumours of a reunion. At the annual Rock 'n' Roll Hall of Fame dinner in New York, challenged by the Beach Boys' Mike Love to 'get off your ass', he did so, singing 'Satisfaction' and, backed by Dylan and Springsteen, 'Like A Rolling Stone'.

If anything it was the remaining members who now denied Jagger. In February the singer Terence Trent d'Arby performed 'Honky Tonk Women' and 'It's All Over Now' in a pick-up group including Wyman and Wood, neither of whom were said to be averse to it becoming permanent. Things deteriorated further when, simultaneously courting the Stones, Jagger announced the delayed dates of his own concerts; this, said Watts, was the last straw – 'a decision which virtually folded up twenty years of the band.'

By then, March 1988, Jagger may have regarded the event more as a commitment than a genuine extension of his career: once and for all he intended to find out if there was anything behind the intimations of genius that constantly came over him. The itinerary announced that spring was restricted to seven dates in Japan – a previously untapped market with no comparative experience of the Stones. First reports were encouraging: it was said that two hundred thousand fans would pay in excess of three million pounds, of which a third would be Jagger's. Rehearsals took place in New York. The musicians featured on *Primitive Cool* (minus Beck) were joined by backing vocalists and dancers auditioned by Jagger; he also supervised financial arrangements for the tour. 'He gets this tight reputation,' his lighting engineer Patrick Woodroffe told *Vanity Fair*. '[In Japan] we had to work with a much smaller set than before, but we didn't want it to look bad. So the set people came in, and Mick said, "Screw the money. It's got to be great no matter what it costs." And then the set people left and the accountants came in, and Mick said to them, "Look, you've got to make sure those guys don't spend too much" . . . You could call that being manipulative, but the result was that we had great sets.'

The tour, known officially as Suntory Dry Beer Live Mick Jagger in Japan, opened in Osaka on 15 March. Eleven thousand fans received a two-hour, twenty-song show including 'Brown Sugar', 'Tumbling Dice', 'Satisfaction', and 'Jumpin' Jack Flash'. Technically the event was a success, if lacking the spontaneity still associated with the Stones: no botched intros, no duplicate solos, just a tightly choreographed package in which, try as they might, the backing musicians remained just that. The eye never moved to them as it did to Richards and Wood. In Tokyo Jagger was joined on stage by Tina Turner; they duetted, as before, on 'It's Only Rock 'n Roll'; as before he ripped off her dress. The tour ended on 25 March, the critics evenly divided along ethnic lines: in Japan (where audiences varied from impassive 'salary men' to mothers holding up small babies, as if for Jagger's inspection) it was regarded as a triumph. Western observers detected elements of burlesque and buffoonery – even of boredom as Jagger sang 'Satisfaction' for the four or five hundredth time on stage. He returned to New York amid rumours of multi-million-dollar offers from British and American promoters. In London it was further reported that an Australian financier, Gunter Roth, had offered twenty million dollars for Jagger's ashes on his death. He wanted to make egg-timers out of them.

First there was the matter of the lawsuit arising from 'Just Another Night'. On 18 April – while Jesse Jackson and Michael Dukakis, both of whom sought and failed to secure his endorsement, contested the Democratic presidential primary – Jagger appeared in court at White Plains, New York, to hear evidence that his debut solo single plagiarized the 1982 album *Just A Touch of Patrick Alley*. For a week the court was entertained by Sly Dunbar, the drummer on *She's The Boss*, demonstrating the different techniques of his calling (in a bizarre twist, Alley then claimed Dunbar had played on *his* album); at one stage Jagger himself broke into song. On 26 April he was cleared of all charges of copyright infringement. 'My reputation is really cleared,' he announced. 'If you're well-known, people stand up and take shots at you.' Alley, a small, dishevelled figure beside Jagger, was unrepentant. Outside the court he made an elaborate and detailed statement: 'I'm honest! Innocent!' Jagger rapidly exited by chauffeured Mercedes. News programmes led with the story on all three American networks.

· XI ·

AFTERMATH

Next Jagger did what the failure of *Primitive Cool* made inevitable: for the first time in two years he summoned the other Stones. The meeting in the Savoy Hotel, London, on 18 May opened with a long, rambling and at times impassioned oath of allegiance to the group, Jagger expressing his 'sadness' at recent events. Obeying the rule which makes it impossible to hear anyone claiming to be unhappy without putting forward similar claims oneself, Richards retaliated, and for a minute the two men were in sharp contention as to whose chagrin and remorse was greater. Despite each having respective (or, in Jagger's case, residual) commitments to his own career, the Stones, says Wyman, 'all felt intuitively right for getting back as a band'. ('We sat down, rowed like crazy for a day and stopped slagging each other,' said Jagger.) An album and possible tour were mooted. Leaving the suite Richards, clutching his vodka, milk-pale and wheezing, buttonholed Jagger in the corridor. 'You can't hire a band like us on the street-corner.' He play-punched him – surprisingly hard – on the arm. 'This thing is bigger than both of us – *capisce*?'

In fact Jagger's face remained blank as a mirror. His re-formation of the Stones must have been galling to a man who, a year earlier, had denied they would ever play live together again. For a month he became what the American press now realized him to be – and their British counterparts had insisted he always was: a family man, endlessly concerned with his assets, his holdings, his antiques, his gardens and his wine, a figure of fun and nostalgia, for ever refuting the disparity between his actions and his words. When that spring Jagger prevented his daughter from appearing in a film in the role of a prostitute the British media were enchanted; a month later, when Jade was expelled from St Mary's Calne for illicitly meeting a boyfriend, ecstatic. Amidst widespread amusement that the very embodiment of sexual excess had been offended by Jade's behaviour, Jagger maintained the defensive: 'That was so minor,' he told *Vanity Fair*. 'Jade and I were laughing about it, but the English press love to make it into this whole deal of how strict I was . . . I wasn't strict, it was the school. I just told her that she was an idiot.' (Jagger was also said to be impassive when in March 1989 Jade's name was mentioned in connection with a cocaine trial in London – and when she subsequently became pregnant by fellow art student Piers Jackson; after the birth of her daughter Assisi on 2 July 1992 Jagger, the press proclaimed, was 'knocked out' that his wife and first grandchild shared a birthday.) On his own, 26 July, he dutifully attended Hall's opening night in *Bus Stop* at the Montclair College Theater, New Jersey – further evidence, the tabloids insisted, of going 'from rock 'n' roll to rocking chair', from 'Mr Raunchy to Mr Wrinkly' and 'dare we say it, sixties' sinner to starting senile'. Even *The Times* was left wondering 'whether the Rolling Stones [had] anything to offer but a past'.

In fact at that very moment Jagger was outlining plans for a new album. In August he wrote material with Wood in London. On leaving Heathrow he confirmed that the Stones would, within a year, be re-activated. In New York he met Richards to confirm it. While at the Hit Factory Richards himself took the opportunity to play Jagger an acetate of *Talk Is Cheap*. Returning from the bathroom he saw the singer through an open door dancing to the opening track; Richards retraced his steps, coughed and walked in to see Jagger, tapping his fingers, yawning, his changeling face registering almost abject boredom.

There followed three weeks of rehearsals for Jagger's final commitment to *Primitive Cool* – a solo tour of Australia. This singularly lucrative project began when, at a press conference in Sydney, after praising Bruce Chatwin's *Songlines* for its vivid portrayal of aboriginal life, Jagger announced his intention to retire from touring at fifty ('You can't be nineteen for ever . . . I'll just want to sit back in a chair'), a gambit which, as the *Herald* noted, 'did nothing to harm ticket sales whatever'. Three days later Jagger made a surprise appearance at the Kardomah Café, playing an entire two-hour set before seven hundred startled fans – another event afforded full prominence in the morning press. The first show, at the Brisbane Entertainment Centre, trailed by an advertisement stating 'Please note: Mick Jagger performs entire concert', promptly sold out.

In all Jagger gave sixteen concerts, sponsored by Reebok, followed by one each in Auckland and Jakarta (where he arrived after a London businessman and his pregnant fiancée had been shot by local police – not the ideal time to be a British tourist in Indonesia) over five weeks. It was also in Jakarta that Loewenstein approached Bill Graham with the insistence that 'Mick and Keith should be working together'. As in Japan certain critics held that the events' technical proficiency and elaborate stagecraft – in Sydney Jagger appeared on a *Mad Max* set replete with walkways, a chain-link fence and dry ice – tended to conceal the absence of less contrived excitement. To compound his problems, both the local press and word of mouth had foretold the event as a kind of surrogate Stones-*fest* (Wood or even Richards was rumoured to appear), an impression failing to correspond to Jagger's own perception of the tour. Dressed in a series of garish jackets, scarves and T-shirts (successively removed as the concerts progressed), gum-chewing, drawling, Jagger was widely criticized for extending his sense of distance into detachment; the audience was left with an endlessly polished entertainer whose performance veered between irony and sarcasm.

Jagger indulged the more sentimental side of his character off stage. In Sydney, as he had on previous tours, he visited his maternal relatives; he watched cricket; he tolerated the presence of overwrought fashion reporters questioning Hall about her designer swimwear. He even contacted his old schoolfriend Paul Ovenden, last seen when Jagger attended a Christmas party at Ovenden's house in 1961; they used to drink in the Oddfellows Arms together. Ovenden had since settled in Melbourne and, hearing of Jagger's appearance there, left word – more, he says, in hope than expectation – with the local ticket agency. On the afternoon of 6 October the phone rang in Ovenden's home and his daughter announced that a man purporting to be Mick Jagger wanted to speak to him. For forty minutes the two reminisced about school, about Dartford, about basketball – a remarkably unaffected conversation, says Ovenden, in which 'Mick was quite unlike the image people have of him . . . If anything he was self-denigrating.' As the call ended Jagger invited Ovenden to his concert at the International Tennis Centre. He declined, having to work that evening driving a taxi.

In New York and Paris, meanwhile, Richards was giving a series of more-or-less conciliatory interviews to promote *Talk Is Cheap*. To *Option*'s question, 'How are things between you and Mick?' he answered, 'I love the guy . . . I respect him. There's also animosity but that's par for the course. You can't tread the boards every night like Mick did, acting like you're semi-divine, without something rubbing off.' In *Rolling Stone* he also dwelt on the stabler aspects of the relationship. 'I love Mick. Most of my efforts with him go to trying to open his eyes: "You don't need to do this – you have no problem, all you need to do is just grow up with it" . . . I tip my hat to Mick. I admire the guy enormously.' The following year he announced on *25 × 5*, 'We needed a break. Mick needed to find his own feet and see what it's like . . . It's easy to go a little crazy inside the Rolling Stones bubble if that's all you do.'

Richards' placatory tone concealed the fact that, even in point of timing, he harboured doubts about the group's reunion. Jagger's summons of the other members in May had come at the very moment Richards finalized plans for a year devoted to his own activities. 'Mick suddenly called up,' he told *Rolling Stone*: ' "Let's put the Stones back together." I'm thinking: "I'm just in the middle of an album. Now what are you trying to do? Screw me up?" ' The point was echoed in *Talk Is Cheap*, released that October: in a reference widely interpreted as an allusion to Jagger and his solo albums Richards sang, 'Now you want to throw the dice/You already crapped out twice' before reiterating the song's title: 'You Don't Move Me'. Jagger himself returned to London on 5 November, confirming, or perhaps fulfilling his forecast to Richards of October 1983: five years to develop a solo career in tandem with the Stones. Their meeting in the Caribbean that Christmas – after a series of solo concerts by Richards extolling the very opposite virtues to Jagger's – marked the formal end of their separation. They were said to have spoken, repeatedly, and at length, in a manner one observer described as 'surprisingly like old friends'. (In private Jagger continued to admit to 'mixed emotions', while Richards advised his wife, 'I'll be back in a fortnight – if not overnight.') For the first time since 1985 studio time was booked in Barbados and Montserrat. The other Stones were placed on standby.

While in the Caribbean Jagger also contacted the producer Chris Kimsey, last employed on *Undercover*. Kimsey in turn introduced Matt Clifford, a former cathedral chorister and graduate of Birmingham University. 'I went down to Barbados,' he told *Vanity Fair*, 'and the next day found myself flying to Mustique and having lunch on the beach with Princess Margaret . . . Being with Mick is going in the deep end, head first. He can get on with anybody on any level. He's an expert at making you feel at ease – just the opposite of the standard rock star.'

Jagger and Richards met in Barbados on 13 January 1989. In the space of a weekend they wrote, embryonically, three songs – including Jagger's aforementioned 'Mixed Emotions'. A film was made of the event and shows Richards, guitar in hand, cigarette clamped Capp-like to his lip, still contriving to warble:

'You're not the only one . . . with Mixed Emotions . . . You're not the – '

'Only one.'

'Only one . . . yeah. We need another chord . . . another chord in there . . . I think we have to take another minor – '

'Yeah, one more minor. F and G.'

The result was that by mid-January the first phase of the reunion was complete. With three songs already written it was clearly going to be permanent. On the eighteenth Wood was summoned to New York, where he joined Jagger and Richards, and also Mick Taylor, at the Waldorf Astoria for the annual Rock 'n' Roll Hall of Fame. 'Guys,' said Pete Townshend, making the induction, 'don't try and grow old gracefully . . . It wouldn't suit you.' Jagger jumped up in his leather tuxedo and bow tie, shaking his head, grinning, shuffling in his boots and grey silk trousers. 'It's slightly ironic,' he lisped. 'Tonight you see us on our best behaviour, but we're being rewarded for twenty-five years of bad behaviour . . . I must say I'm very proud to work with this group of musicians for twenty-five years . . . of the songs Keith and I have written.' As the applause died Jagger paid tribute to Stewart ('a great friend, a great blues pianist, whose odd but invaluable musical advice kept us on a steady bluesy course most of the time') and, more pertinently, to

Jones ('whose individuality' – here Jagger's voice altered to convey irony while not ruling out the possibility of respect – 'and musicianship often took us off the bluesy course with some often marvellous results.'). Richards interrupted him, as he was known to on stage, as Jagger quoted Jean Cocteau. The lights flared, the audience stirred, the three Stones and Taylor played 'Satisfaction', also 'Honky Tonk Women' and 'Start Me Up'. The next day Watts arrived in New York.

Immediately Jagger was pressed by Bill Graham and by the Toronto promoter Michael Cohl to tour America. He, Loewenstein and their lawyer John Branca received offers in Barbados (Jagger at one stage admitting, 'I'm only doing it for one reason – the money'), where rehearsals continued through February and early March; Wyman, who joined the group on the ninth, reported that 'probably because of the long layoff, it was like a young band again'. (Jagger's 'revitalization' vindicated.) 'We got on marvellously and the music felt good.' A week later Jagger released a statement: the Stones would tour the US and Canada – with a possible sequel in Europe – that autumn. Cohl guaranteed the group a staggering sixty-five million dollars with additional payments for merchandising, publicity and a pay-per-view television special. The still-inchoate album, it was said, would be released in August.

Recording began in Montserrat. From 29 March to 1 May the Stones completed fifteen songs – a rate of speed unknown since *Aftermath*. Much of this derived from sheer pressure of time (as Jagger said, 'If you've got an afternoon to do the overdub, you go in and do it'), as well as the physical confines of their surroundings – Richards was heard to remark on the benefits of working on a 'Godforsaken island' as opposed to the city. The only distraction came as, on 30 March, Wyman announced his engagement to the nineteen-year-old Mandy Smith. When a charter jet of journalists (prone to such headlines as 'Old Bill and Me', 'The

Wonder of Wyman' and 'I'm Glad Mandy's Rolling Me Down The Aisle') was reported leaving London, Jagger ordered the bassist to Antigua where Wyman gave a series of interviews, citing Picasso and Chaplin (the latter of whom would have appreciated the Karno-like atmosphere) as successful older husbands, not forgetting to mention the tour. In Montserrat Jagger was quoted, straight-faced: 'Love has no boundaries and I wish them every happiness for their future together.' (His had been among the voices raised loudest when Smith, aged fifteen, had appeared during the recording of *Dirty Work* in Paris.) An employee of Air Studios remembers 'much falling about' by the other Stones in Wyman's absence and the general feeling that the marriage, afforded front-page coverage in England, could only stimulate interest in the tour – a charge made crisply by Christina Appleyard in the *Mirror*.

In May Jagger returned to Olympic, his first use of the group's original studio since the recording of *Sticky Fingers*. On the second he was conveyed by outsize limousine to a cricket match at The Oval, an operation causing inordinate grief to the ground's already querulous gatemen. For a month interest in the Stones was sustained by speculation surrounding the date and place of Wyman's wedding (2 June, Bury St Edmunds Register Office) and whether Jagger in turn would follow suit; on 5 June he, Hall, Richards, Watts and Wood were among the guests at the reception at the Grosvenor House Hotel. (When the bride's young family asked Jagger for his autograph, he invited them to 'Fuck off.') According to the *Mirror* the singer 'lavished two hundred thousand pounds on a genuine Picasso etching as a gift for his old chum', with whom relations in the past had, in fact, been ambivalent. There was further merriment when the journalist Piers Morgan reported Jagger to have been 'knocked out with a single punch in a five a.m. hotel brawl' with, of all people, Watts. The article quoted Richards as witnessing the drummer deliver 'a walloping right hook' to Jagger, who 'landed in a plateful of smoked salmon and slid along the table towards the window', before ending reassuringly, 'The two have patched up their row and will join the others on the Stones world tour later this summer.' Domiciled in Kensington, Jagger willingly used this and the commotion surrounding Wyman's wedding to generate interest in the group. His willingness did not, however, extend to attending the opening of Wyman's restaurant four hundred yards from his front door.

Next there was an elaborate, exotic, and expensive detour when, in mid-June, Jagger flew to Morocco. This excursion was suggested when Bacchir Attar, son of the Joujouka tribal chief friendly with Jones in 1968, wrote offering to assist the group – then in the process of recording a track called 'Speed of Light'. Declaring it ideal for just such assistance, Jagger accepted with alacrity. On 16 June he arrived in Tangier, grinning widely, carrying his own black Slazenger bags, instructing his driver to stop at the rooftop home of Paul Bowles, known to Jagger through William Burroughs, where he addressed the author in his curiously disjointed, halting speech.

'The thing [about Joujouka] . . . They did have this sort of odd historical connection which was kind of . . . appealing . . . somehow – '

'*Joujouka?*'

'Very tenuous,' Jagger admitted. 'But it did have, sort of . . . There was this coincidental thing where, when I was writing the song, I said, "This'd be great if we could have someone like Joujouka on it" and, like, the week after . . . Very coincidental.'

'Yeah.'

'So now we've got to rehearse it . . . I don't know how quickly they can learn . . . What do you think?'

'They've been practising, haven't they?'

'I think so.'

'I believe it.'

'We live in hope,' Jagger laughed. 'But you're quite ... pessimistic ... about most things?'

'About most things. Yeah.'

The interview ended with Jagger complaining of tiredness after being woken that morning by his youngest children bearing Father's Day gifts. At his old haunt the Hotel Minzah he was incensed, yet again, by the price demanded for what, by western standards, was a relatively modest suite. Eventually housed to his satisfaction he appeared next morning at the Palace Ben Abbou to record the Joujouka ahaita – an unusually high-pitched horn – and massed tebel drums; the effect was to insinuate an infectious, danceable rhythm into an otherwise banal song, a stratagem earning Jagger reproof from some quarters for exploiting native music and praise from others for his willingness to experiment. On his last night in Morocco he was asked what associations the visit had called up for him.

'I just went into Bacchir's bedroom ... There's a big picture of Brian there ... It sort of evokes that period.'

'It's really a music that's associated with madness and healing.'

'Yeah ... a pretty psychotic time, that.'

In London he gave an interview to the journalist Steve Grant. The Stones, he said, 'have never had anything in common apart from the music. You've got a lot in common because you've done a lot together, but you're never going to have everything in common. Everyone has a different general disposition.'

'Who's the leader?' asked Grant.

'Me.'

Jagger also, as before, watched the Test match at Lord's and won five thousand pounds on the Irish Derby by predicting the first three horses past the post. By early July he, the Stones, Clifford, a brass section including Bobby Keyes, three backing singers and the organist Chuck Leavell were housed in a disused high school in Washington, a hamlet of two thousand west of Waterbury, Connecticut, rehearsing for the tour. On the eleventh Jagger appeared on the caboose of a train in Grand Central Station. After a short, perfunctory announcement he took questions from the 450 journalists wilting in the indecent heat.

'Is this' – a long pause – 'the Last Time?'
'I don't see it as that. It's the Rolling Stones in 1989.'
'Some commentators have charged that the only reason you're doing it is for the money.'
'What about love and fame and fortune? Have you forgotten about them?'

The tour itself was preceded by the now-familiar surprise performance: on 12 August the Stones gave their first American concert in eight years in the setting of Toad's Place, a nightclub in New Haven. Elsewhere ticket sales were reported to be brisk: four concerts at Shea Stadium sold out overnight, two in Toronto in six hours. Background interest in the tour, fuelled by a succession of elaborately staged interviews, was high; even the comments of an irate Washington resident, Michelle Coulette ('It's like an army ... You're afraid to take a walk because Stones security goons will stop and question you') generated headlines. On 17 August 'Mixed Emotions', accompanied by a suitably high school-ish video, was issued – a jaunty rocker existing with 'It's Only Rock 'n Roll' and 'Respectable' in the second tier of Stones singles. It reached number thirty-six in Britain, number five in America.

The accompanying album was released a week later. *Steel Wheels* opened with 'Sad Sad Sad', a typical Stones belter diminished by unusually banal lyrics; the single; 'Terrifying', a jazz-rock outing suggestive of the group's Ohio Players–*Black and Blue* period; 'Hold On To Your Hat', originally drafted by Jagger and Watts in Barbados, though credited Jagger–Richards, a rocker in which the singer advised the subject to 'get out of [his] bed', to 'get out of the sack' before reaching the unsurprising conclusion, 'I'm over with you, baby . . . Get up, get out.' It could have been off *Exile*. It could have been off *The Rolling Stones*. It was followed by 'Hearts for Sale', wherein Jagger distinguished himself on vocals, guitar and harmonica (as good, said Chris Kimsey, as the old blues players – the gaps were as important as the sound) and 'Blinded By Love', a slab of speculative country-rock in the style of 'Far Away Eyes', for whose lyrics, relating to Cleopatra, Delilah and the Duchess of Windsor, Chris Jagger received a credit as literary editor.

Things improved on side two. 'Rock And A Hard Place', an extended fusion of funk and brooding rock, in one stanza of which ('We're in the same boat . . .') Jagger reiterated the theme of 'War Baby'. 'Can't Be Seen', wheezed, not sung, by Richards, derived from *Talk Is Cheap* – as did 'Almost Hear You Sigh', an elevated ballad in the style of 'Beast of Burden' whose straightforward, loser-in-love lyrics, reminiscent of *Look Homeward, Angel*, again earned Chris Jagger a credit; the remodelled 'Speed of Light', now styled 'Continental Drift', whose ingenuity exceeded its effectiveness as a filler between 'Sigh' and 'Break The Spell', an authentic blues snarled in the threatening tone of 'Stray Cat'; finally 'Slipping Away', Richards closing the album, as he had *Dirty Work*, with a ramshackle ballad.

Steel Wheels earned generally favourable reviews – its very existence reduced certain critics to the role of amanuenses for the group's press releases – ('He's Back . . . Old Giblet Lips . . . The Queen of Tarts, the Robin Naughtyfellow of Rock 'n' Roll Trollopry . . . The Midnight Rambler, the Dartford Knife Grinder, Jumpin' Jack Flash . . . Thass 'im, old Mick Jagger'), tending to advance the record beyond its rank. In a long notice in *The Times*, David Sinclair praised the group for their 'resilience and compatibility', resulting in an album of 'tremendous vitality that combines moments of mild experimentation with a general restatement of first principles ... Like a carefully preserved vintage hot-rod, the Stones are still firing on all cylinders.' *Steel Wheels* reached number three in America and number two in Britain, the group's highest placing since *Tattoo You*.

After completing a much-maligned video ('Hi, I'm Mick Jagger ... Hope you have fun selling these clothes') to promote the group's designer accessories, Jagger was spirited by dramatically secretive means – his already airtight security enhanced by State Troopers responding to threats that, after twenty years, the Hells Angels still sought revenge for Altamont – to Philadelphia, where the tour opened on 31 August. The sixty thousand crowd was confronted by a set, strongly reminiscent of *Bladerunner* (or that summer's *Batman*) of boilers, girders, trusses, ropes and chutes, of flame-throwing pipes and hoses, the whole to represent an aptly named urban jungle. At the horn and drum climax of 'Continental Drift' the pipes fired, the lights flared and Jagger, grunting, strutting, waving his arms, appeared on stage: 'Start Me Up'. After a perfunctory 'Bitch' he came forward: 'Shadoobie, shadoobie ... *Shattered*.' The song began, a percussive assault of bass, guitar and drums before, twelve bars in, the sound system – all 550,000 watts of it – died; Jagger was left there muttering invective. Things recovered in 'Miss You'; spectacularly in 'Midnight Rambler', 'Paint It, Black' and '2000 Light Years', Jagger crouching, howling, prowling in the suddenly fanned fog. Though denied the theatrics of earlier tours he continued to indulge his obsession with props. In 'It's Only Rock 'n Roll' a giant screen back-projected images of Elvis, Buddy Holly and the early Stones. In 'Sympathy' Jagger introduced himself from atop a hundred-foot-high tower; 'Honky Tonk Women' was illustrated by two sixty-foot inflatable dolls –

Angie and Ruby – manufactured, the press were assured, of untearable riptop nylon; 'Satisfaction' – a song Jagger once vowed never to sing after the age of forty – was again the finale; fireworks; curtains. Tom Moon, music critic of the Philadelphia *Inquirer* praised the concert as 'a fantastic two-and-a-half hour party', the *Daily News* adding, 'They cheered Mick Jagger's contemptuous trademark strut . . . He looked incredibly fit and still moves with agility – communicating his sassy, sneering body language to ecstatic fans.'

He was undeniably fit. If, as more jaundiced critics observed, the man who sang 'Little Red Rooster' was no spring chicken, if his centre of gravity had shifted from his hips to his arms and flailing legs, if at times his stiff, karate-like antics again suggested the declining Elvis, Jagger still, at forty-six, retained the ability to interpret – to illustrate – a song. Illustration, after all, had been his original function – to provide the emphasis of Richards' music, not its demented counterpoint. On stage Jagger's movements were more intentionally restrained than since 1966 – the point at which, arguably, caricature had overcome performance. His clothes too were subdued: black shoes, breeches, a succession of jackets inevitably removed to reveal one of the numerous tour T-shirts. On certain numbers he stood stock still, agitating rather than playing guitar, his still inimitable voice amplified by three backing singers (including Bernard Fowler, whose unmistakable Brooklyn tenor was said to be 'substituting' for Jagger – like something out of Jan and Dean). At any moment there were fifteen musicians on stage, supported by a cast of three hundred technicians, projectionists, engineers and electricians responsible for a thousand tons of equipment, the – largely successful – idea being to replace the air of unpredictable charm surrounding the Stones with one of steely professionalism; or, as Jagger said, 'There used to be tremendous ups and downs . . . I think [people] thought being lackadaisical was kind of hip . . . Now the tenor of the moment has changed – everybody seems really focused and proud of what they're doing.'

Easily bored himself, Jagger's intuitive sense of *pacing* – of what would and would not hold an audience's attention – led him to insist on certain standards. 'Ruby Tuesday', 'Gimme Shelter' and 'Jumpin' Jack Flash' were all included, as was 'Brown Sugar'. He persistently quizzed Cohl about the age and composition of crowds, which he summarized to *20/20* as 'sixty per cent never [having seen] the Rolling Stones before, thirty per cent having seen them once and ten per cent old haggard Stones fans with lots of kids and no money trying to relive their past'. He was careful to introduce each pre-1970 song almost apologetically as 'an oldie'. And he continued to insist that the audience 'Get up', 'Strut', 'Dig it' and generally 'Enjoy [themselves]', an urging entirely consistent with his biography in the tour programme: 'Mick is basically about fun and he's never seen the music as anything much more. "Don't get too serious about it, it's only rock 'n' roll" has passed into common usage. He likes to smile and laugh. He's worked hard on the preparations for this tour and the reward is seeing a lot of happy faces out there.' It was written by his brother.

The Rolling Stones had always travelled in style; now their progress was little short of presidential. Over the sixteen weeks of the tour Jagger was flown in a series of chartered 707s, DC-9s and Learjets; limousines met him on arrival; whole floors of hotels, under the inevitable aliases, were booked to ensure privacy. Where once he was visited backstage by Abbie Hoffman and members of the Black Panthers now access was afforded to Meryl Streep and Barbra Streisand. In New York Jagger's very presence caused a tremor, halfway between joy and horror, in the local press. Of the group's opening night at Shea Stadium the *New York Times* wrote:

Mick Jagger, pursing his famous lips, articulated every torn and tattered phrase and maintained his personality without sinking into caricature ... Songs like 'Paint It, Black', 'Sympathy for the Devil' and 'Gimme Shelter' presented the acidic world view that squared with the Stones' position as a band that helped define the morality of a generation ... The larger social power of their myth, combined with the continuing magnification of their celebrity, also helps to explain why people will pay so much to see them. The band's concerts in New York are expected to gross nearly $12 million.

In California three weeks later Jagger appeared, alone and without prior notice, in a community centre outside Oakland, gazing silently at the broken windows, the bulging walls and fissures presented as evidence of the recent earth-quake. Immediately he offered to donate funds, eventually totalling half a million dollars, from his three concerts at the Alameda Stadium to disaster relief. 'It was spontaneous,' says Maria Hookes, a federal emergency worker from nearby Watsonville. 'He'd seen the news coverage and wanted to help ... There were people coming up to him, asking for money, autographs, anything. He was literally giving them cash from his pocket. I think the whole thing – the poverty, not just the physical damage – really got to him.' On stage that night Jagger made a short speech: 'Our hearts go out to those of you who suffered, but we know that you northern Californians have an incredible spirit ... and I don't have to tell you it's a wonderful place to live.' Others noted that the arrogance characteristic of previous tours – in Hall's words, 'the nice, gentle, gentlemanly guy I live with [becoming] this incredible egomaniac' – was leavened by a new sense of civility. When, tired of travelling and missing his wife, Wyman entered his hotel suite he was met by a note even the bassist considered 'supportive', signed by Jagger.

The tour ended, as in 1981, on 19 December. From

Mustique Jagger returned in the new year to England where, on 25 January, Hall opened in *Bus Stop*. Her own view – 'Modelling's so much easier than acting, and it pays so much better' – was one the critics gave her no reason to retract. Backstage there was a cast party attended by, among others, Jagger and Jade, whose relationship with Piers Jackson the press had recently discovered. In early February the Stones, in a revealing sequence of arrivals (Jagger with Watts, Richards and Wood, Wyman with his son Stephen) landed at Narita airport, Tokyo. After regrouping at the Hotel Okura, and attending the Mike Tyson–Buster Douglas title fight, they gave the first of ten concerts on 14 February, before which, the *Sun* insisted, Jagger had sent a 'scorching' Valentine's Day fax to Hall in London. As in 1988 the crowds at the Tokyo Dome, a variety of businessmen with briefcases, mothers and small children, applauded politely before lapsing – as if by prearranged signal – into abrupt silence. Even Jagger, with his prior experience of Japan, looked uncomfortable in the extended gaps between songs. (For Richards the greatest shock may have been the six-thirty p.m. start, at which time the guitarist had been known to be eating breakfast.) Elsewhere Jagger responded with enthusiasm to aspects of Japanese culture: saki, geishas, the bath houses and Kabuki, mugging gamely with the samurai warriors sent to meet him at the airport. After a CBS reception – which he alone of the Stones attended – Jagger was said to have left on the arm of a 'mystery blonde', later identified as a record company liaison officer. Despite imaginative treatment in the British tabloids no evidence emerged that the assignment was anything but professional – or that Jagger's deportment in Japan was less than that becoming the 'esteemed visitor' the *Asahi Shimbun* deemed him to be.

A more critical reception was widely anticipated in Europe. At a chaotic press conference on 22 March – Jagger tripping over his microphone lead, cut short by the ringing of his own phone – dates were announced in Holland, Germany, Spain, Portugal, France, Scandinavia, Italy . . . and Britain. Explaining the decision to introduce a new set (designating it thus the 'urban jungle' tour) Jagger insisted, 'We want to make it more exciting for everyone, including the people working on the show' (omitting to mention the financial motive), adding on a personal note: 'Obviously you have to be in good shape, but hopefully . . . it's still do-able.'

His qualms arose from the disparity between the adoring American market – where a host of surrogate acts including the Black Crowes, Guns N' Roses and a reanimated Aerosmith had emerged in the Stones' absence; where they weren't just a group but a habit – and more cost-conscious, *ennuyé* Europe, where a healthy dose of iconoclasm, never far from the surface, had recently seen Bob Dylan jeered from the stage. There were conflicting reports about the rate of ticket sales in London. In Rotterdam there were pockets of empty seats when the Stones opened on 18 May. The morning press remained unconvinced, though in Germany, where memories existed of Jagger goosestepping across stage in 1965, Pallenberg's brief reappearance ensured, in one reviewer's words, that 'it was just like old times'. There was also a reference to the tour's one indisputable technical hitch when in Hanover Jagger appeared, spotlit, on top of a hundred-foot scaffold to sing 'Sympathy', only to find his radio mike inoperative. The ride down, according to the engineer who accompanied him, was 'distinctly chilly'. A documentary was made of the two concerts at the Olympic Stadium, Barcelona, and shows Jagger cavorting, like a spoiled child transported into middle age, among the props, ramps, gantries and the ever-pliant Wood. 'Shattered' having been finally discarded, the audience was treated to an extended 'Street Fighting Man', accompanied by – yet more – giant simulacra. In Paris *Le Figaro* hailed the group with the inevitable *Les Stones Roulent Toujours*, before attempting the first cogent analysis of their motivation: '*Cet amour de l'argent, qui les a sauvé des paradis artificiels leur remet même de faire encore de bons concerts.*' Jagger, the report concluded, remained 'a great, perhaps the greatest, performer'.

The designation was hard earned. Jagger's regime on tour was akin to a training athlete's. He neither drank nor smoked; he ran a minimum of five miles daily (and the equivalent of fifteen on stage), accompanied by his personal trainer and masseur. Later Clifford would be summoned to perform vocal warm-ups, for which, inexplicably, 'Angie' was invariably chosen; then more exercises, Jagger flexing his trunk, touching his toes, balancing on one boneless leg, grunting to Dunn and the stage manager David Stallbaumer; then pyrotechnics; Jagger hawking in his throaty trademark snarl, *Start me up . . . Start me up . . . I'll never stop*, his movements a continuation of the circuit-training backstage, flips of his legs, his hands constantly reeling, his voice somehow matched by the taut unfriendliness of his face: Twist and Shout.

The Stones, having politely declined Dick Taylor's request to have the Pretty Things precede them, opened the first of four consecutive nights in London on 4 July. 'They worked their ramshackle magic,' allowed *The Times*. 'Jagger strutted, preened, shimmied and sang with a fervour that the years have done nothing to diminish . . . He went through half-a-dozen jackets at least, frequently exposing his non-existent midriff.' Even the *Guardian* abandoned its proprietary brand of critical sang-froid: 'Mick Jagger boasts that he has probably made love more times than any other man on earth,' trilled Joanna Coles. 'Judging from the female reaction in the seventy-thousand crowd which saw the Rolling Stones at Wembley last night, he would have no trouble doubling his score.' In less excitable vein Adam Sweeting commented in the same paper: 'In his huntsman's frock-coat and with his obsessively trim physique, Jagger exudes a nervous fussiness . . . Where there used to be an inkling of insurrection and sexual braggadocio, there is now business acumen and mocking campness. You can picture Jagger picking at his smoked salmon and totting up the VAT while Keith sprawls across his bed and unstoppers the Remy Martin.'

Other critics alluded to the comic disparity between Jagger and his guitarist, a relationship, compared by *Punch* to Laurel and Hardy, occasionally descending to the level of buffoonery, as their rendition of 'Midnight Rambler' proved; the significance of the original was lost in the rapacity to entertain. Jagger's reaction to the World Cup semi-final occurring simultaneously in Turin – news of which was relayed to Wembley – lacked the aplomb of his performance in 1982; when England scored (in, as it turned out, a particularly emotive passage of 'Almost Hear You Sigh') he looked physically startled at the apparently spontaneous applause interrupting a Watts sonata. 'Is the tension getting to you?' he asked acidly at song's end. The absurdity of Jagger – said to be earning ten thousand pounds a minute throughout the two-hour concert* – singing the *angst*-ridden refrain of 'Satisfaction' was seized on by the *Mirror*, though even then the full force of critical scorn was mitigated by events happening elsewhere: at that precise moment, at the London Arena, Frank Sinatra was singing 'Young At Heart'.

The backlash followed in Glasgow. After a concert at Hampden Park on 9 July, Douglas Fraser wrote in the *Scotsman*:

There are those who write off the Stones as having toppled from several of the thrones they once

* For the year August 1989–August 1990 Jagger's income, inclusive of record sales, royalties and performance fees was conservatively estimated at fifteen million dollars.

occupied. But as they enter their rhythm and blues dotage they are using this tour to let the world know – in case it hadn't already realized – that they have conquered a new pinnacle . . .

Because, despite all the sturdy work of the Rutles, the pre-fab four, and the definitive heavy metal spoof of Spinal Tap, the Stones have taken the send-up of rock and roll to new heights.

By cramming us all into the great football arenas of Europe they remind us what it's all really about – recycling your old hits, cramming in the punters and making an obscene stack of money.

The tour officially ended on 9 August, though due to Richards having enigmatically injured a finger ('The first cancellation ever,' he insisted) two London dates were rearranged at the end of the month, exactly a year since the tour's opening night in Philadelphia. By then the Stones had performed to 110,000 people in an outdoor concert in Prague, leading Václav Havel to praise the role played 'by models like Mr Jagger' in promoting the Czech revolution. An Australian tour was also scheduled but failed to occur.

On balance the critics enhanced Jagger's reputation. They discredited themselves. When the concerts were viewed as concerts relatively little could be said against them; in two hours Jagger delivered twenty-four songs extending over four decades; his ability to engage an audience, notwith-standing Wembley, remained intact. Such criticism as there was was inevitably accompanied by an attempt to place Jagger in his wider context: a dilettante Englishman indulg-ing in a last-ditch cash-in, or a nostalgic rerun of past glories. The two million who paid to endure often archaic conditions, exposed to the sun and, in London, to wind and rain, assaulted by a sound of such blaring incoherence as to blur the distinction between songs, wherein Jagger was reduced to the dimension of a prancing ant, had little cause for complaint: they went home, as did the audience at the London Arena, having been in the albeit distant presence of a legend. In finally eliminating the elements of fear, risk and danger (with their concomitant threat of physical menace) once associated with the Stones, Jagger succeeded in perfecting the form to which, even in highly charged adolescence, his instincts had drawn him: mass funny entertainment.

For some time – since at least 1978, when their names had become linked – the media had agitated for Jagger's and Hall's marriage. There were periodic intimations (the birth of their children, Hall's acquittal in Barbados), periodically denied. By 1987 the British press had focused its attention on Jagger's parents, specifically on Eva, who was reported to have instructed her son to 'marry – or else'. She denies it. 'Provided the children were looked after, I was happy for things to go on as they were. Besides, it's none of my business.' Jagger himself maintained the defensive. 'I've always thought getting married more than once was a waste of time ... Marrying Bianca was one of those mistakes we all make ... Never again ... If two people love each other they shouldn't be worried about a piece of paper.' Now, eight years after their reconciliation, Hall (who wanted to marry so badly, a friend told *Vanity Fair*, 'she used to travel everywhere with an orange blossom and a plastic ring in her suitcase') drew Jagger's attention to its premiss: marriage, babies and happiness – though, as he always maintained, not necessarily in that order.

In mid-November they, their two children and Dunn were on holiday in Bali. On the twenty-first (the night that, in London, Margaret Thatcher decided to resign) a holy man named Ida Banjar was summoned. Over the next six hours he recited chants, burnt incense and advised the respondents to acknowledge their Karmas. History fails to relate whether, as tradition requires, the husband also beat his wife with a banana. After eleven years of bachelorhood, and more than thirteen with Hall, Jagger was married.

Elements of the press, who entirely missed the event, became indignant and ecstatic in the same breath. Under the headline 'IT'S ABOUT BALI TIME, MICK', the *Sun* quoted Eva as endorsing Hall as 'definitely the right girl for Mick. She has a job and is homely at the same time, which to me is the perfect combination ... We've been pulling Mick's leg for some time about getting married.' Hall herself, as she later told the journalist Stephanie Mansfield, 'was *sooo* happy the day we did it. I was beaming. I have never been so happy in my life. I couldn't stop smiling. I was lying there, going to sleep with a *huge* grin on my face ... My mother and Mick's parents were really happy. It meant a lot to them.'

Jagger's next priority was his parents. On 7 December 1990 Joe and Eva celebrated their golden anniversary; what became a joint celebration took place at the Nayland Rock Hotel, Margate. 'Mick was there with Jerry,' says Herbert Scutts. 'He was charming ... very relaxed.' After dinner Jagger proposed a toast and presented his parents with a gold chalice. Eva's memories are of a 'beautifully arranged, but crowded room', Scuttses tending to predominate over the less profligate Jaggers, and the presence of a large number of men in raincoats of no known affiliation to either family. A small disturbance ensued when a journalist introduced himself as 'Mick's brother' to Chris Jagger, but it passed when Dunn intervened.

Intrigued, the press belatedly enquired into Jagger's marriage. Rarely have journalists discerned the need to repair with such haste, and in such profusion, to Bali for Christmas. Their efforts were rewarded. The wedding was reported as of dubious validity. Ida Banjar later repudiated the entire ceremony, apparently unconvinced of the couple's Hindu credentials and complaining of the absence of supporting documentation, including Jagger's birth certificate.

No legal paperwork was ever completed, qualifying Jagger as one of relatively few people to answer the question 'Are you married?' (as he did to *Vanity Fair*) by replying, 'I think so.' The fact remains unrecorded in the London Registry.

On 16 January 1991 – the day on which Allied aircraft first bombed Baghdad – Jagger recorded 'Highwire', a diatribe against not the war itself but the munitions dealers supplying it. It was released to little effect as a single. 'Highwire' also appeared on the live album *Flashpoint*, issued on 8 April. Promoted under the slogan 'The Rolling Stones' Greatest Hits' it duly included 'Ruby Tuesday', 'Paint It, Black', 'Sympathy for the Devil', 'Brown Sugar', 'Jumpin' Jack Flash' and 'Satisfaction'. Jagger's on-stage patter was restricted to polyglot song introductions and a general twitting of Wyman ('Tonight we thought we'd try a number we don't do very much . . . Which album's it from, Bill?' Long pause. 'He doesn't know, he doesn't *know*') whose recent autobiography had revealed a not wholly idolatory attitude towards the singer. *Flashpoint* also yielded a second studio single, 'Sex Drive', purporting to deal with physical privation on the road and deriving heavily from James Brown. The accompanying video saw Jagger notionally being recycled on the psychiatrist's couch, surrounded by women in see-through cellophane dresses. Promptly banned in the US, it also fuelled rumours of a romance with the model Lisa Barbuscia to whom, according to the *Mirror*, 'Mick took a shine . . . He kept kissing her as he went through their sexy scene. When the shoot was over he asked her to call him.'

In the meantime Jagger was reported to be suffering from cancer, a rumour aired periodically since the sixties. He completed *Freejack* in Atlanta, auditioned musicians for a putative solo album and moved in early summer to London where, revising a lifestyle described by the judge in his divorce case as 'quintessentially peripatetic', he paid £2.2

million for a listed mansion on the slopes of Richmond Hill. Downe House, less than a mile from the old Station Hotel, purchased from the advertising executive Tim Mead, included six reception rooms, original Adam ceilings, a gym, Jacuzzi and nursery; buying it, says Eva, 'was one of the shrewdest things Mick did'. Even then, rumours – somehow never far removed from Jagger and Hall – persisted. Press reports alluded to the divergent tastes preferred by the couple: he, the modern look, 'all glass and spotlights'; she 'a frivolous art deco style'. An unnamed friend told the *Evening Standard*: 'We expected to find the ideal family situation – a cosy kind of place where children could easily move about from one room to another . . . What we found was a kind of fortress, furnished to suit two people who had very different ideas and obviously wanted to spend time alone.' Further comment followed the revelation that 'the man who carried the banner in the sexual revolution can no longer even slip into his wife's separate bedroom – they have papered over the connecting door'.

As so often with Jagger, the critics missed the significance. Downe House, with its Georgian decor, its box hedges and rose garden, its bay windows overlooking the Thames, was a home, not a playpen – ideal, his mother insists, for 'putting down roots'. Within a month of exchanging contracts Jagger made the headlines again: Hall was pregnant.

There might be thought to be relatively little news in a forty-seven-year-old man moving with his family to the London suburbs, surrounded by analysts, lawyers and his own financial adviser. Nonetheless news there was, and a media watch began at Jagger's gate. On 23 June he, Hall, his parents and Jade visited Richmond: But was Mick, asked the *Mirror*, beaming with satisfaction? 'Heck, no . . . He wore the wall-to-wall scowl of a bloke who'd forked out a fortune to please the missus.'

Actually Jagger wore the wall-to-wall scowl of a man see-ing an agency photographer scaling his front wall. Having made his annual excursion to Lord's, Jagger had met his family that afternoon at the Imperial War Museum; the decision to view Downe House was reached on the spot. 'As soon as we arrived,' says Eva, 'there was a creature at the gate. You'd really think, by now, they'd have better things to do. Mick spoke quite sharply to him.'

Having discerned qualities in Jagger other than the rampant anarchy of his youth, the press changed tack. In a long article in the *Evening Standard*, Rory Knight Bruce strived to explain 'How Jagger Joined The Gentry'. There was talk of 'hobnobbing' with Hugh Trevor-Roper, the Pinters, with Paul Johnson; of Jagger quizzing his youngest daughter's headmistress about the school's religious education; of pipes of port and Eton – all accompanied by the inevitable charge of snobbery. (The reason why Jagger 'never achieved his potential' according to Philip Norman, being his reluctance 'to take a risk for fear of what his posh friends may think'.) Some of this dated from as early as 1964, when Jagger had been overheard discussing art with the Marquess of Bath, a cultural avidity often confused with social climbing – one continued under Gibbs, Fraser and Cammell and accelerated by Faithfull. If it left Jagger struggling to emphasize the more primal aspects of his character ('I couldn't give a shit about gardening,' he told *Vanity Fair*; 'I think wine is so boring . . . Nor am I interested in decorating') even as Hall, less aware of the implication of such things in England, was insisting the opposite ('He knows about food and wine and antiques, and he's very refined'), his defence – borne out by the facts – might have echoed Fitzgerald's: 'Riches have *never* fascinated me – unless combined with the greatest charm or distinction.'

On the subsidiary charge of conservatism, aspects even of Jagger's youth suggest he was favourably impressed by *Areopagitica*, by Raine and Emerson with their conversion of liberty into a socially acceptable doctrine, rather than by

Utopian dreaming. As early as 1967 William Rees-Mogg described Jagger, whose father's school motto was 'You have the perfect liberty to do as you like, provided you do the right thing', as 'heavily influenced' by John Stuart Mill with his belief in self-restraint, in freedom as a moral principle. Six years later Jagger informed the world, 'All you have to do is make sure that whatever you do doesn't bother other people . . . Everyone has to be tied down to something, but within discipline there's a lot of room to move' – a near textbook definition of libertarianism. Jagger's 'room to move' might retain the power to shock – the 'Sex Drive' video, his insistence since 1978 on the serial letters CUN for his albums (before which it was COC), his employment of a secretary named Crotch – but much was merely an extension of Mill's belief in 'vagary and caprice' as proportional to society's strength, as innocuous – above all, as *English* – as Benny Hill or a McGill cartoon. That – his Englishness – may after all be the key. Whatever the subsequent course of Jagger's life, four-tenths of it has been spent in Dartford.

When, in summer 1991, Downe House was refurbished Jagger rented a suburban home in Barnes distinguished only by its ordinariness. He walked on Putney Common; he even cycled to Olympic studios. When, on 2 July, Hall turned thirty-five the family appeared en masse at the Indian, Chris Jagger, Joe and Eva mingling with Paul Channon and Lord Hesketh. 'Gentleman Jagger,' breathed *The Sunday Times*, 'sends toffs weak at the knees (and vice-versa).' Again Eva demurs: 'He likes people who are funny, whatever their background. So do we.' That August Jagger exchanged telegrams with Václav Havel and Boris Yeltsin; he watched cricket with John Major; he talked art with Getty and Charles Saatchi. Perhaps his most fruitful encounter was with Tim Renton in the Nubian Room of the British Museum. 'Before 1963,' he informed the arts minister,

'British pop was unexportable ... Alma Cogan doing versions of Rosemary Clooney, Cliff imitating Elvis.' Then Jagger made his pitch: UK artists accounting for twenty-five per cent of the world's record market, why not a National Music Day to celebrate the fact? The idea, seized on by Renton and his successor David Mellor, endorsed by Equity, the Musicians Union and the Arts Council, was formally announced on 12 February 1992. Jagger stood fielding questions, including, 'Have you joined the Establishment?', exactly twenty-five years after elements of the Establishment had embarked on proceedings to jail him. The event itself earned mixed reviews: in a lofty critique George Hill admitted to 'an overwhelming impulse to duck out ... The tendency to play Scrooge [being] all the stronger on this occasion because some areas of the world of music in Britain are in the throes of grief and uncertainty. A day of celebration must seem to many musicians to have the hollow ring of a *danse macabre*.' When the day dawned, 28 June, Jagger appeared (but failed to sing) at an open-air session on Clapham Common before headlining a blues concert described by Robert Sandall as 'short but twitchily charismatic', at Hammersmith Odeon. After performing 'I Just Want To Make Love To You', accompanied by Watts and Wood, Jagger left the stage and declined to return for an encore.

A meeting had meanwhile taken place with Richard Branson. The chairman of Virgin Music, a known admirer of the group since 1969, made overtures to sign the Stones on the expiry of their CBS contract. A long-time Virgin artist remembers being introduced to Jagger in the boardroom. 'He had one, completely normal voice talking to Richard, then a Godawful, put-on Cockney when the tealady appeared.' There was said to be rival interest from Polygram. Finally, on 20 November 1991, after dinner at Mosimann's, Branson made the announcement: 'The Rolling Stones are the greatest rock and roll band and I am honoured they have chosen Virgin Records.' The deal gave the group a thirty-three per cent rise in advance payments from six million to eight million dollars an album, thirty-five million dollars in all, including rights to their records since 1971. 'We are looking forward to a successful relationship with Virgin,' Jagger informed the press. 'I'm not saying it's not a lot of money,' he later told Stephen Schiff, 'but Virgin does hope to make a profit on the deal. They could probably be recouped with one new album and one boxed set of reissues.' When, less than four months later, Virgin was sold to Thorn EMI Jagger assured Branson he was 'happy to be working for a British company'.

Parallel negotiations continued with Ahmet Ertegün to revive Jagger's solo career. A contract was signed, as it had been with CBS, for two albums – the difference being that, with the relative failure of *She's The Boss* and *Primitive Cool* and their negative reception by Richards (not to mention the obligation to Virgin) Jagger acknowledged the doctrine of co-existence: whatever the direction of his musical career, his films and his book, his primary interest would be the Stones.

He recognized as much to *Vanity Fair* in February 1992. 'Keith and I seem to be getting on all right. The tour got all that out of our systems … We had a good time … Which is why I can blithely talk about doing it all again.' To the same magazine he contended, 'I wasn't *trying* to be rebellious [in the sixties] … I was just being me. I wasn't trying to push the edge of anything … All those songs we sang are pretty tame, really. People didn't think they were, but I thought they were tame. A lot of it was bullshit, the whole idea of "Let's Spend The Night Together" and a lot of other things – it was so ridiculous.' On other aspects of his past – on Faithfull, Jones, on Altamont and Bianca – Jagger insisted, 'I'm not interested in all that shit.'

The impression was of a middle-aged, affable Renaissance figure, a man who read biographies of Dickens and Shaw, enjoyed cricket, who danced and sang 'Sex Machine' while viewing expensive paintings, who scrutinized bills and micromanaged budgets; who viewed his career with an expected modesty – 'I wouldn't claim anything extraordinary and wonderful' – if an equally disarming certainty that it was a great one; who stressed his peripatetic instincts at a time, others suggest, they were diminishing; who, above all, resisted the lure of the pigeonhole, concluding, 'People find it hard to accept multifaceted people – that you can be a person who has children but yet you can go out and get wild and crazy and mad and drunk, and then go out on the road and be completely sober because that's what you have to be . . . I don't find life quite so simple, that everyone's just got these tiny personalities and that they can only behave in one kind of way.'

Jagger's own multiplicity was revealed in the background to the interview. Unknown to its readership, the magazine had originally commissioned celebrity writer Nancy Collins, whose questions on Jagger's past – on the 'shit' so summarily dismissed – provoked a crisis. At Jagger's insistence Schiff – *Vanity Fair*'s critic-at-large, a connoisseur of dance, of opera, of fine art – was substituted. The two got on well together.

Another reminder of Jagger's past followed in February: despite having toured the country without incident in 1988 and 1990 the Japanese government refused him entry to promote *Freejack*. For twenty-four hours he waited at Narita airport, signing forms, giving statements, while Justice Ministry officials debated his twenty-two-year-old marijuana conviction. (Before flying to Tokyo Jagger had asked whether his black-listing still applied, and been told he was free to find out.) Finally, on 17 February, the authorities yielded. Under the headline 'JAPAN RELENTS AND ALLOWS FAMILY MAN, 48, TO ENTER', *The Times* reported that 'officials who still see the singer as a threat to morals have not yet grasped that Jagger, father of four (*sic*), grandfather-to-be, and friend of members of the British royal family, is not the man he was in 1969 ... When he was in Tokyo with the Stones in 1990 he was interested not in finding drugs but in finding the best jogging circuit near his hotel.' Jagger himself was said to be 'not entirely distraught' that elements of his prior reputation survived: it was the publicizing as much as the manner and style of his life that still fascinated.

Freejack was coolly received, reaping only fifteen million dollars at the box office in the first two months of release. The critics were agreed that Jagger, in Kevin O'Sullivan's words, 'was no Olivier', though he retained a 'certain dark presence', curiously offset in *Freejack* by a series of effete, lisping accents. The same month he released *Rolling Stones At The Max*, filmed during the 1990 concerts in Turin, Berlin and Wembley and shot in giant-screen Imax, a format dependent on a 'rolling loop' projector advancing the film horizontally instead of the conventional vertical direction – causing David Sinclair to write: 'The vivid quality is impressive, but the sheer scale of the enterprise is breathtaking. As you look out over a sea of waving arms and swaying heads, then up to the top of the screen, where a distant helicopter buzzes in the darkness over the stadium, you get an extraordinary impression of what it must be like to be on stage with the Rolling Stones.' Due to its technical demands, the film was seen at just seventy-seven theatres worldwide, only one of them in Britain.

Next Jagger was approached by the producer John Griffin to appear in the stage musical *A Slice Of Saturday Night* in the role of Eric 'Rubber Legs' De Vene, an ageing nightclub performer fixated on Elvis; film scripts, if not in their previous number, continued to arrive at the office; there was talk of Jagger financing, writing or even directing his own feature. If the portents were discouraging (one thinks of *Renaldo and Clara*, of *Give My Regards To Broad Street*), if suspicions lingered that, Imax notwithstanding, Jagger translated more easily on to the small screen than the large one, if his few starring roles failed to ring bells in the far universe, then no one would bet against the logical extension of his career into production. When, in March 1992, Jagger attempted, and failed, to install satellite television in the Caribbean hotel of the England 'A' cricket XI (wanting to allow them to watch the World Cup final) he was heard to remark, 'I should be in this business,' with more than the usual air of saloon-bar levity.

The press, meanwhile, considered: Jagger's marriage, his homes, his children (doorstepping his seven-year-old at Ibstock Place), his conservatism, his parsimony, not omitting to mention Hall. On 3 December 1991 the couple were sighted walking on Barnes Common, a scoop afforded full-page coverage in the *Daily Mirror*. On 11 January Jagger was equally expansively pictured buying flowers for his wife at Chiswick House. The next afternoon Hall gave birth to a daughter at Portland Hospital, a private clinic patronized by members of the royal family. The birth certificate, filed on 27 January, lists the family's 'usual residences' as Downe House and Mustique.

Jagger, present at the delivery, was said by a spokesman to be happy: 'He didn't mind if it was a boy or a girl – just so long as the baby was healthy.' At a ceremony in Richmond, attended by Joe and Eva, by Watts and the former Conservative cabinet minister Paul Channon, the child was christened Georgia (possibly in deference to having been conceived in that State's capital city during the shooting of *Freejack*) May (the month filming was complete).

Almost immediately Jagger was seen in Phuket where, witnessed by the journalist Howard Sounes, he was joined in the Amanpuri Hotel by a teenage girl with whom he 'drank beer, danced ... and kissed on the lips'. According to an unnamed source, 'Jagger would get up early and do aerobics with the girl by their private pool ... He was

obviously very close to his friend and they had a great time.'
His wife, quoted later in the *Daily Mail*, admitted, 'I confronted him and asked who he was with in Thailand . . . A
man is supposed to be with his woman when she's just had
a baby.' Further reports tied Jagger to Lisa Barbuscia and,
more persistently, the fashion model Carla Bruni, herself
linked to Eric Clapton and Donald Trump. On the eve of
their fifteenth anniversary together Hall informed *Hello!*,
'It's a miracle we've managed to stay together so long,'
adding, 'It's difficult in the entertainment business because
there's always attractive people around and so many young
girls who chase after Mick' – an admission provoking comment with which Julie Burchill in the *Mail On Sunday* can
be associated:

> Jerry Hall thinks that it's a 'miracle' that her relation-
> ship with one Mock Jogger has lasted fifteen years,
> considering that so many *preety* women chase him. I
> don't. Because what she fails to mention, and so resol-
> utely refuses to discuss, is that perhaps they don't just
> chase him – they catch him. And he doesn't appear to
> struggle too damn hard, either.

Warming to her theme, Burchill offered a character study
of Jagger: he was, essentially, 'a figure of fun', a 'half-
centenarian rebel rocker', 'laying pipes of port rather than
groupies' who, unpardonably, 'is about to become a grandfather'. And finally: 'When I was a teenager, we girls
thought Jerry Hall was a real dweebie for running off with
someone like Jagger when she had a beaut like Bryan Ferry
. . . Well, I bet she's sorry now. Serves her right.'

Burchill was right, of course. Hall must have regretted
ending a simple affectionate affair and being saddled with
Jagger, than whom no one was less simple. What was the
attraction? Hall couldn't point out that Jagger was a composite father and husband – that (again, *pace* Fitzgerald) he

was one of those people, relatively rare in England, able to sustain conflicting ideas and still function, that he loved his wife and spent time, but not all the time, with his children. Apparently he already seemed odd enough. Hall might have mentioned Jagger's undoubted intelligence, his humour, his ability, as a friend puts it, 'to carry on just as easily in the Ritz as in the taxi taking him there', his random generosity (paying money to a sixties pop star, underwriting charities) leavened by a financial acumen responsible for an eighty-five-million-pound fortune. Supposedly a hell-raiser and boor, he turned out to be an award-winning song-writer and adviser to government ministers. A generation raised on Freud will have no difficulty in attributing to Jagger the self-confidence of the elder child, nor the values of thrift, energy and perseverance instilled in his youth. There are not many major cultural figures whose upbringing impinges so directly on their culture. Even at the height of Jagger's legend, a landscape fixed variously between 1964–72, he was rarely as wayward as the subordinates around him. One part of him, says Keylock, remained firmly 'fixed in the real world' – the world of tax lawyers and accountants, of strategy sessions and brainstorms. If, at fifty, Jagger gave fuller vent to the qualities that earlier (Oldham insisted) remained hidden, if he reverted to the primary instincts of his youth – instincts that had gained him a fortune, five houses, the ability to pick friends and straddle lifestyles, to resist the demand 'only to behave in one kind of way' – then Hall may not after all have retracted her opinion: 'Mick still has glamour for me ... On tour, I get so proud looking out at the audience. There'll be tens of thousands of people wanting Mick and I'll think, *That's my man.*

'He's not at all the wild man of rock and roll that people think he is.'

If such people still existed they would have been unsurprised by Jagger's next move: on 29 July 1992, three days after celebrating his birthday in London, he flew to Los Angeles allegedly to join one of the numerous women – Carla Bruni or the model Kathy Latham, among others – whose company he kept in nightclubs around the world. In a long interview in the *Daily Mail* Hall was said to be 'devastated' and – as she had been in 1982 – 'on the verge of a nervous breakdown'. In a further twist a letter claiming to have been written by Hall to her husband was quoted in the press:

> I want you to have your freedom and I won't be mad if you fuck other girls. Oh my darling Mick, the thought of losing you breaks my heart in two. I'm truly sorry I was jealous. I tried to punish you and was unsympathetic . . . I'll be good to you. I respect, admire, trust, need and love you through all my being.

Jagger himself would admit only that, 'My family is very important to me and I care about them very much. However, they must remain a private affair.'

The imbroglio – quickly overshadowed in the media by those involving Woody Allen and the royal family – was a defining example of Jagger's talent for ambiguity, vagueness and paradox: whereas other men left their wives or didn't, were themselves left or weren't, Jagger occupied the middle ground. Undoubtedly he saw other women, just as Hall was known to socialize with other men; undoubtedly his behaviour in July 1992, just as it had in July 1982, precipitated a crisis; undoubtedly both parties engaged in conduct unusual in other middle-aged parents. Even so, to draw the conclusions reached (even in Britain, where they should have known better) by certain observers only proved how elusive Jagger remained. By October, three months after the scandal broke, he was back together with Hall in London.

For the remainder of 1992 Jagger continued to record and mix tracks that became his third solo LP, *Wandering Spirit*.

Originally planned to follow the Stones' 1989–90 world tour, it was delayed first by the filming of *Freejack*, then by the collective bargaining with Branson in 1991. Late that autumn Jagger returned to Olympic Studios. There and in Los Angeles he recorded material with a group of musicians (of whom only Clifford, Lenny Kravitz and Billy Preston were familiar names) known collectively as the Red Devils. The resulting album, released on 9 February 1993, was a return to the blues. There was a competent cover of James Brown's 'Think', as well as the inevitable touches of rap, reggae and country. Lyrically, too, *Wandering Spirit* returned to the premiss of *Some Girls*, of *Undercover* and *Dirty Work*, of arguably every Stones album since *Aftermath*: the man pursued by the lover from hell. Remarkably, when Jagger, approaching his fiftieth birthday, spoke of having his 'gun' unholstered by an encroaching lover, he still carried conviction.

The question of ageing, of adapting his behaviour to that of a pentagenarian grandfather, continued to fascinate Jagger's detractors. Not one of the reviews of *Wandering Spirit* overlooked it. In November 1992, apparently reconciled with her husband, Hall had told *McCalls*: 'I've always hoped that one day he'll outgrow these things and it won't happen again.' Pete Townshend's 1983 profile in *The Times* was quoted at length, critics being divided on whether, as predicted, Jagger was 'still beautiful when he's fifty . . . [his] talent still as strong at fifty because his ambition is not dependent on his youth.' *Wandering Spirit* gave no evidence.

If anything it was Richards who proved more personally mature. His own solo LP, *Main Offender*, released in October 1992 (though proving, like Jagger's, the inevitability of any intelligent rock star finding at least part of his audience ridiculous) gave evidence of a man at ease with his past. When, in one of numerous interviews to promote the record, Richards returned to his taunting of Jagger ('I hope the man comes to his senses. He should stop that now, the old black-book bit. Kicking fifty, it's a bit much, a bit manic') – and Jagger retaliated by walking out of one of Richards' solo concerts – rumours spread that the group's future was again in jeopardy. In early 1993 the two met in New York to discuss it.

———

Jagger continued, as always, to inhabit different worlds, altering his very appearance to suit his surroundings. In France he was the amiable *châtelain*, patronizing the Amboise market, drinking *eau de vie*, hosting parties notable for their absence of skull-faced rockers; in Mustique dining with Princess Margaret on the beach; in New York and London, immaculately made-up, coiffeured, doing the circuit of theatres, galleries and the inevitable clubs. He lives comfortably but unobtrusively within his means, preferring the taxi or bicycle to the available Mercedes. In profile he looks strikingly unchanged from his youth: the same enormous hands and head, the Beatle bouffant (his own – Jagger's one great fear, according to Eva, that 'he'd go bald like his father' not having been realized), rail-thin, his teenager's trunk and torso. The difference is all in the face: the eyes, the S-shaped curves to his cheeks, the furrowed chin wrinkled as if by the sheer weight of his mouth. At fifty he inclines to simple knife-point trousers and Jermyn Street shirts, invariably over a T-shirt or vest. He looks, at a glance, somewhere between sixteen and thirty – a remarkable achievement in anyone with three small children and a granddaughter.

England, the 'petty, boring, unambitious' small-town of his youth, seemed more accommodating in middle age. In the nineties Jagger reviewed his many options: he spoke nostalgically of London and without insult of Dartford; he acquired his first British home since Cheyne Walk. He watched and played sport, he attended openings, he tended his garden. At weekends he visited his parents in Westgate, or vice-versa; they went for walks together. Discussing what? 'History, politics, the family,' says Joe. 'The usual things.' Now eighty, Jagger's father remains active, playing golf, writing, reading, organizing the local Residents' Association to oppose construction of a nearby block of flats. In full maturity Jagger's instincts seem less exotic, less divergent to those of his parents than once appeared possible. Joe, too, admits to being 'against the establishment – if the establishment is wrong'. The old, familiar type of despotism, wherein government imposed itself on the governed, having ceased to exist, the tyranny of the majority – exerting itself not so much in politics as in the entire realm of social life – continues to engage the Jaggers' interest: 'Mick,' says Joe, 'was always taught to express himself. All he did was to find a way to do it.' Strange as it is to consider Jagger, in Rees-Mogg's phrase, advancing the sound traditional values of Britain, insofar as those include paradox, irony and a broad streak of libertarianism, it is hard to think of a more traditional character. Jagger, in short, not so much rejected as revised the standards of his parents, brilliantly realizing his talent for mimicry and exposition, 'expressing' himself – and in the process taking the risk that all this might help his career.

Relations with Richards also improved. It did not take a genius to predict, for this writer did so, that Jagger would be reconciled with his partner. Hard as it now is to recall, there was a time when ostensibly sane observers regarded them – the one an art connoisseur and grandfather, the other with his engaging Dean Martin slur – as twin princes of darkness. The image became proverbial, accepted. Possibly they subconsciously played up to it. If, again, they revert to the original strategy of their youth, to make music – not, as it turned out, an insuperable challenge – superior to that of their peers *and get paid for it*, who can blame them? There will be other Stones albums, other tours. The strategy still holds. Jagger can still look down over the park, the terrace gardens cut symmetrically like baize, across Paradise Road to the club where, thirty years ago, a shaggy-haired boy in a sweater sang the blues.

EPILOGUE

'You're a comical geezer,' James Fox told Jagger in *Performance*. 'You'll look funny when you're fifty.' There was a fad in the sixties for magazines to commission 'projections' of how rock stars – the Beatles, Dylan, Cliff Richard – might look when they reached the age Jagger reached in 1993. His own projection was the most comical: a bronze balding dome with sagging jowls and pitted cheeks. That Jagger celebrated his fiftieth birthday still hawk-faced, still hirsute, still *recognizable* was only the latest joke in a routine that seems to have begun in 1963. Before then it was possible to see Jagger for what he was – an ambitious but by no means exceptional grammar-school boy motivated by money and vague longings for America. A number of his letters from then have survived: what strikes the reader is how little they contain that might not have been written by hundreds of contemporaries who disappeared, around their eighteenth birthdays, into sales jobs or minor positions with the civil service. That Jagger turned out as he did was due, in roughly equal parts, to the accident of being born in the Baby Boom, the first generation to discover music as a conflict with its parents; his talent for mimicry, on which early British rock was largely founded; and Keith Richards. It hardly needs repeating that without Richards Jagger would now enjoy the status of a Peter Noone or, at best, a Paul Jones.

Jagger was always rock's most complicated character. From the classic Rolling Stones image that Albert Goldman described as 'sado-homosexual-junkie-diabolic-sarcastic-nigger-evil' to the wine-loving father of five, it is tempting to see his journey as that of a young outlaw into a pillar of the establishment. But the truth is different. Alone of the rock aristocracy, Jagger will never be pictured entertaining sick children or inviting *Hello!* into his beautiful home. He may have given up drugs but he remains notably interested in sex and rock and roll. *Wandering Spirit*, released on the eve of Jagger's fiftieth birthday, was his most satisfying album in a decade. He spent the birthday itself recording with the Rolling Stones.

The very idea of Jagger at fifty is a joke we never seem tired of. It will be remembered, though, that when the Rolling Stones formed, most of their material was written by sixty- and seventy-year-old men. It may only be recently that the group has approached the status of the originals. Jagger has already survived twenty years longer than the most optimistic forecast made on his debut. It is curiously tempting to bet on him lasting twenty more.

SOURCES AND CHAPTER NOTES

Formal interviews and on-the-record conversations are listed as follows. Inevitably, many requested that their comments remain anonymous and therefore no acknowledgement appears of the enormous help, encouragement and kindness I received from a number of sources.

CHAPTER I

An account of MJ's first day in New York appears in Bill Wyman's *Stone Alone*. Other sources included contemporary newspaper reports, the recollections of Barbara Collett and the late Ian Stewart. For the account of the Rolling Stones in Seattle, newspaper reports and my own memory are entirely responsible.
('Under My Thumb' (Jagger–Richard) © ABKCO Music)

CHAPTER II

Interviews with Joe and Eva Jagger; with Tony Smith of Dartford Grammar School; with MJ's former schoolmasters Richard Allen, Walter Bennett, John Mackereth, Arthur Page and Walton Wilkinson; with his former classmates Gareth Bolton, Alan Dow, David Drinkwater, Peter Holland, Paul Ovenden, Mike Richards, Clive

Robson and Graham Walder; with his former tutor Walter Stern.

I also spoke to the three former members of the Blue Boys, Bob Beckwith, Alan Etherington and Dick Taylor, as well as to Bob Clash, Ian King, Edith Keep, Keith Richards (12 February 1977), Carol Ward and John Keeble.

CHAPTER III

Interviews with Walter Stern, Don Short, Dick Taylor, Bob Beckwith, Alan, Andrew and Winifred Etherington; the late Alexis Korner and Ian Stewart; Eileen Giles, Jane Hamill and Alan Freeman; conversations with Jean and Chrissie Shrimpton, Ben Brierley, Dean Martin and Jimmy Savile. In the course of my research I visited Edith Grove, the Wetherby Arms and the Station Hotel, Richmond, alas much altered by improvements since Jagger's day.

A full account of the Rolling Stones' early years – including a description of life in Edith Grove – is given in Bill Wyman's *Stone Alone*.

CHAPTER IV

Interviews with Ronnie Wood (9 August 1971); with Tom Wolfe, Gered Mankowitz, Tom Keylock, Joan Keylock, Andrew Etherington, Anthony Phillips, Edith Keep, Chris Farlowe, Don Short, Jeff Griffin, Ben Brierley, Achmed D'hou and John Birt.

Much of the material relating to Marianne Faithfull in this chapter was derived from A. E. Hotchner, *Blown Away*, and from Mark Hodkinson, *Marianne Faithfull*. Philip Norman's *The Stones* and, again, *Stone Alone* also provided a number of quotes and anecdotes.

('Get Off of My Cloud'; 'Paint It, Black'; 'Out of Time' (all Jagger–Richard) © ABKCO Music)

CHAPTER V

Sources included Gered Mankowitz (and his book *Satisfaction*); interviews with Tom Keylock, Frank Thorogood, Don Short, the late Alexis Korner, Albert Clinton and others associated with the Gay Hussar restaurant; members of the staff of *Rolling Stone*; official depositions relating to the Inquest into the death of Brian Jones; and Dr Johnny Johnson.

Material on this era has been derived from the following books: A. E. Hotchner, *Blown Away*; Mark Hodkinson, *Marianne Faithfull*; and Tony Sanchez, *Up and Down with the Rolling Stones*.

Detective Sergeant Constable declined my request for an interview.

('Street Fighting Man'; 'Jumpin' Jack Flash' (both Jagger–Richard) © ABKCO Music)

CHAPTER VI

Further interviews with Tom Keylock and Frank Thorogood; Canon Hugh Hopkins; with Don Short and Jeff Griffin. The Granada film *The Stones in the Park* provides a documentary record of the events of 5 July 1969. Additional material was provided by Ben Brierley, Kathy Ward and the late Ian Stewart. Sections of MJ's FBI file were supplied by Kevin O'Brien of the US Department of Justice.

Published source material includes Stanley Booth, *The True Adventures of the Rolling Stones*, invaluable for its description of the 1969 tour of America.

('Wild Horses'; 'Monkey Man'; 'Gimme Shelter' (all
Jagger–Richard) © ABKCO Music)

Chapter VII

Interviews with Tom Keylock; with Ross Benson, Jeff
Griffin, Mike Oldfield and the late Alexis Korner. A full
account of MJ's wedding (sometimes referred to as 'Les
Perrin's finest hour') was supplied by Don Short and Eva
Jagger; printed information was obtained from the General
Register Office. Additional discussions with Clive Robson,
Ryan Grice, Winston Stagers, Tom Wolfe and the late John
Cheever.

Robert Greenfield, *A Journey Through America with the
Rolling Stones*, though disparaged by Jagger, provides a
unique insight into the group in 1972. Tony Sanchez, *Up
and Down with the Rolling Stones*, Mark Hodkinson, *Marianne
Faithfull*, and Barbara Charone, *Keith Richards*, all proved
useful source material for this period.

('Sister Morphine' (Jagger–Richard–Faithfull) © ABKCO
Music; 'Tumbling Dice' (Jagger–Richard) © Colgems–
EMI MUSIC, Inc.)

Chapter VIII

A number of the quotes attributed to MJ in this and other
chapters were taken from David Dalton, *The Rolling Stones
In Their Own Words* and Miles, *Mick Jagger In His Own
Words*. Other sources included Jeff Griffin, Ron Wood, Paul
Wasserman, Vincent Lorimer, Peter Barnes, Ross Benson,
Keith Richards, Joe and Eva Jagger, financial discovery
documents obtained under public disclosure laws and Jerry
Hall's illuminating *Tall Tales*.

('Fool to Cry' (Jagger–Richard) © EMI Publishing Ltd)

Chapter IX

Conversations with Congressman Norman Dicks; the late Senator Henry Jackson; Ross Benson; Jeff Griffin; Gered Mankowitz; Andy Peebles and with Mick Jagger (14 October 1981). Published sources referred to include Jerry Hall, *Tall Tales*, and Victor Bockris, *Keith Richards*.
('Send It To Me'; 'Indian Girl' (both Jagger–Richards) © T.M. Musidor B.V.)

Chapter X

Conversations with Joe and Eva Jagger; with the late Ian Stewart and Alexis Korner; with Denis Compton, Godfrey Evans and Colin Ingleby-Mackenzie; with Patrick Alley, the late Steve Marriott, Nick Miles and Herbert Scutts.

A lucid, though by no means comprehensive account of the rift between MJ and Keith Richards can be found in *USA Today* (April 1986).
('Tie You Up (The Pain of Love)'; 'Winning Ugly'; 'All The Way Down' (all Jagger–Richards); 'Had It With You' (Jagger–Richards–Wood); 'War Baby' (Jagger) © CBS Grammofoonplaten B.V.)

Chapter XI

Interviews with Jeff Griffin, Maria Hookes and Paul Ovenden; with Joe and Eva Jagger and Tom Keylock. Previously published interviews with MJ as quoted.

Other sources included Anthony Haden-Guest, Cecilia Lewis, Don Short, Tom Wolfe and, again, Bill Wyman's *Stone Alone*.
('Hold On To Your Hat' (Jagger–Richards) © CBS Grammofoonplaten B.V.)

BIBLIOGRAPHY

Aftel, Mandy, *Death of a Rolling Stone* (Sidgwick & Jackson, 1982)

Bockris, Victor, *Keith Richards* (Poseidon Press, 1992)

Bonanno, Massimo, *The Rolling Stones Chronicle* (Plexus Publishing, 1990)

Booth, Stanley, *The True Adventures of the Rolling Stones* (Abacus, 1986)

Carr, Roy, *The Rolling Stones, An Illustrated Record* (New English Library, 1976)

Charone, Barbara, *Keith Richards* (Futura Publications, 1979)

Dalton, David, *The Rolling Stones In Their Own Words* (Omnibus Press, 1980)

Dalton, David, *The Rolling Stones* (Alfred A. Knopf, 1981)

Dimmick, Mary Laverne, *Annotated Bibliography of the Rolling Stones* (University of Pittsburgh Press, 1979)

Elliott, Martin, *The Rolling Stones: Complete Recording Sessions 1963–1989* (Blandford, 1990)

Flippo, Chet, *On the Road with the Rolling Stones* (Doubleday & Company, 1985)

Greenfield, Robert, *A Journey Through America with the Rolling Stones* (Granada Publishing, 1975)

Hall, Jerry, with Christopher Hemphill, *Tall Tales* (Elm Tree Books, 1981)

Hodkinson, Mark, *Marianne Faithfull* (Omnibus Press, 1991)

Hotchner, A. E., *Blown Away: The Rolling Stones and the Death of the Sixties* (Simon & Schuster, 1990)

Jasper, Tony, *The Rolling Stones* (Octopus Books, 1976)

Mankowitz, Gered, *Satisfaction* (Sidgwick & Jackson, 1984)

Miles, *Mick Jagger In His Own Words* (Omnibus Press, 1982)

Norman, Philip, *The Stones* (Book Club Associates, 1984)

Sanchez, Tony, *Up and Down with the Rolling Stones* (Signet, 1980)

Scaduto, Anthony, *Mick Jagger* (W. H. Allen, 1974)

Wood, Ron, with Bill German, *The Works* (Fontana, 1988)

Wyman, Bill, with Ray Coleman, *Stone Alone* (Viking, 1990)

Index

· 433 ·

Vicious, Sid 192, 304
Vicuna, Victoria 349
Vidal, Gore 257, 269
Vogue, Sheldon 355

'Waiting On A Friend' 337
Waits, Tom 369
Walcott, Caspar 375
Walters, Dave 301
Wandering Spirit 416–17, 422
'Wanna Hold You' 357
Wanzenberg, Alan 352
'War Baby' 378, 393
Warhol, Andy 106, 192, 239, 240,
    247, 264, 276, 306, 308–9, 312–13,
    315, 318, 331, 337, 343, 375
Wasserman, Paul 291, 301, 310,
    311
Waters, Muddy 31, 38, 40, 45, 54,
    70, 93, 265, 298, 320, 342
Watts, Charlie: American tours
    (1966) 124–9, (1981) 342;
    background 59–60; Blues
    Incorporated 55, 59, 62, 65;
    BJ's death 204, 205; BJ's group
    63; BJ's sacking 197; British
    tour (1990) 401; drag act 129;
    Glasgow riot 97–8; Hyde Park
    concert 207; Japan (1990) 398;
    jazz 371, 372; 'Loving Cup'
    255; marriage 85, 101; on
    Stewart's role 367; orchestra
    372; relationship with MJ 194,
    359, 379, 389–90, 413; Rolling
    Stones 74, 76, 117, 158; Rolling
    Stones role 361, 371, 393;
    'Satisfaction' 112; song-writing
    role 299, 393; 'straight' 249;
    'Sympathy for the Devil' 173;
    Wood's wedding 362; Wyman's
    wedding 389

Watts, Shirley (née Shepherd) 85,
    102, 128, 359
'We Love You' 147, 158, 165
'We Want The Stones' 109
Weeks, Willie 285
Weidenfeld, George 352
Wenner, Jann 194, 314, 329
'When The Whip Comes Down'
    321
'Where The Boys Go' 331–2
Whitehouse, Mary 177, 255
Who, The 66, 160, 189, 340, 347
'Wild Horses' 218, 225, 240
Wilkinson, Walton 39, 41, 48, 50
Wimbish, Doug 373
'Winning Ugly' 368
'Winter' 268, 280–1
Winter, Johnny 280
Wohlin, Anna 197–201, 203–4
Wolf, Peter 346
Wolfe, Tom 103, 106
Wonder, Stevie 263, 312
Wood, Krissie 307
Wood, Ron: American tours
    (1975) 292, 294, (1981) 343;
    arrest 294; *Dirty Work* 367–9;
    drugs 302n, 336n, 348;
    European tour (1990) 399;
    fatherhood 307–8; Japan
    (1990) 398; joins Stones 288,
    290, 292; marriage 362; New
    Barbarians 327; on MJ 292,
    315, 323–4; on Stewart 367;
    relationship with Margaret
    Trudeau 311; relationship with
    MJ 285, 379; Richmond 99;
    Rolling Stones relationships
    332, 336, 371; solo LPs 285,
    371; suggested as BJ's
    replacement 196; Wyman's
    wedding 389